PLAYED BY EAR

Daniel A. Lord, S.J.

PLAYED BY EAR

with an introduction by R. Bakewell Morrison, S.J.

LOYOLA UNIVERSITY PRESS

Chicago 1956

IMPRIMI POTEST:
William J. Schmidt, S.J., *Provincial of the Chicago Province*
September 20, 1955

NIHIL OBSTAT:
Austin G. Schmidt, S.J., *Censor Deputatus*
November 25, 1955

IMPRIMATUR:
✠ Samuel Cardinal Stritch, *Archbishop of Chicago*
November 29, 1955

Printed in the United States of America

Library of Congress Catalog Card Number: 56-7099

P-PLA-D-OE

Designed by William Nicoll

CONTENTS

INTRODUCTION

"You are tone deaf," he said to me. And my hopes of singing in that novices' choir went glimmering. I hope that my introduction for *Played by Ear* does not merit Father Lord's verdict, for it was he who was testing the new novices' voices.

That little incident of our overlapping years—early Jesuit years—may serve to indicate how long I have known Father Lord. We continued, throughout our lives, always being somewhere around each other. I lazed with him on many a sun-baked sand bar. I debated and dreamed with him on roof tops. I worked with him. And it was not always he that judged me; I had my innings, too, listening to *his* efforts, when manuscript after manuscript of his came to my desk for censoring. Neither of us was art critic to the other, I am sure. We knew each other well.

Father Daniel A. Lord, S.J., will speak for himself in this book, but I must hint something at what he does not say, as he listens and records the years, and the voices and heartbeats of men. I want to hint, merely, at areas where his pen did not reach, as time closed in upon him.

He dreamed, for example, of beauty, though he did not often say the word. He rather wanted to create it than to talk about it. He tried, in pageantry especially, and in his rhythmed prose, to make his dream come articulate—his dream of celestial beauty.

With human voices, human gestures, human beings—and rhythm, and color, and sound—he attempted to impress the fact of beauty, the philosophy of beauty. He was hungry for the sight, the feel, the sound, the taste of it, the very smell of it. His hunger was for the beauty of God; and so, with all his resources, he tried to make that beauty recognizable and real to others, to all others; they, like himself, had to be hungry for beauty.

> Thou heavenly, new Jerusalem,
> Vision of Peace in prophet's dream,
> With living stones built up on high
> And rising to yon starry sky.

He tells, episodically, his story. As an orchestra leader picks out first one instrument and then another, he hears them selectively, one at a time. Then he is not done with it; but retaining each as a part of the whole, he adverts especially to another and another until though not finished with them all, he must lay down his baton. He has by no means completed his list, or his appreciation of the instruments; he simply has not had time to tell of them all, as he "plays by ear."

Of the untold, the unreviewed, the unplayed instruments, there were still some of the best, some mighty dear to his heart. His sodalities, his pageants, his Eucharistic Crusade—of these he did not write in this book. And we can scarcely do more than catalogue his unbounded outpourings on these themes. The volume of his work was tremendous, and defies accurate listing. Its impact was, and will remain, incalculable.

He wrote exactly thirty adult books and twelve booklets. His pamphlets must number nearly three hundred. He wrote forty-eight children's books. He wrote twenty-five plays, twelve pageants, three musicals; and he published five separate musical compositions, not to mention the tunes incorporated in his pageants, some written in collaboration with others.

These pageants of his were sometimes spectacular, in size, in the number of actors called for, in staging. He may have colored all his later work by his initial experience of a pageant. Before he had ever done one, he had seen and sighed over the St. Louis Centennial at the foot of Art Hill in St. Louis. The setting is still here of quiet, nearly brooding majesty, seen across still lagoons, against the hill. He always wanted room.

So he contrived with light and every artistry to create vastness. At Toronto in his last pageant, *Joy for the World,* Hazel, one of our recent tornadoes, expiring there, called for his utmost ingenuity for the show to go on. He "produced" twice at Detroit. His last there, *Light Up the Land,* was tremendous. Memories of it still live vividly. He indeed loved pageantry—whether in Jamaica with a thousand actors or in lesser auditoria, as for instance in *The Dreamer Awakes* in St. Louis, *The Restless Flame* in Milwaukee. The casts of his pageants will never tire of boasting, I believe. And his audiences have, indeed, something of color and majesty to remember—of beauty—which will stay with them.

His youth work will never be forgotten, though in *Played by Ear* he does not expatiate on it. National conventions first, beginning in 1928 in St. Louis, and then the uninterrupted series of Summer Schools of Catholic Action brought him an enthusiastic and ever-growing audience of young people who, but for him, might never have been caught up in the Students' Spiritual Leadership Movement. But they responded to the magnetism and solidity he always knew so well how to communicate. He was massive but never ponderous.

He had still other preoccupations. He never ceased marveling at the magnificence of the Catholic nun. His play, for example, *Everynun,* demonstrates this admiration. It is typical of its author. He could express in music or in dramatic action what he could not say, even to a friend. He could dramatize his love, his ambition, his hope, his very self, but he was not one to tell, man-to-man, what was in his heart. He seems to express himself in symbols, not in personalities.

He did not "build" the present Queen's Work building, inasmuch as he bought it ready-built, but he built *The Queen's Work* —six stories of unwearying activity, seconding our Lady's efforts to bring her Son closer to all mankind.

His final illness was protracted, a weary series of "bouts at the hospital," until, in October 1954, he went there for the last time. He was dying. Short of a miracle, he was certain to die—how soon? Yet he worked steadily on, until, not many weeks before the end, utter exhaustion stopped him. Finally, a few twilight days. Then, death!

He wanted, and he left, no monument that could crumble, no human relic to identify him, exclusively, in time. He had been too omnivorous in his reading, too spendthrift in his writing, too exuberant in his speaking, too outgoing in his counseling, most of all, too sensitive in his sympathy, to let himself be limited to one field—unless his speciality was being all things to all men that he might gain all for Christ! In that I'm sure he was single-minded; to use a Pauline expression, he was "straitened."

He was, indeed, quixotic. He was the fruit of many generations, achieving, very nearly, the all-but-dead ideal of the Jesuit *Ratio Studiorum:* "eloquentia," the man who, with judgment, could express himself to his fellows, to the world, in deed, in worth-while thought, and reasoned truth, and comprehension of God. His were the interests, the ideals, the hopes, and more, the practices, of those men of yesteryear, who had felt, as he felt it, the Christian *ethos,* the faraway thunder of the Trinity, the instant majesty of Christ, the tenderness of the Mother of God.

Played by Ear is very strictly a Jesuit's book. Father Daniel A. Lord, S.J., was, first and foremost, a Jesuit. It was not that he had any formula at hand to guide his writing, any rules that indicated to him what to write. He wrote, he tells us, when and about what the moment suggested; and the moment was largely determined by what he sensed or directly had heard that the young Catholics of this country needed to hear. He was always, I know, acutely aware of his audience, in sympathy with it, appreciative of its needs.

Though the reader of this book will surely not feel that it was written for adolescents, or takes, in any way, an adolescent point of view, Father Lord does seem to look through the eyes of the young, for the topic, the method of treatment, the implications of what he is writing. He would not be himself if, when he wrote, he had not had an adolescent audience in mind. This audience had kept him from growing old, had kept him from being crotchety or one-sided. So many youngsters perennially needed his counsel, sought his direction, instruction, encouragement, warnings; and he knew how to be one of them without artificiality, understanding them, while managing to remain himself, essentially and always, adult indeed. He just was never stodgy!

You can read *Played by Ear* and see how he worked at and gave expression to his ideas, and to a truly amazing variety of immediate objectives, while he never for a moment forgot that it was all for the Greater Glory of God and the Honor of His Blessed Mother. He said: "I never wrote without A.M.D.G. and B.V.M.H. on the page." (A.M.D.G. et B.V.M.H.: *Ad Majorem Dei Gloriam et Beatae Virginis Mariae Honorem*—"To the Greater Glory of God and the Honor of the Blessed Virgin Mary.") Those initials were truly his sign, his hallmark, his slogan, his life.

He was voluble in writing about his family. One can wonder at that. Perhaps the reason why he talked of them at length was because he could represent them; as they did not speak for themselves, he undertook to speak for them.

As the reader progresses, he cannot but be stirred by the extraordinarily ceaseless character of Father Lord's work. And yet, though incredibly spendthrift of his energy, enormous in his output, his expression, really, of himself was meager. Another—as, for example, Gide—may attitudinize and talk about himself. Perhaps because Father Lord refused and rejected the iniquities of such as Gide, he only shyly and in symbol reveals himself in his work. The issue must be impersonal if he is to be at his best.

This is why, I believe, his autobiography is so clearly *not* the record of his inner self—as Augustine gives his inner self to us. But, sooner or later, the candor of Father Lord is going to remind people of St. Augustine; the Augustine of the dialogues and debates, rather than of *The Confessions* and *The Soliloquies*.

Father Lord was always "ready." He had made himself ready by the most grueling and unremitting self-discipline imaginable. No man could pour out material that was so "solid" as was his without an amazing sense of orthodoxy, and a completely wholehearted identity with the mind of the Church. It is true that he had studied the faith in a rigorously exacting school; but, without that, his mind was the mind of the Church. As Tertullian said it, long ago, he was just naturally at one with the mind of the Church. He never deviated, he never wavered, the needle of his spiritual compass never quivered or hesitated in pointing to the truth: to the teaching of Him who named Himself the Truth, the Way, and the Life.

Father Lord could argue. With his brilliant mother wit, with his extremely agile and fertile ready mind, he could debate tellingly, but you just can't be so ready with views, with positive and intransigent dogmas and certainties, unless you know and feel and love consistency and truth.

Nor were his decisions on right and wrong always easy ones to produce. All the big questions of today came under the review of his typewriter. And he was as Catholic in what he taught on the amusements of men—on music, drama, poetry, pageantry, dance, song, play—he was as unwavering in counseling, in consoling, in meeting the most sensitive and pain-racked human need, the most thundering and ravening human desire—as he was firm in the sound, equable, refreshing consistency of his faith.

He did not deal with inconsequential questions. Though I do not recall that he ever mediated a strike or settled a major industrial problem in a wage dispute, he unwaveringly taught and practiced honesty and honor, fair play and fair dealing. His aim was for the questions, the problems, the moral perplexities of the moment, of today. He never burked these problems or failed to give concrete and practical answers. His long-sustained series of letters answered on his popular radio broadcasts are evidence of this.

Father Lord could philosophize for you with depth and still at random; he could theologize; he could play, dance, sing; he would teach—always he was a teacher—and he would learn, and listen. Many notable priests seem to have but one string each to their bows. Father Lord could and did canvass the problems of the world in the macrocosm of all men's needs, and in the microcosm of the human heart, at grips with life. He saw and judged them all, fairly and soundly, with the Heart of Christ.

He was selfless in a very baffling manner. Usually recognized at once, in any group where he appeared, he never called attention to himself; he simply made others aware that he was there. We are frequently conscious of this phenomenon. I have watched this elusive factor at work, for example, in a Jesuit recreation room where many priests mingle informally; and always some drift toward foci, so that you have islets of persons rather than a common group, a solid whole. Now, wherever he appeared, Father

Lord seemed always in focus. An extremely sensitive man, Father Lord "felt" others, even sooner, perhaps, than they felt him. He could freeze, grow cold inside, manage not to be at his best, in the presence of someone he knew, or fancied he knew, to be hostile. It was not that he feared opposition—to a degree, it stimulated him; but he was quickly aware of personal animosity, and he reacted to it with a feeling akin to horror.

He did not mind being known as the master of the obvious. The obvious, to him, was whatever he encountered that could be passed on to others. He was happy in his power to reveal *as* obvious, with his magic hand and nimble art, what had not seemed so before.

I believe that the best way of explaining Father Lord is to insist that he, throughout, was a most insistent person. From his earliest days he "wanted." And he came to know just what it was that he wanted by doing, by working, by trying, by *never* giving up.

Less inclined than most, perhaps, to fisticuffs or brawling, he was a fighter of the first water. He had a truly "fighting" heart. Would he tell you, as I, for him, am trying to tell you? I think not. Was he like Joan of Arc in that he held a King's secret?

PLAYED BY EAR

IN SEARCH OF A TITLE

During the course of my writing life I have named a good many "literary items." That may be a pretentious description of the things which I have written and launched into print, yet the name of each item has always seemed important to me. I wrote for the reader who runs (or rides a bus or auto) as he reads, who picks up his reading material as the Pony Express picked up the mail. And I felt that the title had . . .

To be short.

To give a fairly honest foreshadowing of what the article or booklet or book or play contained.

To be sufficiently attractive to make the fingers twitch a bit as the eye was arrested and the rushing passer-by paused.

Now as I sit down to tell my story, I fumble for a name.

Naturally, I think simply of "My Story" with my name down as the autobiographer. But to me "story" always suggests fiction; and I'd like to keep this very much according to the facts. Some years back a famous churchman wrote his life's story. A monsignor who was consultant for an important book club wired the chairman: "This is a *must*. Be sure to pick it for your readers. What a magnificent piece of fiction!" It was picked, and it had a fair share of imagination, of fiction, and of what the churchman hoped deep down he was and had really accomplished.

I thought of calling it "The Story of Father Lord." The motion pictures have discouraged me there. In recent years we have had more than our share of "Stories of . . .," mostly delightful, and mostly doctored by writers who preferred glamor to truth. I recall such a film story of a well-known composer; had I been the victim, I should have hied me to a hermitage and prayed the heavens to cover me against the laughter of my friends. The scenarists had even (as they did in many another "story") invented a heart interest right out of their file cabinets. I hope the victims of the stories were at least well paid for the nonsense written about them.

I paused on "Reminisce," but dismissed it, since I have written too long with my heart set on teen-agers to offend them with a word out of their normal vocabulary. Anyhow, if you say that word right, you can prolong the last syllable into a protracted hiss. And who wants to challenge readers to mention his book and hiss?

"By Way of Explanation" was a little like what I had in mind. But this is more than just an explanation. Or so I hope. Not being a scholar, I thought of "No Footnotes, Please!" as a promise of continuous reading without the eye being constantly deflected to the bottom of the page or challenged to turn back to the small print in the rear of the book.

In all honesty, I felt the book might well be called "Happy, Happy Days," for mine have been just that—happy, blessed, fortunate beyond the possibility of gratitude enough to God—days I would willingly share with others, days I might well wish for my friends and my readers. And that made me pause on another title, "Kind Friends and Gentle Readers," which I rejected on the grounds that it sounded Victorian. I paused briefly on "I'm Happy To Recall," but passed on without a second glance.

Enthusiastic as I am about the generations through which I have lived, I liked "Across Exciting Times." For the years from 1888 to the current year have been the world's most exciting. I have said—so often that I have long since lost all idea of how often—that "I was lucky enough to be born into the most exciting period of history; I shouldn't have missed it for anything." Yet my own contribution to the times has been too slight for me to seem in my title to lay even slight claim to these wonderful and exciting times.

I felt there was too much irony in "Worth Telling?" The question mark was really my attitude toward the story; yet the reader might retort, "But you continued to write it." So I thought of calling it "On Request" or "Request Number." In my dealings with young people, and older ones too, I have often sat down at the piano. And when I did, it was my custom to look around and ask, "Any requests?" or "What do you like?" With that cue, I would start off and play by the hour. The truth is that, much as I enjoy the chance to talk about myself (who doesn't?), I doubt that I should have attempted this had it not been for the kind nudging of friends. "Don't Nudge" might have been a title. And since in the past months so many friends and gentle strangers have written, "Are you going to give us your life's story?" with a display of pretended reluctance I rushed to my typewriter.

That leads me to a title which for a bit intrigued me: "Under Gentle Sentence." For I am writing this with the recent announcement of the doctors still vivid in my mind. God graciously sent His messengers well in advance; the Angel of Death did not strike me, as he struck my Protestant minister grandfather, with a heart attack in the line of duty. I did not fall as he did from the pulpit of my last sermon. Cancer is a kindly warning, but a very definite one. And when God's gentle sentence was passed and announced by the doctors, as a sympathetic jury, I thought instantly of writing of the goodness and zest and joy of the years. It is thus that I write.

So it would have been easy to title this book "With Gratitude to God." For God has been amazingly good and I am humbly grateful. I recall a famous cynic who said in effect that, while he did not know anything about the dealings of God even with his closest friends, he had to admit that God, in His dealings with him personally, had always been a gentleman. With me, God has always been the lavishly generous father of a wasteful and prodigal son. I can look back over a life in which God visibly and tangibly played the most gracious roles. From the vantage point of the years I can see nothing that God might have done and failed to do. Indeed, the words of rebuke which the Church puts into the mouth of the Savior during Holy Week have always seemed directed straight to me: "My child, what could I have done for you that I have not done?" That made me think of the title "He Never Failed Me." But as my name would follow as the author, I felt it might for a moment cause some ambiguity. And heaven knows the extent of my failures.

"But for His Grace" seemed too much of a protest. And "I Am What I Am" was a little affected.

Since, however, one cannot start a book of this sort without a sense of overwhelming gratitude, I dwelt for a little on this: "Gratefully Yours"—as in all sincerity I have often signed my letters. Paraphrasing that a little, I liked "With a Bow to Many," and so many would rightly bow back to me, knowing in their hearts that I meant them.

When one begins his story, he thinks naturally enough of his ancestors. "The Last of His Line" flashed through my mind, for I knew it worried my father, ancestral-conscious, that with me his branch of the family would come to an end. With a gesture to my mother, whose life I wrote after her death, I thought of "A Son to His Mother." But when someone laughed and parodied the title to become "Mrs. Lord's Little Boy," I decided that would never do.

The mingled strains of Catholic and Protestant, the blood lines which all came from the British Isles, though the paternal ancestry has been American from early colonial days, caused me to play with the titles "Mingled Faiths" and "From Many Lines." But who cares for ancestors these days? And really, like most Americans, I know surprisingly little of mine.

I wish I had the courage to call the book "A Son of the Society." But though I am humbly proud to boast of my connection with the Society of Jesus, I could not be sure that the Society would be equally proud to admit my descent from the noble lines of Jesuits.

Like most men who have written extensively, I have actually written much of my story as I went along. My mother's biography was the story of my early days. *Hi, Gang!* was the story of boyhood days. As one grows older, the events of youth stand out with greater clarity and beckoning charm. If anything, I have drawn too eagerly upon them, forcing my own memories on my patient readers. The fact that I lived through the Gay Nineties, now so fascinating to the modern young people, has been a challenge to write of those days. The fact that I recall so happily the stories of his boyhood which my father poured forth in the twilight of a long series of Sunday evenings made me imitative almost without the consciousness that I was so.

So I felt that in honesty I might call this "Filling in the Spaces," omit what I have already told, and add what seemed to be worth while by way of connection and explanation.

Shakespeare had, really, the perfect title when he called one of his less good plays *Much Ado about Nothing*. Let Shakespeare be freed from even the flattery of imitators.

Then suddenly I decided that I would violate my own principles, that I would pick a title which did not tell in advance what the story was and did not clearly state what the book was about.

"Played by Ear" intrigued me.

As a small boy, I had dreams of becoming a concert musician. As only a slightly larger boy, I knew that demanded talent, labor, and training beyond anything that I had or could hope to attain. I suddenly turned from the printed music page (which I had learned to read with some skill and fluency) to play by ear. Many a surprised listener during the years has stood back of me as I thumped the piano for a room or hall crowded with young people and said, "You're not playing that the way it was written; it sounds right enough, but it's not what the composer wrote. Are you playing by ear?" And I had to confess I was doing just that.

And as I began to write this story, I knew that I would write it "by ear."

It would be a fluid story, told as I remembered it.

It would not be history, except personal history . . . the things vividly remembered, the people who had been close and dear.

I would write as through the years I have come to play: the melody would be completely true, I hope; but the harmony might be my own embellishment.

I beg you not to imagine that it would be impossible to write a precise history of at least the last thirty years and more of my active life. Thanks to the world's most perfect secretary, Marian Prendergast, I am blessed with the world's most perfect files.

Through one of those gracious acts by which God seemed most providential, Marian Prendergast walked into my room at St. John's Hospital in the year of grace 1926, applying for the post of my secretary. Blessedly, she is with me still. She has been not merely a secretary but an unconscious historian, a skilled archivist, the keeper of my records, the wonderful associate who knew more about what I had done, was doing, and planned to do than I knew myself. She handed me in advance the schedules I was to undertake. She kept the correspondence which made up a large part of my life's work. She filed away the record of work done, statistics and programs and the minutes of meetings, most of which she had seen in the making, all of which she kept with meticulous and unostentatious zeal.

Besides this, since I had been from childhood an instinctive diarist, I had early begun to write the record of the days. On my travels this took the form of letters sent home to my secretary. The records were impersonal, exact, full of names and places and events, of references to talks given and audiences met, of ideas suggested to me by others, of councils and interviews, and of projects that quickly came to life or quickly withered before fruition. When I was in the office, I developed the habit of writing to Sister Marie Clyde, once of Webster College and later of Loretto Heights in Denver, a similar résumé. I have always felt that diaries should be complete and yet impersonal enough for anyone to read. The records of the day-by-day doings turned out to be a very complete diary—at least of the outer self, which is probably the most interesting.

Yet I have no intention of turning back to these bulging files and these comprehensive records. I prefer to rely on the memory of things that stood out, of faces that smile through the years, of gatherings that at the time seemed significant or full of promise, of events in which I was privileged to play a happy part.

So I am giving you a story that is "played by ear." I hope that the melody is pleasant and almost gay. I hope that the harmony which I improvise will fit the melody and be correct and not unattractive. Melodies go on endlessly; harmonies have a way of changing with the fashions of the musical moment and the instinctive wanderings of the fingers.

As I have hit many a wrong chord on the piano and struck with conviction many a false note, I may do the same thing here and now. Perhaps it were better if I had followed the example of St. Cecilia, patroness of musicians; for she won her place as the guardian of all who attempt to make music by singing to God silently in her heart. Much disharmony would have been avoided if more of us bad musicians had been silent and had made music solely for God and the angels.

To complicate things even more for my readers, I decided to write the story in the form of letters. You see, letter writing has been for a lifetime my hobby, my speciality, almost my main "apostolate." If I settled down learnedly to write a history, I should feel ill at ease. If, instead, I wrote to the kind friends who had asked me to tell them about myself, what life has meant to me, what God has done for me, what friends have given me, what life in retrospect seems to mean, I could write informally, easily, as I have written in the thousands of letters I have dashed off.

Sometimes I have visualized myself in a sort of continuous "paper chase." I imagine the youngsters of our crowded cities have long since foregone that wonderful game. It was the English boys' magazines of my youth which introduced me to the "paper chase," the fast runner heading off as if he were the fox and dropping behind him as he ran a trail of torn paper. His pursuers, like the hounds of the English fox hunt, followed his trail and eventually caught, cornered, and "slew" the human fox. Thus have I seen myself. Running rapidly all through life, but scattering behind me these uncounted letters to friends, acquaintances, strangers, all of whom have written to me first, I have felt that anyone who cared to follow the trail of my letters would soon catch up with me and corner me for the "kill."

So the story comes in the form of letters. I write with these friends in mind. After all, I hope that my readers will be my friends, too—the same kind of friends to whom I have written steadily through the years, the same types who listened patiently while I sat at the piano and "played by ear."

TO A YOUNG FATHER AND MOTHER

Dear Both of You:

Really, I think you are wonderful! Married eight years, aren't you? And this is your fourth child! Proud of you, very proud indeed; and I think that God must be enormously pleased.

Of course, I am grinning ear to ear that you named the youngster after me. I almost said "unfortunate youngster." But I don't mean it that way. I've always liked my name. Daniel Lord was I christened—no middle name at all. When I was confirmed, Sister Mary Thecla, long since gone to God, persuaded me and another boy and a solitary girl to take Aloysius for our middle name. So I became, in common with a multitude of good little Catholic children, a client of the model of purity. It was a good and wholesome influence in my life. As for the "Lord," I thought that was a grand name. Had I not become a Jesuit, I'm sure that I should have called myself Dan Lord; merely that. My boyhood chum, John Pierre Roche, used to bemoan his three-car name and taunt me with the folly of ever calling myself anything but Dan Lord. But as a Jesuit, Dan Lord would have been a little curt, offhand, perhaps undignified. Yet Dan Lord I have always been to my friends. People have paid so little attention to my middle initial that my name on a program is likely to read Daniel A., Daniel J., Daniel S., and occasionally as a concession to my Irish maternal ancestors, Daniel P. The P is undoubtedly for Patrick.

At any rate, I am pleased that your little lad bears my name. In years to come he may want to know something about his namesake. So I am writing with that in mind. Like your boy, I was not named for a saint, not even for the great prophet who defied the lions and foretold the exact date of the coming of the Messias.

I was named for a grandfather who was a minister of the Dutch Reformed Church, a branch, unless I am much mistaken, of the Presbyterian Church. On the bookcase in my office still stands the chalice which was given to Rev. D. Lord (like me, he was christened without a middle name) by his congregation of Nyack, New York. Your lad is named for a Jesuit; and though, as I discovered when I looked it up in later life, there are ten canonized Daniels in the Roman Martyrology, he will probably always think of his name as coming from a notably uncanonized mortal. Maybe he will be the first modern Daniel to win to sainthood.

The psychologist was wise indeed who suggested that a smart child would be careful to pick out the right parents. I was lucky in mine, as your boy is lucky in his.

But ancestors, the first of our birthday gifts, are also, naturally speaking, the more important. In my question periods as a lecturer, I am often asked a question that seems to bother a good many people: "How does it happen that in a single family you'll get such a wide variety of children? In the same household you'll find the innocent lamb and the black sheep. Fiction loves the story of the two brothers, the hero and the villain. Yet they have the same parents, these children. Now can you explain the fact that the youngsters will have so little in common?"

I've answered that usually with the aid of a blackboard.

For we forget that mother and father are just two of our innumerable ancestors. We forget that before our mother and dad were their mother and dad, a pair apiece; and then the spreading out of that family tree . . . each bearing within them the genes and chromosomes which they pass along to their descendants.

We are the heirs of the ages, we say casually, not realizing how true that is. We, the children, are the net product of generations of ancestors. Think for a moment how complicated that can become. We can believe that we had, let's say, great, great, great grandparents who numbered among them a blonde, brunet, carrottop, titian redhead, premature gray, bald, flowing-locked, straight-haired, waved, tight-curled—and on and on through the range of hirsute adornment and natural coiffures. Nobody should be at all surprised when a very great variety of hairdos turns up in a single family.

And those same ancestors may well have numbered a hero and a traitor, a coward and a saint, a villain and a martyr, someone with a great gift for mathematics and someone who could not add two to two without getting five or seven, a musician, a scientist, a thwarted lawyer, a poet, a businessman, a woman with homemaking instincts, a flirt, a home wrecker, and on and on and on. Since each transmits his traits to his descendants, by the time four generations have been born and have watched their children arrive, a pretty complicated assortment of family traits results.

I believe it was Ibsen who used to draw up the family tree for each of his dramatic characters back to the third generation of ancestors. He would then work out the traits he thought each ancestor possessed, and how they were transmitted, and how they reappeared and were modified, and their changes through combinations and recombinations. He seemed to insist on transmitting the oddities. But then, it's the oddities of our ancestors that the family is likely to remember.

Hence the endless jokes about "the nuts on my family tree," and "If your family has a family tree, you are certainly the sap." As youngsters we sang a currently popular song that ran, "I think I hear a woodpecker knocking on my family tree."

My ancestry, you may tell that little namesake of mine, was Irish and English. There must have been some Scottish in it, or I cannot explain the Douglas which was my father's middle name. About the Irish and English my family was inclined to be a little aggressively proud, though in our immediate household the English paternal side was soft-pedaled.

When I came to visit Ireland, I was notably annoyed to discover that the Queen's County in which my grandmother Langdon had been born was gone from the map. But I had never been allowed to forget that it lay within the Pale. All the women of the family had been Catholic; all the men had been Protestant; and before they died, each of the men asked for a priest, the faith, and the last sacraments. That was the kind of women we had in our family.

My grandmother Langdon, who was a lady if ever I knew one, used to talk freely of her father and not at all of her mother. Her father was unforgettable for the simple reason that he hated priests and all things Catholic. When the pastor of the parish church called on the family of growing children, the father of the house slipped out the rear door, sought refuge in a tavern, and remained there until he could spot the shining rear of the clerical coat heading back down the street. But his vast brood of children were all baptized in the Church; and on his deathbed he followed the example of the other Protestant husbands, and, said my grandmother in complete complacency, "The priest came because he was sent for, and your great-grandfather saved his soul, a favor he owes to his good luck in marrying a Catholic girl."

The Irish of those days had a strange way of losing all touch with their families. I think that I recall my grandmother stating that she had eight brothers. Apparently she was the eldest child of the family, and despite a great reserve of character and acute shyness and physical fear was the first to come to America. One might have thought she came to prepare a way for the rest. But she paid little attention to what happened to them. Of the eight brothers she had no knowledge. Maybe they came to America, and maybe they didn't. My conviction is that they followed her to the United States and scattered, as the Irish of those days did, in the various tenement districts of the land. Apparently the Irish of those days had never discovered the postage stamp; and a cablegram or a telegram was used only in the event of sudden death. Let a messenger appear at the door waving a yellow envelope, and the house instinctively set up a wail. The banshee was no surer sign of death.

If my grandmother was the eldest of the large brood, my great-aunt Lizzie was the youngest, and heredity played its tricks when it put the two women in the same family. Grandmother Langdon was a Jansenist of Jansenists. In her faith only Catholics had the slighest chance of eternal salvation—and very few of them. As a youngster I sat and saw her shake a solemn gray head as she mourned the fate of humanity. She was not slow in transmitting to me the conviction that even my generous and wonderfully good father would never rejoin us once we got to heaven—"provided, that is, that we ever get there."

Her favorite entertainment was to spend Sunday afternoon in Mount Carmel Cemetery, and many's the tombstone off which we ate our picnic lunch of fried chicken and deviled-ham sandwiches. Her first husband, a railroad man of some sort, had been killed in the line of duty—pinned between cars. Her second husband was the type about whom the Irish never make mention. His name was Kelly; he had stayed briefly, disillusioned her and her daughter, my mother, with the male of the species, and disappeared off the horizon. We never mentioned him. Later on, I calculated the facts, and wondered if the migration of mother and daughter from Cincinnati to Chicago had not actually been a flight from the unspeakable . . . and never spoken about . . . Kelly.

My grandmother's family name had been Lawlor. When I came to Killarney, I found a tombstone bearing the name Lawlor. You see, the haunting of graveyards had become a transmitted family trait; I even wrote and sold in later years an article on a wonderful old Irish cemetery that I discovered in Wilmington, Delaware. Standing before the tombstone with the ancestral name, I asked a caretaker if he knew the Lawlor family who owned the lot. He shook his head. "They're strangers here," he replied in what to me is a lovely if unreproducible brogue. "What do you mean by strangers?" I asked him. "They've not lived here much more than a hundred years," he answered. Rally Patricks and Michaels-Come-Lately!

After the lapse of the full octave of missing brothers, my great-aunt Lizzie arrived in the States. She was not just the start of a new octave; she was in an entirely different key and tempo. I should guess that she came to Chicago because her older sister was established there. Never for a moment did she slightly lean upon that stiff ramrod of a woman. She married a man named Clinch who had gone home to God before I was even aware of him, and for him brought into the world a sturdy and healthy family of four sons and a charming and quite brilliant daughter. He left her, on his departure, one of those combination grocery-saloons which once on a time were common enough on Chicago's West Side. A great convenience, this arrangement; for while Mother picked out the groceries in the front of the store, Father could pick up his schooner in the rear; and the children, unrestricted by any nonsense about minors and the law, could oscillate between their parents.

If my grandmother, the eldest of the family, was austere, my great-aunt was the soul of joviality. If my grandmother was convinced that mankind, with rare exceptions, was doomed, my great-aunt loved all mankind with a vast and trustful love. If my grandmother was the complete lady, corseted to rigid erectness, speaking the most precise English, laughing not at all and smiling rarely, my great-aunt was the hostess of an old Irish tavern, with a laugh that rang out to the joy of all listeners, with a capacity for food and good conversation, and with a brogue that was authentic, high, and fluent.

"That brogue of hers," I heard my grandmother say time and again, "is a sheer affectation. Nobody in Ireland ever spoke with a brogue, nobody. Your Aunt Lizzie picked it up on the West Side of Chicago."

Of a Sunday afternoon, when we were not haunting a cemetery, we visited my Aunt Lizzie, sat in the little apartment back of the combination store, ate one of those wonderful Irish meals, and gossiped. That is, my female relatives gossiped. I used to take my place on a cracker barrel and count the growlers which came and went on a Sunday afternoon. The social life of the West Side was well lubricated in those simple days. Or I wandered about reading the labels on packages of groceries. For the first time I discovered "Imitation Strawberry Jelly, a Coal-Tar Product," and turned violently against jelly which was made, horrible thought, from the same stuff we used to burn in furnaces.

Or, under the leadership of my cousin Joe, I slipped down to the nearby brewery, borrowed horses, saddled them under the eyes of the lenient stablehands, and raced like mad up and down the Burlington right of way. In the fashion of all small boys, we kept from our mothers what we were doing. The horses must have dreaded our coming. We ran them as I had seen the ponies run at Washington Park race track. They say that a horse knows, the moment a rider hits the stirrup, who's master. I was master of the horse at eight and ten; when I remounted in my forties, the cow pony out in Wyoming knew who was master, and never let me get him out of the corral.

I can still see my cousin Will, the gentlest Irishman I ever knew in my life, with a velvet voice, a gracious little wife, and a successful family. The daughter of the family became Mother Clinch of the Sacred Heart nuns, of whom I am accustomed to boast, though our busy lives have given us slight contact. The other boys were out of my age range, and remain misty figures on my memory's horizon.

Many things fascinated me in that household besides the growlers, the groceries, and the proximity to the horses. For one thing there was a pasteboard box about the size of a laundry box into which was pitched the money taken in in the store. Apparently the Irish of those days distrusted banks. No wonder that in a later day they followed Father Coughlin in his denunciation of bankers. The family bank was that box, and out of it the boys seemed to draw whatever was necessary for their needs in the running of the store. Over them hung the prospect of golden days ahead: the Burlington Railroad, which provided us with our race course, would some day have to expand; and when it did, it would buy out the store at a fabulous price and the entire Clinch family would be able to retire in peace and plenty. The dream of the expanding railroad took years to develop. The peace and plenty, like many a financial mirage, never came.

Then there was the family "surrey with the fringe on top" long before the song made it famous. We had moved to the South Side of Chicago; and, playing safely on the autoless streets of the period, we would sight the oncoming surrey down the avenue. We sent up the cry, Mother rushed to the kitchen, a gigantic meal was miraculously summoned into being. Aunt Lizzie laughed her way up to our apartment, Cousin Will cared for the horse, and Cousin Joe and I played catch until supper was announced. There was much laughter in the house that night, and each time a quarter was left in my hand when my great-aunt departed. I always understood the lads in the English boys' stories who lived in anticipation of the visits from those relatives who pressed upon them a shilling or a crown. For me, a shilling or a crown was always a quarter, no more, no less.

One thing bound the women of the family tight—they had the deep Irish faith. We lived in a parish with a diocesan priest as pastor; Aunt Lizzie felt herself ecclesiastically blessed by living in rundown old Jesuit Sacred Heart Parish. I knew no Jesuits; but to hear her talk of them, I had the feeling that she was spiritually shepherded by something close to the archangels. I'm sure that predisposed me to my future associates, even if I later learned that archangelic qualities, like Jesuit villainies, can be vastly overstated.

But life for all the women centered about the parish churches, Holy Angels and the Sacred Heart. They felt a smug complacency in their faith, even if they served God in fear and trembling; and though they had a great capacity for friendship on the widest scale and without question of religious belief, they felt sorry for all who did not share their religious certainties and the warm devotional glow that permeated their souls on any slightest contact with altar, confessional, Communion rail, shrine, or votive candle.

America's melting pot was quietly waiting for two divergent elements or ingredients.

My Irish Catholic mother was waiting in Chicago to meet the son of the Dutch Reformed minister. And the melting pot gurgled in anticipation.

Among my grandfather Lord's effects was a document that left upon my memory an indelible impression. I could easily, had I skill with brushes, paint it; though I could not on a typewriter possibly record anything on it. I remember the exact format, the texture of the vellum on which it was hand-lettered, the long line of English kings from William the Conqueror to Victoria the Good that ran down the left margin, and the "Family" that began with the Great William and continued in the same carefully lettered script down to Revolutionary times. From then on, a succession of hands had penned in the names of the children of the last of the line. The names of my father, his sister Catherine, and his brother James were the last to be written down. The line stopped there.

I was, I think, in fifth grade when the "pedigree," as we called it, fell under my eyes. I came to school proudly to announce to Sister Mary Blanche that I was descended from William the Conqueror. She answered in the scornful disdain of one of German-Swiss ancestry, using, I regret to report, the current equivalent for "So what?" Further study of the family tree persuaded me that I was also a descendant of Henry VIII. This too I reported to my beloved teacher with much pride. "If I were you," she retorted, "I'd never mention it again." Not having any knowledge of English history as yet, I missed the point. To this day I regret that I do not know whether I descend from either the England-conquering William or the lady-conquering Henry.

I am only certain that the Lord section of the ancestry came to America in the early colonial days and—though there are Lords of French ancestry in Canada—have never left here since.

Once the porter of our Jesuit house on Farm Street in London stopped me at the door: "Isn't yours an English name?" he asked. "Yes," I answered, "but the family has been in the United States a long time. I think they left England two hundred and more years ago." "Oh," he said without the trace of a smile, "I wasn't here then."

My mother, who regarded the whole matter of the family tree as at least silly and probably slightly scandalous and shameful, somehow managed to rid the house of its brooding presence. I looked for it in vain in later years; and when I questioned her about it, she turned upon me that glazed look with which she shielded herself against the annoying. Sorry, but I have no way to prove royal blood, noble ancestry, or my right to claim relationship with some of the more distinguished Englishmen and early American Tories who probably hung from some famous historic trees . . . and gibbets.

Apparently the men of this family were professional men.

When, some short time ago, I visited New Brunswick in New Jersey, I came into the shadow of my grandfather Lord's alma mater, Rutgers University. Somehow I had learned that he graduated from that old college at a time when it was largely a training school for Dutch Reformed ministers. Later on he took six months out from his ministry to graduate in medicine at Rush Medical College in Chicago. In six months' time any college graduate could master all that anybody could teach them about the medical practice and surgery of those days.

While he preached in Bridgeport, Connecticut, pastor among others for P. T. Barnum, and near the Roosevelt family's estate in New York, and in a Prairie Avenue church in Chicago, he practiced medicine on the side. An old nun at Mercy Hospital in Chicago pointed out to me during my college days my grandfather's name on the records of their physicians of the '70's. I liked it that the Sisters of Mercy who taught me had once been served by a physician who was to be my granddad.

For one of the brightest spots in my ancestry is that wonderful Protestant minister. Of him, too, I brag. Whenever I have been asked about my religious vocation and whether or not I had any relatives who were religious, I answered promptly: "One cousin, a Sacred Heart nun; one grandfather, a Presbyterian minister."

He came into my orbit to sweep me away by sheer personal fascination and kindliness. I was five when in 1893 Chicago broke out in the excited rash of the World's Columbian Exposition. Our family was properly excited too when a letter in his illegible scrawl (which unkindly he bequeathed to me) announced that my unknown grandparents Lord would visit the Fair and stay with us for six weeks. They came and I was conquered. I have no slightest recollection of my grandmother Lord which goes back to that time. But that incredible grandfather! That fairy grandfather right out of the pages of the most delectable children's story! That master of wit and monarch of kindness! That relative who fulfilled all the dreams of a small boy!

Who can say how much of what he possesses is owed to any one person? Who can say that from this ancestor he inherited this and from another that . . . that he is gay because of . . . and gloomy because of . . . and loves books or music or science or painting because of this ancestor or that?

How can one blame or thank a definite ancestor for an itchy foot or sticky fingers, for a curious eye or a too-passionate heart, for restfulness or restlessness, for ease in virtue or easy virtue, for this taste or that distaste, for a zest in living or willingness to die?

Yet so much of life seems for me to start with those six weeks that I have myself loved youngsters and tried at times to give them a little of what I know that minister grandfather gave me. Whether his wife ever bothered to go to the Chicago Fair I doubt. Later on, I am sure I knew it would not have interested her in the least. She had already retired into the dark recesses of her own strange, brooding nature. But he—well, he was up with the dawn and long before my rising time was singing the gayest of hymns in the family bathroom as he splashed about in his very English cold bath. He was off before breakfast to raid the neighborhood bakeries and fancy food shops for crisp rolls and melons and unusual fruits. He had completely fallen in love with my mother, and proudly proclaimed her the world's greatest cook.

"When we are bankrupt, Iva, my girl, you and I will set up a muffin shop. You will bake them and I will sell those which I have not already eaten."

I cannot imagine that his glowering wife grew more attached to the bright, gay, laughing papist girl over whom her husband was making his unecclesiastical fuss. The time was to come when she would have her revenge.

Breakfast over, that wonderful grandfather tucked my little hand (little by comparison with later spread; even in those days a hand with piano fingers) into his, and off we trotted to the Fair. He was a short man, but to me he seemed mountains high. We did the Midway from gate to Illinois Central tracks, and not in any condescension to a child's love of circus, side show, and carnival, but in the sheer zest of living. We did it in a sort of delightful zigzag that sewed it up forever in my memory. And all the time he laughed and talked, paying me that greatest possible compliment one can pay to a child, the compliment of remembering he is and pretending he isn't.

Then we made our pilgrimage day after day to the Fair proper, as distinguished from the Midway, perhaps slightly improper. He had the curiosity of the Gay Nineties for electricity, that new and glittering toy. We walked through the Electrical Building, and when evening came on sat together on a Fair bench watching the little figures of the men who crawled the eaves of the great white buildings turning on each circuit of lights, until the Fair became outlined in that incredible marvel which Mr. Edison had just given to the world. He had the newly awakened alertness to anthropology, and we did the Anthropological Building stem to stern; and as we paused at each exhibit he talked of nations and races and primitive peoples and civilizations that had lived and died and left their records behind them for our delight or warning. We walked leisurely and sedately through the Art Gallery, and in the Aquarium paused to look eye to eye into the strange faces of the fish which, I am sure, found our flat human countenances equally weird. We did the State Building, and under his guidance I had my first contact with foreign lands when he paced me through the buildings that had been erected to the glory of strange lands not yet to me a spot on a map or a blot or shining patch of history.

When he died years later, part of his collection of books and some of his china and bric-a-brac descended to us. I learned then that each year he had, in the quiet of the Mohawk Valley hills, pursued with avidity some new project. Lying flat on my stomach I paged through the glorious volumes he had purchased—the Nile and the reconstructions of temple and palace in Egypt's Memphis and Thebes; beautifully illustrated books on Chinese art; Persia and its creative achievements; and book after book of history and myth and biography and the bulging science of that day. I was back with that granddad once more, unconsciously, I'm sure, hoping that, more than the books, he had left me his joy of life, his dancing curiosity, his great concern for people.

For I came to know that he had fled to the hills of mid New York, not only to hide away his witch of a wife, but to serve the farmers and small villagers around Jordanville as their dominie of a Sunday and their physician of body and soul all through the week. If I had once in a lifetime a choice of ancestors other than my wonderful mother and my exactly right father, I would reselect that grandfather. He crossed my path for a matter of a total of weeks. We visited him in his parish, and I sat beside him as he made his parish rounds, feeling the respect in the voices of his parishioners and neighbors, feeling his affection and high humane regard that reached out to envelop them. He returned to Chicago to celebrate his golden-wedding anniversary, but there was no

Chicago Fair to which he could now take me. And perhaps I had lost the quick receptiveness of a five-year-old.

He must have been a very young, aspiring minister when he met and married the dour, humorless woman who moved in my memories of him like a dark, hardly distinct shadow. She was a member of a prominent family which gave its name to much of Pennsylvania. They had money; I fancy my grandfather never had much. Once I heard him brag, never to forget it, that when he came to die he would leave his manse in the hills, his own and unroofed of any mortgage, the insurance that would safeguard his wife, and a trunk full of sermons which no one would ever be able to read. That horrible handwriting he left as a legacy to me—that and more than I can ever thank him for. I am glad he left no millions.

Of my grandmother's family I never knew anything, except the comic story of my grandmother's two sisters, spinsters who lived to an interminable age in Germantown outside of Philadelphia. They lived the sort of life that has become subject matter for the *New Yorker's* type of fiction and, I should guess, for the psychologist. They did not, for instance, hesitate to lean from their bedroom windows and command the driver of the Germantown horsecar to wait until they had finished dressing and were ready to descend for a shopping trip. To them the public conveyance was their privately controlled chariot; and apparently they had reduced the driver to a state where he accepted their assumption of ownership.

As for my grandmother herself, I should prefer not to retell, as I retold in the story of my mother in some detail, the dreadful days when, after my grandfather's beautifully spectacular death, his wife descended upon our little home and brought with her the only ugly days I can recall throughout childhood. She had never forgiven her son for marrying a Catholic, as my Irish grandmother had never quite forgiven her daughter for marrying a Protestant. But where the Catholic grandparent accepted the accomplished fact and dwelt in something akin to pity under the roof provided by her son-in-law, the newcomer set herself to wreck the marriage she had not been able to prevent.

We children moved on tiptoe. A Brontëlike figure, she sat in her bedroom all day long, her meals served to her on a tray. Upon the return of my father from his paralyzingly long day's work, she swooped down upon him, dragged him into what had become her lair, closed the door in melodramatic finality, and hissed at him the faults of my mother and the wrongs she herself had suffered since the dawn.

The intolerable situation was solved when she returned to New York to live among people whom she did not despise. Yet there was a macabre touch to the whole memory that seemed to add danger and threat to the lines of my inheritance. Into each life, I suppose, some madness must fall. Surely there is no family without its strange dancing or skulking skeletons back of the raincoats and umbrellas. And I have lived with the feeling that sanity and a good disposition must be fought for and guarded against ancestry known and ancestry half-suspected of fell designs.

For my father had never disguised the fact that he had a brother James who was physically weak and mentally retarded. He adored him and served him with strong young arm and broad young back. He had to be carried across the farmlands and down the roads by my father, a vigorous youngster. He had never matured and never mentally developed. Evidently he had lived to young manhood without being able to do any work. I loved the unknown Uncle James, remembering him, not from any experience, but from the vivid tales of my storytelling father. And yet he represented with my grandmother Lord the possible blight that might touch my own mind and paralyze my own will.

Whenever strange melancholy or a love of closed doors or periods of intense desire to do nothing seized me, I thought, "They too are part of me," and turned from the threat to the laughter of my grandfather Lord, the unshaken sanity of my mother, and the calm, loyal fidelity of my father's attitude toward his family.

How strangely limited is the swing of our personal knowledge! How circumscribed is the vision we have of those whose characters and ideals, shortcomings and heroisms, national characteristics and acquired skills help make us the people that we are! At best we seem to go back a couple of generations. Then the clouds of obscurity settle in, and our ancestors become anonymous figures without face or history, distinguishing characteristics, or differentiating achievements.

Yet we carry them in our bodies and in our dispositions. Our hair curls or does not curl, we crook our fingers or carry them straight, we have a gift for music or slaughter the simplest tune, because of them. We are the sum of the ages. We are the burning glass that concentrates the multiplied lines of our ancestors.

I could have wished that into me had come some of the other lines of nation and race. With years I have come to regard my Irish ancestry as precious, for it brought to me my faith and some of my joy of life and love for music and verse. I find the English in me stronger with each year. But it was an English ancestry that made my remote ancestors rebels who fled their native country to find the freedom of the colonies and ultimately the challenge of American opportunity. I should like to say that I have some of the ebullience of the French, the calm scholarship of the Germans, the creative genius of the Italians. I can understand the enthusiasm with which my good friend, Father William Markoe, dashed on occasion into my office saying, "Do you know? I am sure that I have Negro blood in me. My family came from Haiti, and it seems there is hardly a soul in Haiti who hasn't a touch of the color." Yes, I can understand the eagerness to share some of the characteristics of all the people who are God's children.

But fortunately for me, I have been born in an age that has grown world-minded. When we say these days "Our Father who art in heaven," we are less reluctant to accept the corollary that all men are our brothers. We have abandoned, thank God, the anthropological myth of the superior and inferior races, the master and the mastered peoples, the empire builders and the colonies. If we are not entering an age when the bloodlines will converge in each of our bodies, we are entering a period of history when, please God, the bloodlines of the world will converge in our sympathies and our wills.

I am even—forgive the adverb—glad of my strongly Protestant ancestry. It has given me, I hope, a tolerance for those of other faiths. I have kept through life the Catholic conviction that Christ was no man to clutter up the earth with a lot of ambiguous statements resulting in divergent churches and discordant beliefs, all equally true. But I have a conviction that finding the truth is a long, hard quest and that I am simply one of those fortunate souls who found the grail without the need for weary searching and to whom the faith was given undeserved and without effort. Who am I to condemn one without it? And should I not pray that others have my good fortune?

All this, my very dear young parents, is a sort of gush of explanation that some day you may want to pass on to that precious little namesake of mine when he asks, "Who was I named for?" I hope he won't be such a grammatical purist that he will put it, "For whom was I named?" I like grammatical mistakes made in the struggle of youth with the octopuslike tentacles of our language.

God bless you and your lad and the fine ancestry I happen to know you are passing along to him! "It's a wise child that knows his own father," said the tiresome cynic; but that could be modified into, "It is a wise child who bothers to learn his father's ancestors, to copy the best, to avoid the worst, to cultivate the strong in the family strain, to root out with the glorious gift of free will the blights and dangers that lurk in all of us."

Oh, by the way, after I had written the story of my mother, Hollywood discovered it. One of the producers for Metro-Goldwyn-Mayer bought an option on it and planned to film it. Just one element in the life caught his dramatic fancy, and he was quite willing to risk a feature film in order to present that climax. I remember so well his enthusiasm when he came to St. Louis to talk to me.

"What a climax that story has," he cried. "I can just see it now. The young Jesuit with the Irish mother and the Yankee father comes to his ordination. And there, watching him made a priest, is the Dutch Reformed minister grandfather."

"Wait a minute," I protested. "My grandfather had been dead for years before I was ordained."

"What difference does that make?" he shouted me down. "That's the story I want . . . all those different elements, the jovial Aunt Lizzie, the dour Jansenistic Irish grandmother . . . the lovely Irish mother . . . then the other side of the family, Protestant, Yankee . . . and you coming down to bless them all with your fresh newly made priestly hands."

I was patient with him.

"My grandparents were all dead for years. I doubt very much if I sent even an announcement to the remaining Lord side of the family. There should be plenty of them somewhere. But while we never had any family quarrels or feuds, the Catholic and non-Catholic branches never met. East is East and West is West, and never the faiths did meet."

He waved me away impatiently. "Don't raise silly difficulties," he said. "I'm telling this story the way it's going to be filmed. I can see the camera coming down to take in the Irish Catholic faces, then crossing that church aisle, the broadest and least crossed space in the world, to swing past the Protestant Yankee faces. And then we'll pick out your Protestant minister grandfather, and he'll make the break, walk up the aisle, kneel for your blessing, and after you come down from the altar you'll bless him first . . ."

"Not," I retorted stoutly, "until I've blessed my father and mother."

He didn't even hear me.

Well, Hollywood got interested in war pictures, or how to dodge the motion-picture code, or backstage musicals, or mystery yarns, and the option lapsed. But I've been tempted again and again to recall the picture my producer friend had summoned up. Of one thing I am sure: had he been alive, grandfather Lord would have been at that ordination, and had I been permitted to bless him, I should have leaned forward to say, "Thank you!" for far, far more than I could ever repay.

But then, as life moves along, we come to thank our ancestors immediately after we have thanked God.

And I am very, very grateful for what mine bequeathed me beyond wealth (of which there was little) or fame (of which there is almost none). May that little namesake of mine think some day of his ancestors with the gratitude that I feel now for mine.

TO ANOTHER YOUNG FATHER AND MOTHER

Dear Both of You:

Nothing has ever pleased me more than the kind letter which, like yours, told me a child had been named for me. There have been many, though I stand abashed in the presence of a memory like that of our late St. Louis archbishop, Cardinal Glennon. When he was a young man, tall, handsome, a brilliant orator, the genial ruler of a great archdiocese, it became a positive fad to call boys by his name. There was even a sort of informal club made up of boys called John Joseph Glennon Kelly, and Schwartz, and Polizinski, and Thompson. For years the archbishop gave an annual reception when he received and blessed his namesakes, who formed a sizable queue around the episcopal mansion and took a deal of time in the greeting and blessing.

Boys named for me have been a handful by comparison, but each has been a source of happiness to me personally, and a new reason for trying to be less a disappointment to God and to those who bore my name.

I hope you will call him Daniel or Dan. Danny is fine for a born comedian. Danny Kaye, for instance, or that incomparable Danny Thomas get a fillip just because their names seem right. But once I was old enough to battle for my rights, I became Daniel or by preference Dan . . . a blessing I wish upon your young son.

Some time ago I wrote another gracious couple about the wise choice of ancestors. Oddly, in that letter I got as far as the mother and the father and then stopped. Knowing you, I am tempted to lay before you the story of my mother and father and to say, "Go thou and do likewise." Pardon the slip of grammar. When I lapse into the biblical, I forget the proper number. "Go ye," I should have said; and however little I may think of the product of my parents who happens to be myself, I know that I was blessed with parents given to few boys in the long course of history.

It annoys me a little that in the Roman Martyrology there is no separate listing of saints under fathers and mothers. I am sorry that a tender impulse did not impel that cataloguer of sanctity to develop a special category of "holy mothers"—and I don't in this case mean the foundresses of religious orders, wonderful as they are. Probably divine providence withheld such a classification on the quite obvious grounds that there would be too many qualifying for admission. The Church has been singularly blessed, and humanity through it, with holy mothers of wonderfully fine Catholic families. Watching patient young mothers suffering from the physical exhaustion brought on by tender wrestling with a twenty-pound mass of muscles and nerves, and looking at the lovely lines of patience written into the faces of old mothers, I think that to the "holy mother" might well be added, without exaggeration, "and martyr." The martyrdoms our mothers suffered because of us and through us must make them not unworthy of rank near Agnes and Philemon and Cecilia.

No one has bothered to list male saints under the category of "holy fathers." There again, holy father is the dear name kept by the sons of religious orders and communities for the saint who thought up their way of life and set them the example on which they pattern their characters.

But throughout my happy life I have been lucky enough to know many a holy father of a family whose life was in the pattern of those who think first of the importance of their homes and the value of strong, well-trained children. American Catholic fathers rate a special place in history. Men have never worked harder. Catholics have never made more generous sacrifices for the advancement of their Church. Husbands have never been more loyal and in a way long-suffering. And if they have loved their children, they have, perhaps, loved them less wisely than well. The enthroned paternal tyrant of England's Victorian days, the Christian sheik ruling with despotic whim many a European home, never seems to have place in American life. Even in *Life with Father,* the blustering Mr. Day is more the subject of laughter than of fear. And in Catholic homes I have seen and felt much more of love than of domination, of paternal service than of paternal commands, of determination to pass on to the children everything possible of faith and joy and opportunity rather than a demanding of awe and servility.

Defying the philosophical principle that no one can give to others what he himself does not have, American Catholic fathers have miraculously created a generation of children with far greater opportunities than ever they themselves possessed. They have seen to it that their children's chances for education were better. They have worked for laws that would make their lives more secure. They have perhaps spoiled their children with too much loving, but so, apparently, did the father of the prodigal son whom the Savior presented as the sublime example for the fathers of our race.

If I have any slightest eloquence, I could expend it gladly on American Catholic mothers and fathers. Heaven must be full of them. And without too much hesitance, I suggest that many of them knew their purgatories while on earth at the hands of none-too-grateful or gracious children.

There is one lovely prayer over which I invariably pause when it recurs in the Breviary. I suggest it as a perfect petition for parents. The sacred writer asks God to spare him the blight of great poverty or great riches. He wants instead what is sufficient for calm and happy living, not too little, not too much. In other words, he prays for the great blessing of being Middle-Class. Quite deliberately I put that noble sector of society into capital letters.

My mother and father were definitely middle-class. I never heard my mother suggest that she was a daughter of the Irish kings. My father laughed good naturedly at the "pedigree," and, as far as I recall, never would follow my begging insistence that he study with me the heraldry of that long-since vanished family tree.

I was a young fellow in the days when it was the fashion of the clever to bombard the bourgeoisie with abuse and to laugh ribaldly at the middle class. The French men of letters who hated God and God's sturdy yeomen of the respectable mid-section of society set the fashion. Shaw and Wells and Galsworthy and Ibsen and Sinclair Lewis followed the pattern in other lands. It was a disgraceful thing to admit that one was middle-class. Bourgeoisie was a dirty word. And like all the young men who read widely in that period of preparation for catastrophe, I was infected with their venom. All goodness came from the proletariat. Middle-class virtues were at the root of all our evils. We venerated the superman who had risen above their morality and their ideals, who crushed their homes and laughed at their peaceful, commonplace marriages. Businessmen were laughed to scorn. It was the rebel rising from the mob or the dictator ruling on top of the mass who rated history's applause and the panegyrics of that strange age.

Years later, in Rome, I sat with the great Jesuit social pioneer, Father Joseph Henry Ledit, and heard him plead the cause of the middle class.

I cannot quote him verbatim, but I quote him from vivid memory of his words:

"We must fight with all our strength for the salvation of the middle class," he said. "They are the only strong natural defense of our Christian civilization."

How strange that sounded with *Main Street* still sneering at this bourgeoisie and *Babbitt* becoming a common noun, an insult hurled at the businessman of America! William Allen White, from the heart of Kansas, had whipped out at Lewis, when he invited him to come to any of the small midwestern cities, by-pass Main Street, and visit over on Oak or Elm or Chestnut or Maple, and see the quiet, tree-sheltered homes out of which had come the real greatness of our land. Not much could be hoped for from the depressed and suppressed inhabitants of the tenements of Mean Street. Almost less could often be hoped for from the sons and daughters of the metropolitan Gold Coasts. But from the shaded residential streets of American cities, from the parents who had to struggle a bit to give their children advantages they themselves might have missed, came our generals and presidents, our scientists and scholars, our fine fathers and pure mothers, our physicians and honest lawyers and farsighted men of commerce and enterprise, our heroes and statesmen, our poets and musicians and artists, our martyrs and our saints.

Father Ledit, living then under the shadow of Mussolini's fascism, with Hitler's glowering menace rising to darken one horizon while Stalin and Trotsky battled it out in another direction for the control of men's destinies in time and eternity, needed only to wave a gesturing hand: "How they hate the middle class, all of them," he said. "Never does a tyrant rise without the proclaimed intention of wiping them out. They are his enemies. He can mold the mob to his whims. He can bribe the rich and powerful with promises that they will sit in the seats of the mighty. But the middle class see through him, reject his false promises, despise his cruelty and greed, win his inexorable hatred; and he sets himself to destroy them utterly.

"There will be no middle class in any land where communism takes over. Hitler leaves no place for them in his Nazi tyranny. Mussolini is dedicated to the wiping out of these enemies of his despotism. The wholesome, the healthy, the free in heart and the open in mind, the loyal, the honest, the frugal, the idealistic, the gentle, the kind—all these come from the middle class; for them we of the Church must battle. Once they are gone, civilization will yield to the brutality of tyranny; the brute state will take over in place of the Church of Christ."

I have watched the progress of history and I know how right he was and how clearly his thesis has been vindicated. Democracy is the government of the great-hearted middle class. Christianity will always remain a religion of carpenters and little housekeepers in their small homes on the side streets of a thousand Nazareths.

All this is by way of saying how important I think parents like you, the mother and father of my new namesake. For I know that when Christ spoke of the "salt of the earth" He included in the very center of that savor people like my mother and my dad. The real light of the world is made up of the candles on the altars, the votive tapers in convent shrines, and the bright illumination of family living rooms. God lighted those Himself. We can be mercifully spared the floodlights and the conflagrations.

My father was a grocery clerk.

In sort of abashed ostentation, I have always said that "he dealt in tobacco." He did. Dealing in tobacco, in this day when the money of the world is controlled by the insurance companies, the liquor manufacturers, and the tobacco companies, sounds extremely aristocratic. He sold tobacco, but he sold sugar and salt and fancy canned goods, and staples and imported foods and drinks. He worked a painfully laborious day that took him from the house at seven in the morning and returned him at seven-thirty in the evening.

Children's idea of income is always a matter for adult laughter. My dad had a way of saying that "On my magnificent salary of eight dollars a week" and "Of course we're rich, with me bringing home eight dollars every Saturday night." Multiplication had just enlarged my horizon to the extent of making me apply it to events around me, when it led me to a terrifying discovery. Our weekly cleaning woman, Annie, in those days of munificent incomes was paid a dollar and a half a day plus her three meals. I can still see myself sitting at the table, a scratch pad before me as I did a sum in practical arithmetic: "Annie gets a dollar and a half a day, works six days a week . . . that means she earns . . ."

With a horrified scream I rushed into the room where my mother was entertaining guests.

"Mother," I cried in agony, "I've just figured that Annie earns more every week than my dad!"

For years the memory of twenty-five dollars a week lingered on as the sum total of my father's wages. I recall that Mother once mentioned in a burst of confidence that he had asked for a raise from Stanton and Company, the "fancy grocers" in the heart of downtown Chicago, with the guarantee that, if he got this increase (whatever it was), he would never again ask a raise. He got the raise, was briefly named "manager" (maybe on the principle that "We can't give you much more money, but we'll let you call yourself by some title if you want to"), and I am confident that never did his salary top thirty-five dollars a week.

Consider his working week, the Saturdays in July and August when the store closed at the hour of three, and the fact of never a vacation, and the whole financial picture looks pitiful.

Thank heaven for the wages-and-hours law! In those primitive days it was not even a twinkle in a legislator's eye.

In my book-length story of my mother, I paid tribute to the gambler (my father) who made his most successful gamble when he picked out a little Irish Catholic girl from a West Side boarding house and asked her to take over his future. He had no idea, nor had she, that he was marrying a financial witch. All he knew was that he was simply off his head about this young beauty and that he was offering her whatever she could make of his life and the less-than-just-modest wage he had begun to earn. Maybe he dreamed that the title "Lucky George," as his gambler friends had dubbed him, would be the basis for their financial security. He became Lucky George all right when he married my mother; he was the first to proclaim that to the amused, when listening, world. But his gambling days were over. He had won his big stake when she said her "Yes," and from that time on money would be scarce enough but absolutely regular and secure.

I would guess that they were about matched in formal education. The son of a long line of professional men, my father had scorned school and, like my mother, probably never bothered to finish eighth grade. The little girl who lived with her widowed and then deserted mother had to work as soon as she could get a job. She was always extremely courteous to the clerks who waited on her, and by preference she selected a girl clerk to serve her; for she never forgot and often talked of her days behind the glove counter when she had waited on the fashionable trade and known what it meant to be snubbed, bossed, and insulted.

Without formal education, with no appreciable income by any standards of our day, this young couple, with my grandmother Langdon, who was more a part of the household than the living-room furniture or the gas range, set up housekeeping in a home of their own. Never again would they live in a house that they did not own. They would be freeholders, independent with their heads held high. My mother had left forever the boarding houses in which she had spent her youth.

The Chicago Belt Line cutting through the heart of Chicago's old West Side has long since obliterated any sight or memory of their first cottage, but for years of my childhood I heard Mother and Dad talk of it in affection and with bursts of laughter. It must have been a maximum of four small rooms, with frame walls to keep out only the weaker winds and milder forays of winter. I doubt if it had running water or inside plumbing, for they used to mention the water that froze in the washbowls and the need to scrape frost off the windows to see how bundled up they must be before they ventured out. But they owned it. It was their very own. And Mother seemed to regret that she could point only to elevated-railroad tracks as the scene of my entrance into the world. Patronizingly I have felt a little sorry for youngsters whose birthplace is a magnificent modern hospital with its sanitary obstetrical floor.

The fact that at two years of age I had pneumonia could well be attributed to the rigors of winter in that relative lean-to. But no one ever commented on my near brush with death as other than an act of God.

Our life could be chaptered from that point on in the rising quality of the dwellings in which we lived. Our little frame two-flat building on St. Lawrence Avenue near Forty-fourth still stands. It represented a tremendous rise in fortunes, accomplished, I'd guess, without a comparable rise in Dad's wages. My mother supervised the building of the two-storied apartment building on Vincennes Avenue near Forty-third. She reared it in the shadow of the fabulous mansion which had been erected and deserted by Storey, a seemingly incredible financial genius who ended a bankrupt. I have often wondered if she thought the sight of its unfinished grandeur might deter my father from grandiose dreams of quick fortune by reckless gambling.

They were not content, however, until, early in my high-school days, they had purchased a house. Dad's English instinct to have a home that was his castle unshared by another tenant now was gratified. My mother with her shrewd financial instincts preferred a building where the rents paid her on the first of each month meant that she herself lived rent-free. But she loved the small house in Chicago's last-annexed suburb, Austin; and like every spot in which she lived, she made it in the truest sense a home.

Once a literary purist rebuked me for my careless use of the word "home." "You never call a house a house," she said primly.

"Do you know that you call all houses homes?" I hadn't noticed that, but it was true. Why not? I never lived in a house; I had always lived in the home which my mother's skill had filled with warmth and affection and good living. Maybe from practical experience I had no knowledge of houses—only of homes.

Briefly during my early teens, as we moved from one spot to another, we boarded. The return to a boarding house brought back all the ugly memories of my mother's youth; she hated every moment lived in the house of someone else. And with her usual genius for real estate we were soon out of it and back, in that dear domestic expression, "in a home of our own."

I have often talked to parents during the course of my priestly life about homes and homemaking and children in the household and the fun that one can have in a family. I am afraid that I based much of it on my own personal memories. And all of them are sublimely happy. When in the question period following a public lecture someone in the audience has protested that I talk like a millionaire and evidently expect them to give their children a mansion, I laugh inwardly and feel more than a bit patronizing. Ours were tiny houses. For years I slept on a cot in the living room, and when I was very small and inclined to roll out of bed, dining-room chairs were placed against the small sofa to serve as a nonhumiliating fence to hold me safe.

It was a big day in my life when I finally had a room of my own. I was still a youngster, but it remains one of the bright days of all time.

Money must have been a pressing problem. To the eternal credit of my parents, I never heard them mention it, discuss it, much less wrangle about it. But that is a tribute they can share equally. Of a Saturday evening my dad simply tossed the pay envelope on the table in the kitchen. On Monday morning my mother gave him the money he would need for carfare, lunches, and incidental expenses of the week. For the rest, his was the generosity and trust, hers was the financial management that came in its small way close to genius. When I hear moderns protesting the terrible lack of money, once more I smile. Times are changed, no doubt of that; and money has no longer the purchasing power that once it had. But I wonder if in domestic matters it is nearly as much a question of "how much income" as it is of "how well managed and with what generosity, loyalty, good humor, and love."

What our household knew was the frankest and most hearty possible love. For that I think my father can be thanked.

Not so long ago a fine physician friend of mine, Dr. Leo Bartels, and I sat discussing problems of his patients and my penitents. As always, a main problem was marriage. Said he in the course of the discussion: "No girl ought to marry unless she is off her head about the man. She must be madly in love with him, or the marriage just won't work." I shook my head in disagreement. "Not in my books," I said. "I think it is much better when the man is more in love with the girl than the girl with the man." "If that's the case," he retorted, "he's going to be a slave. She'll have all the power, and in a household that won't work. Let the girl do the main loving. Let the man feel that he is loved more than he loves. Then he can manage his affairs, resist her inclination to dominate and often, heaven help us, to make him change the work he loves for the work she wants to see him do."

We could never agree on that, I saw; for I was remembering the vastly successful marriage of my mother and father. And I know now that he was the lover and she was the deeply beloved.

Not that my mother wasn't the most devoted and the tenderest of wives. But in the balance of affection, the scales weighed with the enormous richness of his love for her. I am certain that my mother never gave any other man a passing glance. Truth to tell, she disliked most men and distrusted them all. I think her distrust in a singular sort of way extended to her husband. He had been a gay blade and he showed no signs of rusting. Though we could have accounted for every least second of his days and nights, she regarded his frank love-making with a slightly cynical eye, and would, after he had kissed her enthusiastically and gone out of the room singing gaily in his melodious off-key, look at me quizzically and say: "Do you think he really means it? Or does he just think that he does?"

He adored her. No doubt of that. Yet one evening he and I sat together in the front row of the theater gallery, the seats we affected since they were the ones we could afford. Rarely did we go anywhere together, he and I; but for some reason Mother had not been able to go, and we went to the play together, just the two males. As always in those formal days, we carried opera glasses. I recall vividly my shock and surprise when my highly proper and entirely devoted father and my mother's unabashed husband and lover took the opera glasses and during the intermissions trained them thoughtfully and appreciatively on every pretty woman in the boxes and the front row of the balcony below us. He even followed the progress of the formally dressed ladies up and down the aisle, relishing their charms, as far as I could make out, much more than he had enjoyed the development of the play.

I could not have been more than ten, at which age adults take it for granted their children are unobservant. A fellow feeling for him kept me, I am proud to report, from even suggesting to my mother his devout use of the opera glasses. I too thought that pretty ladies were to be admired. And I believe that even then I could understand how, having admired them with wholesome masculine relish, he would hurry home to the wife whom he proclaimed in tones of genuine gusto to be the most beautiful, charming, clever, and altogether desirable woman in the world. Whatever my mother's clouds of cynicism, I never doubted he meant to the full what he protested with such enthusiasm.

Never did he enter or leave the house without kissing her vigorously. I am tempted to use the old English word "buss." His English ancestry would have approved his busses. Never did a Saturday evening pass but he brought her a bouquet of flowers and a small box of candy. That was part love and part, as I have discussed in her life's story, her excellent training. She expected his tributes and she got what she expected. She was quite capable of adjusting her hat, like the fabulous wizard in a nursery tale I particularly loved, and freezing the birds out of the trees and his ears off his head. It was the privilege and duty of a husband to love his wife wholeheartedly. She would wait for him in the doorway, come evening. She would give us an affectionate whack that sent us scampering down the street to meet him. She would stand waiting for his embrace and return it with frank affection. But as I recall it all now, it was he who loved and she who accepted. She gave him absolute fidelity, but he gave her a sort of bounding and boundless affection. And between them they created the atmosphere of domestic peace and love in which I confess I thrived.

Perhaps I found it an ideal beyond the possibility of imitation. For when I have talked of the love between my parents, listeners have often countered with a natural enough query: "If you saw such a successful marriage, how does it happen that you didn't marry?" That puzzled me at first. Later on, perhaps rationalizing, I decided that I had seen such perfection that I doubted I could match it myself. Having seen a husband who seemed casually to attain to the heights set by the most arrant romanticist, I searched my soul, perhaps unconsciously, to decide no such domestic virtues lurked in my own soul. I could admire without hope of imitating. And knowing the perfect, I did not wish to blemish it with a poor imitation. Too much perfection may be discouraging.

I am glad I cannot write, "I never knew them to quarrel." On the principle that the exception proves the rule, I can recall one majestic quarrel between them, that rises with horrifying volcanic fury along the calm sky line. Briefly, it happened thus. He returned this warm Saturday afternoon tuned to concert pitch. He kissed her rapturously and she pulled back in horror. He, who to my knowledge never took a drink, "reeked of the stuff." She said nothing, and he said too much. It was explanation that did not explain and protest that was eloquent of guilt. She disappeared briefly, returned with her hat and purse, and walked down the front stairs, an avalanche of indignant scorn that would not be stayed in its course. An hour later, hand in hand, my father and I circled the neighborhood, calling, in heavy casualness, at the houses of her friends. She was not there or anywhere. Then as night drew on and the clock ticked horribly, he sent my brother to bed, and he and I, wordless and sick with misery, sat together in the living room, convinced that the end of the world had come and that judgment was a matter of minutes away.

I shall never forget the leap of my heart as her footstep sounded on the porch stairs, the sweep of his eagerness as he flung open the screen door and wrapped her in his arms, and the complete disregard for me as, tightly embraced, they went to their room. I slept that night in a great peace. But it was peace following the nearness of terror.

Even during the dread days when his mother tried to drive the wedge between them, they did not quarrel. She was calm when she reached the point where the decision was his to make and he must make it. His usually smiling and happy face took on the tense, agonized lines of a man being torn apart by the two women dearest to him. But there were no angry words between them. And when the dark, lowering figure disappeared from their horizon, they never referred to the subject again. In fact, I have no memory of their ever "throwing things up to each other," hashing over the past, reliving former mistakes, or boasting, in the fashion of people who love less, that they can forgive but they can't forget.

If I have been accused of being idealistic in my attitude toward marriage, if I have been convinced that the power of women for man's good is beyond words, if I have felt it was the privilege of a man to be tender to women and gentle and considerate, her free courtier, I am afraid I must lay gentle blame upon the domestic life of which I was an observant part. I was convinced that homes could be happy on a minimum of money. I was sure that husbands and wives could love each other deeply and for life. I was certain that fury and anger and recrimination and spats and quarrels are no more the common events of married life than wrecks and collisions are the constant concomitant of good automobile driving.

Ours was a house of good food.

Isn't that a trivial subject suddenly to bring into the story of my life? Not at all. "Feed the brute!" is the cynical injunction given by the wise mother to her about-to-be-married daughter. And many a household goes on the rocks, not of angry seas, but of poorly cooked dinners and sloppy suppers.

When my father married my mother she had never cooked a meal in her life. Nor had her mother, an exquisite seamstress, cared for the kitchen. It fitted badly into her natural aristocracy of character. "She'll make a poor wife for a poor man," my grandmother Langdon told the aspiring suitor, in a final effort to frighten this Protestant wooer from the door of their boarding house. Undaunted, he married her anyhow in the priests' parlor of Chicago's old St. John's, and bore off in triumph one of history's great cooks.

It just came natural to her. She loved food, and she loved to see her man well fed. She flourished in a prediet day. She had married a man who sold food all day long, and who had a combination of inherited good taste (his own gourmet father provided that) and access to the choicest foods of the day. I cannot recall a badly prepared or casual meal in our house. I cannot recall my mother more completely at home or more gay and joyous than in her own kitchen. She was Cinderella who had been rescued from the ashes of a glove counter to find her throne room between the icebox and the kitchen gas stove.

With something approaching deep pity I have regarded men and women who "don't like this" and "can't eat that," and "never touch this" or "I don't know, I've never tried it." I have something that is almost intolerance for picky eaters and for people whose diet is limited to two kinds of meat and the plainest of kitchen garden vegetables. I watch in scorn eaters who draw back from anything they have not eaten constantly, and who turn away in a sort of emotional tremor from some strange dish.

When a neighbor at table regards some experiment of the chef with repugnance, and, instead of tasting it, utters an intolerant, "What's this stuff?" I want to turn the dish upside down on his offending head. I might, except that I am personally too eager to taste the novelty and test the flavor that I have thus far missed.

Adventuring in food is one of the great adventures of life. And thanks to the brief shopping excursions with my grandfather, my father's employment in a "fancy grocery," and my mother's miracles with saucepan and skillet, my youth prepared me for something approaching a lifetime of experimenting in food. To this day I find no recreation more stimulating than a chance to take my place in a kitchen and for appreciative eaters to launch into the concoction of dishes which, I sincerely hope, no one has ever compiled before.

We had a stern rule in our family: anything that was brought to the table was good enough for us children to eat. The rule did not long hold for my invalid brother. For me it was not a law but a challenge. "What's new for dinner?" was easily my dad's greeting as he sat down to dine. And when he came home laden with packages from his store, my mother unpacked them with the gaiety of a child emptying a Christmas stocking. So it was that, as a youngster, I grew familiar with brands of cheese and unusual foreign canned meats; truffles and paté de foie gras were familiars; and curries and chutneys and unusual jams and preserves. The cuts of meat were indefinitely varied on our table, and the ways of cooking vegetables were a triumph of my mother's cuisine.

Butchers soon developed the highest respect for her ability to pick the precisely right piece of beef, and they looked at her admiringly as she waved away some cut they were trying to dispose of and indicated instead the choice piece they had been saving for a connoisseur. She shopped with a meticulous regard for pennies, and we would walk for a mile to find the shop where lamb chops were selling a penny less a pound. I have never forgotten the day she flared indignantly: "You mean," she demanded, "that roast beef is now a quarter for two pounds? What robbery!" Mercifully she did not live to see steak selling for a dollar and a half a scant pound.

In the summertime our kitchen became a redolent cannery, and city folks though we were, we went through the cycle of ketchups and preserves and jellies and jams and pickling and bottling. Root-beer time was a little like the coming of the circus; with the fillip of fireworks when the bottles, set to ripen in the sun, exploded on the back fence in an aromatic fountain of brown foam and fury. Watching the sight was almost more fun than drinking the stuff.

The challenge of our male "sweet tooth" excited my mother to feats of dessert making. She became a champion pie baker, and her cakes were mountain high and light as the clouds on the uppermost peaks. She became famous for her doughnuts, so that I fed the neighborhood children out of her bottomless doughnut jar. She discovered the male love for puddings only to gratify it. We took turns churning the ice cream which she made to rich perfection. And her concoctions of fruits and nuts were enough to delight Dr. Sam Johnson had he not missed her cookery by several generations.

Breakfast in those days, when food was also entertainment, might well be cooked cereal, corn bread, lamb chops, and heaps of toast. Sunday dinner was an event which left Mother groggy from labor and Dad groggy from gorging. And picnics meant the preparation of hampers of food that might well have sustained an army making a beachhead but actually melted before the might of appreciative trenchermen.

We have a Jesuit rule that reads, "While at meals the body is refreshed, let the soul also have its food." This becomes the excuse for reading at meals. My mother believed that food was a precious and important element. Always she preferred quality to quantity. Rarely we ventured down, she and I alone, to Rector's, the best restaurant of its day. For forty cents each we could get a fresh crab-meat salad, and the crispest of lettuce and the freshest of mayonnaise. For another fifteen cents we could top it off with raspberry water ice. Coffee, butter, and delicious hot rolls came just as unpriced incidentals. We ate appreciatively, and left feeling that life was good.

But she who had never heard of St. Ignatius or his Common Rules knew that more important than food for the body was the food for the soul. So I lived, from the moment of dawning consciousness, in an atmosphere of books. Why I did not turn out much, much better than I did has always been cause for personal apology. Ours were premovie, preradio, even pretalking-machine days. Where the modern, "thrown on his own resources" by the breaking down of the family TV, is a restless and lost ghost of himself, we were constantly left to entertain ourselves.

The symbol of wealth in our day was a simple statement of fact: "Oh, they have a piano and everything." The everything was never specified. The piano was the mark of wealth. How they managed it, I do not know; but once I had reached five, we had a piano. The "everything" with us consisted in a constant flow of good books. Public libraries were still in the currently predatory mind of a Scottish ironmonger who later would put his name over noble arches as Andy Carnegie. If you wanted books then, you bought them. We did. Magazines were all a dime, *Munsey's,* the *Strand* straight from London and reeking with mystery and horror, *McClure's, Harper's, Scribner's.* Somehow we managed them. And, I'm sure at the cost of many a new bonnet she might have had, my mother bought and brought home, read, and then interchanged among her literate friends, the classics and the books of the year.

Before I could read, she read to me. I was saturated in Greek fable, nursery rhymes, Aesop, the Grimm Brothers, Anderson, and Andrew Lang. How she, without formal education, searched them out and discovered them for us is one of the mysteries and wonders of God's grace. She read me Lamb's *Tales from Shakespeare* and swiftly graduated me to listen to her reading of *The Merchant of Venice* and an hilarious fairy tale called *The Taming of the Shrew.* The year that Lew Wallace hit the literary bull's-eye with *Ben Hur,* she read it aloud night after night through one whole winter.

I can close my eyes today as I write all this and see vividly the little scene around the dining-room table. The dinner was cleared away; the dishes were washed; homework had been prepared; Dad had returned and relaxed after a taxing day; my brother sat quietly in the beginnings of a strange apathy that was the first stage of his illness; and Mother picked up the book she had been reading, and with the light from the welsbach burner falling on the page and the lower half of her beautiful, animated face, would read. She read beautifully, as few women I have ever heard. She phrased with complete understanding. She mimicked the characters as they spoke their dialogue. She could make the vivid passages come to life and adventure race. She read us *Treasure Island* and *Robinson Crusoe* and moved on to *David Copperfield,* and reaching above our heads, she attempted and achieved the exquisite prose of *Vanity Fair.*

She read in the most perfect brogue the weekly meditations of the current Mr. Dooley and, in a swift shift to German dialect, the popular adventures of a newspaper creation whose butcher shop and dog antedated the comic strips. She discovered for us George Ade and his fables, and read O. Henry before we bothered about who this mysterious writer could be. We thrilled together to Sherlock Holmes, reading the great stories as they appeared, one a month, in the current magazines.

Forgive me if, in slight senility, I feel so sorry for the youngsters with their noses buried in the most dreadful time killers and anesthetics of the mind, the comics. Forgive me for a complacent gloating over the mother who stored my mind for all future days with the richness of great fiction, high adventure, unforgettable characters, and the lilt of beautiful prose. How can one be sufficiently grateful for favors like that, or wish more heartily he could share his blessings with a generation apparently determined not to read?

High-speed color printing had not yet developed for children books that make reading ability unnecessary. Yet I recall with fullest detail the first time I was allowed to pick out a book to be entirely my own. I walked the counters of the department-store book section, and settled at long last on *The Story of George Washington in Words of One Syllable*. I can still see the way in which the editor had split up *sur-vey-or* to make a three-syllable word (essential for the story) look like a single-syllable word. That was the first little book cell around which was to cluster my growing library. I got books for my birthday and for Christmas and major feasts.

Once I was five and could stretch part of an octave, I was started at the piano. Of that enough for the present, except that Sunday evening became a time when we gathered in the living room and I played through my repertory to a patient family audience. My father was tone deaf. As they say of General Grant, he knew two tunes; one was "Yankee Doodle," the other wasn't. Providence was merciful, for he could sit through my performance at the piano not knowing that my left hand was hiding completely from my right hand what it was doing.

The atmosphere of our house was thoroughly Catholic. Yet out of tactful respect for my father, grace was never said at meals and there was no family prayer. Mother, Grandmother, and the children went off to Sunday Mass. The days were prefrequent-Communion, so once a month was the accepted custom for receiving Holy Communion. Yet, though Dad slept late on those

Sunday mornings and though in childish logic I grew to worry because he did not share the blessings which evidently meant so much to my mother, I knew very well that any departure from my mother's way of religious conduct would excite his just wrath as promptly as it would bring my mother's punishment and God's ultimate rejection.

In fact, I cannot believe I knew the meaning of mortal sin when for the first of a hundred times my mother told me, and meant it, the story of Queen Blanche and the young St. Louis. "I would rather see you dead at my feet," my mother would quote, dramatically becoming the mother of the young king, "than feel that you had ever committed a mortal sin." Just the other day, a dear and gracious mother wrote me how, when her young son lay grievously ill, she had suddenly found herself praying, not for his health, but that, if he ever would offend God mortally, he would be allowed to die. Mothers are the same when they are good and great. That same prayer was the prayer of Queen Blanche, my own mother, and the mother of this lad of the present generation.

No wonder (if I may be permitted another aside) that people who have read my story of my mother write to me in surprising numbers to say, "I marveled how like she was to my own mother."

My father, a country lad, loved to talk of the country. He had no slightest interest in ever returning. When we finally achieved a lawn and space for a small garden, he regarded it with reluctant eyes; mowed the lawn when I failed to do so; but let the land lie fallow. To my mother the country was a necessary evil, a place that had to be if we were to have milk and pork chops, spinach and peaches. That anyone would voluntarily visit it, much less live there throughout a lifetime, baffled her. It was almost impossible to drag her to a city park. She regarded outdoor exercise as something for small boys and professional athletes, and had been brought up by a mother who safeguarded her skin and complexion with hats of the broadest brims and the constant wearing of gloves.

If the custom of our neighborhood called for a summer holiday in the country, she sent me off with my grandmother to the hospitable farm or to the lake. She stayed home where civilization provided what she regarded, not as luxuries, but as the sheerest essentials of life. Once she made a summer excursion to the Wisconsin lakes, feared the small life in the tall grass around her, avoided the water in anything less than a sizable launch, detested the discomforts of the summer cottages, sat on the porch in the midst of the cardplaying of chattering ladies, and wished she were vacationing on the corner of Madison and State or Broadway and Forty-third.

She raised a true son in me, a city dweller who vastly admires the countryside from the comfortable seat of a moving car, whose thumb if slightly green is green with some life-destroying poison, and who spent the four years of his early Jesuit life at Florissant hardly able to distinguish growing corn from a field of potatoes.

Once during my priestly life I was invited to address the rural youth gathered in a great Catholic rural-life conference in Spokane, Washington. It was a delightful meeting; but when my time came to chairman and address these young people, so skillful with livestock and adept in the coaxing of green things from the ground, I confessed my complete futility on the farm. "When first we had a little garden of our own, or rather, space for a garden," I confessed before them, "my mother, who believed her son should try anything and everything, set me the task of raising some vegetables. A little quiet snooping convinced me that radishes were almost foolproof. So I planted the seeds according to the directions on the highly ornamental package and waited trustfully for the burgeoning of the magnificent radishes (little less than melons in size) promised by the optimistic artist employed by the seed company. But he had reckoned without my ability to blight. Once the promising young green appeared above the soil, I made daily excursions to my truck garden, each day pulling up half a dozen radishes to find out how far they had developed. I then thrust them back into the earth to resume their interrupted course. That was my first and only attempt at farming. With that confession before you, we shall continue the discussion of your conference under my expert chairmanship."

Forgive me, my dear young parents, if I have talked of mine at such length. But my mother and father are subjects about which I grow easily prolix. And perhaps I write this way in the hope that some day your little Dan, my namesake, may think of you with the love and gratitude I feel for mine.

For my father was a man who lived for his wife and children, who made life for them peaceful and full and rich and cushioned with love.

My mother was in what I think the realest sense of the word a career woman. She had taken up, almost without preparation, the career of wife and mother, and she made of that career a magnificent success. I say that, knowing that I may seem conceited, almost arrogant. Am I suggesting that I, one of the products of her career, am so notable a credit to her? Heaven forbid! On the contrary, I am amazed that, considering all she gave me, I was not far, far more worthy of her dreams and her labors.

She herself never thought that hers was the most important natural career in the world. With years she grew in her reverence for the career of a good nun. She thought there were no women like "the sisters." For herself, God had chosen another career, a career of turning a house into a home, of preparing those meals which would build strong bodies and contented minds. She knew the importance of accepting love and deserving this dear domestic wage from the man who gave it so freely. She had not the slightest thought that for her to write a book would be a more important achievement than to bring a son to full maturity. She was not a trained musician, but she created around her the harmony of graceful living. She was the sentry at the door of her home to bar the way to temptation and to hold out sin. She had a full-time job making her family happy and watching the growth of the most tender of all God's growing creatures, the souls of children.

Next to the faith, which comes most often from faith-filled parents, certainly the best gift of God is parents like mine.

I cannot but wish and pray for you the strength to be to your son all my father and mother were to me.

Lucky your little Dan if he can in his old age feel the gratitude and honor, the love and respect, which are in the heart of his namesake.

TO A YOUNG SCHOLAR AND TEACHER

Dear Bill:

From the vantage point of your mellowed Ph.D. you are kind to ask me about my education. Education, my own included, has given me endless subject for thought and interest. Though I spent only three years teaching in a classroom, I consider myself an educator. Teaching others in a variety of mediums is really my life's work.

I have often wondered if I am an educated man or merely a man on his way toward an education. In all honesty, most men would claim for themselves only the effort to learn, not the mastery of knowledge. In the course of the years I acquired a bachelor of arts degree, which, I suppose by the very force of its name, means someone in a position to marry arts, science, and literature, not someone already taking these lovely creatures to his breast. I was solemnly proclaimed a master of arts, when I could ask in all honesty what art I had ever mastered. I never gained my doctorate of philosophy, though I had three full years of philosophy itself. It has amused me that that degree is given to men for years devoted to every conceivable subject under the skies or under the earth; seldom to men who have specialized in philosophy itself. I was several times created and re-created an honorary doctor of letters, and on each occasion my acceptance of the kindly and gratuitously bestowed degree implied only one thing: I liked to be known as a doctor and to be called a doctor, a man with a right to teach others.

When I was a young novice teaching catechism at Florissant, my father, a convert recently in the faith, stood on a hill watching me come back with my apostolic companions from the little village school where we taught the fundamentals of faith to local youngsters. He bowed to me in his unfailing courtly fashion, and quoted strictly by ear, "Blessed are the feet of those who come teaching the good news." I hoped I might merit that "blessed" for long years of my life. It would be such an enrichment to make the good news, which is knowledge, truth, and wisdom, one's very own and tell it convincingly and persuasively to others.

If I were a true scholar, I should at this point dash back to the library, and demand from the librarian a copy of *The Education of Henry Adams*. For it is long years since I read that enlightening study of a man's growth and development. Instead, since I am not a scholar, I quote and mention it from hazy memory. The sole point I wish to make is that the sizable volume is the story, not of a man's schooling, but of a man's life. The education of Henry Adams was partly in formal classrooms, mostly in the lovely university which is the universe. He speaks of his professors with gratitude; he is most grateful for the men and women who taught him, never suspecting that he was their avid pupil. A professor's gown may be the outward sign of a teacher's skill. Some of the world's really great teachers never wore the gown nor had the right to wear it.

The only thing I personally can claim for my education is that I have tried never to allow it to stop. Each time I rounded out a period of my formal education, I echoed with approval the name of the day: Commencement Day. And I refused to think of it merely as the start of a new phase of life, when what it seemed to me was the start of a new course of learning. Education with me, please God, will end with death; and then, in divine contradiction, I hope that it really begins.

Some time back I was placed in the position of being forced to analyze formal education. What are children supposed to learn from school? What does a successful student get as a result of much classroom attendance, laboratory practice, lecture, and research? Instead of going to the masters of pedagogy, I did a little thinking back over my life, and then over the lives of men and women whom I regarded as well educated. You need not flinch. This is no discussion of pedagogy. This is no summing up in learned synthesis of what the big educational conferences have not achieved. It's just a fumble out of experience.

If I had any claim to education, it was certainly not a claim to a vast storehouse of facts. The quiz kids on the radio programs long ago discouraged me. And I was pleased when they discontinued "Information Please!" Those experts made me feel like a dolt.

When I pick up a popular article on the atom, I am lost in a few paragraphs. Once I walked through the library of our Biblical Institute in Rome. Oh, what a disheartening experience! To look at the backs of the books and to confess I did not know even the meaning of their titles! To look at the little cards that subdivided the library into major sections, and not know what subjects the sections contained!

For years I read through all information quizzes in current magazines and failed an appreciable number of questions along any line. When I am trapped into listening to one of the TV quizzes, I admire but have no desire to imitate the courage of the victims, who aren't quite sure what queen darned socks with Cleopatra's needle and whether Aida is an opera, a famous surgeon, or the name of a Pullman car.

Then, in my own personal summary, I decided that the net result of education was the creation of pleasant, useful habits. A habit of that sort is something that a person does easily, well, without effort of much conscious planning. And I found I had a lot of such habits. I have the habit of reading and certainly the habit of writing letters. I have the habit of talking easily with friends and meeting strangers without much struggle. I have the habit of music, and though my performance at the piano is totally without technique or polish, I use music constantly for my own enjoyment and some pleasure for others. I have the habit of theology. I doubt if I could pass the examination which was relatively simple when I finished my theological course years ago; but I never rise before an audience, large or small, without using theology . . . and more important perhaps, the philosophy that has been theology's handmaiden and my pleasantly accommodating companion.

I have the habit of interest. Few things fail to interest me and I seldom venture out without events and places and people passing within my range which catch and hold my attention. I have the habit of curiosity, which probably isn't much different from the habit of interest I've already conceitedly claimed. But when a stranger tells me about the unusual trade or profession which is his, I ask him questions out of a real desire to know. I am fascinated by new places and strange foods and unusual customs and books that are different from the general run of books. Life for me has been endlessly exciting and challenging . . . would titillating be the word for the way life affects me?

My grandfather Lord comes instantly to my mind when I think of an educated man. Although he lived in the back hills of the Herkimer Valley, he was keenly alive to the new in world events and medicine, took up a fresh subject for each year's study, assembled around him a library of the most variegated interests, loved every moment of the World's Fair, and found conversation even with a child endlessly delightful.

If the test of education is the contentment of mind when one is alone and left on one's own resources, I have known some beautifully educated people. Another test is awareness, the live mind that turns quickly and sympathetically to almost everything. I have met many without much formal education who are educated. I am not too sure that all the specialists I have met with are educated men and women. Some of them are alive only when they are (to use their own tiresome phrase) "in their field." The Universal Man who was the ideal of the Renaissance has apparently given way to the Pinpoint Man, and the point and the pin seem to be constantly shrinking.

But before we find ourselves engaged, my dear young educator, in a duel of footnotes at forty ems, let me skip lightly (with due allowance for creaking joints) from the abstract to the concrete. I cannot lay claim to a profound formal education. I am diffident about suggesting myself as an educated man. But I can, as you asked, talk about my education.

What's the old psychological saying, that every man's education begins four generations before his birth? Could be. We'll skip that, referring you back to what I have written elsewhere about the education, slightly formal, of my parents, about the education I received at the finger tips of my minister grandfather, about my grandmother Langdon who always talked to me as to a fully matured adult. I have told you about the way my mother, endlessly and with keen perception and intelligent interpretation, read to me. I could mention the fact that I spent much time among adults; the fact that my brother was an invalid and that I was not encouraged too much to associate with my contemporaries made that inevitable.

In recent years the psychologists grow eloquent about the education that is soaked up almost through infantile pores. Adults for a long time paid little attention to the presence of youngsters among them. Aside from such adages as "Little pitchers have big ears," children were just part of the furniture. Now we know differently; we know that in those years of infancy and the clumsy, half-tipsy years that precede the so-called age of reason, children learn all the basic things of later life:

How to walk.
How to talk.
How to eat.
How to get along with people.
The basic principles of right and wrong.
The basic sense of truth and lies.
The sense of religion.
A reasonable care of health.
An attitude toward exercise.
Manners.
Interests which can from the first tiny seeds be developed into the vast thing known as culture.

As a teacher later on I used to flatter myself that, given two weeks' steady contact with boys in a classroom, I could give you a pretty fair picture of their home lives. Their conduct in class was a demonstration of the sort of homes they lived in. Their alertness or inertness told the story of their parents.

Perhaps when I say I flattered myself, that is just what I was doing. But early I learned not to use rich home and good home, poor home and bad home, as synonyms. Some of the worst-mannered and dullest boys I ever taught came from the homes of the rich; some of the most polished and alert came from the very poor. In fact, it has never ceased to amaze me that too much opportunity, too many chances to see and hear and go and come, seem almost as bad as too little or too few. Those parents are wise who ask God not to give them too much wealth or too deep a poverty. Children thrive better with plenty of chances for which they have to do more than a little struggling.

Lovers of the old saw like still to quote: "Charity begins at home." The cynic long ago added the tag line: "And usually stays there." And without cynicism: "And if it does, it does not stay there." When a child reached my tutorial hands, and as his pedagogue I took him by the moist little palm and began to pull him the rough way of knowledge, I knew that I was working with a pretty "set-in-his-ways" individual. Nothing sounds more stupid than to say of a child entering kindergarten or first grade, "Today he begins his education." He is merely taking his first reluctant steps toward formal education. Hitherto, if he has had good parents, he has taken willing and unconscious steps in an education more effective because more informal. The teacher because of his profession is called upon suddenly to take the already formed and pretty well solidified mass of humanity and see what he can do to fashion it further. The change henceforth will not be notable. If he has heard at home, "I ain't got none of this and I don't like nothing like that," he may be taught the horror of the double negative; deep down inside, the single negative will always seem to him pretty weak and sissified, and in lapses to the natural, he'll slap the double negatives on with a feeling of their essential rightness.

If he has dropped his things all over the house, leaving them for someone else, mother or a maid, to pick up and put away, he'll go right on doing it. I recall once saying to the wife of a naval officer: "It must be wonderful to be married to a man trained to the meticulous neatness of a battlewagon. You certainly don't have to go around after your husband picking up his dirty socks." "That," she said with pained irony, "is what you think. Annapolis made him a consciously neat person; and when he's on the ship, he thinks things should be shipshape. At home he lapses right into the habits of his youth, and does as he did at home when he was a boy. He scatters his gear all over the house and the women of the ménage pick it up."

So I have hardly a conscious recollection of my going to school. I am too preoccupied and have been all my life with the training I got before school. Mine was an infancy when kindergarten, both as a word and as a fact, was novel indeed. No schools in our neighborhood had one. A few of the better-circumstanced sent their children to private preschools that bragged they were using all the new methods later associated with kindergartens. But my parents didn't. Instead, when I look at the equipment of a modern kindergarten pupil, I have a surge of affectionate familiarity. My parents provided me with all manner of building blocks. None of them were streamlined in the style of today; indeed, when I finished my childish structures they were rococo indeed, with pediments and capitaled columns and lots of stone gingerbread flanking the flights of stairs. We had no paint books; but we had boxes of paints in which we messed with freedom, preferably doing our murals on the butcher paper that came wrapped around Sunday's roast. Nobody in those amazingly pacific days thought that toy lead soldiers made a lad belligerent; so we had our cavalrymen and Indians and Civil War soldiers and English Hussars and French Zouaves. We loaded and unloaded our small farm wagons; and our wooden Noah and his family embarked over and over again with their animals into our toy arks.

I was very young indeed when I pedaled my tricycle, ironically called a velocipede—as if velocity were possible on its iron-tired wheels. And though nobody thought of this as social studies, we could buy a pasteboard police helmet and dickey for a quarter, and play fireman in a similar suit when the mood was on us.

My mother and father, who loved cards, gave us their old decks and taught me little casino before I was six. And I could recognize the various American writers on a pack of "authors" cards before any contact with their books. We played games like messenger boy and pachisi; and since Mother and Dad and Grandmother were not caught up in the throes of soap operas or obliged to spend time listening to quiz programs, they had time to play with us youngsters in what was, I believe, a highly effective substitute for the kindergarten of the future. I'm all for kindergartens, mind you; it's just that I feel that I got mine at home. No, no clay modeling; that would have messed up the family carpets, and children were to be children and not messy herds.

All of this, of course, indicates something which has been criticized in me by many a formal educator: the sneaking but often-expressed conviction that schools are just supplements for homes that have not been too successful. A child learns more in the first five years of his life than he ever learns again, and learns eagerly, willingly, in the spirit of zestful fun, in the atmosphere that he knows and loves. The transfer to a formal factory for hammering knowledge into his head is what makes many a child drag himself unwillingly to school. He is told he is learning instead of learning without knowing he does. He is taught by a stranger instead of by his nearest of blood. Study becomes a chore as later on work will be a chore. Before school days began, it had been an unconscious delight.

Whether or not anyone deigns to agree, I lament the fact that our schools are so magnificent and our homes so mediocre, that our teachers are trained professionals and many a parent is a reluctant amateur. I regard with horror the attitude of many educationists that the child must be rescued from his parents as soon as possible and turned over to people who have a formal degree to prove their competence for the job of child training. I am a little sad that the best hours of the day are spent away from home, and in an atmosphere made so elaborate, that the parent stands in our civilization a fair chance of becoming atrophied. Alas that the modern parents should be regarded by too many pedagogues as in the same class with the appendix or the useless fins of a whale!

Educationists, too, have protested when they thought I overpraised the cocurricular, which once on a time we called the extracurricular. At least I am glad that this part of education has been advanced from *extra* to *co*. That is a step up. They plug for class; I am likely to plug for comradeship. They love the laboratory; I like the gym and the school little theater. They feel that the English class is the spot to master the mother tongue; I put in a plea for the school paper, the debate, public speaking. They feel that students learn most from their teachers; I incline to think they learn a powerful deal from their fellow students.

As you can readily see, my dear young educator, I am entering a strong plea at this point for preschool training such as I feel was given me. All my life I have loved lots of people, rejoiced in crowds, met strangers with zest, because, I am sure, of the variegated social life of my parents. Once more, please note that money and social life need not go together. Social life can be singularly without extravagance or elaborate formality. I think back to the constant flow of parties in our home. My grandmother and mother, left alone by the long working hours of my patient father, rejoiced in the constant visiting of their neighbors. And they were much more called upon than calling. Hospitality was their métier rather than social rambling. I recall with relish the poker club to which my father belonged throughout the years, and which my mother welcomed in genuine delight, displaying her approval in the delicious supper that rounded off the final pot. I have never forgotten how, once we had become established in a house instead of an apartment, my mother quietly informed her women friends that henceforth on every Wednesday afternoon she would be at home, and they were most cordially invited to drop in without need of announcement or further invitation. Wednesday was one day when I dashed home from school to dip into the wonderful plates of salad and sandwiches and cakes with which she regaled her visitors. And never were there less than three, though seldom more than eight, who came and spent the afternoon in formal informality.

I could not list the succession of card clubs to which my parents belonged and which they entertained regularly in their turn. I just know that my young eyes popped when the time came for their taking over our little living room. We were not exiled, we children. We had been trained to take a silent and auxiliary spot; but as long as we behaved, we were permitted to sit and watch, to feel the genuine pleasure with which my parents played host and hostess to their friends, to hear the spontaneous laughter that greeted my father's undoubted wit, and the gay ripples of my mother's gaiety setting a key for the others.

I have been inclined to envy the children of large families. That is because I am almost relationless. The strange way in which the Irish of that day lost track of one another meant that my mother was almost without kin. She had never had a brother or sister. Aside from the Clinch cousins, she had no other relatives. My father's brother died young; his sister was separated first by geography and then a strange family chill. I had my one invalid brother. So I have often said of myself that I am a little like Melchisedech, without family. It seemed a disadvantage compared to the training that should be received in the give-and-take, the sharing and partnership, in a family of many children and a widening circle of cousins.

On the other hand, a family like mine could not settle down into the slackness of a ready-made social circle. My parents had, in a sort of way, to forage for friends. They could not depend on the going and coming of brothers and sisters, aunts, uncles, and cousins. I had to seek out companions. They were not handed to me by providence. Then, too, I did not have to accept what blood and the ties of kindred had presented to me. The right to pick and choose was mine. As the old saying goes, you can pick your friends; your family is forced upon you. I have noticed what seems a slightly perilous social apathy in big families. They grow so content with the fact that they have been handed a great many associates that they do not seek friendship or go out making new acquaintances. I had to. I still have to. My parents did before me. It could be a bit of a blessing.

Because of that constant flow of social life around me, I was trained from infancy to be at home with people, to greet friends easily, to meet strangers without shyness.

Indeed, my mother transmitted to me a kind of contempt for shyness. I find it hard to be patient with children whose fingers go into their mouths and whose shoulders are crushed against the protective shelter of a wall. My lip involuntarily curls in disdain when, in a crowd of the teen-agers with whom I have worked, I spot the timid violet creeping into the shelter of the potted palms and hanging back when a dance or a game is announced. My shortest temper is for those who can't be coaxed into taking part, who clot together in larger gatherings with the few people they have long known, who greet strangers as if they were hiding a bomb behind their backs, and who swallow their tonsils when they are introduced.

We children were trained, as soon as we could be trained to do anything, to meet the family guests easily and decently. Hating a limp, dead-salmon handshake, my mother taught us to shake hands firmly but without the grip of a monkey wrench. We were required to say "Sir" and "Ma'am," until my mother ran across the path of a little girl who was setting unconsciously a new fashion by greeting her elders with their proper names. So we were then taught to say "How do you do, Mrs. Brown," and "Thank you, Mr. Kelly."

During the course of the conventions which later on became part of my life's work, I have taken time out at assemblies to remind the young people that their manners were the high compliment or the telltale betrayal of the kind of parents God had given them. "The manners you display at this meeting and here in this hotel shout aloud, not the sort of school you come from, but the kind of home in which you were reared. If you want to have people respect your parents, good manners, please. If you want to act like boors and hicks, remember you are proclaiming for all to see, 'My parents are ignoramuses, common vulgarians too.' "

Watching recently the teen-agers who are driving the audiences out of neighborhood theaters and ruining the business of unfortunate drugstores they haunt, I notice the magnificence of the high schools that claim them, and find myself despising the parents who begot, and then had no idea what to do with, a race of huns and vandals. I could be bitter about it all.

Manners, to my mother and father, were a sort of prelude to morals. In that, they were sound philosophers. The supernatural builds on the natural, the scholastics have agreed. You build faith, hope, and charity on natural virtues like consideration, courage, gratitude, and a decent respect for the rights of others.

We were taught "Thank you" as one of our first word combinations. It was demanded of us as our most frequent phrase.

If we forgot to say "Please," we just did not get what we asked for.

When an older person entered the room, we were expected to rise and greet him.

When we passed in front of anyone or in any way disturbed others, we were taught that "Excuse me, please" was the least we could do in apology for our inconveniencing them.

A certain type of youth we have all met—once confined to the male of the species, now overflowing into the supposedly gentler sex—seems to consider good manners sissified, a confession of weakness, a protestation of missing manliness. Some parent failed to impress on these social hulks, floating loose and perilously in the social sea, that good manners require the strength of self-control and self-mastery. They are the first approach to making friends and influencing people. They are in simple truth the only natural thing which makes possible the living together in congested cities or small houses of large groups of human animals. Pigs may squeal and jostle at the trough; elephants may crash against one another and impeding trees in a stampede; steers may crash down upon their wounded fellows; the jungle animals may abrogate the codes and the rules of good manners. When storm troopers or Russian reds, teen-agers on the loose, or subway crowds charging into an already jammed car take over the world, you may join me in my nearest desert and share the hospitality of my hermitage. A mannerless world strikes me as being only less slightly terrible than a world without morals. I have found that morals and manners have a way of coming very close together in happy association.

Again, I am abashed that I do not show and have not shown through life more completely the education I received in my preschool days. From eternity, my parents must be more than a little disappointed.

Our little two-flat frame building on St. Lawrence Avenue was almost directly across the street from the Forestville Public School. It was so named from an adjacent street that had been pushed through a forest long lost to memory. On the other hand, the nearest Catholic school lay beyond a main car track, a railroad crossing, and a busy boulevard. As my mother thought any child of five was ready to take up piano lessons and go to school, and yet as she did not dare trust me to make the eight-block journey to Holy Angels, she led me across the street and entrusted me to the gentle ministrations of Miss Florence.

Miss Florence had another name. It was long and difficult; so in consideration for her young pupils, a consideration which showed itself in her whole loving attitude, she bade us call her by her first name. To this day I have a faint and roseate memory of my first teacher. Because of her I have had a strong affection for public-school teachers, regarding them as a charming breed, heroic souls serving an ungracious public at wages notably less than those of the head janitors (or custodians, or engineers) of the same schools. It is evidently America's conviction that tending boilers is a higher art than tending the budding mind, and emptying wastebaskets is more difficult than filling human hearts.

It is baffling to realize that the human memory can turn back to find the first two years of school an absolute blank. The one event that I can recall is the visit to our school of some invited teachers. We were put through a course of simple arithmetic. Could that have been first or second grade? I was selected to go to the board and draw a square, which I did. Then a visiting teacher asked a trick question: "Is it possible on a flat board like that to draw a box?" I nodded emphatically, and she challenged me to make good my impossible boast. On the board I carefully outlined a transparent box, with all six sides clearly displayed. I recall that the teachers laughed at my triumph and the discomfiture of the questioner. It was the first time my ears had ever been delighted by the sound of laughter which I had caused to spring forth. It was one of life's most delicious sounds, and the delight I feel in it has never died. Let me confess the weakness early, without, I regret to say, shame, sorrow, or firm purpose of amendment.

Out of those early days I can salvage just one fact about my education, and that is to the discredit of the system to which youngsters must submit. Any of my friends can tell you I have one of the world's most horrible handwritings. My script defies description, so to speak. For that, my dear minister grandfather is partly responsible; I lay the finger of heredity upon him. Yet he is not totally to blame, for my schooling subjected me to a series of experiments in penmanship of which I certainly did not approve and to which I inwardly objected, for all the good it did me. And my experience there has, I am afraid, been the experience of many a student who has played guinea pig for professional educators.

We began to learn to write by printing. That was right enough. When we transferred to script, we stepped into a species of slant which, with mild flourishes, was fashionable in that day. Indeed, the sign of a "beautiful penman" was the ornamental capitals and the number of curlicues which spiderwebbed across his page. We did not go in for much ornamentation as yet; but we wrote or struggled to write with a free, bold hand.

Hardly had this begun to take shape when a new system was introduced. Some pedagogue (or author of a highly profitable textbook) persuaded the schools of my city that children should be taught vertical writing. This necessitated a new grip on our pencils or pens, a new position of our hand, and a readjustment of our eyes, accustomed to script slanting to the right, to make and admire letters that went straight up and down. The letters tended to be squat and square and very businesslike, somewhat in the form of a regiment of dwarfs solidly planted on the battlefield of our youthful pages. By seventh grade it was discovered that vertical writing was slower than slant, and another system called Spencerian took us over. It was severe and without adornment, but the letters followed the lines of the Tower of Pisa, and we had to readjust our muscles and minds to the new slant.

My first year of high school with the Christian Brothers brought me face to face with the mysteries of the then-young Palmer method. We did Slide-O-Slide-O-Slide hour after hour. We were taught to hold our fingers totally without movement, and let our hands slide back and forth on the muscle of our forearm. It was hard, almost impossible to make my fingers, long in control, yield their sovereignty to a forearm muscle which up to that time I did not know I had. So the year was a battle between fingers and arm, with dire consequences to my penmanship.

The next year I fell into the power of the Jesuits, who are proverbial masters of dictation. For six years with them, I took down thousands of words that they hurled at me and I acquired the habit of learning through the point of my pen. I got the thoughts right enough, but in the process I had completely destroyed my penmanship. The little guinea pig had tried his best to conform; in the end he had been taught six different ways of writing, had mastered none of them, and ended with handwriting which is one of the world's fastest and most illegible.

You may, my dear young educator, use that as a Parable of Modern Education if you are so inclined.

Since a happy country is a country without a history, you may decide with me that my two years in Forestville Public School were happy ones. I recall no single incident, no name of a classmate, not the face or the name of the teacher of second grade, nothing on which I can lay a typewriter key. They must have been years of mental peace . . . or mental blankness.

For at the end of the two years, my mother decided that she would let me risk the Forty-third Street car line, the rush of the trains over the railroad tracks, and the traffic of the intervening thoroughfares to find my way into a Catholic school.

Old Holy Angels—called, with fashionable overtone, not a school but an academy—occupied one floor of our combination church-school on Oakwood Boulevard. The nun who welcomed me to third grade was, though I did not know it, a novice of the Sisters of Mercy, wearing, without due right to wear it, the habit to which as a novice she was still aspiring. She was Sister Mary Blanche, of whom in later years I was to write much. For she became one of the big influences in my life, a superb teacher in those early days, one who loved children, was a power with us boys, and could slowly develop the dependence of a pupil into the friendship which bound her to many of her pupils for the whole of life.

Again I pause in amazement to realize that education can be an almost unconscious affair. It must be a sort of mental osmosis, soaking up what is around it without conscious effort. The only thing that made Holy Angels different from Forestville, beyond the fact that our Catholic school was almost a shack compared to the public school's relative splendors, was the presence of religion. St. Patrick hung beside Abraham Lincoln on the walls. Christ, the founder of Christianity, had a place near Washington, the father of his country. And if we had been familiar with the portraits of Clara Barton and Barbara Fritchie, we now became familiar with the faces of Mary and Anne and Elizabeth and Catherine of Siena. The teachers had the ageless quality of nuns. Their habits endlessly fascinated me; and when Sister Mary Blanche paused near my desk, I could not keep my fingers off her crucifix, dangling at her side, or stop itching to touch her beads.

The subjects seemed a simple flow from the subjects we had had, but catechism was new and different and exciting. Actually, much of the excitement came from the fact that at this point my grandmother Langdon took a hand in my education. It had been the wise policy laid down at the very start by my mother that no help should be given children with their homework. Let them do their assignments themselves. Let them struggle with the problems and come forth with what answers seemed right to them. Homework was for children and not for their parents. From that policy we never deviated in the whole of my education. I recommend it strongly to parents who wish their children planted on firm feet and sturdy pedagogical legs. It eliminates many an educational parasite.

But catechism turned out to be different.

Night after night I stood before my unsmiling grandmother and recited the lesson that had to be memorized for the coming day. Since this was the Faith, with a capital F, and since she was inwardly sure that some day before God's judgment seat I would have to pass a final examination in what the small book contained, there was no trifling with the text. I must repeat it in the exact words. My phrasing must indicate the precise punctuation. I must say it with conviction and stress its meaning with intelligence. By the time I came to my first Communion I could recite the entire little volume without the briefest hesitation. Wonderful as it was for my religious training, I cannot but feel it must have been an amazing exercise for my memory. I have never been one to talk down the value of the memory; somehow it has always seemed to me that what we know is right there in the memory, conscious or unconscious. I am glad of the stern taskmistress who made me letter-perfect in the rudiments of my faith; I am grateful for the muscular exercise of my memory.

At the mid-term it was decided that I could move up to fourth grade. And by the end of the year I was promoted to fifth. I had mourned a little leaving Sister Mary Blanche and my fellow third-graders; and I hailed with proper rejoicing the fact that Sister Mary Blanche, like myself, had been promoted to fifth. It was on my part at least a very joyous reunion.

What did we learn in those simple days? I recall bright moments like the opening of our first geography, a vast volume that made the other books seem pygmies. I was fascinated by a first glimpse of English history—atavism, I'm sure, plus the sheer glamor that has long attached to the story of Britain. My favorite subject must have been English, for I can recall the vast skill I developed in diagraming sentences. Probably like pyrography, which I also attempted, diagraming sentences is in the limbo of outmoded sciences. If so, I am sorry for the present generation, remembering what that practice did for my later mastery of Latin and my facility in writing when speed became an element much to desire.

What I remember most clearly about grammar school was the competition between a group of us for the largest number of books read each week. We were spurred on by Sister Mary Blanche, who loved books simply and intelligently. We considered it a feat comparable to athletic victories to score high in the records of books taken from our school library, read, and returned in jig time. I cannot recall that any of these books were ever assigned for class reading. They seem to have been the object of supererogatory love.

Our playground was a quadrangle of gravel and cement, destructive of shoes and fatal to clothes. Toward the end of my school days we began to show signs of developing school teams; originally, play was a matter of our own animal spirits, vast ingenuity, and sheer physical energy. We raced and wrestled and threw one another about, played tough games like prisoner's base and something that sounded like pum-pum-peelaway. In the latter game two lines formed on the far ends of the yard with one boy in the center. Each side in turn raced across the yard, and the one lad in the center tackled, threw, and made prisoner of another boy. Then the two in the center of the yard tackled the line as it charged to exchange sides. At the end all the boys except one man of might, muscle, and dexterity were in the center. And when he tried to break through, the pile-up was mountainous. At the end of the recess we returned to class breathless, our shoes scuffed and the soles worn through, our clothes in rents and tears. It was a very, very nice game indeed. Gentle, too, as you will notice.

Teachers should be a discouraged race if they paused to recall the names of those who taught them in grammar school. I remember faintly Sister Liguori as a stern disciplinarian. I remember a gentle Sister Mary Gregory. Sister Bonaventure was large and generous, and smiled when she bore down upon the most unruly. And Sister Mary Michael came to us with the clear foreshadowing of the heights to which she would someday rise among the authorities of the Sisters of Mercy. But how vague their faces, how unsure I am even of the classes in which they taught me, how misty it all seems over the years!

Indeed, I was not too much surprised by the deflating experience which happened to me as a middle-aged priest. Educators can expect no more. The successful-looking gentleman on the Pullman engaged me in conversation, gradually revealing the fact that he had been a student at St. Louis University during his freshman year. I confessed that I had taught there in that year. We compared notes, he asked for teachers of the period, and then, looking off into space, he said: "There was one young teacher I had in freshman English. I've often wondered what happened to him. Do you remember anything at all about a Mr. Daniel Lord?" Oh, what an impression we make on our students.

Characteristically, my father left the guidance of my education entirely in the hands of my mother. Non-Catholic though he still was, he raised no objection to the tuition required of the parochial-school pupil, when he was entitled to send me free to the public school. And in an equally characteristic attitude my mother was quite content if I finished each quarter third or fourth in class (she was stern if I dropped lower), provided I brought home a round one hundred in deportment on my report card. She tolerated nothing less than perfection in conduct. She did not demand that I be brilliant; she did think it lay within the power of any boy or girl to be perfectly mannered and absolutely obedient. She never taught me lessons in authority; authority was simply right in any argument. There was just one side in any dispute, the teacher's; and it would have been a waste of time for me to argue against that.

So convinced was I that the wrath would fall upon me for failure in conduct that once, when my report card showed a terrifying 98 in deportment, shamefully and with a bungling forgery I scratched out the mark and changed it to a blotted 100. She could not believe that the palpable trick was other than the slip of a teacher's clumsy pen. For weeks following the deception I lived in remorse and fear, vastly relieved when my crime came at length to light. She was horrified when she discovered that I had cheated, I was properly punished for my crime, and I held the line so carefully that I did not again deflect the two points that had pulled me from the bright North Star of unblemished classroom conduct.

During those years of grammar school my contact with the extracurricular and my growing respect for it advanced notably. My mother started me off in music at the same time I entered first grade. Once I had applied for Holy Angels, I was entered in the drawing class. Drawing was an "extra" in those days. Somewhere in the family was a tradition of skill with pencil and brush. It missed me completely. But we had to find out that it did before my mother was content. Dancing, however, was something else. Music would train my fingers to some dexterity; something must be done to weed the falls and tumbles out of my feet. For in no acrobatic sense I had developed into an amazing tumbler. Over my constantly broken knees I was long forced to wear leather guards, or between the time I was dressed to go out and the family could assemble I would have fallen and torn the knees of my stockings twice or even three times.

My mother entered me in the ballroom dancing classes that met on Saturday afternoons in the neighborhood. This was followed by a year of what was then called buck and wing, later known as tap. She had no expectation that I would become a Fred Astaire or even a bleached Bill Robinson; she was determined that I would not stumble over my own feet or climb recklessly on the insteps of others. Jesuit though I became, I was deeply grateful for the dancing lessons: I have talked with some understanding to ballet masters and choreographers who did dances for our varied musical productions; I have watched good dancing with some appreciation; and I have crossed the vast empty reaches of lecture platforms with less alarms and excursions.

How varied are the elements which enter into a single educational experience! When we moved to the better economic environment of our newly erected two-apartment building on Vincennes Avenue, the lower floor was taken by a young doctor, fresh from Rush Medical College, my grandfather's alma mater. Dr. George Troy Bailey (G.T., his friends used to say, as in Get There) not only watched me through an almost fatal illness, but became a powerful factor in my mental development. We played ball together in our small back yard, and for the first time I learned to handle a fast pitch without danger to my fingers, and to throw a straight ball and not a long sidearm pitch.

Then, with the wonderful courtesy which some men have for small boys, he turned me loose in his library, an excellent one. During my sixth, seventh, and eighth grades I was reading everything I could carry away from his bookshelves. The Index of Forbidden Books had not dawned on my consciousness, so I fell under the spell of Dumas. I came in contact with the florid imagination of Jules Verne. I paged through exciting books of travel. Here was a new and different education, and I lapped it up, hardly knowing what I got. In the case of the French novels the names baffled me; I solved the problem by remembering the character's first initial and the approximate number of letters which followed it. Never did I ever pretend to pronounce it. So the Three Musketeers to me were just P- - - - - -, A- - - - - -, and A- - - - -, and D'Artagnan was simply a chap named D-apostrophe-A.

I cannot tell you what subjects I took, except to parrot the subjects I know are required of all grammar-school pupils. But I can tell you about our school entertainments, the small plays in which I played small parts, the wonderful introduction that came to me when I met Gilbert and Sullivan by being borrowed for the Midshipmite in a parish production of *Pinafore*. I could dwell on the educational value of a deck of cards and how I mastered euchre well enough to be my mother's partner at the parish card parties. Once I trumped a partner's ace. My mother had moved ahead and I was left to the tender mercilessness of an outraged card enthusiast whose game I had stupidly ruined. All that is extra- or cocurricular; but once again, it is part of the difficult and essential art of getting along with people. Education without it might well be education for misanthropy or a hermitage. Education that accompanied or was accompanied by all this gave me much that life has proved valuable.

A year of schooling was lost when I was stricken with a near-fatal disease and spent a year recuperating. There again, was it lost? Or was it a year when I practiced patience with ill health and learned to live with myself and grew to appreciate the gentle care of my mother and the endless cheerfulness of my father, and could read a great deal and be the companion of adults?

I had graduated scholastically top boy in my class; two girls of course outranked me. One of the reasons why I have opposed coeducation is precisely the fact that in grammar school it seemed to me that girls always outranked me. From my dealings with high-school students I am convinced that they continue to outrank boys for those four years. Girls develop both mentally and physically faster than boys. They are more docile and less distracted by athletics, hobbies, and temptations. Their leadership in almost all the studies forces upon boys a sense of mental inferiority. They feel themselves less intellectually competent than girls and come to wonder if the male may not belong to a somewhat inferior sex. As a consequence they profess a great distaste for the subjects in which girls excel. They disdain literature and the arts and turn toward the utilitarian subjects in which they outshine the girls.

For some it brings about a dislike for education. For others it means a neglect of the cultural subjects which should teach them how to enjoy life rather than merely how to earn a living. It inclines them to surrender, as American men largely have, the nicer things of our civilization to the women—good music and art galleries and libraries with their books and lectures and interest in the so-called cultural pursuits. It makes boys study with one standard: "How much more will I earn if I master this?" instead of asking: "Will this make me a better and more attractive person?"

At any rate, since I had a higher average than the other boys in my class, I was awarded a scholarship to De La Salle Institute, staffed by the wonderfully devoted Christian Brothers. A remarkable fact in education is the intense loyalty possessed by the graduates who call themselves "Christian Brothers' boys." Most schools can envy the Brothers their alumni associations and marvel at the unique manner in which they have gained and held such fidelity among their former pupils. I know that on many occasions I have found myself professing publicly the fact that I too am a Brothers' boy, though I was under their care for exactly one year.

For in those days, a period of educational interregnum, the Brothers in high school taught only commercial subjects. I disliked the subjects deeply and did badly in them. Not, of course, as badly as I would have done had not my mother demanded high scores even in the bookkeeping, which I found ridiculous, and the shorthand, which added another reason for my bad penmanship, and the Palmer method, which I thought was playing stupid games to a rhythm without music. Most of the class left me flatfooted in business arithmetic. Typewriting was worth learning, though I felt we gave it too little time ever to grow at all expert. So I came to life only when the English period rolled round and I was back on dear, familiar ground.

Fortunately for me, De La Salle brought me the friendship of a man whom I felt to be a saint. Brother Paschal was young and delicate. He had the lovely manners which fared rather badly at the hands of our not-too-well-mannered class. His voice was gentle, and he was more himself during the ten to twenty minutes of morning prayer that preceded class. I am afraid that during those prayers I paid more attention to him than I did to the God I was expected to address. For he prayed with such relish and fervor, eyes almost closed to shut out the world of our classroom and reveal the inner world of the spirit and truth, that we were reverent despite natural irreverence and devout at the least devotional period of our lives. I felt that I loved him as a young brother might love an older one who had all the qualities he himself had missed. He taught us well and patiently. He lived before us a startlingly Christlike life. And if he went on to be novice master of his order, I was not surprised. And if he was touched for long years with the compliment of illness, that was another clear sign of God's approval.

I tried my hand at the athletics of the interclass leagues and was so overwhelmed by the masterful athletes of the school that I retired in chagrin to the library. There I met Brother Jerome, who belonged on the playing field but who at least kept such perfect order and silence among the books that I got an extra half hour of reading each noon and plowed my way through bound volumes of back magazines to the enlargement of my vista of the generation just ahead of my own. I can still hear his threat to the occasional whisperer: "Silence, or I'll drop-kick you through the transom without bothering to open it." No one doubted that he easily could and well might.

As principal of De La Salle there ruled one of the remarkable men of my youth. Brother Baldwin was short, plump, ruddy of complexion, jovial of manner, quick and clever of mind, understanding of boys, and a gentleman even in the face of some of the professionally tough kids who come from the Chicago Stockyards district. He was, I learned, of Polish nobility; his brother was one of the top executives in the great Marshall Field Company; and I have no doubt that he could have been as successful in business had he not given himself to our ungracious selves.

He had one trick that gave me the brightest moments of the year. We wrote our English compositions in copybooks, and regularly he dropped by, collected them, marked them himself in penetrating and witty comments, and returned with the books under his arm to spend half an hour reading passages from the best and making complimentary remarks that greatly encouraged the lucky authors. Because of him I threw new energy into my writing; and since I had plenty that I was not using on the distasteful studies, I found that my efforts paid off. When the copybooks came back I avidly read the comments he had written in the most polished handwriting with red ink at the end of the final paragraph. And if he liked what I had written, I was fired with new enthusiasm to be an author indeed.

But alas for the mistakes of the best of teachers! I had written this particular composition in a fit of disinterest, and his penetrating critical eye caught this and noted it in a paragraph of criticism that touched the heart of the weakness, the poverty of the thought, and the raggedness of the style. Admiring him and aiming at his approval, I set myself to undo the fault.

He had an excellent pedagogical trick which consisted in demanding that, once he had criticized a piece of writing, we rewrite it according to his suggestions. Fired with interest, I did this time much more than just follow his suggestions. I scrapped the original and offending composition, worked out a fresh and different treatment, wrote it from the ground up in a new approach, and handed in what I was sure was an excellent piece of writing. Then I settled back to accept modestly the bouquet he was sure to pin on the composition.

Only he didn't. He wrote a perfunctory little comment stating he was glad that I had followed his suggestions and that the piece was somewhat better. It came to me with the crash of a falling idol. He really had not bothered to reread what I had so patiently and under his inspiration so carefully rewritten. He just took it for granted that I had made the suggested changes without troubling to discover that here was something so different that it was my compliment to him, my tribute to his interest, my brave effort to win his approval and to merit his touch of accolade. I did not lose my admiration for him. But I felt cheated, and my work became almost perfunctory instead of shot through with the enthusiasm he had formerly generated.

One Sunday to our parish church came a tall, ascetic-looking priest who mounted the pulpit and talked of higher education. He explained its need, the importance of the classics, the value of philosophy, what the Catholic leader of the future would need in education, mental training, inspired outlook, and strength of will. He did not bother to announce himself, but he made it clear that the education of which he spoke was to be found at an old school called St. Ignatius in the heart of Chicago's decaying West Side. My mother sat spellbound, intent on every word. When the Mass was over, she approached one of the curates to learn that the speaker was Father Cassilly, new dean and principal of the school he presented eloquently.

As we walked home she said only this: "Is that what you are getting at De La Salle?" Thinking with repugnance of my business course, I uttered an emphatic and indignant, "No, indeed!" That was all the discussion that preceded one of the significant shifts of my life's course. Assuredly she talked it over with my father, for throwing up a scholarship and starting once more to pay tuition would mean sacrifices in their financial arrangements. We took one detour to look at the new St. Cyril's College just opened by the Carmelite fathers on our own South Side. She found that a little unsettled and insecure and in the process of formation, and what she wanted was something that would take me into a fixed and established educational pattern.

So we gave up the scholarship to De La Salle; and in 1903 I was entered in St. Ignatius High School on what was then West Twelfth Street, and a new period of my education began.

I find it hard from this period of carefully standardized education properly to appraise my education of the next six years. The educational associations were not yet a beam in the glittering vision of the country's pedagogues. Columbia's Teachers College was still a foundling. No one had felt himself powerful enough to wrest the guidance of American education in any particular direction. It was certainly the day of the most individualistic teachers in the most completely independent schools. And the Jesuits had taken fullest advantage of that situation.

Their course from the end of grammar school to the A.B. degree ran seven and not eight years. No break marked the end of high school and the beginning of college. Rather, the system was a fulfillment of what later on I discovered was Loyola's famous *Ratio Studiorum*. There were three preliminary classes: third, second, and first academic. These melted into a class called humanities. Then came poetry and rhetoric classes. And the course was topped off with what was called simply philosophy, after which one received a sheepskin and the right to say he was Jesuit-trained.

The teaching was notably paternalistic.

Each division of each class (and the academics might have as many as four or five sections) had one teacher who was responsible for its direction. He was always a Jesuit, usually a priest, sometimes a priest-in-the-making called a scholastic, and he handled the Latin, the English, possibly the Greek, the history, and the mathematics of that class. So at the beginning of the year you knew that, for better or worse, you would have one man as your intellectual director for four hours at least each day. If he was a priest, he also taught the class its religion.

The consequence of this was that each class was a family, closely knit, thoroughly acquainted with the Jesuit in charge, and subject to his inspiration and his deep knowledge, or to his caprice and whim. The system obviously could work effectively in either of two ways.

The studies were designed to create a man of culture, someone who might nicely have come out of the Catholic Counter Renaissance and the Catholic Counter Reformation. The academics laid down the foundations. One was supposed to master Latin well enough to read it fluently, speak it a little, and appreciate it well. English was studied as a tool for the expression of thought. Mathematics were basic—algebra, geometry; and history presented the broad outlines of the main flows and ebbs, a thin sketch that expected the later filling in with color.

Humanities, as the name implied, introduced the student to the beginnings of real culture. He was now expected to read the Latin classics and to make some headway into the Greek masters. He was to have enough skill in handling English to understand the men who throughout its history had handled it well. Mathematics now turned to trigonometry. History began to display a flush of color. And the added sciences appeared for the first time on our horizon. Chemistry came first, with physics the following year and analytic chemistry the next.

Poetry class was a tribute to the emotional development expected of a cultured man, and ranged the field of poetry in the three languages. Rhetoric turned out to be the study of the classic oratory with strong stress on the development of our own ability to speak convincingly, straightforwardly, with polish and the power of persuasion. This meant the study of the great orations of Rome, Greece, England, and the United States.

The course climaxed in a solid year given over to philosophy. Two and often three hours a day were devoted to a systematic study of scholastic philosophy. We dipped lightly into the history of the other philosophers, read some philosophical English, and did some more serious thinking along religious lines. For religion had been part of every course, ostensibly growing toward theology as our minds grew better able to appreciate the vast revelation back of the Catholic faith.

Theoretically, the course was magnificent.

Practically, it had its problems.

Yet often, as my priestly life progressed and I have spoken to small college bodies on Catholic campuses, I have bragged in this fashion: "I am a graduate of a small college in a run-down building situated in the very center of Chicago's darkest Ghetto. Yet I would not trade what I got there for the most spectacular college education the universities of the world could offer." And I have meant sincerely what I said.

Perhaps it was the boys in that vast, dirty, dangerous playground who most impressed me. They streamed to St. Ignatius from all over the city. Most of them came on foot or on the trolleys of the period. One rich youth was driven to school in a closed carriage; but he soon bribed the coachman to stop the carriage three blocks away, while he slipped out and arrived at our highly democratic campus on foot.

My first impression of them was that of noise, enormous confusion, great boisterousness, scuffed shoes, a professional carelessness of dress, and a vitality that overflowed with wholesomeness and the love of life. When first I walked into our playground, I was fairly overwhelmed. At noon four games of softball took place simultaneously, with the outfields overflowing into the infields of the other games. We could play a regulation baseball game in that yard and did, to the grief of many of our opponents. For our batters had discovered the enormous convenience of a jutting classroom building just back of left field; any long hit into that sector of the diamond bounced off a wall, and by ground rules was a single. Many a succession of singles we banged off that convenient building, until our opponents decided our team was made up of nine players and an abutting wall; and they got the aim and started using it for their long liners. Any man who slid to base could spend the rest of the game and most of the following week pulling cinders out of his hands and cheek. That discouraged strange teams from sliding; and they ran into the bases standing up, to be met with the full impact of a glove and a ball.

In the winter it could be flooded for an ice rink, but you had better keep your eyes open for the hazards of clinkers that rose, black icebergs, through the thin crust of the surface.

My second observation about the boys of St. Ignatius was most reassuring. Here were the most amazingly pure boys I have ever been able to imagine. They came from middle-class homes—and again I bless the strong middle class—and often from poor homes. They were the Irish of the West and South sides, the Germans from the North Side, the Poles from along the growing Polish colonies that flanked Milwaukee Avenue, and the slightly more acclimated Americans from the rapidly developing suburbs. Yet at the end of six years I could say that never once had I heard from a fellow student a dirty story or a filthy expression. Nobody ever made a tempting suggestion to me. None of the pornographic literature that flowed through the schools of Chicago from restricted Custom House Place and later Armour Avenue ever was brought to my attention by one of my associates. They were just good normal, noisy, reluctant, sometimes disobedient, destructive boys and young men. But they were so good that I look back at them in admiring wonder.

Later, when as a scholastic I taught at St. Louis University, a young country-school teacher, Clyde Brown, joined my English class. He came for the credits and with a deep distaste for Catholics. At the end of the year he informed me that he was applying for instruction in the hope of conversion. He must have seen my amazed look. "I'm surprised myself," he said, "but I've been as student and teacher in a good many schools; and since I've been here, I've not heard a dirty story or a smutty remark. I figured something must make the difference, and maybe it's the Catholic religion. I'd like to try that too." He was baptized after the college year ended.

At De La Salle I was associated with a great many fine young fellows who later made notable success in life. The mayor of Chicago, Martin J. Kennelly, was a fellow classmate, as was a former United States senator and any number of distinguished professional and businessmen. A late glance down the records of my fellow alumni of St. Ignatius revealed a surprising record of later success. When my father mentioned to a non-Catholic friend that his son was attending St. Ignatius College, the friend said in disgust: "Why send him there? They graduate nothing but priests and professional ballplayers." Said my father shrewdly: "If he makes a success at either, my son won't do too badly."

The records of St. Ignatius are not studded with spectacular luminaries. They are filled with substantial successes—physicians, dentists, lawyers, advertising men, journalists, businessmen, men in politics and in the trade unions. Any parents who trusted their boys to St. Ignatius need make no apologies to them for stunting their success in life. Better, the number of successful marriages, the rarity of divorce, the fine Catholic families of excellently trained children, are more convincing tribute. And when Cardinal Mundelein asked the Jesuits to assume the education of his seminary at St. Mary of the Lake, he was turning to men who had given him and the Chicago archdiocese a succession of fine pastors and religious priests for the service of God and souls.

My first meeting with Jesuits was my introduction to Father Francis J. Cassilly, one of the great men in my life. He moved through life with the speed of flowing lava and the impenetrable character of a glacier. He could cow a hall full of rioting youngsters with one ringing order and two steely eyes. The entire student body of the combined college and high school was approximately five hundred; he was dean of one and principal of the other, and he juggled the management with fluent ease. He was a stern man who had no favorites and asked no favors. Yet he had the most amazing sense of public relations. He could turn a high-school elocution contest into a gala Hollywood opening. He persuaded the student body that tickets of admission were rare and precious and that, if he allowed them an extra pair, it was a sign of great condescension. He could transform the junior choir, made up of tousle-headed little roughnecks, into polished choristers, with a skillful choirmaster, porters who arrived before the production to shine their unaccustomed shoes, and a carnation in every lapel.

I even think he may have been a great educator. He insisted on high grades. He could send down to the Rhodes scholarship examinations six applicants and see five of them pass those tough examinations in Latin, Greek, and history. He believed in the extra- and the cocurricular to the extent of giving the school a fine band, a delightful glee club, prize-winning debaters, good publications, and classic plays.

He liked me in his chill fashion, and I never to the day of his late death lost my reverence for him. He was to me the best dean I had ever known, either as a student or a teacher or a later observer.

Probably deep down, I knew that he was one of the people who could see right through me. He spotted my faking the moment I began it. He knew when I was substituting fluency for knowledge and eloquence for facts. He could spot an effort to dodge work, and he could smell out a poor job even before you had laid it before him. You can't but admire a man like that, even if well into middle age you remain afraid of him and in his presence have an anticipation of what it will be like to stand before the wise, all-seeing Judge.

The fault with the Jesuit education of that day was precisely the human breakdown in a good system. If you hit good teachers, you were on the top of the educational world. For four or five hours a day you sat on your end of the log with a great teacher on the other, and that, in the stale cliché, makes a great education. But if you hit a poor teacher, you were stuck with him for the same length of time, four hours a day for a full year. And in some cases he advanced with you, and you came back to find you had him for another year.

I started out with an excellent teacher. He was little Father William Feld, who in a moment of confidence told me that, from the day he had left his angry home and his anti-Catholic parents to become a Jesuit, he had never had a single personal line from any of his relatives. He started us off talking Latin before we had finished the first declension. His opening greeting to the class was an astonishing, "Salvete, fratres!" to which we answered with a bemused silence and then a salvo of laughter and delight. He confided to the class in the course of the first week that, while lesser Jesuits might be rectors or be permitted to teach philosophers, the best teachers were in the early academics. And we found the comment totally without conceit, and answered it with a nod of our heads. We had one of the really brilliant professors right up there in the front of our classroom. He made us love Latin. He made English seem a challenge and not a chore. He tossed off the algebra with fine theory and no particular application to any aspect of life. And he reveled in elocution. In no time at all he had us all on our feet learning to make gestures in the three planes, lower, middle, and upper. He taught us how to manage our unruly feet so that, as our right hand went out compellingly, our left foot went back in balance. He trained our voices to speak with scorn, to rise in fury, to drop in pleading, to match the eloquence of the classic speeches we were to memorize.

Class from dawn to eventide was fun. We learned a lot, and I know now that he was far from a brilliant man. Later he took to writing poetry himself, and that was the giveaway. But he was a pedagogue, and he led his responsive class by highly competent hands.

I had one brilliant young chemist, Mr. Joseph Wilczewski, a Jesuit scholastic, who made analysis live for me. I had some excellent teachers of religion along the way. I came into association with the keen young minds of the teaching scholastics, none of whom, unfortunately, ever taught me in class; but when I sat that first day in the classroom of Father Edward Gleeson, I knew that I had met a man in the tradition of the Irish hedgerow teachers, the professors of the old days, a lecturer who could make the ancients seem more modern than today's headlines, a mind that cut through fluff and nonsense, and eyes that penetrated the soul of a student and knew just exactly what was stuffed away there.

He began by taking it for granted that we knew nothing, not even how to read the textbook or to digest a lecture. He ordered us all to secure uniform notebooks. Each day he lectured, and each day he assigned a portion of the difficult Latin texts in philosophy. The following morning before class began he inspected our notes on his lecture and went over with cruel scrutiny the synopsis we had made of the assigned section of text.

The first man assigned to defend a simple thesis rattled off the proofs with the convincing fluency of a district attorney. When he had finished and sat back complacently, Father Gleeson fixed him with a repellent eye. "A waste of time. Anyone can prove anything and leave an audience totally unconvinced. Proofs are unimportant. What you should have done was spend ninety per cent of the time explaining what you were talking about. You defined no terms. You explained no adversaries. You told us nothing about the state of the question. And your proofs were fireworks shot vacantly into the thin air. They impressed you and nobody else but you. Now tomorrow you will come back and do it all over again. You will take practically all the time to make the question so clear to us that by the time you come to the proofs you will hardly need the proofs. We'll be nodding our heads in agreement and will be all ready to accept the proofs which, actually, were already contained in your explanation. That will do for today. And I hope the rest of the class will not waste any time giving a pyrotechnic exhibition that in the end is a matter of smell in the air and falling sticks."

He walked out of the room, leaving us deflated but informed.

The next day the young man gave a brilliant explanation of everything about the subject, proofs of his thesis that were a matter of brief minutes, and got at the end a curt nod from "Paw" Gleeson: "Better," he said. "And that is the way we do it henceforth."

As a matter of fact, that is the way I have tried to do it henceforth throughout life. I have tried to make clear what I was talking or writing about. I have explained as thoroughly as I was permitted the subject under discussion. Usually proofs were hardly needed if both parties understood the subject at hand, the meaning of the terms, and the data that had surrounded the question in the first instance. I had met a great teacher, for a great teacher is a great master of exposition. Argument makes you mad. Proofs drive their victim into the corner where he bristles and closes his ears against what is being said. Calm exposition, clear explanation, definitions that make the words you are using intelligible to those who read or listen—once that is cared for, proofs follow, rest on interested ears, and reach a mind already more than half convinced.

With a brilliant teacher, a ruthless drillmaster, a man who allowed no fuzzy edges around the class's thinking, with two and three hours concentrated each day on the subject of philosophy, we were amazed ourselves to discover the ground we could cover. He was a man without poetry in his soul; he preferred stark truth. He did not embroider; he cut down to skeletons. He did not love words, but he was very much in love with the facts back of words. And he gave us a great year, a great training, and a basic outline for the whole of an intellectual approach to the life we must live.

I have always felt that that sector of my education was rounded off by a master pedagogue. No one in the class ever felt that to Father Gleeson he was a person. He was rather a sort of human filing cabinet into which was being tucked method and truth. He was not someone to be loved but someone to be whipped into mental shape. It was not the father-and-son relationship of most Jesuit classrooms; it was the sergeant and the raw recruits who must be so readied for the battle ahead that they could dodge the enemy and be ready for the counterattack, bear the blows without wincing, and, in the course of time, strike the blows that would mean victory. None of us felt any tenderness for Father Gleeson; we held him in a kind of reverential awe. I never could have imitated him; but I felt him eminently worthy of imitation by those who could.

It was my Sacred Heart nun cousin, Mother Elizabeth Clinch, who quite without knowing it planted another educational seed in my mind. She spoke in gentle rebuke of the boastings of a confident collegian. I had managed excellent marks—never topping the class, however—by the familiar student practice of burning the midnight electricity just before examination time. During the term I gave my subjects a modicum of attention. There was much too much of interest in the exciting world around me to make me think class more than a necessary interlude. I suffered it as the interruption to the more interesting things of life. Always there would be the examination week when all else could be pushed aside while I boned up on the neglected subjects, concentrated with fierce intensity on the matter that must be mastered, went into the examinations fresh from a soaking of my mind with what the examination would demand. I could get enough in those fervid hours to make a good mark, come out with a smile, bring home a passable report for family inspection, and return to the ways of the leisurely scholar of all the ages.

So casually and with a shrug of my shoulders I bragged to Mother Clinch: "I've yet to find a subject that I couldn't master in a single night before an examination." She looked at me with the genuine pity of a woman whose fine mind had kept her steadily at the top of her class through school days and now made her a marvelously successful teacher.

"There is," she said gently, "a world of difference between passing an examination and knowing a subject. You will find some day very soon that subjects you learned that way you never learned at all. They skimmed the surface of your mind; they never even briefly got inside."

It was my turn to regard her with pity. How little she knew of the ways of a smart collegian, I thought! She had had too much religious life already to understand the ways of the world. I felt a little sorry for her and lived to know her absolutely right. Education began all over again when I started to despise examinations and relish class.

One summer I got a glimpse of an entirely different approach to education. My mother, with her practical mind working rapidly, decided that my handwriting would be an incurable handicap unless I availed myself of the rising mechanical devices that made penmanship, good or bad, unnecessary. Off she shipped me during the summer holiday to a downtown business school. My slow pecking at a typewriter, begun at De La Salle, was now subjected to the experienced direction of a calm lady who sat at a desk surrounded by the human woodpeckers and who trained us to use the old Remington typewriters of the period. We were each handed a book. We were each assigned to a typewriter, to which we felt chained like galley slaves in a rower's bench. And, believe me, we were on our own. If we wanted to sit all day at the machine dreaming, we could dream. If we itched to complete the lesson rapidly, we could beat out the task on the machine at our top pace. At the end of the first day I turned in my complete assignment. The teacher turned a chill haddock eye over my paper, with a blue pencil the size of a policeman's club circled eight mistakes in the first four rows of type, tossed it back to me contemptuously and said: "An assignment is complete when you turn it in with a maximum of three mistakes. Do it over tomorrow."

It was assembly-line education, and for a good many reasons I grew to respect it. The teacher was there to help, but if you didn't want her help, you need not think she was weeping silently in the depths of her frustrated soul. The machine was there for you to use, but it would not explode under your hands if you failed to use it. You could type assignments just as fast as you cared to. If you wanted to occupy desk room, the school didn't care. It had your tuition, and you could not expect anyone to lean over and plead with you to take the education offered. Years and years later I found something of that same method in the professional schools and graduate departments of a great university. It was very, very different from Jesuit paternalism. A nice debate might well be joined at this point.

Never have students been able to jerk a tear from my not-too-stony eyes by the sad story of how far they have to travel to school. Once I had moved from Forestville Public School, I never lived near the school I attended. I walked about eight blocks to Holy Angels. I walked sixteen blocks each way to De La Salle. And I traveled for a solid hour on the Toonervilles of our day from my home to St. Ignatius. To the long walks I can give credit for tireless legs that have pumped hard for me during a lifetime of pretty steady use. To the trolley ride to and from West Twelfth Street I owe an amazing amount of good study time. Few other boys came from my part of the town to my school. So I soon discovered that it was a choice between dawdling, looking out the car window, and wasting time, or putting in the two hours of transit on my homework. I chose the reasonable alternative, with the result that on the Madison Street car and the Lake Street L I did so much studying that I had most of the evenings free for pleasanter pursuits. I was never delinquent with a written assignment. I knocked out book reports with ease. The slowly bouncing cars of those primitive transport systems turned into excellent studies. Living far away from school was for me an unmixed blessing. No boy or girl has ever wrenched my heart with the sad tale of how far they live from school. It was my personal good luck.

Some time ago I wrote the story of Claude J. Pernin and his influence on me into a fairly sizable booklet. It would take volumes for me to explain the impact he made upon my life and the part he played in my education.

In 1905 I was entering the Jesuit class of humanities with one proud acquisition. By dint of turning in reams of manuscript, most of it worthless, I had impressed the moderator of *The Collegian* with my complete fitness to represent the academic classes on that quarterly journal of the school. So I returned to find my name lowest on the roster of editors, a very junior reporter. But there it was, and I was pleased and proud. And then I was knocked back on my heels. The Jesuit moderator at whose door I had laid the treasures of my priceless manuscripts had been transferred to another school, and a newcomer was announced as taking his place.

Claude J. Pernin, S.J., I read. And inwardly groaned.

Moving at a terrific rate around the school was a short, plumpish, swarthy figure who never traveled at less than racing speed and who never seemed to notice any of the boys along his path. This I was told was the new scholastic moderator. On the board two days later went up an announcement: the staff of *The Col-*

legian would meet with the new moderator in his classroom after the final dismissal bell. I looked at his signature, fierce, determined, in deep black ink, the signature as distinctive and forbidding as the racing figure in the corridors.

We gathered promptly, the ten or twelve men, most of them collegians, with me the sole high-schooler, and sat in the desks waiting. He planned a dramatic entrance, made it, talked briefly, and whirled out leaving us flattened. I have no clear recollection of what he said, only that I had been blown upon by a dominant personality who had every intent of making *The Collegian* the outstanding literary journal in college circles, who would tolerate no inferior writing, and who wanted a thing called deadlines carefully observed. He ended with a military "That is all," and left without time for question, comment, or rebuttal by the startled editors. "That is all" was a hang-over from his days, I discovered later, as a cadet in St. John's College of the future Fordham University, New York.

Little did I know that his manner was the brusque effort of a young, inexperienced teacher to impress a group of young fellows. Once he broke down and told me how he tried that same trick on the printer who got out the issues of *The Collegian*. "I remember," he said, "that the printer asked me if I wanted halftones. Never before had I heard of a halftone. So I countered: 'Did my predecessor use halftones?' I demanded. The printer nodded. 'Then,' said I impressively, 'this year we will have wholetones.' I stalked out on that, never realizing why the printer regarded me as something out of the looney hatch."

A wholetone would, of course, have been a perfect reproduction of that classic painting of six Ethiopians dressed in black shoveling coal in an unlighted coal hole at midnight.

More than anything else in the four wonderful years that followed, my association with young Mr. Pernin taught me how much a single man could do for a single growing lad. I soon found him fascinating. Once he realized that brashness was not necessary and that we did not demand the building up of a cold front, he settled down to be what he was in fact—the most brilliant conversationalist I've ever talked with, a man who knew books with deep, personal love, a mind avid for everything around him, a heart that expanded in the company of men, the best teaching instincts I've ever known, a perfectly wonderful guy who treated us all as if we were strictly contemporaries.

Never did I have the good luck to have him teach me in a classroom. Nor did I belong to the debating society which he built up in the high school and with which he made a clean sweep of every debating club in the city of Chicago. For me his classroom was his smoke-filled bedroom overlooking noisy Twelfth Street. His classes were the informal talks about books and drama and men and travel and life as the most exciting of adventures. He never recommended a book; he reluctantly closed a book at the last page and said, "This is terrific. Who wants it?" And we, his growing band of disciples, all reached out eagerly to begin reading the book still hot with his enthusiasm. His father had been the inventor of a system of shorthand, and for a time a wealthy man. Young Mr. Pernin had lived in New York, in pleasure-loving little Detroit of those social days; he had been a newspaper reporter, a haunter of good theater, a clubman, a *bon vivant*.

For four incredible expanding years he was the ideal on my horizon. He introduced me to the new authors as they came along. He despised people who could not tear the heart out of a book as he did. He talked with a scintillating cleverness and a depth of perception that was never show-off and always genuinely alert and alive. He welded a little cluster of us, boys from various parts of town, different classes of the school, unjointed ways of life, into a band of readers and observers and talkers. He was that one-man university of which you read, the most fascinating personality I was ever to know in my life, a Jesuit of the mental caliber I had expected in the sons of Loyola's dramatic tradition, a friend of a lifetime.

Under his eyes I expanded. I wrote thousands and thousands of words of voluntary manuscript, most of which he dismissed with a flick of his stogie. At his nudge and urging I read scores of books unrelated to class or to assigned subjects. He encouraged all of us to keep our eyes open for the unusual. One wealthy member of our gang he sent on a pilgrimage of unusual Chicago restaurants, and we listened to his reports and finally read the pilgrim's clever article in a kind of foretaste of the metropolitan columnists of the future. He taught me to know and love light verse and to copy it in my own style. He was bored with long sentences and demanded that mine have the crack of a whiplash. He was the greatest teacher I ever knew, and the biggest single influence in my education . . . after, of course, my mother and my grandfather Lord.

More than all, however, I think he taught me that a little personal interest can make all the difference in the life of a young fellow—that we learn best under the approval of a man interested in us—that formal education can readily give place to informal, and that the quick give-and-take of alert minds is probably what Plato sought when he walked with his disciples in the beginning of the peripatetic school of philosophy.

There is much more of Claude J. Pernin in my life's story. I regard him over the years with the gratitude of a full heart.

Graduation and an A.B. terminated what I thought was the conclusion of my formal education. Little did I suspect that, in the words of Scripture, "Now I begin." Yet how can one look back over those formative years without a wistful wish to share them with the young people he had known and loved throughout life?

I had learned at home. I had been given the best that Catholic education could afford. In the basement of our parish church I had worked at the art of meeting people and building friendships. I had joined clubs that gave me a wide variety of human experiences. For my part, I have but one sadness: that from so extraordinary a training I took really so little, and that from so wonderful a preparation I had so little of fulfillment.

This letter, Bill, has outgrown the proportions I set for it. But education is a fascinating subject as education is a challenging and exciting thing. It is what has made America great and the Catholic Church of America uniquely wonderful. Thanks for your patience in listening to me reminisce. Now turn back to your life's career as a Catholic educator, and do unto others as another generation tried so beautifully to do for me.

TO A YOUNG MAN CONSIDERING HIS VOCATION

Dear Dave:

Vocation is a mighty important decision, isn't it? I wonder how many of us would ever have the courage to make a definite choice of any state of life if we did not have the example of someone in the same profession or field who strikes us as being a great guy.

God has the first word on any vocation. When He gives us our character equipment, our potential, our abilities, our tastes, He is planting the natural seeds of a vocation. And then comes the silent call that is the most inarticulate and yet compelling voice in the world. I'm convinced that the vocation to be a doctor, a lawyer, a craftsman, an artist, is just about as clear a call as the vocation to be a priest.

But we have the last word on a vocation. In the end it's a matter of free choice, a highly human act by which we say, "This, with the grace of God and the development of my abilities, will I become."

And along the line are the mother who prays, the nun who believes in us, the companions who have the strangest and most effective way of making our characters take shape, and the person who is the great inspiration, our argument to show that we too can do as he has done. Your father is a great lawyer. Law may be your future. On the other hand we are sometimes discouraged from a profession simply because of the enormous success of a person for whom we have love and respect. He is too successful;

we dare not aspire to a field in which he is pre-eminent. He has done so well that his path is dizzy with heights and swift ascents; we choose a smoother, less adventuresome road. It's not easy to know how far an individual affects our ultimate choice, unless, as happened in my case, love and admiration and the challenge of a personality all work together persuasively.

However, this is not a discussion of your vocation, but a sort of retrospect on my own. Sometimes seeing how another man has done a job is a way of discovering whether something of the same might appeal to us. So let's turn from you to me for a bit. And who so willing as an old gaffer to tell a young man how he got that way?

What makes any young man even think of being a priest? Concretely, what makes a young fellow suddenly—or with painful drag of his feet—decide that he is going to be a Jesuit?

Actually there are a thousand different paths to the priesthood, and every man who travels altarward seems to mark out his own. I have never known any man the record of whose slow climb has been like my own. Most men with whom I talked vocation find me odd in my approach. Nothing is a more fascinating subject for novices in a Jesuit novitiate than the answers to the question: "How come you came here?" And each answer seems to all the listeners a little strange.

Not too long ago, Father Kane of Nova Scotia edited a book on *Why I Became a Priest.* He invited a number of priests each to contribute a chapter, and the chapters line up to prove once more the high individuality of the Catholic priesthood. No two men came to the novitiate or seminary for the same reason. The roads were different in all cases, and even the glimpses they had of the goal must have made them think they were not looking at the same thing.

In the end, I doubt if I decided to become a priest. What I found myself being forced to accept as inevitable was my designation as a Jesuit. Oh, incidentally I would be a priest, if I could stick it out. But when I made the final decision, I did not say, "Now I shall go and be a priest." I said, "Looks to me as if I was doomed to be a Jesuit." I was neither grateful nor glad. That came later. Right then and there, I knew that the good Lord had picked on me, and I was irritated that He had not pointed His gracious finger at somebody else. Any lad of my age could have had my vocation by naming his own price.

It is amazing to think back to the men whose entrance into the priestly preparation of a novitiate I have personally watched.

I think of a wonderful friend who arrived at the novitiate with all the magnificent starch of Irish dignity. He was unsmiling as he bowed to us who had arrived a day before him. He shook hands with elaborate courtesy that soon awoke our suspicion. Never, he later confessed, would he have taken that final step to the novitiate if he had not braced himself with bottled courage. He wasn't by any means drunk; but he was fortified with a courage other than his own. He became a leader among us novices, a marvelous priest, a power with people, a fine scholar, and a saint in his unflinching acceptance of a painful death.

I recall another lad who up to the morning of his departure had not the courage to tell either his mother or his father of his intentions. When to his surprise he found that they had known it all the time and had with difficulty hidden their delight, he grew morose, wanted to cancel the whole deal, and almost did. He had a trip to make with a change of trains in a large city. He managed to meet a convivial school chum. He handled affairs so that he missed the last train that night for the novitiate. He arrived late in the hope he would be rejected for this first delinquency. Instead he remained on to become a very wonderful priest and one of the most zealous apostles of the down-and-outer that I've ever known.

There was the son of the rich merchant who arrived in St. Louis and recalled the injunction to give all he had to the poor. Under the impulse of what he felt was a positive inspiration, he cupped all his money in his palms, told the porter to stretch out his hat, and dropped the bills and the coins one by one into the grip of the wide-eyed Negro who by this time was kneeling before the unexpected fountain of plenty. When he left the Pullman and got into the station, he suddenly realized he hadn't left himself carfare to reach the novitiate. He had to borrow the money to take his final step.

Men have found their path to the priesthood along the ruts of battlefields, in the wards of hospitals where they were interning as young doctors, or when they decided after winning a law case to plead the cause of Christ. They have made money merchandising and then decided that buying and selling the cheap stuff on the counters was a horrible waste of time. They have loved books and felt that the priesthood would be a lifetime of books. They have seen the need in human eyes and been unable to resist that appeal. They have fallen in love and then fallen out, and in the vacuum that followed determined never again to love any but the Ultimate and Best. They have wandered in all simplicity and innocence into God's house, a little surprised that they are there. They have battled their way as aviators and top sergeants and ballplayers and plumbers and brokers in the melee of Wall Street.

Just about the only way of finding a vocation that I have not personally known of was Martin Luther's blast of lightning. I am not impressed with the vow he made under a shattered tree. Fear is a motive, but I've usually seen much better.

And never have I known a man to become a priest in a twist of thwarted love. One eminently successful Jesuit of my friendship was for years very much in love with a beautiful and thoroughly selfish girl. He would have married her any of a dozen times. She dangled him, and when she finally married someone else, his sigh was not wistful but actually relieved. He knew that for years he had pursued an illusion. The real life was vaguely there ahead. He found it. Sometimes we have mentioned the girl, whom both of us knew well. He has always a general air of relief and escape. The priest of fiction who sits of an evening mooning over a lost love is in the same class as invaders from other planets. Maybe he exists. I've been spared knowing him.

On the other hand, I have known, as all priests have, of men who started the road to the priesthood for stupid or wrong motives. One young fellow arrived at St. Stanislaus Novitiate with the misapprehension that our beautiful locale was really the setting for a country golf club. He brought his matched woods and irons, his best sport clothes, and a sense of general relaxation. He lasted two days. Boys have come because their mothers have forced them. I could cheerfully strangle the mothers. I pray God that the reluctant sons have the sense either to find a real motive for staying or take the first outbound bus. Families have picked on one lad to do their praying and sacrificing for them. Some of these apparently fortuitous choices have also been God's selection and became saints. Pleasing the family is a poor reason for attempting the hard life of the priest.

We know so little about the motives that inspire others and the reason back of the most obvious and public actions that with time a person hesitates to say, "This is why we did that," or "He became a priest for the reason that . . ."

I know why I did. Or do I? For after taking into consideration the prayers of my mother, the Catholic atmosphere of my home, Mr. Pernin's example, and the grace of God, I'm no longer sure what brought me to Florissant.

The fact is that almost any boy of a normally good Catholic family at sometime or other considers the priesthood as his vocation. He may in succession determine to drive a garbage truck, to operate as a great surgeon, to be a circus performer, and to be a priest. The ambition to be a priest rises first of all from the great Catholic respect for priests and high regard for the vocation of the priesthood. Then no tiny Catholic but has a clear sense of the importance of priests to the world and to himself personally. He thinks it might be wonderful to be that important in his turn and to someone else. Finally a man has grown old indeed and out of touch with youth if he forgets or discounts the high courage, the idealism, the desire for personal sacrifice, that motivates much of early conduct. We may outgrow our own splendid virtue, our instinctive love of adventure, our desire to do noble things for others; we must not forget that once we had these things and that young people easily possess them in every age.

For all these reasons the supply of priests, however pressing the counterpleading of the world, continues. God cares for His race. Parents are splendidly generous in every generation. And human nature is capable of the heights.

Just to prove that one can be the exception, I had never been an altar boy. My mother had been shocked at the casual conduct of some acolytes in the sanctuary. She heard that back in the sacristy they roughhoused in unrestrained schoolboy fashion. She quoted to herself with emphasis, "Familiarity breeds contempt," and when she was approached by the zealous young curate who saw in me a natural altar boy, she returned him a polite but unequivocal no. I had almost finished high school before, on a Sunday morning, Father Bernard Naughton came out for the eight-o'clock Mass unattended. My mother leaned over to me. "Do you think you could serve him?" she asked. Though I had never been "on the altar," I waited until he had soloed the prayers at the foot of the altar, then slipped into the opening in the altar rail, and without difficulty or too many blunders I served my first Mass.

It was late June. Father Naughton cornered me when Mass was over. Would I like to serve his seven-o'clock Mass every day? I thought it an excellent idea, mentioned it to my mother, who promptly seconded the motion; so, though I never put on a cassock or surplice (I was too long and gangling for any supplied by our small parish) I served all through that summer and the next. My memories of Father Naughton are affectionate. Yet no slightest inclination impelled me to walk his way. He was not my Father O'Malley bidding me be "going my way."

The memory of every Catholic must hold in pleasant suspension the face and character of the priests who served his youth. I can close my eyes and see Father Gilmartin standing, gentle, red-faced, fatherly, over my sickbed that threatened to be my deathbed. I am vivid in my recollection of the fatherly Father Tighe who fought his parish sternly until they invested the incredible sum of $125,000 in a magnificent new church. Poor man, he couldn't build a baptismal font for that now! But the parish loved him for the splendor he gave them, and he died looking upon his work and knowing it was good. I fell briefly under the fascination of Father Judge, straight from Ireland, and with an irony that was a blend of acid and high explosive. I think of the little figure of Father Campbell leaning far out of the pulpit and patting the congregation gently on the head. I did not know that he had come to thoroughly bigoted Austin, walked undaunted when the local inhabitants took pot shots at him, and put up the first Catholic church in that section of Chicago which bragged it had kept Catholics entirely out.

Deep down inside was the recurrent thought: It would be nice to be a priest. "Nice" was a weak word. It was about the strength of my impulse. But with adolescence even that adjective disappeared or at least burrowed. Many a youngster must go through that same tearing period. He must know the rack of adolescence and suffer in a fashion that he finds difficult to explain. For many a youngster is torn apart. He lives in the light of his mother's purity and inspiration. He knows that she is drawing him to goodness with her prayers. He can't understand why he seems to struggle against her and the grace she wins for him. He drinks in the atmosphere of his home and school, deeply and pervasively Catholic. He looks in admiration on the sister who teaches him and marvels that his own strange, new impulses are so alien to her simple, crystalline purity.

For adolescence has let loose within him the forces he cannot account for, much less explain. The peace of childhood fades before the onrush of passion. In himself he seems to discover a terrifying new creature, animalistic, selfish, flung about in instincts that rise from nowhere. He is beset with anxiety. The world, the flesh, and the devil move in as if to take over. The world has suddenly become exciting. The flesh is fierce and demanding. The devil turns out to be a skillful and persuasive promoter, most eager to take over his controls.

And in the preoccupations, distresses, turmoils, and sudden sense of complete unworthiness, the desire of the priesthood may well die. Die is too strong a word, perhaps. He may soon find the desire is hiding away, showing itself rarely and then in a discouraged, futile, furtive fashion. To be a priest is too difficult an enterprise. It fits in incongruously with the present temptations. A wise confessor may reassure him that his experiences are in no sense novel or unique. The careful preparation of his parents for this upheaval may cause him to regard the troubles with an almost calm eye. But if he fights the battle alone, unaware even of a name to attach in confession to the problems he faces, he may be much too disturbed to give place to any further consideration of a priestly vocation.

As the excitement and interests of high school and college either serve to neutralize or pre-empt the emotional space taken up by adolescent temptations, or as he develops new calm and strength through the sacraments and a well-adjusted outlook, the thought of vocation may recur. But it may be buried with a new avalanche, this time of the preoccupations of his school, his friends, his hobbies, sports, his early dating, all that make up the taxing and delightful adventures of those years in school.

It seems to me in retrospect that my earlier nudges toward the priestly vocation were gentle and hesitant indeed. I felt far less inclined to the altar than I felt toward the stage. I might not often think of myself in the pulpit, but I could get a very clear image of myself pleading before an enthralled and hypnotized jury. Yet there must have been a deep-down inner impulse, the result, I'm sure, of my mother's prayers and the inspiration in which Sister Mary Blanche held the possibility of priesthood.

But I put the idea aside. For the truth is that I was having much too much fun. High school and college had brought me a world of excitement, a wealth of delightful experience, and the best and most sympathetic of friends. When one of the lads in my class mentioned casually that he was becoming a priest, I can still hear my own voice crying out in repudiation, "Well, I'm certainly not."

Yet I could never have guessed that the very fun I was experiencing, the friends with whom I was associating, and the interests that engrossed every waking moment were a kind of negative preparation for the day of vocation. I hadn't time now for the fierce temptations of adolescence. The wholesome character of my friends cushioned me against the evil just beyond their charmed circle. Sin became difficult, for goodness and activity were much more delightful.

How wonderful in retrospect appears the providence of God around a possible vocation! Almost throughout my life I knew no bad people. Once I met at the house of some friends a dazzlingly attractive organist. He was a mature man who took a great fancy to this fourteen-year-old boy, invited me to come with him to the choir loft of his beautiful and highly fashionable Protestant church where he promised to transfer my clumsy fingers from the piano keyboard to the manuals of his glorious organ. I accepted willingly, made a date for a near evening, mentioned it to my mother, only to meet with her stern and unexplained refusal. What strange maternal antennae had reached out to make her sense in this charming stranger what I had not guessed? For less than a month later, angry fathers pursued him out of town on the confessions of the little fellows in his own choir.

One week end threw me into the company of a strangely unfamiliar group alien to my normal crowd. I walked through the slightly riotous week end more bewildered than tempted, more inclined to dislike than to be attracted. I returned in positive relief to the kind of young people with whom I had long associated. I realized that I liked companions much better when they were good.

No young man or boy of normal circumstances and temperament misses the multiplied temptations from inside and out which come during those growing years. The difference in constant peril of yielding and strength against assault and inner betrayal is, after the grace of God, certainly the kind of associates he knows. And mine were the best. For them I can never sufficiently thank a protective Providence. I think of Bart Burns and Harry Moylan, my close friends of grammar-school days. We played ball, we walked, we rowed in the park, we cycled, we sat on the tall stools before a soda fountain and sipped our ice-cream sodas, we formed ourselves into a little trio which we christened The Three Egotists, a secret society that had no secrets to hide from God or our parents. I think of those wonderful young men who made up our small clubs, the Pit Club that first met one Sunday afternoon and continued together for three happy years; the splendid associates of high school and college—John Frank Quinn; Pierre Roche; Emmet Royce, who had the highest gaiety, a tremendous sense of comedy, and who never needed the slovenly humor of an off-color joke.

Most of the boys of my acquaintance bounced into love and out again with the springy confidence of youth. They found girls attractive. They danced with them and played tennis on the court we had laid out one energetic spring. They, and the "they" certainly includes me, picnicked, went on hayrides, and drove a little in the newly invented toy that was the auto, and danced down the streets of our suburb in the full of the moon, and, without knowing it, lived with God's arms around us . . . all of us.

How happily I could draw up a catalogue of the good young people I have known. I think of the little girls who with an equal number of little boys made the loud and happy and boisterous and altogether delightful guests of my birthday party as I attained to six. I think of Clara Barton and Virginia Falkenberg, who sweetly wrote to me, grandmothers now, when the papers carried news of my illness. Clara was the daughter of my mother's closest friend, which guaranteed her, of course. Virginia's father was the one wealthy man of our neighborhood. Of a hot summer evening he drove down St. Lawrence Avenue in his tallyho with his cropped-tailed teams, picked up the children of the block and carried them off to whisk through the parks and stop for frosted lemonades topped with luxurious-looking orange slices and cherries. At seven I rode behind with Virginia in her pony cart, sometimes permitted to take the reins over the little Shetland while she played the Golden Princess that she was.

From the vantage point of age a man can look back to those days and the bright faces that filled them, knowing how much of virtue is based on natural goodness and how the good girls of his early years are one of God's great blessings to his whole character. I can think of Rosemary Quinn and Audrey Quinn, my first dancing partner; and Clare Sullivan and Clare Thorndyke, who with her brother Everett were among my closest friends. With reverence and a lifelong gratitude I think of Nell Collins, whose dignity was gracious, whose purity was immaculate, whose mind was singularly alive, and who had a beauty that the years served only to ripen and mature.

My youth fell in a happy period of history when the mechanical entertainment of juke boxes and motion pictures and the radio and accessible autos lay in a less fortunate future; and the entertainment world had not fallen into the hands of the soiled, smutty, and intolerably lazy. Because we had no entertainment but what we furnished ourselves, we learned to have fun without gadgets. We played cards and games of our own devising. We danced the strenuous two-step and the graceful waltz, the ground-covering barn dance and the polkas and schottisches of the period.

When we took a girl to the theater we knew it was drama without a blush. There was no need for Legions of Decency or motion-picture codes. Vaudeville was cleaner than a Walt Disney nature film. Every Monday the great Cole and Castle each sat in a stage box and watched the acts. Any comedian who said damn or hell was fined five dollars. If he had the slightest touch of blue to his songs or jokes, he was warned once, and fined on second offense. Yet we saw all the great in the theater and watched the rise of the men and women who lived in the golden age of the American stage. The dirty hands of money-mad managers had not as yet throttled the drama in America. A city like Chicago ran simultaneously fifteen legitimate theaters and four vaudeville houses. New York had no monopoly on the theater, for every small town had its opera house, to which came the traveling companies often headed by the greatest stars of the day.

We were enthusiastic about the clubs which formed an important part of our self-created recreation. It often surprises young people of this generation when I tell them that in a single year at college I belonged to a parish dramatic club, a neighborhood card and dancing club, constantly attended dances given by other clubs, and once a month went as a regular member, the youngest, to a formal dancing club on the Near West Side, where not a tuxedo but full evening dress was required for admission. It was white tie for the men and correct formal dress, long white gloves and all, for the girls, and we arrived in four-wheelers and danced the cotillion with a skill that meant most of us, boys and girls, young men and young women, had spent a good many winters at dancing school.

When I sometimes meet men with a Puritan or Jansenistic background who shake their head over dancing, I laugh. I am sure that my Jesuit vocation was safeguarded on the dance floors of my youth. When I see graying heads shake over time spent in social life, I recall the blissfully happy evenings of play rehearsal, of parties in the basement of the parish church, and the parties that moved in a happy cycle from home to home. We were much too gay to be much tempted by sin. We were too busy to have idle hands for the devil to fill. Our clubs were made up of the kind of girls we boys expected some day to marry, and it was our duty to see to it that they stayed good and worthy of Christian marriage.

This may seem odd coming from a Jesuit, yet I cannot pay too much tribute to the wholesome social life of home and parish and school and supervised club. If during years when I gave the consideration of vocation no slightest nod my vocation remained possible, I can thank largely the social life that made the days and nights gay. I am convinced that the devil thrives in an atmosphere of gloom. I am convinced that the truly happy can easily slip ahead to become nicely holy. The social life I knew in my youth was not too far removed from the spiritual life.

The whole incident of my loss of faith startles me even today.

During my early days in college I had read widely and not wisely. A young architect friend who had been trained in the state university threw my way books I might never have otherwise seen. And the reading of the condemned and Indexed books which I had taken blithely from Dr. Bailey's library began to back up on me. The literature of that period was an overflow or corollary of the scepticism of the eighties and nineties. Evolution was its god, and Darwin was his prophet. The attack on morality was fierce and sinister. The plays which came from England and the Continent were anti-God, and anti-Christianity, and were preparing the way for the atheism of communism and the communism that is an outgrowth of atheism. With the voracious appetite of an eager reader I read them all.

The morning remains clear and frightening when I woke with the realization that I had lost my faith.

It was a strangely terrible experience, yet one that, since it happened that way, I would not have missed for anything. I was about eighteen, in college, determined to stop at the end of my sophomore year and transfer to a law school, no particular one in mind. And I lay in bed looking up at the ceiling which blocked out the sight of God, the vision of the supernatural, all but the blank, alarming conviction that my faith was dead.

I looked the facts clearly in the face.

God had become as distant as the nearest fixed star and to me as nameless.

The whole scheme and pattern of religion looked fantastic and totally improbable.

Man was an animal of the high levels, but the thought of free will was absurd, largely because morality was such a bother and annoyance.

I wondered if anyone could prove that Christ had ever lived, much less that He was God.

And the Church seemed filled with the flaws and mistakes and evils which I had had thrust upon me by the writers who delighted to dig them out and turn them into high melodrama.

I lay in bed with the morning sun streaming through the window and held myself in a kind of suspended animation. Religion class had been up to that time a matter of memory and endless repetition of what seemed formulae and clichés. I had done no Catholic reading beyond the juveniles of Father Francis J. Finn and Father Henry S. Spalding and Father John E. Copus, and a few translations from obscure European writers. Faith had been a matter of inheritance. And the cleverness and charm of the writers who had engrossed and, without my realization, captivated me, seemed to prove that against my faith was arrayed the wit, the wisdom, the science, and the literary skill of the world.

Yet even as I faced the startling facts as they were mustered before me, I could sense the consequences of the loss of faith. And they appalled me. No eternity. No certainties under my faith. No plan or rule for life. No helps beyond my own very limited abilities. Life without light and heaven emptied of God.

I think I prayed to God, if there be a God. I know that it suddenly swept over me that I had read all the other side and, strangely enough, nothing of my own side. I had let the enemy plead his case; I did not know if there was a convincing defense. What next?

Events blur with the passing of time, especially if the events are lived in emotional intensity, and for a time the events of my mental and spiritual life were very intense indeed. My father was just on the verge of entrance into the Church. He had gone to listen to Father Bertrand Conway and had returned carrying *The Question Box*. Years later I had the privilege of meeting the great Paulist and telling him that his sermon had put the capstone on the arch of my father's faith. And I added, "And your book brought me back step by step from a sophomoric scepticism to the faith." It was actually the first of that long series of Catholic books which have presented our side of the question and made such a defense of God, Christ, the Church, and Christian morality that the other side seems fireworks, froth on the beer, icing on the cake, and veritable moonshine. I went back to school determined for the first time to get something out of our religion class. And when later I came to philosophy under Father Gleeson I was disposed to listen to a skillful advocate presenting what he evidently knew to be the God-given truth.

Young Mr. Pernin, sensing my troubled state, began tossing me the new Catholic writers like Henry Harland and the editors of *The Yellow Book*. I came across and devoured F. Marion Crawford. For the first time I discovered that my beloved Oscar Wilde, after a life of the most devastatingly logical paganism, had ended his misery in the arms of the Church. I came in contact with the brilliant mind of Robert Hugh Benson, and learned that he had found in the Church the only answer to the problems of the questing soul and the intellectual storm-tossed by the incredible contradictions that take over once faith has been ejected.

The loss of faith and the current legend that Jesuits were men of deep study and an almost chill scientific approach to the faith may have combined to prepare once more for my vocation. I have often apologized to God, whose truth fills the visible world and the soul of mankind, for that brief loss of faith. I have been grateful that it forced me, the born Catholic, to do something like the laborious study of the convert. Many have asked me if I am a convert. It has been my great good luck to receive the faith without deserving it. Yet in a kind of way, I have known the upward climb from doubt and confusion. I have dwelt intellectually with the enemy and the adversary. I have heard and read his arguments. And I have struggled to establish myself on the rock of Peter. And the study of the years has kept me there, contented, tempted often enough, in touch with the new doubts and objections that rise and fall, yet convinced with absolute assurance that either we are right or no one is, that God has given us truth and means us to possess it, that the voice of Christ is the truest voice in history, and that that voice of His He transmitted to His teaching Church.

Yes, all this too was preparation for vocation.

My great admiration for Mr. Pernin had grown with association. I had finally found a Jesuit who struck me as being what I would like to be—not as a Jesuit but as a mind and a man. We were in most things different. He was short, I had grown taller than either my mother or father. He was dark and swarthy, I was blond with the annoying acne of an adolescent. He never seemed to know that the world possessed a race of women; I liked boys and girls and gravitated to either group or a blend in one crowd. Though he was at heart highly sentimental, our relationship was the most casual one. It was mind with mind, interest with interest; and, as I hope to indicate later, no one could flay me the way he could.

Yet in him I found almost everything that interested me. He had been everywhere and done everything. He had been a successful young newspaper man and loved club life. He knew the theater thoroughly. He was a great reader and a perfectly marvelous speaker. I knew he had come from a family far better circumstanced than mine. I even discovered that he had been briefly in love (the only woman, except a mother to whose memory he was devoted, that ever seemed to light his horizon). And an inner conviction rose that perhaps I could imitate him without going the whole way and becoming a Jesuit.

Providence arranged circumstances with masterly skill.

I had fallen out of love with the girl who had been a sort of protecting interest for two and a half years. Nell Collins was now interested in someone else. Incidentally she married still a third man. I had briefly come close to the fire and had not been burned. An invitation to play the lead in a short one-act play had thrown me into the company of a remarried divorcée, beautiful, clever, synthetically blonde, and headed for a career on the English music-hall stage where she did remarkably well. She made it abundantly clear that she would like a partner for some dramatic sketches which might do well in vaudeville, and to a young fellow of twenty that was blending temptation with opportunity.

The skillful handling of this problem by my mother brought me through unscathed. And for a moment, that late afternoon of the early spring, 1909, I could sit in Mr. Pernin's room completely relaxed. Philosophy classes were interesting and stimulating. I was doing a musical show that interested me with our parish dramatic society. I had fairly settled in my own mind that the law course which I had postponed would begin after graduation. My world was good and I was at peace.

Then Mr. Pernin, looking at me through the densest possible screen of stogie smoke, asked a question: "What are you going to do when you graduate?"

God alone knows why I gave the completely unintended and utterly absurd answer: "Oh, I don't know. But sometimes I have thought I might be a Jesuit."

Even as I said it the whole thing sounded ridiculous. I did not think I'd be a Jesuit. I did not want to be a Jesuit; in fact, I could think of nothing that I wanted less. The life had little appeal for me. Jesuits who had taught me had not much impressed my young arrogance. I was having much too good a time in life. Though for the moment I was interested in no particular girl, there were a number of charming young ladies on my horizon. And what I had said was hardly out of my mouth when I wanted to pull it back and cancel it out with laughter and emphatic denial.

Instead, he leaned forward, not smiling, but almost grim, touched my knee with that hand which he himself described as looking like the forepaw of a mole, and said, "Dan, I've been waiting for months to hear you say that. I couldn't say it first. But now that you have said it, where do we go from here?"

I stood up with a jerk.

"No place," I answered. "I'm frankly talking through my hat. Forget it. It was a slip and a stupid one."

He waved me back with authority and obediently I sat again in his comfortable chair.

"That may be true," he said. "You may have no more vocation than the chair you sit in. You may have been talking out of your head. But for your own sake and for mine, I'm going to make you think it through. I can think of no more wonderful life for a man. I've loved every moment of mine. And though I could not lift a finger to persuade you, I am going to be unpleasant about it if you don't give yourself a chance to settle that question calmly and reasonably."

"If," I said with a real chill in my voice, "you want to do me a favor, you'll regard the whole thing as nonsense and drop the subject for good."

"Not when there is a chance that you may be able to know the joy and happiness of the Jesuit life," he answered. And on that we resumed our normal talk about books and life and the world around us.

But he would, unexpectedly and with the sudden thrust of a great duelist, from time to time look at me, and say simply, "Well? What have you decided?" And I would answer, "Nothing! Absolutely nothing."

In a short life of Father Pernin, called *My Greatest Teacher,* I have told the story of that evening when, at the close of school, he came to our house for a farewell dinner. I have told how I took him upstairs to my room, closed the door, and said in a voice that was rich in annoyance and disgust, "Well, I've decided. I'm going to apply for admission into the Society."

He grinned at me and shook my hand. "It's the happiest moment I've known in years," he said. He walked across the room, broke a wild flower out of a vase that my mother had placed there in his honor and thrust it into the none-too-neat lapel of his rusty suit. "I have not worn a flower in my buttonhole since I became a Jesuit," he said; "but the occasion calls for no less."

And we walked down to dinner, after agreeing not to say a word about what was still our secret. I have elsewhere told at length of breaking the news to my mother. She and my father, with graduation in sight, pulled a few strings and got me an appointment to see the executive director of one of Chicago's largest and best-established family estates. To the disappointment of my on-the-minute mother, I kept postponing the interview. At last, it all came to a head in the elevator of Marshall Field's. She was buying me a summer suit for my graduation, and as our elevator reached the men's clothing floor, she said, "Isn't this a good day for you to see the director of the estate?" I answered somewhere deep back near my tonsils: "No point in that just yet. I'm thinking of going to Florissant." We stepped out of the car and into the racks and counters of summer suits. She did not look at me, but asked very softly, "Then do you think you had better buy a light-colored suit?" I shot back in something like fury: "The lighter the color the better." Which is why I arrived at Florissant in a very light suit, which later on I had dyed black for clerical use.

With her usual tact and determination not to intrude, she did not bring up the subject again for a good many days. Then I told her the news. I had graduated, and had given a flamboyant speech in the fashion of young orators; I had put in a leisurely day, and then, without reporting my reasons, I had gone back to St. Ignatius, made my formal application for membership in the Society of Jesus, and returned home in the depths of depression. I told her out in the kitchen, in the brusque, heartless fashion of youth: "Well, I'm going to be a Jesuit." She smiled a misty smile, and then said, "Do you think I have been praying for anything else for years?" And we sat on kitchen chairs and wept together. What chance has a lad of missing the great gift of vocation when his mother has prayed for nothing else for years?

Vocation is an odd and inexplicable thing.

Father Cassilly, who had, I am sure, a deep affection for me, never once mentioned vocation to me, and I think I must have been about the only one in the class to whom he did not give a little talk. He concentrated instead on a brilliant young fellow, class leader for many a semester, clever speaker, and end on our high-school and college football teams. Father Cassilly's heart was set on the future of this lad; over me he only shook a head heavy with hopelessness. I was much too frivolous. I brought young ladies to our school events. He even called my mother to the parlor to warn her about the fact that I always seemed to be arriving in the company of three or four attractive girls. My mother answered him with a wisdom which, I am sure, escaped him: "As long as it is three or four, Father, I shall not worry. I shall begin to be troubled when he settles down to one."

During the spring of my senior year I was deep in the production of one of our parish musicals. I had been keen to see my beloved Mr. Pernin in the audience. Instead, he developed a frightful cold, and gave the tickets to Father Cassilly. Years later he told me the incident:

"I gave him the tickets, told him I couldn't go, but begged him to take my place. Then I explained why, how you were thinking of becoming a Jesuit, and how, though I was imparting to him the strictest possible secret, I felt he might want to see you outside of the college setting. He went. It was after midnight when he knocked at my door and woke me up. He came and sat briefly on my bed, shaking his head as he so often did over the foibles and frivolities of youth. 'Claude,' he said in sad disillusionment, 'any thought you had of that young man's becoming a Jesuit, you might as well give up. If you'd seen his show, you would have. Throughout the thing, he danced with girls. There were costumes in it that showed the girls' calves, almost their knees. One girl sang a song that was, well, not indecent, but certainly made me nervous. He's a thoroughly worldly young fellow, and if his affection for you brought him to the novitiate, he wouldn't stay out the week.' "

Mr. Pernin's cold was not improved by his sleepless night, but he managed to make a later performance of our production. Yes, I danced. Yes, the girls of our lovely little suburban parish were fresh and attractive. Yes, I had written the show and so plotted it that, in slightly prophetic fashion, I lost the leading lady to another character. Yes, the costumes did show the calves, a remote and taboo territory in those days when skirts made unnecessary any other form of street sweeping. And the "nervous" song (Father Cassilly was unconsciously anticipating bebop) was sung by a girl in a Holland costume. It concerned the fact that Dutch boys gave the girls they courted petticoats; and she had so many suitors that she was simply swathed in "a pretty pink petty from Peter, and here's a blue petty from John, and there's one trimmed with yellow from some other fellow, and one that I haven't got on." By modern standards it was positively prim.

At any rate, Mr. Pernin declined to give up his faith in me, and Father Cassilly returned to devote himself to that bright and shining vocation in the other lad. The other lad went out with his first girl at our senior party, married her within six months, and fathered a fine family, the oldest son of which became one of my Sodality leaders in later years. Father Cassilly watched the departure of his "very worldly-minded young man" to the novitiate in complete incredulity. When I met him later, a priest though still very much in awe of my former dean, he was still baffled about how I ever made the grade. For that matter, I have often been baffled myself.

God's totally undeserved and gratuitous favors are a rare sign of His protecting love.

On the advice of Mr. Pernin, I told almost no one of the decision. "Have a wonderful last few weeks," he said. "If you tell people, they'll expect you to give up your tennis and parties and picnics and dancing. Live your normal life. That will be the best preparation."

"Shall I," I asked out of a sense of the fitness of things, "read a history of the Society of Jesus, or any spiritual books?"

"Certainly not," he replied. "You'll have plenty of that for the rest of your life."

We shook hands and he went off to the holiday villa of Jesuit scholastics. I returned to an even gayer than normal life. The world had never been so bright and my friends had never seemed so attractive. The only way my plan could be pushed forward would be first to push it entirely off my consciousness. I might have stumbled into a vocation without any deserving on my part; I might easily stumble out of it if I did too much thinking about the awful leap I soon must make.

Though by this time Nell Collins was deeply interested in a far more promising young man, a member of our dramatic club, a wit, already marked for great business success, I told her my decision and she was gracious enough to shed a few tears. I had been squiring the daughter of our dramatic-club mother, the gracious Mrs. T. J. Sullivan. I told Clare, and she too in womanly fashion cried a bit. I was vastly flattered, of course. I told my closest friend, Harry Moylan, who thought I was lucky. He had been working since eighth grade and saw no percentage in it. He regretted that the real-estate partnership he had planned for the two of us would never be a reality; he envied me my good fortune. I told Everett Thorndyke, my close associate of many happy adventures, and he greeted the announcement with a sincere and fervid "Well, you damn fool!" Years later, when I re-established contact with him in his cherry orchards of Oregon, he took it back. He had come to know my great good luck.

One close friend had to be told, and with ulterior motives. So I wrote to John Frank Quinn in Joliet, his home town and the scene of some very pleasant partying, to come and spend the week end with me; I had news for him. He arrived, certain he knew the news. A small neighborhood theater on the North Side had just staged a play that was obviously by an amateur; yet as it was a morality play and about the devil, Frank decided I had written it and wanted to tell him the real man back of the obvious pen name.

Instead, after we had had dinner, I said, "Look, I'm going to Florissant. I'd rather not go alone. You're coming too, in case you don't know it."

He looked at me in surprise. "You?" he asked, a little as if I were the last possible candidate for the cassock. I nodded. He thought it over for a moment and then said, "I think I will." Of course, his decision was not as sudden as that; he had been thinking of priesthood and the Jesuits on and off for years; he too had a mother who prayed and a social life that kept temptation to a minimum. He too was a close friend of Mr. Pernin and with years became closer to the maturing Father Pernin than I. So the decision came, as vocational decisions do, out of a wide variety of factors, including the fact that I knew him to be a very frequent communicant with one of the most remarkable gifts of prayer that I have ever known in a boy or young man.

When he gave his answer, I said: "That's fine. Now let's forget it. We'll go out to Forest Park and have an evening, and in the morning we'll talk some more." Forest Park was our suburban Coney Island. It had just installed one of the maddest rides that ever made the passengers scream in a blend of fear and delight. When the heavy cars began their falling flight down the precipitous incline, they caught the electric power of a third rail.

The momentum of gravity was aided by the power of electricity to create a sickening experience which—long before power dives in planes—we loved. Yet we were scared stiff on that first fall into space, and for years the two of us laughed as we agreed that to the normal reasons for vocation had been added the fear of sudden death. We claimed we got our vocations to be Jesuits on a roller coaster.

Frank Quinn's father was one of Joliet's most important citizens, so the news of his vocation soon was newspaper copy. I was included in the item as "his college chum who would accompany him," so the news broke among my own friends. But we kept up a polite pretense of secret. There were no farewells. No good-by parties. No gifts to take along with me. On the final Sunday morning on my way to Mass my mother and I stopped to say good-by to her friends and mine. That afternoon a number of my beloved gang came by. My dear friends, Charlie and Rhoda Crowe, a charming young husband and wife who had come to love each other in our dramatic club, stayed till the rest had gone. I walked Nell Collins home for the last time and then heard my mother cry as I had never heard her cry before.

The next morning it was my turn to cry. I did so, unabashedly. At the St. Louis-bound train the Chicago novices met. Frank Quinn and I gravitated together. The others came from lower classes in school, and I was a little abashed to realize that I hardly knew their names. In the days that followed they became lifelong friends. The train pulled out, but my tears would have made a ship more appropriate; and so I was launched on my way to Florissant.

During the years that followed I had many a chance and privilege of helping young men and women, boys and girls, reach the joy of priesthood or religious life. Hundreds have complimented me by their willingness to talk to me. Other hundreds, picking my name off a pamphlet or hearing me on a platform, have written and started a correspondence that ended in some sort of decision.

You notice that I write, "some sort of decision." To my deep regret we have often discovered, my confidant and I, that no vocation was there. I recall sending away to become a highly successful writer one young man for whom I had a deep affection. One of my dearest students decided with my fullest approval that he was meant to be a husband and father and not a Jesuit priest. On his return from special surgical studies in Europe a very great young doctor consulted me. I had long known and admired him. He had great surgical skill and the offer of a post in one of the city's least Christian hospitals. Yet he wondered if God wanted him to be a Jesuit. In the end I sent him on to work in his hospital to do great apostolic work in a pagan field, and to give great honor to God and the Church. So it has often been with the girls who talked or wrote about vocation. So many of them belonged elsewhere, and we decided this and sent them off to the vocation for which they were fitted. I think of Curley, whose story I later wrote up; Curley who never should have been a nun, yet who struggled, against my advice, for eight years to wear a habit and lead the life; then with my strong approval she gave up the vain effort, married, as she should have done in the first instance, and mothered a wonderful Catholic family.

Yet I have not hesitated to quote my own instance in talking vocation to others. In the end no one can decide whether or not a person has a vocation but God and himself. And God seems to have the last word. For, as in my case, he may find himself saying, "Yes, I'll go," while everything within him cries, "Indeed and I will not." The best I have been able to do has been to sit as referee while the young person struggled to reach a decision only he could make . . . or she, as the case might be.

Often I have met these singularly blessed children of God who from infancy are marked for religious life. I have met little acolytes with the stamp of the priesthood all over their pious little shining faces. (Sometimes they failed, but usually the pull was strong and evident.) I have met girls who danced all the way to the novitiate. I have seen the most heroic struggle against odds that seemed insuperable. There was the girl whom I wrote into a booklet called *All American Girl*. Rarely does she write to me from her cloistered solitude, though I know she prays for me in penance as she does for the world she left. She struggled against wealth, education on a pagan college campus, protesting parents, the fact she was an only child, two engagements to be married, success in the movies, athletic ability that included championship form as a swimmer and crack aim with a pistol. In the end and just under the wire of canonical age limitation, she reached the contemplative convent and made good.

I have watched young men and women in complete distaste for religious life almost court temptation, and seem to race wildly down the primrose path. Then to their own surprise even their wild flight has brought them up sharply to the door marked with the cross.

Not for a moment am I unaware that the story of the rich young man is relived a thousand times every current year. I have known too many rich young men and rich young women who could not sell what they had, give it away in a burst of generosity, and follow the call of Christ.

But what makes it possible for a person to follow his vocation? I can only say that I know myself thoroughly, and bow humbly and gratefully before God's fatherly goodness.

I did not want to be a Jesuit. I felt God would do me a great favor if He picked somebody else.

I cannot say that I knew much of the Jesuit life except the exaggerated legends which friends and enemies had alike confected.

Indeed, I cannot claim that I, as a boy and young man, really liked them very much. For Mr. Pernin I had an overwhelming respect and affection. If there was a natural impulse involved, it was the conviction that I should be able to give up what he gave up and choose what he chose and develop as he seemed to develop and become what he had become. For Father Cassilly I had an awed reverence, the feeling of a gob for a great admiral. For Father Gleeson I had an intellectual respect that was glacial and chill. For most of the others around me I had a certain admiration but no real affection. And few of them excited me to say, "I would be as they." With later years my admiration for my fellow Jesuits grew and grew. I did not bring that admiration with me to the novitiate.

I had no taste whatsoever for prayer. I found it hard and a struggle. Frequent Communion was born in our generation, or rather, reborn. I never practiced more than monthly Communion with the Jesuit devotion of the Nine First Fridays.

Mary was remote. I did belong to the Sodality of Our Lady from my first Communion. Sister Mary Blanche moderated our Sodality to high attractiveness and a vital interest in things Catholic. The Sodality in St. Ignatius was dull, pietistic, a matter of a few hurried prayers, a bit of charity, a concentration on self which bored me, and a cloistered air that had little attraction for us who pretended to be "live wires." That I went to the weekly meetings and said the Office was almost a matter of routine.

I did not particularly like study, though I found it easy. Mr. Pernin's love of books guaranteed me that Jesuits would continue to love books and I could too. Yet I did not find that same love for books in the other Jesuits who taught me. And I would not certainly enter religious life just to get a chance to read.

Yet all the time, my mother prayed. Wisely she said nothing of her prayer or of her hopes, but she never, any more than did St. Monica, allowed discouragement to color her attitude or bring her prayers to an end. Sister Mary Blanche wanted me to be a priest, and she too prayed.

The atmosphere of my home was thoroughly Catholic. My father had a wonderful attitude toward the future. With a family sense that was deeper than he pretended, he wanted me to marry and bring children named Lord into the world. But his only comment on my choice of a state of life was, "If being a cabdriver would make you happy, be a cabdriver, and be a good one."

I knew the influence and the silent idealism of the Catholic school system. I grew mentally in my awareness of Catholic truth and the strength and helps of Catholic practice.

Often I faced up to the dread fact that if I did not become a Jesuit and know the protections of religious life, I would certainly end up in hell. Never have I played on fear as a motive. Indeed, my tendency even in retreats has been to turn toward hell almost in a casual aside. For me it remained a powerful motive, as hell remains a grim, Christ-taught truth.

The good young people whom I had known had never been an even passing source of temptation to me. And when I fell in youthful love, it was with good girls who kept me straight, never threw temptations into my path, and actually were new reasons for me to struggle for self-control and a respect for womanhood.

When the silent voice of the Master spoke, it was seconded by a young Jesuit scholastic whom I vastly admired. There is a tradition in our Jesuit midwest provinces that the number of vocations each year is directly in proportion to the happiness, zeal, and closeness to the boys of the teaching scholastics. It surely was so in my case.

But though I cannot tell with any clarity why I became a Jesuit, I have no slightest doubt about why I stayed. I felt it was the greatest life in the world for me. Indeed, I was not at all sure that it was not the greatest life in the world.

Never have I tried in any slightest way to persuade a young person to study for the priesthood or to enter the religious life. The call must come from God. But when I have sensed a vocation, I have been deeply glad for the lucky person. When we have thrashed through the underbrush that lies in the path of any vocation and seen the road ahead, rocky and steep and dangerous though it may seem, I have never failed to congratulate the young person. God has been good. Life will be wonderfully happy and deeply satisfying. There is nothing like the gift of priesthood or religious life.

And after years of life as a Jesuit, I know that I would not trade it for any other that man has ever lived. I could write to my mother when I renewed my vows as a young Jesuit: "I am happier now than ever. I know now why I renew the vows I made in something of a fog. It is a great life. Your prayers and your home life gave it to me. God has kept it bright and shining. I am very grateful indeed."

TO AN OLD AND GOOD FRIEND

Dear Harry:

Throughout long youthful years you and I were friends. Our paths were very different throughout later life. We met but rarely and then always with the constraint which characterizes close friends whose friendship has been interrupted by time and distance.

Once you asked me a seemingly simple question that turned out to be one of the most complicated in the world: "What makes a Jesuit?" I laughed a little at the time. The question was kindly. But it was a question that had been asked in a thousand varied shades of expression by the wide gamut of human questioners, from those who meant it to be a compliment to those who meant it to be the fiercest insult. A lot of men have written a lot of books trying to answer that question. Historians have been prejudiced *pro* and *con*. So, you see, that question isn't such a simple one after all.

I have been a Jesuit now since the July of 1909. One of the pleasant things which St. Ignatius Loyola saw to was that any young man who entered the Jesuits could consider himself a Jesuit from the moment he crossed the threshold of the novitiate. Our "anniversaries" do not count from vow day on but from the day of entrance. A novice, despite the fact that he is only beginning his training, is nevertheless a Jesuit. Indeed, a youngster so recently arrived that he has not as yet been given his cassock gets a stimulating conviction that he already belongs.

Since 1909 I have been a Jesuit constantly trying to become more Jesuitical. To me a Jesuit is an exciting figure, any way you regard him—or should be. I took my confirmation name from a young Jesuit named Aloysius. So, if you recall, did you. I had a youthful enthusiasm for a great, romantic, and highly adventurous Jesuit named Francis Xavier. Along the course of his days he became a saint. I had never met St. Ignatius Loyola until I was already a member of his spiritually militant company. My esteem for him, my admiration for a great organizer and a man of the most worldwide vision, has grown with the years. I recall a little anecdote of my good Jesuit friend, Father Siedenberg, which somehow expresses one attitude I feel for the man we Jesuits refer to as "our holy founder."

Father Frederic Siedenberg, a very great Jesuit who really introduced sociology to the Catholic educational system and to the Catholic charities of our country, helped found a club of Catholic men called the Medievalists. Once a year they had a *gaudeamus,* a gay evening of good food and drink and laughter and a satirizing of themselves. The Gridiron Dinner in Washington is a modern form of the *gaudeamus.* At one *gaudeamus* the entertainment took the form of a spiritualistic séance, and from the other world ghosts were summoned, each of whom bore some relationship to one of the members. For Father Siedenberg the master of ceremonies and pseudomedium summoned up the spirit of St. Ignatius. Father Siedenberg had recently located his school of social science in a downtown Loop building in the heart of Chicago's financial section.

The summoned spirit of Loyola was very stern.

"Father Siedenberg," he cried accusingly, "how dare you, a Jesuit, move a Jesuit school into a downtown office building? Is this according to our spirit and customs?"

Father Siedenberg shook his head. "The spirit is a fake," he retorted. "That is not Ignatius of Loyola. If it were, he would be saying, 'Father Siedenberg, why did you move your Jesuit school into a second-rate office building? Move out at once and rent space in the city's best.' "

To me that incident perfectly explained Ignatius. He was a great man who thought that nothing was too good and too great for God and for His kingdom and His work. When he sent Xavier out on his mission, he told him simply: "Go, set the world on fire." Nothing less than the whole world would satisfy his tremendous spiritual ambitions. He wanted mankind won for Christ. He could never forget the command of Christ, "Go into the whole world and teach the good news to every creature." It was a universe-blanketing command. He could not forget that Christ had ordered our light to shine before men so that they would see our good works and glorify our Father in heaven. He recalled how the Savior sent the Comforter as a living tongue of flame, burning with eloquence, alive with warmth and brilliance.

Ignatius thought big and dreamed big. He wanted nothing for himself and insisted that his followers refer to the Society of Jesus as "this least company." But where God was concerned he had no such narrow ideas. His company was to work without pause or admission of weariness. His schools must be great. His missionary enterprises must be flung to match the terminus of the widest earthly empire, and then push on into lands as yet unexplored. He demanded that his men think of the Church Universal. They were to be superlative theologians. They were never to accept willingly high office of any sort. They were not to be popes or archbishops. The cardinal's rank was out of the line of their aspirations. But high scholarship and great skill in administering the talents God had given them, a zeal that would not be satisfied until the kingdom of Christ was coterminous with mankind, a flying energy that kept them constantly on call of the pope and demanded that they accept the difficult and dangerous assignment, this, all of this, he took for granted.

I doubt if he could have imagined a careful Jesuit, a timid Jesuit, a conservative Jesuit. He was radical as that Christ who is the true radical: "I am the vine, you the branches." He wanted to get to the roots of things, even if it meant martyrdom, and attempt anything however likely the possibilities of defeat and failure. After all, Loyola had the example of the Failure of the Cross.

I am sure that in the earliest days of his Society, Loyola envisioned a marching army, not a comfortably entrenched company holding safe positions. He bade his men go to any part of the world where there was hope of God's glory and the service of souls. He did not ask them to work for God's glory, but for God's greater glory. He dared his followers to attempt the hard and to challenge the impossible. He turned a handful of first disciples into an explosive center of a new educational world. He heard of the wonderful new lands that had just been discovered and ordered his men to plant the cross and take them for Christ. The thought of death discouraged him not in the least. He made them court danger, whether it was in the bush of South America or in the pursuivant-infested England of the Tudors. One of his most distinguished theologians in the Council of Trent was taunted that he personally had not read a certain obscure author he was quoting. The brilliant theologian retorted: "I have read him, reread him, and written a commentary on him." Ignatius, on the man's return, slapped a heavy penance upon him for what he regarded as arrogant boasting; but he was delighted that he had a spiritual son of such vast learning.

No one can understand a Jesuit who does not understand the greatness of Loyola. Here was a man who set himself to stem the Protestant Revolt and recapture Europe for traditional western Christianity. Here was a man who had only to hear of a newly discovered continent to have men on the way to capture it. He did not cling to the quill in an age of newly invented printing presses. If being constantly on the road meant that his men would miss the long-established custom of Office recited in common, then he would drop the choir from his rule, and did. His was to be a flying squadron, a light brigade, a company traveling without impediments so that it could travel fast and far. Whether his men moved on into the dark ignorance which circles our narrow zone of truth, whether they disputed with heretics as they were stretched out on a rack, whether they were putting up colleges or walking alone into Belgian towns in which there remained not a single good priest, whether they were influencing the progress of the Council of Trent or preaching their duty to reluctant monarchs, Catholic or pagan—Loyola knew them as an army on the march. Trench warfare would have bored him. Holding positions, unless the positions were in terrible danger, he would have left for others. Followers without ambition to do their very best for Christ, best of all captains and kings, were not to his taste.

He must have often enough looked down from heaven to know celestial annoyance when conservatism, caution, respect for convention, and attachment to things as they are chained even one of his Jesuit sons.

Yet he began the training of each of his men by withdrawing him from the world's activities, as he personally had retired to the cave of Manresa. He initiated the new custom of two years of novitiate, because once that was completed his men stood a fine chance of knowing little of the protective calm of an established religious house. They were not to be cloistered monks but soldiers under the range of sharpshooters. They would not work and pray in peaceful monasteries, but would march to battle until the whole world was won for Christ.

And so it was that, once I had been accepted by the Missouri Province of the Society of Jesus, I moved out to a little town called Florissant near the confluence of the Mississippi and Missouri rivers in the lush valleys of Missouri.

Often it has seemed to me that anyone who knew Florissant would know the spirit of the monastic towns of the Middle Ages. Florissant existed before St. Stanislaus Seminary was built. Yet the town took its spirit from that house of prayer and spiritual development and training. Next to the Valley of the Nile, the Valley of the Missouri is regarded as the richest. The first settlers in Florissant did not name their location as much as they described it. To them it was the Flourishing Valley of St. Ferdinand. Flourishing it certainly was: a fruitful valley which the Missouri River regularly inundated, leaving behind black loam of such fertility that poor crops were impossible. And the choice of the French patron, St. Ferdinand, was delightful. One instantly thinks of a later and nationally popular hero in a book and a song, a bull named Ferdinand who luxuriated in flowers and sweeping trees and the charm of abundant harvests.

Father Charles Van Quickenborne brought his pioneer Dutch and Belgian Jesuits across country from White Marsh in Maryland to take up a strip of land that was hardly half a mile wide but ran for several miles back to the bluffs of the Missouri. In the fashion of the frontier they built their first log hut. The great

Sacred Heart nun, Blessed Philippine Duchesne, had already established nearby a school for the education of Indians. And the newly arrived Jesuits looked around for the aborigines who were their quest. They came to convert Indians and stayed to labor for the wilder Indians of the American classroom.

The cut-stone building which was their second structure was waiting to welcome me on my arrival. The Jesuit brothers, for whom I have not praise sufficient to their virtues and obscurely heroic lives, had cut the blocks in the fashion of pyramid builders, had dragged them on stoneboats from now-abandoned quarries, and had put up a substantial and imperishable blockhouse from which the Jesuits of many generations would sally forth to their battles for Christ.

I recall discovering a long crack on the wall and dashing to the rector with news of impending collapse. He regarded me with eyes slightly tired and said: "Yes, I know; I discovered that when I was a novice. The building, you see, still stands."

I was escorted or convoyed to Florissant by a young priest, Father Andrew Ganss, who met us at the train, hurried us into the station restaurant, let us order our own suppers, and then loaded us onto the Hodiamont trolley—and we were Florissant-bound. Frank Quinn and I were close to rage. We had planned an evening of seeing St. Louis and ridding ourselves of what money we had brought, not, I regret to report, by giving it to the poor, but in painting the town at least a mild shade of pink. This quick whisk to Florissant wrecked a wonderfully planned and keenly anticipated last evening of freedom.

We arrived in the dark. We were bundled into two ancient surreys. We bumped over the dirt roads for the three miles from the village. Because I hung back reluctantly I missed the glorious experience of being driven to the novitiate by Brother Louis Verhelst, a wit and a wag, and precisely the guide to whip despondent young men into a merry mood. Brother Kehoe, with one foot teetering on the brink of his grave, drove Frank Quinn and me. We could not imagine why he always drove into a field and then backed up before he made the turns; later we discovered he was blind in the eye that should have picked out the turns in the winding road.

That night the two of us were lodged in the Rock House, as the old building was called. On the floor we left our suitcases crammed less with clothing than with candy and cake, only to find on rising that the red ants of the neighborhood had come in a gigantic safari, carried away most of our hoarded sweets, and made the rest of it a honeycomb of ant tenements. We pitched the food into the wastepaper basket and went hungry for sweets for more than a bit.

Personally, city-bred as I was, the whole idea of Florissant appalled me. The lads of Chicago in their good-natured teasing of the applicants for the Society always called Florissant "The Farm." I had arrived in the dark; I had slept in a high-ceilinged room that I imagined was like the bedroom in any medieval farmhouse; so I rose expecting to walk out into a farmyard, probably pushing the cows and chickens out of the way. The surprise was as delightful as it was unexpected. The buildings were set in the center of a small but charming park. The flowers were in their full summertime glory. Never had I seen lovelier shade trees. Small gravel paths formed square patterns with the beautifully kept lawns. And though the buildings were old, stone-block or red-brick structures, they seemed in pattern with the ancient and quiet peace of St. Stanislaus.

I stood on a little hillock and looked across the luxuriant Florissant Valley to the spot where St. Louis was hidden behind hills. At night its lights would faintly redden the skies. Now it was remotely moated by the pastoral charm of the scene. Once on a time, perhaps a century and a half ago, St. Louis had been a little town which, in mail directions from the East, was "located near Florissant." Now it had swept on to become a metropolis, while the village of Florissant, completely hidden by the hills to the left, reached fifteen hundred population and stayed there.

It was as if one had been whisked up from the twentieth century, reset in an atmosphere of the thirteenth, and from the estate surrounding his monastery looked out over the feudal lands. No railroad approached the novitiate or the town. One absurd Toonerville trolley rattled along to the outskirts of the village and turned tail to return on the same rickety tracks. Two churches lifted their warning spires over the townfolk. But there were no industries of any sort and only the slightest trickle of commerce. The original French settlers were content with fragmentary farms. And incoming Germans of industry, thrift, and labor were slowly taking over. Indeed, while St. Ferdinand's Parish was ostensibly French, the big, bustling Sacred Heart Parish was professedly and successfully German.

Around the novitiate buildings were flourishing vineyards, rich in their purple grapes. The crops grew with a minimum of help from the Jesuits. A beautiful Holstein herd furnished milk and butter and buttermilk, and rarely meat. We had neither electricity nor more than a little running water in the kitchens. The absence of screens on the windows made possible a nightly invasion of winged warriors who battered themselves to death in a fiery holocaust deep down in the chimneys of our kerosene lamps. We slept on mattresses full of rasping, rustling corn shucks, laid across springless planks. Even the plumbing, though not precisely outdoor, was decidedly semidetached and notably unmechanical. The flavor of pioneer days was unmistakable. This was not nearly so much a farm as a deliberately retained monastery. The quiet of the novitiate and its remoteness from active life created an ideal atmosphere for the young men who came to be reshaped into Jesuits.

From the minute of arrival, I loved the place. The city lad settled down into the country atmosphere with a sigh of content. Never did I learn to distinguish growing corn from a field of potatoes . . . until the corn was waist high. I worked in the garden regularly and could not tell one tree from another and had to be forestalled if the vegetables and flowers were to remain unpulled with the persistently aggressive weeds. I tended chickens and carried buckets of milk, but chiefly in the expectation that both would appear on our table. The water supply came from our slanted roofs into vast underground cisterns; and once, during drought days, each of us young fellows was restricted to a daily washbasin of water from which all his ablutions from dawn to dawn must be taken.

I should not have been surprised to see mailed knights-errant riding down our unfrequented roads. The whole place was a new and wonderful world. And in the marvelous system designed by the great Loyola I was absorbed into the mechanism which was not mechanical and into the program that was in no slightest way formalistic.

You need not brace yourself, Harry, against the reminiscing of an old codger who remembers too vividly his early days. I shall synopsize. Perhaps I can even explain. But the very atmosphere of the place was part of the initiation to which I was being subjected; and though some more reluctant newcomers resisted even the atmosphere, I found it fascinating, fresh, a beautiful garden set in a providentially rich countryside, where a man might well discover his soul and turn his eyes toward undreamed of vistas and for four years prepare himself to do battle with the world just outside the invisible but clearly felt encirclement of its secluding and tessellated walls.

A Jesuit novitiate in my day, and surely since, centered round the novice master who became for us father, friend, spiritual guide and adventurer, the perfect Jesuit who was to set us the pattern of the perfect Jesus, orator extraordinary, model of the prayerful life, gentleman to the tips of his fingers, connoisseur of the arts, sweet cynic of the worldly values, stern disciplinarian with a touch of the top sergeant, yet understanding psychologist who never broke the bruised reed of wavering spirits or quenched the burning idealism of the young men under his care.

Father James Finn came from a lake-going family of Chicagoans. Yet he was the universal man who never even mentioned to me that we were fellow townsmen. He was spare as the young Abe Lincoln and had somewhat of his ragged, rugged features. He walked with a cultivated spring, spoke with exquisite perfection of language, had an eye that gleamed with interest in the whole of life, yet somehow he seemed to be boxed in by his own private insulation from the world of crass and ordinary affairs. He was extraordinarily ugly. That was my first impression: "What an ugly man!" From the little curl that persisted in pendulating over his forehead to his long, thin, badly clad feet, he was plain, as backwoodsmen are plain—and poets with no time to worry about their appearance. Then he smiled and you saw his soul dawning on that rugged countenance.

For two years he was the inspiration in my life. Yet for two years he spent his real genius turning me toward that greater Man whom he had discovered, made the center of his universe, and presented to me as the one Man worth loving and serving. Sometimes I thought he must look a little like the Savior, who, I fancy, was lean and thin and often more than sorrowful. The Savior was undoubtedly the most beautiful of the sons of men; yet there was nothing spectacular or even classic about his beauty. François Mauriac suggests that it took some study and a longer acquaintance with Jesus to pierce through His rugged exterior to the radiant beauty of His soul. This novice master who knew the importance of sternness and discipline, of treating each of us kindly and all of us with the same unbending justice, may have been in this like Him, his master and his constantly imitated guide. How can a man be plain and beautiful at the same time? How can he be rugged, and yet in a strange way regal; scrawny and bent by tuberculosis, and yet commanding and gracious and radiating a great charm and wit and loveliness of soul?

Father Finn was all this. For two years he was vital to me. For all my life he has remained an unfading light on my horizon. To this day he could walk into the room and I would feel that I had seen him not later than yesterday evening.

The days between entrance and the first wearing of the cassock are days of real delight to the older novices. Like all new Jesuits, I did everything wrong. I was noisy, without dignity, inclined to whistle and race down the gravel walks and laugh boisterously and break the customs of the house and begin my career of china breaking. Each summer the novices whose first year was ending had a real lift. They could see in the newcomers what heavy-footed worldlings they themselves had been only a few months before. They could be tolerant and patient with stupidity and clumsiness. They could feel mature and experienced and masters of the situation. It gave them a real forward push, as it always does to discover someone on whom we can look down as from a lofty height perilously and painstakingly attained.

We learned, for instance, that first names were not to be used. We would wear the name St. Paul used for the new Christians—

carissime, "dearly beloved." Carissime Lord: I loved what would be my new name. We were told the most fundamental of the spiritual rules in the typed pages read to us by Carissime Mark Gross. He was handsome, six feet and over, and he read with real feeling. For long months we regarded him with awe, thinking he had himself written the dissertations he read. We did not know that these had been compiled by some nameless spiritual forebear and were part of the tradition of all novitiates.

We were instructed never to make an "arsinius." St. Arsinius had joined a monastery from the court of a Caesar to whom he had been courtier. One of his worldly habits, not yet uprooted, was to cross his knees under his habit, a most ungraceful and worldly posture. Rather than embarrass by a reprimand the man so lately escaped the habits of the world, the abbot crossed his own knees, to be followed by the reluctant and slightly shocked monks. The future saint saw what was meant, uncrossed his knees, and never again made an arsinius. Nor as novices did we.

On the Feast of St. Ignatius, July 31, 1909, we put on our uniform for the first time. The Jesuit has no habit. He wears the cassock of the secular priests. Ours was the cassock that had long been worn by Spanish parish priests, a masterpiece of simplicity, a simple wrap-around with two hooks, one at the throat, one over the right shoulder, and a cincture that wraps twice around the waist and is tied in a little knot. From that moment I have found my cassock the most convenient of garments and strangely graceful. It took a week to learn how to mount the stairs without walking right up the front of the long garment. Once that was accomplished, it has served as normal dress by day, bathrobe and dressing gown, quick fireman's emergency garment in sudden stresses, and an outward sign that we Jesuits are entitled to wear a uniform and do.

Perhaps my love of the new and different had almost as much to do with the facility with which I adapted myself to my new life as did the grace of God. But then, isn't a love of the new and different a grace of God? The biggest surprise of that first week was to rise at five o'clock and find that the world around me pulsed with a vibrant life more full and exciting than it would know again until sundown, and that, instead of stepping from bed into a pitch-black world, the sun had been up for a considerable time and the earth was full of light. Never let it be suggested that I have liked five-o'clock rising. Many a time as a novice I begged for an extra hour of sleep. Yet the medievalists who spent their pre-electric-light days from sunup to sundown had much to be said in their favor. It was a wonderful time to begin one's day. I had hitherto missed it by two full hours or more. How had I failed to discover how lovely the earth can be under the bright summer dawn?

The novelty consisted of things quite new and things familiar but in a new setting. We had the intense novelty of praying from rising until seven-thirty. We each got a meditation book and instructions on how to make a mental prayer, but the older novices assured us gravely that, until after the long retreat, we would not really catch the trick. Mass became a daily delight, and Pius X's command for frequent Communion was taken seriously. I recall Frank Quinn's saying with glowing eyes: "Imagine! Henceforth we shall receive Holy Communion every day of our lives!"

My mother had believed that I had some responsibility for keeping the house in shape. I had wiped dishes and run the carpet sweeper; I had cleaned the pantry and swept the cellar of our house. Half my Thursday holiday paid for my "board and room," as I hosed down the porch and walks, cut the lawn, and beat the rugs. When, at the age of twenty-one, I mentioned to Mother that perhaps she ought to get a man to beat those obnoxious, heavy, dust-devouring rugs, she answered, looking at me shrewdly, "My dear, I have a man." So the exercise that followed breakfast was not a surprise. Manualia it was called—a corrupt Latin word that implied the simple fact of work with one's hands. We formed a long line and walked past the chief novice, who assigned us each to a new task each day: working in the scullery, cleaning the kitchen and setting the dining-room tables, sweeping endless corridors and the mud trackings of eager young feet through dormitory and study hall. The huskier were sent to the chicken yard or to help the brother baker knead the bread, a task performed strictly by hand. The more delicate went to the garden to combine labor with outdoor exercise. We had already made our own beds and emptied, in the prewater-famine days, our washbasins.

Now we kept the house shipshape, for we had no servants and did all our own work.

From that moment on, the day was a constant pattern of half-hour changes . . . ten minutes to wash up after work, a period of spiritual reading, an hour of reading or studying in Latin and Greek, prayers said in common, instructions by our novice master, meals, recreation in common, more manual work, and a succession of spiritual duties and physical chores.

I suddenly found myself eating like a plow hand. In fact, I began to worry because for the first time in my life I anticipated food, wondered what would be served at the next meal, and plunged into it with embarrassing appetite. The food was excellent, the supply surprisingly plentiful, and, as my Irish grandmother would have noticed, "Hunger is the best sauce." The really great Brother Van Raemdonck was our cook who disdained the title of chef which he well might have worn. His "feast-day" dinners—the first of which I consumed with delighted surprise on the day I donned my cassock—were a triumph of matching high quality of taste and flavor to the quantity which the hearty appetites of us young Jesuits demanded. Jesuit meals, I soon learned, though never luxurious, were fine examples of hearty food for healthy young men.

I grew aware of the master plan back of our Jesuit spiritual training only with the slow unfolding of the years. But it was no haphazard approach to character, no casual putting of fledglings out of the nest and into flight. As I look back now, it seems to me that the formal elements of our life revolved about a few simple facts.

There was the unescapable fact that was the common life.

Here I was, a young fellow who, though never in any sense wealthy or even by modern standards well-to-do, had always had his privacy. For long years I had had my own room, my own clothes closet, my own desks and library cases. Now I was suddenly thrust into a common study hall. They called it the ascetery; and though I said the word a thousand times, I have never to my memory written it before. Quite obviously it came from the word ascetic, and it took an amateur ascetic to live in it. Along the walls and under the windows were lined our desks. They had a slanting top that could be opened only when everything had been moved off them. They were battered and marked with long years of hard use, those desk tops; though, since none of us ever had a knife, how they got the deep grooves in them, the slashes and cuts, I never could imagine. The top opened to reveal a deep recess, into which it was possible to put about six or eight books, a tablet or two, one's notes, and a few immediate needs. A movable kneeling bench was the companion of each desk. On the tops we placed the little crucifix which accompanied us for two years until we got our beloved vow crucifix on the day we became consecrated religious, and usually a holy card or two, very much in the Barclay Street style. Here we knelt for our meditation, said our private prayers, wrote our letters and our classroom assignments—though as a rule we could work at the long deal tables which crisscrossed the main room. But it was life in common. And it was a great training in give-and-take. Every cough was heard by all. A man with a habit of unpleasantly clearing his throat could become an almost savage trial. Every restless movement upset a kneeling bench. The tops of the desks could be moved only with noise and some confusion; and if a careless hand let one of them drop, the clap of thunder was enough to rouse the most devout from the depths of contemplation.

In this "common room" we began our ascetic life . . . together. And the common life continued all through the day . . . as it was to continue for much of life. Each one had his own fixed place in the common room and in the dormitory, but otherwise we were a mass of men and not individuals.

For we dined in "common," in the big refectory. Each "order" of men was assigned a sector. The faculty ate at the head table. The juniors, young Jesuits with their vows, had their long tables. The brothers under vows ate at their proper tables. And we novices dined at the tables that belonged to us. But we had no fixed spot in our own sectors, so that each day you sat between different fellow Jesuits. On days when the normal silence of the dining hall was broken with gay conversation, you hoped and perhaps even said a little cheating prayer that you would sit between two men whose talk you enjoyed. It was considered real cheating if you helped the prayers out by a bit of wangling to get between two congenial companions.

At night you retired to a common dormitory. We had two main dormitories, and between the beds on brass rings were hung white and spotlessly clean curtains. Inside the square of cotton we had privacy of eye, but no privacy of ear; for the bed next to yours was separated from you only by the width of a small washstand, topped with a tin washbasin that contained the day's supply of washing water. In the small compartment below went toothbrush and powder, shaving kits (used twice a week), clothesbrush, and what cosmetics one had brought along. Once the facial lotion or talcum powder or styptic pencil had been exhausted, it was not replaced. We were to be clean but not ornamental.

To get accustomed to living together, as we would be living for four years, was a task. You soon grew to know the mannerisms which accompanied all the normal occupations of all your companions. You knew exactly when this chap would sneeze. You knew the gestures which accompanied the use of all forks and knives. You could tell the minute the chap in the next bed fell asleep or the nights he was likely to be tossing about.

None of this is too surprising to those who have known military service, except that military units are broken up and shifted with fair frequency. We would be with our companions for a full four years. A large tolerance or traces of incipient petulance were inevitable outcomes of the years.

The common life meant precisely that. If a box of candy came from home, it was laid on the desk of the novice master. It did not reappear until a feast day broke its seals and the candy was tossed into a common dish and served to all. As feast days were not too common, your Christmas candy might appear on St. Patrick's Day, with the bonbons slightly on the cement side and the chocolate turned a sepia brown. You got your writing paper out of the same common drawer. You filled your pen, if you had a fountain pen, from the same pretty thick and sticky ink. After the work of a period in the garden, you washed in basins under taps in the same washroom. You ate, from father rector to youngest novice, precisely the same food. I liked that. I liked it that the top brass got exactly the same food I got. I liked it that they ate off the same indestructible plates and used the same linty napkins and for breakfast must be satisfied with checkered red tablecloths. It seemed democratic, as did the whole routine that came under the name common life.

Actually in this, as in most of the things we did, practice came first and principle later. I have liked that way of teaching. We lived the common life before we got any hint about what it meant. We got used to wearing the same kind of clothes and sharing the identical food and sitting in the plain chairs and borrowing the same books from the same library shelves. The practice became routine before we discovered that we had grown very close together in this companionship. The cleverest and the chap from the richest home could look for no favors or privileges, and would be regarded by the others as a bounder and a slacker if he did. Nobody expected a cushion for his chair or his life. No one asked for fancy food when the rest were eating good, wholesome, substantial diet. When the clothes one had worn from home were shreds, they were replaced from the clothes bins that supplied every man in the community. You didn't put a name on your things. If they had to be identified after their trips to the laundry, you marked them with a number.

Part of this common life was the wonderful experience of getting along without money. Considering the importance of money to the progress of the mare, we did very well indeed. During the course of my third year at Florissant I took out a suit of clothes from my trunk, and found in the change pocket a musty, discolored quarter. I persuaded our father minister to exchange it for some stale candy for myself and a companion as we were about to leave for a holiday walk. It was the first coin that I had had in my hands in over thirty-six months.

For long years after that training in independence of money, I traveled with perhaps a dime, perhaps with no carfare, in my pocket. And, incredibly enough, I had learned never to think of money and never for a moment to miss it.

The four years of Florissant were a surprising training in getting along in a totally male world. There was not the sight or swish of a woman in eyeshot or earshot of the novitiate. When I read later of Mount Athos, where in ancient days the Greek monks tolerated no females, not even female animals in their sheepfolds, barns, or chicken yards, their restrictions seemed to me a little extreme. But I had lived all those months in a womanless world. Again, nobody discussed this. No one said, "This is the rule." It was just a form of life, entirely different from the world I had recently left, a world pleasantly filled with my mother and the charming young ladies who occupied much of my time and thought. Now we had our Lady smiling down at us from a thousand—or so it seemed—statues and pictures. I came to know some extremely attractive ladies of history, falling quite under the spell of St. Gertrude of the mystic heart and St. Catherine of Siena, whom I soon came to regard as the greatest woman of the Christian era, and St. Clare, whose escape to the cloister and her heavenly bridegroom, with the help of the Troubadour of God, had for me as much attraction and thrill as any of history's most romantic stories. But except for the little girls from the Creole and German families who came to my catechism class during my second-year novitiate, there were simply no women. We felt no great renunciation. We did not think of ourselves as preparing for some later fulfillment of a vow. It was a womanless world in practice, and a quite comfortable and gay and happy world at that.

The order of the novitiate was a masterpiece of accomplishment and frustration. The assigned order of the day, indicated by a constant series of bells, began at five o'clock, always an intolerable hour to most of us. It ended with the striking of the De Profundis at nine-forty-five. There was time for all that the training demanded of us—prayer, manual work, meals, common recreation. And there were exasperating little slivers of time when we made a transition from one assigned duty to another. Following Mass, meditation, and breakfast, there was about twenty minutes. Amazing, now that I regard it in retrospect, what I crammed of physical necessity and care into twenty minutes. After the manual work, fifteen minutes were permitted to wash up, put one's tools away, and be in place for the spiritual reading which followed. Of these fifteen minutes one might, with skillful manipulation, manage to save five minutes for some pursuit of one's own. After noon recreation we got a delightful half-hour, from one-thirty to two o'clock, to ourselves. Then or at some other time a good novice made his Stations of the Cross, said his Little Office of the Immaculate Conception or his rosary. But with skillful management of time it might be that he could get to take care of these in shorter intervals and know the splendid luxury of thirty minutes to read, to write, to study, to walk in the open air, just to be free and on his own.

The routine of the day was, without need for theorizing or rules, teaching us to squeeze the most out of time. Into the assigned periods we packed a lot of work, a good deal of spiritual reading, a prompt acceptance of designated duties. But into the fragments of time when we were on our own, the routine was so planned that we could learn to do much in a short space, to be greedy of the moments in preparation for a life that would be fairly rushed and interrupted and occupied. I know that I learned to put things down on the summons of the bell and to pick them up again twenty-four hours later with no wasted motion and no loss of time in an elaborate windup. It was smart practice, well worth mastering.

Here at Florissant were some fifty-seven young men thrown together into a single routine life, living elbow to elbow, sharing exactly the same food, the same order of the day, the same ideals, and the same laws of life. No one ever has been given a sharper experience in the gentle art of getting along with his fellow men. A chap like myself came from a quite limited circle of society. I knew a very small number of young people, and these all congenial. I had the snobbish attitude of the fairly smart adolescent, who admired brains, money, ability, initiative, family prestige, good clothes, achievement. Suddenly I was in the company of men who had been reduced to that blessed common life. We had no money; we knew nothing of one another's families; and an occasional novice who bragged of his was regarded with a blend of pity, contempt, and annoyance. We had the same easy jobs to do and no one had a chance to shine. Most of our work was anonymous, and no medals or marks of distinction were conferred.

On the other hand, we got to know one another simply on the basis of character and disposition, kindliness and charity, a friendly manner and a cheerful attitude toward the life we all shared. We were raw human material in the process of being reshaped from callow adolescents to Jesuits worthy to take the vows of religion. We had to talk to the men assigned us for the noon-hour and evening walks. On the holidays the cry, "Bands for a walk," was a sort of social sweepstakes, for we were on the basis of pure chance to be assigned two companions for the afternoon, and we would walk with them and talk with them for two hours, and we had just better be cheerful about it.

What actually happened was remarkable. Boys naturally unattractive turned out under the pressure of enforced companionship to be delightful fellows. We were thrown, not with men from our own circles of taste and environment, but with men from lives entirely different, backgrounds excitingly different, with experiences that they shared with us to our real broadening of character. We learned to talk about subjects that had never interested us. We forced ourselves to listen to topics totally strange and, to our delight, discovered they were worth hearing.

In the total lack of cliques, the broad companionship of fifty-seven different temperaments, I found social growth and expansion of mind. Dealing with people has never been a problem for me. I learned a lot about getting along with associates in the enforced variety of a novitiate.

St. Ignatius visualized his men as moving with the speed of soldiers, traveling, as he put it, to any part of the world where there was hope of God's glory or the good of souls. He did not like slavery to comfort. He wanted no shackling of his men with pressing demands and needs.

So Florissant was a land without creature comfort.

And once more, strangely enough, we loved the life and never noticed the lack of comforts.

Electricity came to the Florissant Valley long after my departure. We read by kerosene lamps. Our stoves burned wood. There were no machines to complicate life by saving a little labor. Even the bathing facilities were amazingly primitive.

Kerosene lamps were amusing to me and at the same time annoying. Three senior novices were assigned to their care. That was to the peace of all; for every time I touched a wick, I smoked a chimney or sent a sooty smoke signal curling into the air. No screens covered our windows, so on the warm summer evenings all the flying fauna of the valley, from mosquitoes to bull bats, came in the windows. A large part of them headed right for the lamps and offered their innocent lives in fiery holocausts. That didn't help the illumination but it excited in me an unfailing and slightly ghoulish interest.

The wood-burning stoves turned out to produce the most delicious meals. Someone with no particularly architectural genius had put the icehouse and the bakery into one rather limited frame building. A thin wooden partition separated the stored ice (cut from our nearby ponds) from the brick ovens. Yet though it seemed a perfect instance of deliberate neutralization of ice by fire and of oven by cold storage, the brother baker produced the world's most delicious bread. Once electricity came to supplant the wood fires, he never baked a good loaf of bread again.

We did all the work by hand. Sent to the bakery, the huskier novices bent deep over the troughs to knead the dough. We turned huge wringers in the laundry and ironed the clothes in primitive mangles. Milking was done by hand, one cow at a time; but what milk those beautiful Holsteins yielded to the brothers' expert ministrations!

The limitation of bathing was a trial not altogether intentional. Florissant was three long miles of hills and valleys from the Missouri River. Wells were very deep and expensive to drill. For years the community had taken its water from the roofs and rain troughs of the buildings, and usually it was enough. A good rainstorm filled the cisterns buried deep down underground. We pumped up the water for drinking purposes and carried it in great pails to the kitchens. The pumps had a natural overflow, and this fell into large wooden barrels out of which we dipped in tin pans the water we used for washing purposes. One small well supplied a few faucets that were restricted in use. There were exactly three baths in the entire novitiate. So each man was permitted—and required to take—one bath a week.

This was not nearly as bad as it might sound, until disaster in the shape of a drought struck us. For eight months the Florissant

Valley knew no rain. Nothing drained off our roofs and into our cisterns. We were restricted to one basin of water per novice per day. Baths were interdicted entirely. We learned to use that one basin for all purposes, including sponge baths. The rector prayed and the community joined him; a wizard with a hazel switch divined for water; the drillers came, and on the final blast, we found that we had hit a well . . . of sulphur water. The bathing was henceforth done to the odor of sulphur. And anyway, the rains came.

As one who throughout a lifetime has known the luxury—and to me the charity—of a daily bath, I look back to the bathing limitations of Florissant with a slight shudder. Perhaps a visitor would have noticed about us, during that water drought, what Mark Twain refers to unkindly as the odor of sanctity. Living together, we did not notice it. We were healthy, outdoor people, walking a great deal in the open air, exercising freely, and rubbing ourselves down with vigorous towels and young muscles. Yet I still feel that the period of getting along without water was great training. Perhaps it made me relish and value more that wonderful gift of God which is water. Perhaps it made me more eager, once baths were easily available, to use them for my own comfort and the easement of my associates. It was a great experience to learn to get along even without so common a thing as water. Greater renunciations became actually less difficult.

From July 26, 1909, to the Feast of the Holy Angels, October 2, 1909, I lived the practice of the novitiate. Then, by the wise dispensation of St. Ignatius, I was plunged into the theory that lay back of it.

At considerable length I have written of my long retreat in a booklet called *I Walked with God*. I do not intend to repeat that here. I just recall that for thirty days, in silence and a first serious attempt at prayer, under the guidance of a very great director, Father James Finn, I found out what my life was to be, the meaning that lay back of the routine I had been following, and what the career of a Jesuit could become if he gave God half a chance. We had been practicing the Jesuit life; now we plunged into its meaning and explanation.

A good many non-Catholic writers and some Catholics who prefer their own speculations to the facts of the case have theorized about what makes a Jesuit tick. They miss the point completely if they do not understand the long retreat. The Exercises of St. Ignatius are a surprisingly small booklet. Read in sequence, they are jejune and prosaic. Presented by a skilled retreat master, read phrase by phrase and thought through in silence and meditation and prayer, they are one of the greatest documents of all time. Ignatius was a master psychologist. He was an advertising man with a great flair for selling big causes and novel and noble enterprises. He understood men and the motives that can capture the imagination and inflame the wills of men. He did not want a lot of automatons, soldiers moving under the growls of a top sergeant, mercenaries battling with no heart in their fight. He wanted to make clear exactly what was God's plan for His world, how men and women wrecked it by sin, the platform which Christ had laid down for the happiness of mankind, and the cooperation in His Father's business by which men and women can make the earth a lovely place and heaven's happiness a certainty.

So for the four weeks of that long retreat I lived through—with my thirty-eight fellow novices—intense excitement, brilliant illumination, a completely new restating of the meaning of life, the challenge to high adventure.

Life could never be the same from that time on.

In briefest synopsis, the first week was given over to two enormous facts: God's reasons for making the world, man's horrible blunder when he ruins the world by sin.

That Foundation is one of the greatest statements of truth ever epitomized by a constructive mind. Into a single packed paragraph Ignatius, no scholar and on his way to be a saint, sees the plan of God, the relationship of man to that plan, the value and purpose of the lovely world around us, and the use we must make of all the gifts that God's generosity and trust has placed in our hands.

The horrible destructive force of sin in angels, in devils, in our first parents, in any single sinner, and finally in ourselves makes clear that under the fascination of evil is the most completely corrupting and explosive power. Ignatius, like all great spiritual leaders, knew that a man cannot save others from sin unless first he has, with God's help, saved himself. There is no salvation for the world this side of renunciation of the ugliness, selfishness, and ruin of sin.

The second week is given over to the coming of Christ, His life as earth's perfect man, and His glorious invitation to all men and women to join Him in human redemption and worldwide happiness and salvation, and that thrilling call by which He explains His campaign for the war of peace and enlists the heroic and unselfish in the kingdom of His Father. It is a wonderful week, spent walking with Jesus from Bethlehem to the Last Supper. It is a week of challenge: Can you give yourself completely to the cause that brought God from heaven and has won the loyalty of the world's greatest and best?

The third week finds the novice walking with Christ through the battle of His Passion. From the moment of Holy Communion in the Cenacle to the entombment of Christ, he sees Christ struggling with man's vicious enemy. Now the effects of sin become brutally clear as he sees sin reach out to kill man's most perfect representative and to throw even God up upon a cross. Now he watches while the Son of God wins the one great battle of history, and gains for us, His followers, all the strength we need to battle sin ourselves and win for mankind peace and victory over death and evil. Nothing in life can ever seem hard, difficult, or impossible, after we have seen Christ's Passion and realize that He won for our sakes the battle of Calvary.

The fourth week is the week spent with the apostles around the risen Christ. We now have the guaranteed success of the Resurrection, Christ's and our own. Looking back over life, we see the multiplied reasons each of us has for loving God and giving Him the generous service of a lifetime. Brief resolutions are drawn up, and the soul, which has seen Christ's plan for human happiness, offers himself in the glorious prayer, "Take and receive, O Lord, my total self."

Once the long retreat was over, my fellow novices and I sprang back into the routine of our lives. We were now in the spiritual West Point preparing for the battle of right against wrong, of truth against error, of God's high purposes against those forces which are determined that His plan will not prevail.

We now had a cause, the kingdom of Christ upon earth.

We now had a captain and leader, the perfect and inspiring Savior of the world.

We now had a campaign, first the shaping of our own characters into copies of the Savior's and then with Him winning mankind to its own happiness and salvation.

And we had two immediate years to get ready for all that lay ahead.

Life was rich and full and beautiful and exciting. Our companions were fellow officers in Christ's army going through the rigors of an officers' training camp. We had the challenge of Christ's own life and the achievements of the saints. Our Church was the militant force that warred for the peace of the earth and the fullest development of human character and possibilities. Our Society of Jesus was a light company constantly on the march, ready for any emergency, trained to instant obedience, seasoned for tough campaigning, aware of the tricks of the adversary and determined never to miss a chance to advance the cause of Christ anywhere and by any Christlike means.

With the years, a sense of all this ebbs and flows. There are times when the leader and the cause of the campaign seem vividly real and glorious. There are times when the routine presses in, monotony becomes the great enemy, and the spiritual soldiers understand what is meant by the saying, "Most of a soldier's life is spent just waiting." Yet for no Jesuit does that sense of challenge and captain and cause ever completely fade. And the brighter he keeps all three, the more wonderful he finds his life, the more exciting in every dawning day, and the more impatient he becomes with his own failures and inadequacies.

Yet the life of preparation is a life like that of Christ at Nazareth. Christ the apprentice in the carpenter shop, Christ the boy about His Mother's house, Christ leading the unexciting life of a small oriental village, was preparing for the miracles and preaching and Passion and Resurrection of three spectacular years. The young Jesuit for two years knows a life very like this hidden life of the Savior.

Each morning and afternoon I did my trick in the kitchen or in the scullery, behind a bristle-shedding broom down the corridors, cutting grass in the garden, hauling water, helping the brothers. During that time I grew to know and love the Jesuit brothers deeply. Never destined for the studies that lead to the priesthood, these fullfledged members of the Society of Jesus have their own canonized member, once Brother Alphonsus Rodriguez, now St. Alphonsus. He was porter at the door, and model of the humble life. At Florissant the brothers were the solid structure that remained fixed and durable in the swift coming and going of the novices and juniors. To them we owed our wonderful herds and our fabulous vineyards. They cooked our wholesome and delicious meals and baked our bread and churned our butter. A great brother infirmarian took care of a cold or nursed eighteen men through typhoid; in intervals he was brother dentist for the whole community, even to making for us our own tooth powder. Our brothers kept the gardens in parklike perfection and operated our six-hundred-acre farm, with all the staples, and occasional forays into the growing of tobacco. They raised the thousand and more chickens that were blue-ribbon winners. They were bookkeepers and secretaries and printers. And during our novitiate days we were their inept and inefficient assistants, who, I often think, impeded their expert work more than we helped.

Silence was the atmosphere of the novitiate. In itself, that is for a crowd of windy young fellows a great character training. Many a marriage would be saved if husband and wife did not speak until after they had had their first cup of coffee. We never talked before breakfast, to the notable peace of the whole community. To this day, when I return to Florissant, my first perceptive feeling is one of peace. It is so quiet in the midst of a world that is deadened with the constant battering of sheer noise. The buildings seem so calm and restful. Without need for stern signs announcing "Silence," the library invites to concentration. Silence is the lovely and in these days rare atmosphere in which to thrive. And Florissant was during the working week a place of opportunity for the novice to find God around him, to take time to discover his own inner depths, a place of uninterrupted calm, of work done without the constant fracture of clamor and noise and speech without purpose and words spoken for the mere dread of wordlessness.

Yet by way of gay contrast came the periods of recreation. Twice a day we talked fast and furiously and from the stored-up reservoir of speech long contained through the times of silence. True, for half an hour each evening recreation talk was all in Latin, a skillful way of cutting down gossip, garrulousness, unkind criticism, and the youthful smart quips. But with wistful nostalgia I recall those recreations spent *en masse*. In the winter we filled the ascetery with our gay and top-pitched voices. In the summer we sat under an ancient apple tree that dropped shade, twigs, last year's leaves, and apples that never developed beyond the cherry size. For the second half of recreation we might, with our assigned partners, walk in the open air, and many of us did. Or we formed our tight little knots of three, excitedly discussing the events of the novitiate day and episodes in the lives of older Jesuits (who seemed surprisingly contemporaneous), or spun vast theories of life to our own imaginative delight.

On Sundays, Thursdays, and holidays we hiked. We hiked in threes. The chief novice, called a manuductor, set the route and the pace. Never was he more a manuductor. I have often wondered what spiritual wit thought up that name for the second-year novice who called signals for our routine. Literally, manuductor means someone who leads *(dux)* by the hand *(manu)*. And when Thursday and Sunday afternoons rolled round and the bell announced the beginning of recreation, he read out the "Bands for a Walk"; we formed in military threes, though we walked in unmilitary fashion, and swung down the roads, deep in dust or mud, depending on the season, for a two-hour hike.

If the manuductor was conventional, as was Carissime Aloysius Pettit, we stuck to the roads, such as they were, walked from the novitiate to the little iron bridge that spanned the small creek which bounded the sleepy town of Florissant, rested for a bit, and then hiked back. If the manuductor was highly imaginative and given to pranks, as was Carissime Leo Mullany, we hit out through the fields, cut through the woods, and ended up in one of nature's dead ends. When Carissime Mullany was really full of pranks, he then brought out lunch—which on occasion might well consist of brown bread, molasses, and large raw onions. It was Carissime Mullany's idea of a joke, the blend of getting lost and subsisting on incredible food combinations.

Sports took an important place in our lives. But again, they became part of our training for life. The major sport was handball, played against high outdoor walls with projecting sides and space for three players on a side. The game was fast and tough, but any bodily contact was outlawed. Some of the men became highly expert and continued to play handball until the doctor's warning deprived them of a lifetime exercise. We formed teams and gravitated naturally and without resentment into our level of skill. Some of the novices were big-league caliber, and our baseball games were often magnificent exhibitions of the great national sport. We skated in winter when the warm Missouri winters vouchsafed us a rare sheet of ice. We had tennis courts which we kept in shape ourselves and on which we played fair games of tennis. We played a little soccer, but no Rugby. Basketball was for novices a thing of the future. Swimming was dangerous in the treacherous current of the Missouri River, and we built our first swimming pool only when I was about ready to leave for St. Louis.

Whether we knew it consciously or not, sports and recreation were an important part of the training. We were supposed to be friendly with everyone and actually were. Not for a moment would I suggest that in some sort of miraculous fashion natural likes and dislikes were wiped out. There were men in the novitiate in whose physical presence your hackles rose. Some men had only to speak, and you wanted to deny anything they said. There were natural braggarts and show-offs; there were competitors who could beat you in the thing you felt your specialty. I remember the chap with the annoying way of clearing his throat who could translate a paragraph of Latin while I was managing a sentence, and the tall, handsome young fellow who negligently took me out on the tennis court and treated me to a most humiliating trimming. Yet I can say that for two years I lived with fifty-seven young men and never knew an enmity taking tangible form. We played fiercely contested games without wars of words or flying fists. You sat with interest waiting to hear the names of your partners for the week's recreation or the holiday walk; and when you got your assignment, you accepted the companions without resentment or distaste.

When I am asked if I have ever seen a miracle, I could, if I thought it would be understood, tell how for two years fifty-seven young men lived together cut off from all outside interests, without a serious disagreement, a hatred, or a quarrel. That may not be a first-class miracle in any canonical sense, but it strikes me in retrospect as being one of the most amazing experiences of a lifetime. You got along without resentment in the company of men you naturally did not like. You were friendly with people naturally uncongenial. You played fierce games and knew no dangerous flare of uncontrolled temper. You remained friends with men who shared your physically limited movements, and established friendships that lasted for the rest of life.

Part of the training was a training in service.

Everyone was expected to wait on his associates' meals. That continued all through the young Jesuit's life. Aside from a few men who worked the farm, we had no servants; we were servants one for the other. During the first year each period of manual work brought the novice a fresh or different assignment. During the second year he might be assigned to what was, with dignity, referred to as "his office." The assignment of those offices took place shortly before the arrival of the new novices. It was a day breathlessly awaited. The lampadarians cared for the lamps. The castellian was in charge of the toilets. The bookbinder worked on decrepit books, of which we had a full share. And to my horror, I was appointed one of the barbers.

As yet the legend of the "Success from Shears" had not hit the country; Perry Como and Jimmy Durante and the other famous ex-barbers were figures of an unguessed future. I only knew that, when I was read out as a barber, I felt a surge of fierce resentment. It was the others, my victims, who should have felt the surge. Little did they know what was in store for them.

I reported on the next day to my retiring predecessor. He handed me a pair of shears and a comb, and placing the novice due for a haircut in the battered and very solid armchair that topped a low platform, he said, "Watch!" and I watched. No clippers, no razor, no need to resist lotions, hair tonics, or even the simple luxury of talcum powder. Just a comb and a pair of scissors and the swift circuit of a head that wasn't going socially anywhere anyhow, so who cared how it looked?

The second morning my barber professor let me start the operation, and when I had hacked great gashes in a head (which had no mirror in which to watch progress), he took over and repaired the job as well as he could. This happened the third morning. The fourth found me completely on my own. Poor novices! They were in for six months of the worst scalping known to history since the early Jesuits converted the last of the Sioux and Potawatomi.

I cannot be sure, however, who suffered more, the barber or his victims. From the moment I became barber, I hurried into the chapel for all community exercises to sit as far forward as possible. If I sat back, before me I saw heads, heads, and more heads. There were heads ready for trimming, and I dreaded the moment those difficult manes would submit themselves to my primitive treatment. Or worse, there were heads on which I had recently operated, and I had sense and taste enough to recognize the artistic wreckage I had left behind.

Early in my tonsorial career I reached new heights of aspiration and new depths of shame. Carissime John Gerst had the most beautiful head of hair in the novitiate, soft, flowing, with a gentle wave, blonde, silken. He came to me during recreation and said, "Tomorrow my family are visiting me from St. Louis. Do you think—" his tone was plaintive and worried—"that you could give me just a light trim before they arrive?" Here was a challenge. I looked at his beautiful hair and dreamed artistic dreams. Somewhere in my historic readings I had come across the hairdo of the boy pages of the Middle Ages. The page-boy bobs of the ladies were something of the remote future; indeed, the women of those days would have felt shamed and disgraced by any form of bob. Later I was to know young ladies who found themselves in difficulties in convent schools for pioneering in the bobbed hairdo.

At any rate, I planned carefully the exact steps by which I would give Carissime Gerst a haircut to end all haircuts, something which would cause his good mother to exclaim in delight and make his sisters properly envious. The next morning he sat trustfully in the creaking armchair, his rosary in his hand. Novices said their rosary aloud if they did not read aloud to the barber from some pious book. It was both protection against evil and anesthetic. I stood back, admired the hair, and began my creation. But alas that artistic achievement so seldom matches artistic dreams! I trimmed the left side into what I fancied was the roll that had terminated the curls of a young squire. I then worked on the right side. Stepping back, I realized that I had cut the right a little shorter than I had trimmed the left, so I set myself to match lengths. Only, my eye was not too accurate, and I found when the reverse side was completed that it was now the shorter side. Panic now seized me. However artistic the job, the sides of the head must match. So I hacked first one and then the other, while the beads in the hands of my victim went faster and faster. Each side turned out to be the shorter, and the other had to be trimmed to match it . . . until the task was done and the beautiful head of Carissime Gerst closely resembled a freshly plucked chicken. I turned my eyes away in horror from this massacre of innocence. Carissime Gerst took one look into the small pocket mirror which lay on the table and then regarded me in a blend of repugnance, amazement, and incredulity. "Oh, my mother!" he exclaimed, far, far back in his soft palate, and staggered from the room.

At the end of six months I was relieved of my "office" and thrown back into the ranks of those with no particular job. The community had suffered enough. But six months as barber left me with a lifelong respect for any man who does a passable job on my own hair. Don't tell me that barbering isn't a skilled profession! I couldn't make it.

The final six months of the novitiate were lived under the happy attraction of the vows. As a matter of fact, by the end of that first year those novices who cared to do so might be permitted to make their "vows of devotion." These in no sense bound the Society of Jesus; but they were a pledge of earnestness on the part of the novice, a protestation to the Society that he wanted to bind himself, and forever. On the Feast of St. Ignatius, 1910, one year after I had taken my cassock, I walked the long bridge over to the room of the master of novices, knelt all alone before him, and recited the formula of the vows. No one mentioned to his fellow novices whether he had taken these vows of devotion or not. It was each man's personal business. But I told my parents in a happy letter home, and from that hour I never had any doubt about my obligation to the Society of Jesus.

In preparation for the formal vows Father Finn took us through the obligations of the vows, their meaning, purpose, and beauty. He made their binding force very clear. He never minimized our duties once we had assumed them, but he made them seem beautiful and to me deeply desirable. Yet for the three days of retreat that preceded them, God permitted me the training of an almost insane triduum of scruples. I wanted more than anything in the world to take those formal vows; and everything in the world rose between me and their accomplishment. I beat a sentry path to the novice master's door, tried his patience with my raking up of every possible problem and difficulty of the past, insisted that there was a strain of insanity in the family which invalidated any possibility of a Jesuit vocation, and finally listened humbly while he ordered me to put aside this nonsense and move forward to my vows.

God was good. When victims of scruples have talked to me of their ridiculous worries, the insanity which creates impenetrable barriers out of clouds and moonshine, their anxieties, not because of existing things but because they might possibly have reason later on for worrying, I know exactly what they mean. I had three horrible days of knowing scruples at their worst. It was part of God's merciful training for my life as a priest.

With the pronouncement of the vows my first period of Jesuit training was over; and I was much at peace and ready for what lay ahead. For two years I had read widely in an entirely new field of literature. Each day for forty-five minutes we read Rodriguez's *Practice of Perfection and Christian Virtues,* a solid series of tomes, the instructions which an ancient Jesuit novice master had given to his Spanish novices. On my own time I had come into pleasant comradeship with Father Frederick William Faber, Father Basil William Maturin, and a young writer named Father Robert Hugh Benson. In the footsteps of Ignatius I had walked with the saints and read their lives. I stumbled across a world-shaking book by Cardinal Wiseman on the Eucharist. I had gone straight through the magnificent books of the Abbé Constant Fouard, from his study of the Gospels to his history of John the Divine. It was all wonderful material to be storing away for a busy priestly life.

For two years I had been struggling with the problems of mental prayer, and I should be less than honest if I pretended that it ever became easy. Indeed, when my novice master asked me the stereotyped question, "How goes your meditation?" my answer was equally routine: "Badly." Once I varied the monotony with this explanation: "Oh, I don't do too badly when I meditate on death or sin or hell or the death on Calvary. But otherwise . . ." He shook his head a bit sadly: "You have not begun to meditate," he answered; "nor will you till you learn to walk with Jesus Christ, to look at Him and understand Him and love Him and to lay the plan of your own life against the pattern of His."

A great many things got between me and mental prayer. I suppose that, like most young people who have known a gay life, I brought to the novitiate a "dissipated mind." That was not necessarily a sinful mind, but it certainly had the characteristics of a butterfly crossed with a grasshopper. I had always found it easy to think my way through things if I could lay the point of a pencil on a sheet of paper. The point seemed to force me to attention and concentration. The paper, once it began to fill with consecutive jottings, was a challenge and a guide. I asked leave of my novice master to write my meditations as I made them. This was altogether out of line, an exercise of the mind and not of the heart, an intellectual practice and not a spiritual exercise. So I turned back to my own mental process, which seemed to boil down simply to this: I saw things quickly and all at once, or I never really saw them at all. Things came in a flash, never bit by bit and step by step. If I began to think, my mind jumped ahead, hurdling the logical steps until it had raced to the conclusion. No fair race that; for I had not followed the racecourse but had cut across the meadows. I had not taken each of the hurdles in proper sequence; I had leaped the fences to make a short cut.

I have always regarded with admiration and some suspicion men who claimed they found mental prayer easy. I never did. When others taught it to neophytes, I have watched them with envy. My mind either went blank or raced so far ahead that it was all over almost before it had begun. I spent long weeks on Father Roothaan's classic formula for mental prayer. I made a careful synopsis of the almost mathematical principles by which he set himself to guide the praying mind step by step from simple thoughts to profound contemplations. In prayer, as in plots for a story or a plan, I might be blank for a long, long time, and then suddenly in a single bound reach the completed conclusion. The logical steps, the measured forward movement, the accumulation of data—these were not on the pattern of my mind, and I found it hard to change the pattern.

The walk from the novitiate to the Jesuit juniorate is one of the longest in history. Actually just a matter of feet, it is a transition of a lifetime. A separate building housed the young Jesuits under vows. The atmosphere was a blend of spirituality and the classics of literature. We still moved as a group. We still slept in vast, curtain-squared dormitories and studied in asceteries now called study halls. Our recreations were still in common, and on the Oxford University plan we ate our meals in great "commons." We had a rigid schedule of class and study, broken by holidays with their games, walks, and sports.

But we had the lovely intellectual freedom that comes as one opens the world's great books. Two years of Latin, Greek, and English, with guided forays into history, lay before us. I walked for the first time into the juniorate library and sighed in deep content. Walls lined with books—some old friends, but most of them strangers inviting me to comradeship. Since I took my vows in midsummer, I had before the formal resumption of classes a full month to read on my own. Twice a week, after Mass, we walked the three miles to Charbonnier, the primitive little villa, roofed but open to the winds, on the bluffs of the Missouri. But once there, we sang and read and ate Gargantuan meals, and felt ourselves the logical successors of those scholars of the Middle Ages who created and preserved and lived in a world of authors and their books. Yet the training was going on, the deeper training than contact with the classics of the ancients and the classics of my own language. We walked the three miles to Charbonnier, beginning with the Memorare for good weather, and continuing the rise and fall of the road to the measure of mental prayer. We sat together on the cliffs over the sluggish river and sang out our hearts. "The Stone-Quarry Quartet" we christened ourselves, with the subtitle, "All the Voices on the Rocks."

We all took our turns serving one another at table and in the work of the house. We housecleaned and washed windows and worked in the garden and, with the coming of the vineyard season, picked the grapes that were pressed for the altar wines of a countryside. We were inspired by the example of men around us—of Leo Keeler, who in eight months read most of the Latin classics, to follow this with eight months intense consuming of Greek masters, and eight months ruthless plowing through the English great. We heard with pride that Mark Gross had completed the entire reading of Shakespeare in one intensive month. We published our own little newssheet, a blend of gossip and abortive masterpieces. We were still a world utterly independent of money, of comforts, of women, of outside contacts, of anything but the forward drive to becoming Jesuits with the full training and development expected of us.

The men picked to be the faculty for Florissant were always carefully chosen. I recall with awe the figure of Father Caspar Harzheim, bearded, grizzled, unsmiling, speaking Latin or Greek, English or German, with equal fluency, verbally skinning us alive when we missed a word of translation, an old veteran who bore upon his soul the marks of fierce battle for the Lord and who felt he had no higher job than to be drill sergeant for us young recruits.

To me Father James Finn was a saint, gracious as a saint, unbending as a saint, with his eyes never losing sight of the vision. Hence he was sometimes impatient of our fumbles. He had the cause too much at heart; and it was too important and sacred to permit slack service. He insisted on high ideals as the goal of every Jesuit novice.

I heard the ancient saw that told of a Jesuit's progress:

> Young novices look holy but are not.
> Young scholastics don't look holy and are not.
> Young Jesuit priests do not look holy but are.
> Old priests look holy and are.

Around me were the young Jesuits struggling to attain a holiness that was far, far off in the future. And over me brooded old Jesuits who had attained a holiness which seemed to permeate them with a kind of diffused light and controlled power.

I was learning what a highly unspiritual man like Kipling might have meant when he said that "Down to Gehenna or up to the throne, he travels the fastest who travels alone." Genius might move swiftly and furiously all alone. There would always remain for the ordinary man the power and might of union in a glorious companionship for a single united cause. We were better than nature had made us because of the ideals and training of the Jesuit course. The sum total was actually, in defiance of mathematics, greater than the parts which made it up; for to the limitation of the individual member were added the spirit and forward impetus of the whole Society. We would see our provinces accomplish results that could not be accounted for by the abilities of the men who were set to attain them. We would see great universities built with the vow of poverty, and lovely churches cemented to their beauty with red ink. We came to know that we did not merit our reputation; and yet somehow went on earning it. We laughed when we read in some slap-dash author that all Jesuits were cast in a single pattern. We looked at the divergent characters and characteristics about us and wondered how anyone got such an absurd idea; yet deep down, we knew that we had the unifying influence of one leader, Christ, one purpose in life, the establishment of His kingdom, and a remarkable training to which all must submit and in individual fashion react.

Each year we would each make, first under the direction of a retreat master and then, after we had become priests, with our own notes and chosen books, the Exercises of St. Ignatius which had begun our whole training.

Twice a year we renewed vows which had never been suspended, anticipating the event with three days of prayer.

Each day was supposed to be marked with Mass and Holy Communion, with mental prayer and a careful scrutiny of the events of the day and the development of one's own conduct. We gathered for the Litany of the Saints, our only prayer said in common.

Over us was the fatherly superior. He spoke and we obeyed. He was our colonel, and we gave him military obedience. But never could he act through caprice or whim. From the very first day of entrance into the Society we were read aloud our rules and customs. With the years we studied, not the synopsis, but the complete rule as Ignatius had written it and the Jesuit congregations had added to it. Let the superior substitute his own personal preference for the written rule which we knew, understood, and freely accepted, and our obedience was at an end. Ours was government by a clearly explained and freely accepted rule. The superior was the administrator of that rule. Within the limitations of that rule he spoke and we obeyed. Outside those limitations he exceeded his authority and trespassed against the rule.

I found as the years progressed that Jesuit superiors were an amazingly fine group of men. They were chosen by reason of their own fine record of obedience and service. They were usually men without personal ambitions, content to give others a chance while they fell into the routine work of administration. They usually gave their orders with positive reluctance. They asked less rather than more, often demanding too little, I felt, of me and my associates. They were much inclined to set an example rather than to lay down a rule. If they demanded, they first themselves did what they would ask of others. They were tolerant of mistakes and patient with stupidities. Their essential reprimands were very few and always considerate and gentle. They asked when they might in all justice have ordered. They suggested when they could have issued a command.

I myself have never been a Jesuit superior, though I have had the direction of other Jesuits in the work we did together. I have frankly rejoiced that never did I have to give an order to another man. I have been happy that it was my assignment to suggest, to ask, to take along as a partner or associate, to rate no salute or tipping of the hat, to feel that when I got cooperation it came from willing hands and free hearts. Rarely one finds a superior who seems to enjoy being a superior. He is usually less good. The good Jesuit superior is a little sad when he gets his assignment and vastly relieved when he is succeeded by another and is returned to the ranks.

Jesuit obedience is famous in secular history and church tradition. Actually it is prompt enough and ready, but from the viewpoint of the superiors it is gentle, considerate, almost reluctant in its commands, and much more likely to be couched with a "Please" and a "Thank you."

Jesuit religious training, like all religious training, suffers necessarily, I found in my own case, from the same problems and human factors.

Men and women who do the work of the world also receive the rewards of the world. Hard work may mean higher salaries. Ambition means an advancement in authority and prestige. Men of family have the pressures put upon them by each new child, by a demanding wife, by the constantly mounting cost of living. Jesuits get no salary. Whether they do a minimum or kill themselves with work, the visible wages are the same—nothing. Few Jesuits want any position of authority; there are few posts of prestige, and a special Jesuit vow forbids us to aspire to any ecclesiastical honor or post.

In a way this is wonderful.

I am sure that long since he has forgotten the incident, but when I first worked with Mr. Cecil B. de Mille as adviser on his film *The King of Kings,* in his surprise at finding a young priest who was interested in the same type of work that interested him, he began this conversation.

"Do you like your life and work?"

"Enormously."

"Have you ever thought of changing?"

"Never."

"Yet you seem much interested in my work in Hollywood, and alert to the possibilities of the motion pictures."

"Yes."

"Would you consider coming out here, learning the pictures from the ground up, working with me on production, and becoming a producer or director?"

"Not for anything in the world. I love my life; I am completely content in it; and any job that deflected me from that work as a Jesuit would simply not interest me."

"You are a lucky man," he said. And I knew I was.

One evening I sat with Bishop Francis Clement Kelley, a close friend, an inspiring associate, and then bishop of Oklahoma City and Tulsa. He was lonely after his intense years on *Extension,* and he missed the priest friends who had flocked about him in Chicago. In a sudden misguided burst of friendship he said, "How would you like to be my auxiliary bishop?"

I laughed. "You know that Jesuits are never bishops except of missionary spots or places that nobody else wants."

He persisted: "I'd go to the father general, a very good friend of mine, and I'd ask for you. Let's pretend that the Southwest is a missionary country."

I shook my head with emphasis. "One of the reasons I like being a Jesuit," I said, "is that I have vowed not to become a bishop unless ordered by the pope. You're kind, but I have no such ambitions."

He grinned at me, as if the whole thing was a game, which possibly it was; he loved his verbal games. "That's where you are fortunate," he said. And after that we talked of his forthcoming autobiography.

Yet the lack of ambition, the impossibility of real advancement in the sense most men understand it, the fact that a Jesuit has no pressure of wife or family, means that he never feels the goad, the spur, the urge of sheer necessity, or the obligation of making a "higher salary," or getting a better job or a rise in the income bracket. He must of necessity have other motives which impel him to work hard, to do better-than-ordinary jobs, to keep at things when they get dull, to turn out superior achievements. He can be slovenly and go unpunished. He can do poor work and miss no reward. His living and food and room are guaranteed whether he is topnotch or slapdash. He must keep the fires hot within him and his ideals clear and bright and magnetic.

Possibly no one in history has been so completely dependent upon personal ideals and the challenge of an inspiring cause, so energized from inside himself, as the effective member of a religious order. He has almost none of the bread-and-butter motives that force a man to work for his own welfare and the welfare of his family. He is strangely independent, for that matter, of people who depend upon his labor and success for their material needs and comforts. His scale of personal living, his type of recreation, his social life, even the education he can attain, are not measured in terms of personal achievement. Once he becomes a religious and lives within his rule, he is cared for by his organization. He has no need for old-age pension or social security. He may in the spirit of social justice which animates many religious work for social justice for others; for himself, his order gives him the guarantee of essential physical needs, care in illness—a kind of novitiate-to-cemetery guarantee of all that is necessary for bodily comfort and relative peace of mind.

Our novice master emphasized that time out of mind. In substance he maintained that the Society of Jesus gave every one of its members the minimum essentials of life and care. Each of us would find as the years went on a home to live in, three meals a day spread in comfort, an education to which one could bring the degree of responsive interest he determined upon, a job which would be for the glory of God and the good of souls, patient care in time of illness, peace and calm of mind. Each of us in turn would need to determine his own personal response.

Though during the years of training the routine of each day would be carefully marked out, once I was a priest and at work "in the vineyard," I would find myself surprisingly "on my own." Some men, Father Finn insisted, would grow as long as they lived. They would become expert even though their speciality might be, in proportion to their natural abilities, rather a limited one. They would do steadily better work. They would develop into highly effective people. Others would be content to move with the tide of common life. They would feel it enough that they did the essentials, violated none of God's basic laws, kept the basic vows, did exactly what was assigned them.

"Two men," I still seem to hear Father Finn say, "enter the Society of Jesus together. They have approximately the same material gifts of body and mind. They come from the same sort of Catholic background. They start the Jesuit life together and for years will be given precisely the same training. Will they do the same quality and quantity of work? Will they develop into equally effective people? Will they both grow in their capacities? Will they at the end look back over lives which have done equal things for Christ and cause? Indeed not. The training is one thing; the response to the training is quite another. Probably no two will be alike. The work of each will be different. And their impact upon the world of their times will be, under God, their own personal achievement."

I quote strictly "by ear."

Whatever he said, the effect upon me was to convince me that with God's help I must use the potentialities of the Jesuit life as best I personally could.

With years I have come to hold the highest possible respect for what the Society of Jesus offers its members in training and opportunity. Where I have individually failed, I cannot blame the Society; I can only hold myself responsible. I had the chances to become a dozen times better than I am, to do work indefinitely more effective, to have grown vastly more Christlike and enormously more valuable to the cause.

Mentally and spiritually I could have been a giant.

Ignatius planned for a race of giants.

May I from my place too close to the earth confess and regret my failures of response?

TO A JESUIT SCHOLASTIC ABOUT TO BEGIN HIS TEACHING

Dear Brother in Christ:

Jesuit scholastics during the years of their teaching have a fine chance of being just about the happiest men in the world. I know how happy I was. Down the long corridors of the years, I look back and find myself glowing with remembered happiness.

When in 1917 I walked for the first time into a classroom, I felt that my apostolic work had begun. The boys were not far separated from me by any stretch of years; I was near enough to understand their interests and their needs; they were close enough in age to regard me, not as a fossil, an antique, or a museum piece, but as one young enough to be willing to share in the spirit of comradeship. I discovered that the best and most delightful way to learn is to teach. I had a busy and exciting day. There was no time to indulge in the luxury of self-pity. I went to bed exhausted, yet woke with an enormous anticipation of a big day ahead. I had the joy of working with souls, without as yet the distractions of the priesthood. True, I did not have a priest's consolations; I did not start my day by saying Mass; I had to send boys who confided in me to a priest for absolution. Yet I was not torn, as many a priest teacher is, by the desire to be absolving sins and visiting the dying criminal and preaching the gospel in the jungles or the tenements of a big city. I could give myself completely, without any yearnings for higher apostolic work, to the boys and their interests.

At the end of the day a group of congenial fellow scholastics met in our scholastics' recreation room. We thrashed out the events of the day, confessing our ridiculous blunders deliberately to wake the laughter of our confreres. We bragged a little of the superior qualities of our boys, or, when we had some character who was a character indeed, the recital of his misadventures was good for more hilarity. For once in our lives we were bound together in an absolute unity of spirit. Not only were we fellow Jesuits; we were fellow teachers in a small school, consumingly concerned with its athletics and its plays and its debates, knowing our own boys and the boys of the other classes, willing to share our small knowledge and skill, eager to talk and content to listen.

Later on, we might as priests adopt a terrifying phrase: "That is not my field." We would tend to travel our individual and individualistic paths. We would possibly be distracted from the classroom by the confessional and find the lecture platform secondary in attraction to the pulpit. We might even become to some slight degree public figures. Now our total world was bound by our school. We lived it twenty-four hours a day. Our problem students popped instantly into our morning prayers. Holy Communion became the source of strength for a long day of intensive teaching. After the classes were over, we were with the boys in their extracurricular activities, responsible for most of them. They were great days and we all loved them, no one more so than I.

It will probably be your destiny to be given additional and special studies. Few scholastics had this opportunity in my day. The Society of Jesus in the Missouri Province gave its members the straight course of studies and trusted them to continue their work as need and the challenge arose. Indeed, I am rather surprised now, living as I do in the midst of Jesuits carrying their graduate degrees in a score of different fields, to realize that, once I had attained my master of arts degree, I went no further with formal studies.

Twice later, superiors were kind enough to suggest I might go in for advanced studies. Both times nothing came of it, largely through my own decision.

I was finishing my teaching at St. Louis University when Father Francis X. McMenamy, my provincial, stopped me in the corridor. Seldom have I loved a man more than I loved him.

To me he was a saint. To me he was utterly gentle and kindly, a man who looked at you with such melting eyes that you saw in him a father, a friend, a counselor, and a guide. Yet I never had any doubt that he was also one of the world's most absent-minded men.

I followed his gesture that led me to his office.

"How would you like to go to Europe for your theology," he asked; "and then perhaps stay to take a graduate degree?"

At the time my father was fading with a strange atrophy. My mother was going through an emotional crisis that meant continued tears and a distaste for life. My brother was an invalid. I remained almost their only natural support; and though I would be in St. Louis while they lived in Chicago, trains made the trip in a few hours, and I did not feel that I would be leaving them isolated if I remained in St. Louis.

All this I explained to the listening provincial, who nodded, agreed, and said, "Your reasons are adequate; you will not go," and I left, a little regretful over what was a sacrifice, but more than a little relieved.

Two months later I again was stopped by Father McMenamy in the corridor, and again sat in his office. Now, I had no doubt about the number of problems he had on his mind and the number of men whose destinies he was guiding; yet I was a little startled when he looked at me thoughtfully and said: "I am considering sending you to Europe for your theology. Would that interest you?"

I must have gulped visibly, but I mustered my forces, and explained once more the family situation and how I felt that I could not reasonably leave my father and mother to be separated by an ocean—in those preaviation days. Father McMenamy nodded. "Ah, yes," he said in his lovely speaking voice; "I remember now. You told me that before, and I agreed that was ample reason for your taking your theology here. You need not count on going to Europe."

Just before the end of the school year he met me again in the hall. He had a look of disappointment on his face. "Mr. Lord," he said a little sadly, "I am afraid I may have a disappointment for you. I had hoped to be able to send you to Europe for your theology, but now I find it will not be possible to send anyone this year. So you can put that out of your mind if you had perhaps been hoping a bit for a European education."

I think I staggered a little, but I thanked him and that ended the first near brush with really higher education. Incidentally, I have always had a sincere affection and something like pity for higher superiors. During my years as a student philosopher my provincial was the master of calm and peace who had been my college president at St. Ignatius in Chicago. He had liked me then; he continued as a provincial to like me. Because of the intense loneliness of men in authority, he turned to me and to several other scholastics whom he had known when they were boys to companion him on his afternoon walks. We strolled at a snail's pace down Lindell Boulevard and out toward Forest Park. We talked or we did not talk as he wished. And sometimes he would sigh heavily; and sometimes, as if some secret problem had thrown a roadblock across his path, he would stop stock-still on the sidewalk and rub his hand over his forehead. Occasionally I would stand while he drew with the point of his inevitable umbrella (his name, Alexander J. Burrowes, was not the only thing English about him) the vague outlines of some plan that was troubling him. It might be a new building in contemplation. It might be a division of studies or a split in authority. He would talk quietly, using his tightly rolled umbrella both as chalk and pointer, while I stood respectfully sharing less his plans than his sense of isolation. He talked with me because I was a good listener and because whatever his decisions might be I had no interest in trying to deflect them in my direction.

Superiors always seem to me to live in lonely isolation. They are hedged round with power, and it is a hedge that few care to penetrate. Often they must feel that they are the last to know what their men are thinking about. And like all men in high places, they must reach out wistfully for simple truth and sincere friendship.

The second time I was offered higher education was during my last year as a student theologian. Then I was called by my provincial, who asked me how I would like to get a degree in graduate theology and teach it in one of our scholasticates. Since he had asked me, I was free to answer honestly. "I would not," I replied, and I think he was surprised. He asked why, and I continued, with the brashness of young middle age, that I did not like the way theology was taught, there was too much lecture, too much reliance on sheer memory work, a lack of research, and no incentive to a student other than his own strong head of steam. "After two years of my teaching," I said with brash conceit, "the system would be changed or I would be." We pursued that subject no further.

But from what I can see about the theologians and philosophers now studying in our Jesuit houses of higher studies, the method and system have been notably changed. I had a "head of steam" and got a great deal out of my theological studies. Apparently the men of your generation get much more still.

Naturally I have wondered what difference it would have made to my life had I been assigned to graduate studies, whatever the subject. I have always had one dread which was early injected into my mind by young Claude J. Pernin. "Be careful," he used to warn me, "for the best is the enemy of the good." I doubt if I ever understood that clearly until I read Chesterton's sagacious comment that if anything is worth doing it is worth doing badly.

When Mr. Pernin first used his delphic comment, I demanded an explanation. Master of the concrete instance, he pointed to a fellow Jesuit in the community. The man was far and away our best English stylist. No one had read more widely and intelligently in the classics than he. "There is a man," said young Mr. Pernin, "who knows the best. Indeed, he knows the best too well. He knows perfect style; he has read all the classic essayists; and though his style is charming and fluent and crystal-bright, he hesitates to write. He knows he cannot match the best. He is afraid that his style by comparison would seem slovenly and dull. So, since he cannot reach the best, he hardly writes at all. He could do very good work. He does nothing. And it's the best that keeps him from being good."

Chesterton had precisely that same idea in mind. If the job is worth doing, it is worth risking mistakes. If it cannot be done perfectly, at least it can be done to the best of one's limited powers. One can try, since the thing is worth trying. One must risk doing it badly, since it clamors to be done and those who are capable of doing it perfectly may not be willing to touch it.

So I have puzzled sometimes on what would have been my course in life had I known the polishing research of a Ph.D. Suppose I had become so precise and accurate that the large statement, the emphasis, the sweep of ideas necessary in talking to young people or writing for the general reader, would have appalled me. I have seen learned men get to know so much more about some limited field of specialization that they ended by being almost afraid to make a comment on the weather. That was not their field.

Years later, as a young priest, I was talking with Peter Maurin, father of the *Catholic Worker* and philosopher by right of innate genius and zeal for souls. He was telling me of his recent invasion of a great Catholic university campus. He told me how he had grasped by the arm a priest who was a great scholar and a man of power in the world of learning. "I shook my finger under his nose," said Peter, "and demanded: 'What are you doing for the Catholic social revolution?' Do you know what he answered me? He said, 'That is not my field.' "

I would be less than honest if I did not confess I would like a Ph.D. after my name. The honorary degrees are kind, but I do not feel that I have rated or earned them. A Ph.D. means long and laborious years of grinding work. Certainly I would like to know what years of advanced and graduate studies would have added to my store of knowledge. I would like the tools with which the doctor of philosophy has been equipped. It embarrasses me to realize that for the second half of my life I would not have been welcomed on most Jesuit university faculties. Yet I am not sure of what higher education might have done to me.

A very great potential poet, maybe the country's best, never wrote a good line after a Ph.D. in English. Contact with the best had destroyed a great power for good poetry.

My field of vision has been wide if inaccurate. I have loved many things rather than known intensely a few. I have liked to talk sweepingly and I am no master of footnotes. I have worked with experts who knew so much that they never seemed to be able to travel either fast or far under the load of their wisdom.

They could foresee all the difficulties which I could not even guess. They bogged down in problems that had baffled the ages. I never knew until I listened to them that the problems existed. They were so in love with the perfect that they drew back before the tentative, the limited, the abortive. I was willing to run risks; they wanted the guarantee of a certain success.

Again, I would be less than honest if I did not envy those men of great learning who have done such marvelous research along a hundred lines. I am proud of the vastly improved teaching in Jesuit schools. I admire—even if I might not be able to read with understanding—the profound works written by fellow Jesuits in recent years. I like to think that the trained graduates who add a Ph.D. to an S.J. (Sister Mary Blanche to the contrary notwithstanding) are of that rare and precious number who push back the thickets of ignorance and cut their way to the bright palace of the Sleeping Beauty of truth. Would it have been fun to be one of them? Or would I have been a very different person from the rather reckless, somewhat adventuring, man I am—who has sometimes dared because he didn't know any better, and risked because he had never seen the difficulties, and acted as if there were no problem when, in strict truth, he didn't know there was?

I say all this as I begin this little account of my happy teaching days as a scholastic so as to lay no false claims to scholarship and to make no pretenses that are not backed by the facts.

The assignment to St. Louis University was the result of a pleasant event in the course of my last year as a scholastic student philosopher. Frank Quinn and I, fellow students of philosophy, happened also to be deeply interested in the theater. At college together in Chicago we had written a small college musical or two; and we had ambitions to write more. Father Patrick Phillips, dean of the university's college department, had been a scholastic when we were boys at school. We visited his office one significant day and sold him the idea of a musical show. He liked the idea; Frank and I wrote the show; and we put it on with an amazingly good cast. Frank Quinn could have been one of the country's great composers. Instead he became an excellent college dean and university rector. And music knew a great loss.

After one successful musical show Father Phillips looked hopefully toward a second, which is the reason why he asked to have me assigned to his staff and why I found my name listed in a divided job. I was to teach English to the juniors and seniors of St. Louis University High School and to the freshmen of St. Louis University College of Arts and Sciences.

Both schools were in the same buildings on noisy Grand Avenue. The faculties, in those prestandardization days, overlapped. The assignment to English was greeted with great personal enthusiasm by the new teacher. Since the announcement came in the midst of the holiday season, I plugged hard on the texts assigned for the new classes, and I returned to the school full of enthusiasm if a little meager in pedagogy and English classics.

In the fashion characteristic of those days, my first scholastic job turned out to have little enough to do with the classics anyhow. I was called to the office of Father Phillips, who, like the rest of the faculty, doubled in brass, serving as principal of the high school and dean of the college, and handed a list of names and addresses. They were boys who might be interested in attending the high school and I was to hit the pavements and convince them that St. Louis University High School was the school of their dreams. I mention this not because I was a successful solicitor. On the contrary, out of the list I called on that afternoon, I got just one new applicant, and he had already made up his mind to attend, since his two older brothers were students at the high school. For the rest, mothers talked to me from upper windows, doors were barred against me, some of the prospects turned out to be already satisfied with a job, and a few were headed for other educational meadows.

But the one was well worth the effort.

I called at the stately mansion on Raymond Avenue, and found myself surrounded by the most delightful crowd of small boys and girls I had ever met or was likely to meet again. They announced that they numbered eleven . . . they did not know that in time their number would be increased to twelve, the youngest marked by God to be a Trappist. No, neither Mother nor Father was available; but then, that didn't matter; such things could be taken up with their eldest sister, and here she was.

The afternoon was hot. The eldest sister had been working in the kitchen—a not-unusual occupation—and though she was only seventeen, she greeted me with dignity, settled me in a comfortable chair on the veranda, listened to my inquiry about the educational future of her brothers, and assured me that they were all planning to attend St. Louis University High School. The children swarmed about me, I played a bit with them, and headed off for less pleasant homes and far, far less charming families. Later I learned that I promised the children I would return; but I did not keep that promise for almost ten years.

The young man whom I gathered that afternoon for my school is now an extremely successful and zealous Jesuit missionary in Central America, Father George Prendergast. Ten years later the eldest daughter of the family came to work with me as my secretary of the happy years, Marian Prendergast. It was a happy call and a most successful afternoon's effort. And Providence has a delightful sense of humor and a wonderful mastery of the unexpected.

Unexpected? That seems to be the word for the whole of life.

When St. Louis University High School opened, I was given a schedule, and found that I would make my first appearance in any classroom as teacher of English to third-year-high at ten o'clock precisely. How thoroughly I prepared that first class! How thoughtfully I gave myself to the wording of my opening remarks! Did I know that my planned speech was the cliché of clichés? "Boys, I hope we will have a pleasant year together. You be square with me and I'll be square with you." At ten minutes before nine a cassocked courier pounded on my bedroom door, thrust a Latin text into my hand, and cried breathlessly: "Father Phillips says to go down and take second-year Latin. The teacher has been suddenly taken sick, and you're his only replacement."

Thus it was that the preparations of the summer for English, junior and senior, went down the drain. So it was that I never gave that speech, thank heaven, and am spared the shame of having delivered the world's most tiresome talk. So, after anticipating English, I began by teaching Latin. So, proud in my status as a teacher, I began my career as a rank substitute. Teaching is like that, as any teacher will assure you. The suggestion that teaching is not an eventful and unpredictable career is mad nonsense.

My entrance into the classroom was a blend of anticipation and dread. Hitherto I had found mixed in my feelings a horror of my inadequacy as a teacher and a real thirst to teach. My novitiate experience as a catechism teacher in the little country school had been enough to send a man willingly into a lions' cage by preference. I was quick to understand the young Jesuit of provincial legend who after one year in a high-school classroom twirled a globe, picked out the spot farthest from the scene of his misery, and volunteered for the missions. The Chinese of inner Mongolia seemed most attractive after the animal training he had failed to achieve in his high-school classroom.

The boys and girls of the Florissant Valley had found me a wretched teacher, a limp disciplinarian, and a completely frustrated apostle. The boys did not come to class until I had anticipated Tarzan and shagged them out of the branches. The little girls greeted my most solemn pronouncements with giggles, and I ended the year wondering what had ever induced me to join the Jesuits, who made teaching their speciality.

Yet to counteract the lack of experience was an inner longing to teach. Mr. Pernin and I, in discussing my future profession, had often talked of teaching as a career. Louis Mercier, later to become one of the great Christian humanists, had finished St. Ignatius, entered Harvard's Department of Foreign Languages, and later joined the Harvard faculty. I was impressed by the footsteps he had left behind in fairly durable sands of time. Mr. Pernin's answer, however, had discouraged me: "If you want to teach, put on a cassock before you don the scholar's gown. As a layman, join a profession that pays well. As a Jesuit, teaching is a wonderful career."

So I came to my scholastic teaching with feelings that were very much a blend. Would I duplicate the horrors of the Florissant catechism classes? Or would my yen to teach turn out to be a true vocation?

The second alternative prevailed.

I loved the classroom from the moment I faced that unexpected Latin class. Discipline was not the slightest problem to me.

I was much too interested in the boys and the subject to permit them time for nonsense or to allow myself occasion to enforce discipline. Somewhere in my consciousness lingered the pedagogical advice of Father Conroy: "Constant temper and shouting in class is totally futile. Save it all up, and when you have to put on a scene, make it a classic." During the first week in class the high-schoolers tried everything that was calculated to test a new teacher. But some teacher's instinct kept me calm and busy and unperturbed. The classic I played in low key, anticipating the tactics of Jack Webb and *Dragnet.* As I stepped from the classroom on a call from the principal's office, chaos broke loose. I returned to find a mild field day in progress. Instead of storming, I closed the door quietly, walked to the window at the back of the class, and with my back turned I looked out the window silently for ten of history's longest moments. The class were hardly breathing. When the silence and the suspense had reduced them to ragged nerves and pulped minds, I walked slowly to the front of the room, picked up my text reluctantly, looked at them, and said in my lowest possible tones: "I shall think it over until tomorrow. I'll let you know the punishment for this disgraceful conduct then."

They came the next morning expecting the heavens to fall. Instead I said in my most chilly voice: "I've decided to let it drop for just once. But if there is another outbreak . . ." And leaving them cliff-hanging on that phrase, I resumed class.

It was my last problem of discipline.

Not, please understand, that I liked a disciplined and orderly class. I had a sneaking conviction that a quiet classroom was either asleep or paying their devoirs to St. Apathia. I liked a live class. I never had any objections to students moving about. Questions were welcomed. Objections were something that I relished. The nicest compliment was paid me by a singularly uninterested student who caught me after class and bowled me over with, "Gee, teach, you sure have fun teaching us, don't you?" I admitted to myself that I did, and I was not disturbed by his discovery of my pleasure at a blackboard or front desk.

Oh, for the energy of a vanished youth! Father Conroy's pedagogical advice included this masterpiece: "To be a successful teacher, stay away from the furniture." So for three years I never sat down in the classroom. The blackboard was my best auxiliary. I strolled the classroom, never taking up any definite stand, which I now realize is a wonderful way to keep the class alert, watchful, and a little off balance. It is hard not to think of classes and their teachers as pugilists poised for effective blows. In that case, the weaving and bobbing pedagogue has a decided advantage over a teacher flat on his feet.

The college department did not open until two weeks after the high school, so I felt like a veteran when I walked in to greet the collegians. And though I was a youngish-looking chap, they were nice enough to enter into the spirit of pretense and act as if I really were seasoned and tried.

If the first week in a classroom tests every trick that the classes will ever use, the first year brings a new teacher every pedagogical experience he will ever be called on to try. My classes included the most wonderful group of young fellows a lucky teacher ever had to face, and the scrapings of the school. I suppose all principals believe in gathering together all the failures and the reluctant students and assembling them in a single class. This I inherited. And while I loved every moment with the bright young fellows in our fourth year, it was that substandard third that gave me my education in pedagogy.

I recall the boy who joined us briefly. He had come from a public school, and after an hour in my class he was filled with high disdain. He paused at my desk. "Look, I've had everything you're teaching these kids," he boasted, and I felt that probably I should enroll in his graduate classes. "You have?" I said in open-eyed admiration. "What did you read in those classes of yours?" "Read?" he repeated the word as if it were slightly unfamiliar. "Read!" I repeated, saying it slowly and making it sound as if I had spelled it out. "Well," he said, summoning up the vast library of his assigned and supplementary reading, "we read Poe's 'Bells' . . . and Poe's 'Murders of the Ruey' something or other . . . and Poe's . . . 'Bells.'" I thought the bells had been ringing long enough, so I suggested, "You read some Shakespeare? Such as . . ." I hinted. He went blank. So I led him on. "I suppose you read *The Boyhood of Shakespeare."* He regarded me with pity. "Certainly I read *The Boyhood of Shakespeare."* I was not quite satisfied, "And which of his plays?" "Lots of 'em . . . I don't remember the names, but one of 'em was a little blue book like that one there on the desk."

Part of that collection of pedagogical junk was one lad who had the handicap of a rich family, a large income, and, what was for those days most unusual, his own car. With all that equipment, he naturally had no time to get the necessary equipment for class. So if he had a book, he had no pencil; if a pencil, no book; if book and pencil, no paper; and if paper, no pencil to use or book to refer to. One day he arrived with all three—book, pencil, and paper. I was rather stuck for a second, but I gathered my surprised wits, congratulated him on having all the classroom equipment for once, but was rocked again when he answered: "Yes, but I can't use 'em. I broke my arm yesterday cranking my car."

It was a joy to teach the freshmen in college. I had some real brains in that class. My fourth-year-high had at least eight standouts whose submitted work was a constant pleasure. One half the third year was good. But it was from my dullards that I learned . . . that if you put in time, you get results; that if you are patient, they'll respond; that if they have a bad foundation, it's up to you to dig and build them a good one; and that when they don't read, often enough, they simply can't. At the end of the year we were good friends, and they could turn out sentences that bore more than a coincidental connection to the English language. And I was a much wiser and not a bit sadder teacher. Anybody can teach a genius. It's a test and a training to give the dullard and the reluctant insight into the wonderful thing which is knowledge. I'll bet the trainer who trained the hare had nothing like the fun of the trainer who entered the tortoise in that memorable race.

The year was a game of personal badminton. I was batted between class and preparation for class. It was all new and different, and I was spurred on by a terrific sense of duty and responsibility to the boys. A mean distrust that I do not disclaim convinced me that the only way I could be sure they were working was to assign them nightly written work. So each night they got their written assignment, and the next morning I collected a sheaf of papers to submit to the scalpel of the blue pencil. My test was homework. Early I lost all belief in the value of examinations. Father Paul Blakely once said that the way to handle examinations was to toss the papers against the ceiling and flunk the boys whose papers stuck there. When I questioned this ridiculous exaggeration, he pinned me down with this retort: "If a teacher doesn't know his class so well from response in class and written assignments that he can learn nothing about them from an examination, he is no teacher." My own observation soon convinced me that some students simply collapse in the presence of an examination. To give them a low mark for a psychological hazard is unfair. Others can plug for one night (as I had done) and pass an excellent exam. It seemed unfair to give them a superior mark for inferior work and knowledge. So for that first year, and the years following to a lesser extent, I carefully went over their written assignments. I got them to the board for regular quizzes, and gave the examinations the scantest attention.

Please understand that I do not know whether my system, or lack of system, would be possible in the enormous lecture classes which now face college teachers. I am still implicit in my faith in written assignments.

Years had passed when I was approached one day on the street by a successful-looking mature man. "Are you Mr. Lord?" he asked. "I use to be," I confessed. "I'm Father Lord now." "Well," said he with a scowl, "I've been waiting for twenty years to meet you again. You had me in class. Did you ever read the school catalogue?" I admitted that I never had. "Neither did I until it was too late. Well, I read it then and found out that you, who demanded a written assignment for every class, five times a week, were entitled to exactly one a week." I hadn't known that and probably wouldn't have paid any attention if I had. But to my former pupil I felt I had better be a little less arrogant. "So," I agreed, "I got more than I rated. Sorry, but what can we do about it now?" He suddenly grinned, "I can thank you, can't I?" I gazed in bewilderment. "Yes," he said, "I've always meant to look you up and thank you. You see, I have one of the easiest jobs in the world. I am a pulp writer; I write under half a dozen different names—you wouldn't know any of them—for the adventure and science-fiction magazines. I work about four hours a day, have the rest of the time for myself and my family, and net about fifteen thousand a year. And never would I have found that possible if you hadn't demanded those nightly assignments. So thanks, and you can know you have at least one grateful pupil."

I was, of course, fascinated then, as I always was, with the differences in pupils. There was a youngster in my third year who turned in ten and fifteen pages of the most frightfully smudged and horribly misspelled compositions. But they were full of thought and delightfully fresh. I don't know whether he ever learned to spell, and I doubt if he ever learned to write legibly. He didn't need to. He was Jack Alexander, who became one of the top writers and contributors for the *Saturday Evening Post.* I recall the young man whose work was a model of exactitude without vestige of imagination. He became a famous doctor of philosophy in the classic languages. Then there was the lad who wrote with the immaturity of a prefirst communicant. One summer passed, and he returned to give me a simply wonderful burst of imagination and fictional fancy. I would have given anything to know what happened during that single summer that released his romantic nature. And it wasn't what you might think; for he became a priest.

Probably the assets I brought to the classroom, if I can admit to any in the light of honest retrospect, were a real love for books, my own wide personal reading, a terrific amount of vitality, and a liking for the boys themselves. Maybe that discouraged me from ever becoming an expert and a scholar. I fancied that sometimes scholarship kills a zest and love for a subject. I imagined that I had seen men who knew everything about their subject except how to share it with others. I flattered myself that a love for what I was teaching and a love for those I taught would supply for a somewhat sketchy mastery of the topic. In public debate I know how badly I could be worsted if I dared to take such a stand. In my own private attitude, I have not been so sure. Or put it this way: If I had been able to bring to my admitted and unacquired assets a deep knowledge of my subject, what a teacher I might have been! Or do I flatter myself much too much?

Skipping ahead a bit, I was taken out of the high-school classes my second year, and as the university's College of Arts and Sciences in those simple days (1917 through 1920) numbered less than a total of one hundred students, I found myself in charge of the entire English department. So I was teaching fifteen hours a week, the maximum permitted even then; but the teaching included in the next two years the novel, the short story, poetry, drama, public speaking, the history of English literature, and creative writing—more simply called rhetoric and composition. It was great fun; and whatever the students learned, I got a very liberal education as I went along. How often I blessed the people who during my formative years had won me over to the habit of reading—my mother, my grandfather, Dr. Bailey, Sister Mary Blanche, Mr. Pernin, the young men of my own school days who had formed a sort of sporting club for the consumption of literature! I might not have depth but I had a lot of sweep. I might not know much about anything, but I knew a little about a pleasant variety of books and plays and people connected with both.

The classroom collegian has remained to me a subject of absorbing interest. I recall the long, gangling youth who fitted none of the seats provided, who folded himself like the Caterpillar in *Alice in Wonderland,* but who, like the Dormouse, retired into the haze of a perennial doze. That was exasperating; far more exasperating was the fact that when in a low voice I called his name and asked him the answer to the question I had hardly mumbled, or a résumé of what I had just been discussing, he came out of his apparent coma, handed me the precise answer, and retired once more into his blanket of fog.

There was the young fellow who could put a question in such a fashion that I was absolutely sure I had been talking nonsense. For instance, I referred casually to Daniel Defoe's *Robinson Crusoe.* From his sniper's box at the rear of the class he aimed and fired: "Are you sure that it was Daniel Defoe who wrote *Robinson Crusoe?"* Instantly I was not; in fact, if he had asked me to say positively my name was Lord, I would have hesitated.

How relieved I was when he got an appointment as a cadet to West Point and a chance to shoot at brass buttons and eventually at an enemy!

Often I have felt that I should have been quite content to spend a lifetime in a classroom. Years later, when Dr. Fitzpatrick was head of Marquette University's English department, he cornered me as I visited the university in the early days of the sodality movement. "Why don't you get out of that job you're trying to do and come with me into our English department? We need a teacher who loves writing and books. And you could do a job for us in what we intend to make a really great university." I was tempted, though I knew that I loved my assigned job and would not readily win a release from it if I asked. I have envied English teachers who like their subject. I have seen the good they can do. And of course, I am this side of obsessed with the importance of fluent writing and clear, persuasive speaking; and long for the day when appreciable numbers of those who love true beauty and have themselves a strong grasp on sound truth and the saving principles of Christ will write and speak and dominate the communication channels with a mastery of language and the power of words.

During the course of that second year of teaching I stumbled into a unique pedagogical experience. World War I was all about us. Since the draft was something a little different and the men responsible for it were fumbling with too many new problems, the student in college fell under close scrutiny. Was he a slacker? Would it be wise to strip the universities of the nation's future professional men? Had the boy who was getting an education, or who desired an education, any rights which the boy who was not attending school did not possess?

We came back from that first holiday to find that the government, with the aid among others of Father Edmund Walsh, a fellow Jesuit from Georgetown University, had founded the Student Army Training Corps. The letters S.A.T.C. soon took on comic meanings: Safe At The College was one of the milder. And once the armistice had been signed, that became Stick Around Till Christmas.

It is, of course, extremely unwise in religious communities to admit a fondness for anything, for sooner or later you find that the object of your interest and enthusiasm has become your responsibility. So my interest in the extracurricular made me the logical man on whom to dump almost everything connected with this new, totally untried, and highly experimental form of education. It started with the announcement that I was to teach military English. All anyone connected with our university unit seemed to know about military English was that all communications were headed:

From..
To..
Subject..

Some professor with an eye to a quick financial turnover got out a text, with which teacher and students—and I think the military services—were equally unfamiliar. I took it into class and then stumbled on a book of Woodrow Wilson's speeches, dropped the text, and taught them the old Princetonian's dream of a democratic and united world, in some of the purest prose written in modern times. Does anyone read Woodrow Wilson these days?

To my amazement I woke one morning to find that I had been appointed secretary of the new school. I had been selected by Father Joseph Davis, whose deanship of the unit resulted from the fact that he had, with a wonderful schoolman named Frank Thornton, just initiated a highly successful pioneer school among schools of commerce and finance. Father Davis added the S.A.T.C. to his responsibilities, and I was installed as his secretarial assistant. Installed is certainly a large word. I had no office, not even desk space, and I retained all my normal work in the College of Arts and Sciences.

It turned out that my new job was largely one of keeping the unit from tearing the school to bits. Sent to command the unit were two officers whose connection with army affairs had been—let's say—a little unusual. The commandant was a physician and had held the now-obsolete office known as that of contract surgeon in the Spanish-American War. Seldom have I met anyone more charming and gentlemanly—too gentlemanly, it seemed, for his present assignment. His chief of staff was a sergeant of the regular Army shot upward with dizzying speed to be a major. Their control over these play soldiers who didn't want to drill and who resented the interference of the military training with their education was that of a small boy in a cage of Clyde Beatty's less docile animals. I soon discovered that the classes began at full complement and ended with a corporal's guard, while the rest of the young men had climbed out of windows and slipped along ledges and water pipes.

Everyone in the university sufficiently healthy to walk to class was enrolled in the corps. And the medics and dents and law students hated the whole business—except the delightful fact that of a sudden they were being fed, clothed, and housed (if they did not live in St. Louis) and each month presented with the pay of a buck private of the front line. The Navy, not to be outdone by the Army, inveigled a small group to throw in their lot with the Boys in Blue. Only the boys never got into blue. Red tape bound them tight. Their uniforms finally arrived two days after the armistice had been signed, and they never got a penny of pay until the Christmas holidays. As a consequence no cluster of men in service ever looked so bedraggled since the sad figures at Valley Forge. As a consequence the prestige of the Navy suffered at St. Louis University. Even the fact that two smart young St. Louis University grads worked out the war putting on musical comedies at the Great Lakes Naval Base and that one of our football players made history on the navy service teams did not appreciably lift the Navy in the eyes of our student body.

As secretary of the unit I taught classes in military English and did informal sentry duty, keeping order where the military personnel failed. Jesuits don't like disorderly schools. If there is class, they like the students in class. If there is assembly, they don't want the assembly broken up in a sort of general retreat. So, without much instruction from anyone, I would post myself at the foot of the rain pipes and return to the classes the escaping soldiery. Chiefly, however, the barracks were my beat, and a fairly exciting one.

The university for its new and very much toy soldiers had thrown up barracks of the kind that were appearing in cantonments all over the country, on vacant property about two blocks from the main campus. The sketchy program of the S.A.T.C. did little to take up the time of the men, though it expected them to be in the barracks at sundown and to be checked at regular intervals. Knowing that young fellows with nothing to do were likely to rip the barracks apart, knowing too that they simply gave the sentries a wink and came and went as they pleased, it became my self-imposed duty to drop over after supper—mess, if you prefer—roll a light piano into the center of the floor, and gather the crowd around for a song fest. Or I would bring my books over and relax with them while I kept an eye open for the frisky and noisy students who so often disturbed the serious students who wanted to study. Or we'd call the sergeants to line them up and march them back to the auditorium for an impromptu variety show or a motion picture. No USO in those days. No organized plans for recreation.

The food was the subject for the usual soldierly dissatisfaction and complaint. But I sincerely believe they had much more than usual reason. The job of feeding the students was turned over to a contract commissioner who was accustomed to feeding railroad gangs. Our boys, coming from good homes and accustomed to a good table, were a different type. One evening when I reached the barracks, the feeling in the air told me that trouble was brewing. We rolled out the piano, got the impromptu musical instruments tuned, and began our singing. Slowly the atmosphere dissolved from the impending storm to comradeship and boisterous fun.

Not for years did I learn that our song fest had saved a cook. The corps had laid careful plans to kidnap him from the kitchen and his obnoxious pots and pans, string him up with a loop under his armpits, and leave him hanging through a long November night suspended from the nearby electrical pole. They wouldn't have killed him; but neither did his food kill them—precisely. But they would give him the scare and lesson of his life, one that they hoped might improve his skill with a skillet.

One day my chief announced his departure on a brief trip. Would I take over for the day? Ah, yes; some visitors would be dropping by. Nothing much, just a little routine investigation of some sort, a casual inspection of the corps and all that was connected with it. Blissfully unconscious of impending doom, I nodded my approval, only to be faced a few hours later by the visiting committee. Until judgment day, I trust I shall never again go through an inquisition like that. Knowing simply nothing about educational procedure, having only the vaguest ideas of what the government wanted or had asked from the university, I sat down with representatives from Yale, M.I.T., Illinois, and two or three other big-name schools, while they put me through an examination to end all examinations. I located files which I did not pretend to understand. I gave answers about courses and personnel in which my vagueness matched that of the people who had designed the S.A.T.C. I sweated on that cold November day, and thought deep purple thoughts about my chief, who had departed to let the wrathful storm fall on my head. I would have felt less dejected had I known that, though these men represented education at its most elaborate, they had been for a month or more inspecting education at its most confused. They left at last, and I waited for weeks to hear that the Army and Navy had closed out our Student Army Training Corps.

When my chief returned late that evening—returning, I am sure, by a side door and only after some scout had flashed him an all-clear signal—he passed me in the corridor with an offhand wave. "Inspectors come?" I nodded grimly. "Sorry I wasn't here. Must have been pleasant people to meet." And he walked down the hall, leaving me with a quick and intense burn. The war ended; the students sat around waiting for return to their normal way of life; and the committee evidently never bothered to return their report. Professional educators, however, can still give me a nervous tremor by starting to ask me a few technical questions.

Hardly had the S.A.T.C. got under way when I decided that it needed a band. My first call for bandsmen resulted in silence. I then made the interesting discovery that rehearsals might be held at the morning drill and exercise time, from which hated exercises the musicians would be excused. A hint to this effect brought out one hundred and twenty musicians, mostly without instruments. We combed out those who professed, in the wisecracks of the day, "to play a Victrola very well," or who said, "When I was a youngster, I played on the linoleum." We still had eighty passable musicians; some had instruments, some could be equipped from the university band room, but for some instruments must be borrowed or begged. When I approached the commandant he waved his hands in his usual friendly fashion, said he would be delighted at a band, but left the problem of instruments entirely up to me.

Yet after a week's intensive rehearsals under the direction of a young medic who had been playing his way through medical school with a clarinet in a dance band, we marched out on the field and gave the weary and bored civilian soldiers a foretaste of the music that henceforth would mark the time of their drilling. We had some good musicians in the band, though most of them were the flattest of amateurs. One future physician was earning his tuition blasting a trumpet in a summer circus band, and his notes rang out with the positive assurance of Gabriel's horn or the flourish that announced the high dive into a pool of water hardly damper than a piece of blotting paper. I have often wondered what happened to some of my better brass section, though I recall that one tuba player reappeared as a distinguished abdominal surgeon.

Two events stand out in my memory.

Our varsity football team was playing Scott Field Aviators. When our band walked onto the field, eighty-strong and most of them relatively in tune, we made a brave showing. By way of contrast a little cluster of some twelve musicians set up their instruments in the lee of the stands and tuned briefly. Our eighty did some good-natured kidding of this handful, puffed out their cheeks and blasted on their instruments, and then sat back in the stands with a jeering, "Now, little fellows, play!"

They accepted the challenge.

For the rest of the afternoon's game my musicians refused flatly to pick up their instruments and sound a note. The twelve were all professionals, each from some famous dance band, and what they played anticipated Glenn Miller and foreshadowed Benny Goodman at his best. I think our football team won against the aviators; in the battle of the bands we were blown to bits by the very first blast of hot jazz that issued from those beautifully tempered instruments.

The second memorable day for the band is equally seared into my record. Thanksgiving Day was to bring the annual game with our great rival of those days, the local Washington University. We prepared for that with much intensive band practice. In the fiery energy of youth I had written and mimeographed some twenty-five parodies on popular songs, each foretelling the downfall of Washington, then, from their location on the former World's Fair Pike, called the Pikers. The songs not devoted to playing them down were concerned with predicting the tremendous score by which we, the Billikens, intended to massacre them.

Now, football teams in those war days were, in the colleges and services, made up of anybody who could put on a uniform. I had a vague remembrance of a lanky fellow—"Hoosier" we called him in those days before hillbillies had been discovered—who came to apply for admission into our S.A.T.C. A little investigation showed that he had a fair grammar-school education up to approximately sixth grade, so we sent him away. For some reason the usually high-scholastic-rating Washington took him in. He had neglected to mention that he was a star outfielder on an American Association baseball team.

At the same time to Washington had come an all-American quarterback who had finished his college career on the gridiron and plunged into medicine. The fact that he had played his four years, however, was not permitted to interfere with his eligibility in those carefree days.

Thanksgiving Day dawned bright and clear as it was to end gray and sinister. Our band marched out on the field, performed in smart style, took its place in the stands, and ran through, under my directions, the parodies which foretold the triumph of our team and the slaughter of the Washington innocents. We held back our better parodies until the quarter when the prophecies had been gloriously verified. Out on Francis Field trotted the teams, and in the Washington line-up was the all-American quarterback, and at end our rejected applicant from the American Association. Within thirty seconds we knew the worst. The quarterback and the end played their own little private game of baseball. Not basketball or football, but pitch and catch. The quarterback would throw the ball, and the lanky outfielder would slip past our line and reach up and snare the pass as if it were a fungo hit during spring practice, with him back in his familiar left field. The slaughter occurred, with us Billikens on the receiving end.

Back of me I heard the tearing and the crumpling of paper. My mimeographed parodies were turning into snow to add their chill to the general chill of the atmosphere. That day the band refused to play again and the songs we had saved to be sung in triumph were never heard by mortal ear. Father Henry (Heinie) Hermans, who managed our team, and the coach and myself wept together at the end of the game. The band had disappeared to figure how they could eat after they had paid the bets which they had lost.

As I have mentioned so often, my interest in things extracurricular was known, in the words of Damon Runyon, to one and all. I began my career of outside class by prefecting in the chapel for the high-school morning Mass. For that I owe God and my friends an apology. As yet I had not even heard of the liturgical movement. It was my job to keep order, and that I did. But to do something to fill those half hours at Mass, to lead my boys to a better understanding of what transpired before them, to introduce them to the Missal and its use, to make the thirty minutes precious and memorable and a training for life—that never occurred to my unimaginative head. I patrolled the aisles like a sentry. I tapped any student who showed signs of restlessness. But I gave them nothing to fill thirty minutes of suspended animation (except for the workings of the grace of God, rich and powerful, I'm sure). To use the time to train them to love and help offer up the Mass, there I totally failed. Let me confess that, if I have often labored hard to see that other schools made Mass in the chapel an absorbingly alive and interesting period, it is an act of reparation for lost opportunity and a complete failure in duty.

My first assignment to really extracurricular activities resulted in a failure. I was given the college debating society, already half-moribund. The first meeting resulted in such a total lack of interest that, in the fashion of young teachers, I laid the responsibility on the shoulders of the few who came, watched them shrug it off listlessly, and walked away to let the society die. Recently I heard a young varsity debater bemoan the lack of faculty interest in debating. I quietly struck my breast. With perfect right the debaters of my day could blame me for allowing one of the most valuable of the cocurricular outlets to die. I was interested more in other things. I did not fire their imaginations or stimulate their interest. To my eternal debit I let die what could have been an important apostolic work.

For during that first year's teaching I was deep in dramatics. We began with a high-school show. In one of those youthful bursts of energy I wrote it during the course of the Christmas holidays. We staged it during the spring. Chiefly I remember it for the fact that, quite ignorant of guns, I borrowed shotguns instead of rifles to be used during the siege of the Central American ranch by a band of God-hating and Church-hating bandits. The roaring blasts of those shotguns—loaded, thank heaven, with blanks, which, however, left more space for powder—must have been a reflection of the then-recent Battle of the Marne. If the audience applauded the final curtain, my actors were too deafened to hear it.

Frank Quinn, who was teaching at our old St. Ignatius High in Chicago, and I collaborated by mail in the long-distance fashion of Gilbert and Sullivan, and had produced together a war musical called, of all things, *Rouge and Rapid Fire*. It dramatized the adventures of a regiment whose preparations for a rear-line show were interrupted by very much front-line action. How many shows since have used that formula! This was collegiate, strictly male, lots of fun for the cast, and a moderately mild entertainment for the audiences which came to the Odeon and paid good money to see it. Incidentally, our expenses reached the then-fabulous sum of almost twelve hundred dollars. As the highest amount ever spent on a college production in our recorded history was less than half that sum, I was called on the carpet for a lesson in economics.

My defense was simple: "Before I took over dramatics, the university spent five hundred dollars on a show and netted five hundred. We spent around twelve hundred and netted two thousand." I'll never forget the aghast expression on the face of our university treasurer. "What's that got to do with it? I am protesting the absurd idea of spending twelve hundred dollars on a mere school entertainment." When in 1951 we spent one hundred and twenty-five thousand on the University of Detroit *City of Freedom,* I was glad that our treasurer of those days was mercifully gone to God.

On the staff with me was a young Jesuit priest who was to exercise a profound impression on Jesuit education and certainly upon me. I found time to discuss with him the importance of advanced education. Father Austin Schmidt was a perfectionist who did not, however, allow his love of the best to hamper his creation of the good. With time and a Ph.D. in education he became the head of Loyola University's Department of Education, where he set a high standard of teacher training. Then he became director of Loyola University Press, to the great benefit of those who like their textbooks beautifully made.

We talked of what could be done to advance education at St. Louis University, and he settled on a simple expedient. We would borrow a small auditorium on the campus, announce a series of six Saturday-morning lectures on teaching methods, invite the brothers and nuns of the city to attend, and launch a small teachers' college. I doubt if the faculty paid much attention to what we suggested. But their permission was incidental and readily enough given. We wrote out our own announcement cards, and waited for the first Saturday morning that would bring us our first student body other than the boys of the university.

Then, as is so often the fate of pioneers, Father Schmidt ran into a near fatality. Two days before our opening, he was struck with a bug, and through a wretchedly swollen throat managed only the weirdest of unintelligible sounds. Two of us made up the Saturday-morning faculty, and one of us couldn't whisper a word. So it was, in the impromptu fashion of educators, that I went in on the first morning and taught his class as well as my own.

How many would accept our invitation? How many would gather in that small hall? Oh, thank God for the teaching sisters!

Almost one hundred of them came to smile at me when I rose to begin my first class in the teaching of high-school English. It was the most wonderful audience I had ever savored. Indeed, I think classrooms full of nuns spoil teachers for almost any other type of class. They come eagerly, avid for knowledge, intelligent and alert, and with ears that hear and minds that retain. They are appreciative of anything a teacher does for them. They are responsive and quick on the uptake. They make a teacher want to give his best. And when he tries at all, he gets the most inspiring response.

The next Saturday, Father Schmidt was able to take over his own class and did. For six Saturdays we went to the small hall to run our little school-inside-a-school, not dreaming that we were anticipating the much later and really great College of Education of St. Louis University.

Once the series was ended, Father Schmidt and I planned far more elaborately. We could not let slip away that wonderful audience of teaching sisters. Once more taking our case to the president and the dean, perhaps not too clearly but certainly with entire honesty, we pleaded for a whole year of Saturdays, a regular school of education to be opened to the teaching nuns of St. Louis. We got a casual permission, but with one qualification: the university was not ready as yet to admit women to its student body. We must conduct our classes off the campus.

The young directors were undaunted. We approached the Religious of the Sacred Heart at Maryville College and begged permission to use the small grammar school on their grounds which later (with our blessing, believe me) grew into the significant Barat Social Center. They graciously gave us hospitality. We drew up our announcement and let the sisters know that in the autumn a faculty of three would teach them if they cared to accept our guidance. When the summer announcements came, Father Schmidt was sent to get his doctorate at the University of Michigan. I returned, a faculty of one, to beg the cooperation of one of the world's great Latinists, Father Otto Kuhnmuench, and of Father Joseph Murphy for philosophy. He later became a great missionary bishop of British Honduras. I offered a course in the technique of the short story, served as general manager (I did not dare to assume the title of dean), secretary, and treasurer. Yes, bless them; the sisters trustfully paid tuition, all hundred and twenty-five of them. By the way, I doubt if I ever thought to pay the Religious of the Sacred Heart a penny of rent for their building. Will I work out that debt in purgatory?

That was my third and final year of teaching. By this time I had hit my pedagogical stride in the college classrooms. And the pleasant response of the young men plus the wonderful cooperation of the nuns made the year happily memorable. I frankly loved teaching. I think I threw into it real zest.

The next year, when in another department of the university I had been submerged in the mysteries of theology, the president of the university, his term completed, became my dean. One morning when I called at his office on some small matter, he suddenly lifted his long, bony hand. Father Bernard Otting was a saint. With years he developed into a mellow, laughing saint. Then and for the years that preceded he felt that authority and a smile could not be wedded, and that a stern man was probably a holy one. He had discovered that "no" was one letter shorter than "yes" and hence a timesaver. And he believed that a university was a matter of intensive study and not of extensive public relations.

That finger, long and stabbing, had often been directed at me when he was president of the university and I was one of its youngest faculty members, and his "By the way" was a phrase that had power to make even the most guiltless begin to search his conscience.

"By the way," he said, "didn't you run a course for sisters last year?"

I admitted the mild impeachment and watched him shake his gray head.

"I can't understand it," he said. "I simply can't understand it. How did I ever give you such an extraordinary permission?"

"Oh, but you did," I protested rapidly, relying on his steel-tempered sense of justice.

"That's it precisely. I did. But how and why? You were a scholastic. The scholastics are not supposed to teach women. I believe there is a rather recent letter from Father General on that subject. Yet I let you Saturday after Saturday go down to Maryville and teach nuns." He shook his head in bewilderment. "For the life of me I can't figure how it ever came about."

We didn't go into that any further. Perhaps it was divine Providence that had, through very much a side door, opened St. Louis University to the thousands of teaching nuns who from that day onward have been among its more cherished and favored graduates.

Actually, through some other oversight, he had permitted me to launch into what has been something of a lecture career. Grim men, intent on safeguarding small details, sometimes miss larger things that you would not suspect they would overlook.

While I was still studying philosophy, Father Davis, of the School of Commerce and Finance and chief of the S.A.T.C., decided to sponsor a series of public lectures. He assembled several of the university faculty, and for some surprising reason selected young Mr. Leo Mullany and me to augment his roster. He himself was to talk on Francis Thompson; Mr. Mullany would talk on Chesterton; and I was to handle—preferably rough-handle—George Bernard Shaw. It was unusual for a man studying philosophy to make any sort of public appearance. It was a novelty for a scholastic to give a lecture before a mixed audience.

The lectures were scheduled for a series of Monday evenings. On Friday night before his lecture Mr. Mullany got the word that his father had died. There was nothing for it but to catch the midnight train for his home in Waterloo, Iowa. Father Davis wandered over to my room in a slight daze.

"He won't be back for his lecture," he moaned, "and there is no way to cancel it. The admissions are by season ticket mostly, and mostly they have been paid in." How vital it is not to return money once in the treasury! He looked at me skeptically. "What do you know about Chesterton?" he demanded.

"Not as much as I should like to know," I answered honestly. "But I have read a good deal of him and . . ."

"Could you take Mr. Mullany's notes which he left behind with me, bone up on them, and give the lecture?"

It took me one moment of brashness to accept the proposition. But I could not fancy myself using another man's lecture notes.

I had that Friday evening, the periods between class, all day Sunday, and what time I was not listening to professors lecture on Monday. So I dashed to the library, returned with armfuls of books, and set to work to block out my own lecture. By Monday night I had a sheaf of notes ready, and I was waiting when the audience filed into our small auditorium.

Then Father Davis launched my lecture "career" with a classic introduction.

"I shall introduce you and give your talk a slight explanation. I shall explain that you are pinch-hitting and that you have had little time to prepare. In that way, if you don't do too well, people will understand and they won't stay away from your own lecture when you are scheduled to appear next week."

Leaving me properly deflated, he took the platform, explained precisely that to the audience, and I entered upon my first public lecture with this anticipatory prophecy of failure. I swallowed heavily and went out to talk on the sort of subject at which nobody could fail. Chesterton told his own story, but I had fun in listening to him speak through my mouth.

During that last year of teaching the yen for public lecturing returned. Once you have faced an audience, you can't get over the urge. And my urge was deep and doomed to be durable. The Knights of Columbus decided they would like me for a series of talks; and the same series was repeated in the Cathedral school auditorium. I talked on modern Catholic literature—though, truth to tell, there wasn't a great deal of it; on O. Henry, on J. M. Barrie, on the meaning of humor and why people laugh; on the newly sprouting Joyce Kilmer.

But if I was making these delightful side forays into other fields, my boys came first. How the extracurricular seemed to gravitate to me, I don't know. But I found myself in charge of the musical societies and engaged a young organist named George Devereaux to run the glee club and another named Donald Lowmiller to start an orchestra.

For some reason the student publications had been largely allowed to lapse. But in my classes were two university students of far above normal ability. They came to me in a committee,

Claude Heithaus and O'Neill Ryan. They wanted to start a university newspaper to supplement the *Fleur de Lis,* the literary journal of the university. Would I get them the necessary permission and back them up if they undertook its launching? Heithaus was a willing editor. Ryan had a fine knack for persuading reluctant students to buy subscriptions and unwilling advertisers to place their ads with him.

The idea delighted me. First, it was encouraging to have students keenly enough interested to undertake a sizable project on their own initiative. Then it seemed to me that the university needed a newspaper. And finally, it seemed to me that a newspaper would be an excellent laboratory for my English classes. Nothing like learning to write by writing for publication!

The team proved unbeatable. They "drummed up" a fine subscription list of willing subscribers. They assembled out of the small student body of the arts college a good staff. They persuaded the busy professional schools to choose reporters and representatives. And we launched the first issue of the *Billiken* with a flourish. It caught. The editors were rightfully proud. I was pleased as two or three Punches. The university had its newspaper.

But young men have lots to learn, and the second issue threw the fear of ruin into me and upset the school authorities with a first-class journalistic mistake. For some reason my editors grew angry at the law students. Now being possessed of a journal of opinion, they launched a fierce attack, deserved but most undiplomatic, on the offending lawyers. The retort was swift and devastating. The lawyers canceled their subscriptions in a body. The president had me on the carpet. The offending editors dodged me for two days. And that was their good luck and mine. For if I had met them, I would, in my indignation at their gauche conduct, have fired them ignominiously. I looked for them, but they were younger and more fleet than I. When eventually they sought me out, they found me cooled off and waiting for their explanation.

They did not hazard me. They merely dropped their eyes and said, "That's right; we're donkeys. You ought to fire us. But if you don't, we promise you'll never have another fiasco like that. Give us a second chance and we won't fail you twice."

Largely because I knew that the paper, if not managed by them, would drop right back in my lap, I lazily called off the intended firing, gave them back their authority, and retired to my own pursuits. Never again did they make a notable mistake. Each issue of the paper, complete, was laid on my desk. They handled the finances and left the treasury with a surplus. A public apology brought back the lawyers. I had trusted two young men and they fully justified my restored confidence.

At midyear they came as a second committee. Wasn't it only right that the university yearbook, the *Archive,* which had been discontinued for several years, be restored? I agreed that I approved the idea. They were willing, they said, to handle the whole job: make contracts, sell the students on the idea, get the pictures and the advertisers, and present me with the bound volume. And that precisely, with the help of young men they assembled around themselves, is what they did. They ran a small financial deficit, and Claude Heithaus put in his summer working to make that up. He left in the fall to become a Jesuit and a great antiquarian; Ryan went on to fine achievement in the business world. I got some small credit for the origin of the university newspaper, now the *University News,* and the revival of the yearbook. Actually the work was a student enterprise; the credit was theirs. As part of my education, I had learned to trust young people and believe that, given a job in which they are interested, they will carry it through to completion. As far as I know, there has been no break in continuous publication of either of the publications to this date.

I have often thought that my term as a teaching scholastic at St. Louis University must have fallen into a transition period. Who would have suspected that our arts student body of less than a hundred would grow into the ample department with its subdivisions into premedical and predentistry and prelaw and preengineering? Who would have anticipated the number of young ladies who would walk about the sacrosanct corridors and invade the classrooms of that strictly male school?

As a feature of our public-speaking class I used to encourage an occasional comic debate. The students chose some subject that amused them and debated it with a fine regard for the ironies and a real display of wit and humor. Prohibition was just sweeping the country, and their best suggestion was a debate that roused much excitement, and a degree of seriousness underlying the nonsense. Not far from the university was a famous male restaurant and tavern called Garavelli's. It was a normal hangout for the students—an amazingly temperate crowd in those preprohibition days, by the way. With the coming of the Volstead Act Garavelli's appeared doomed. No one had previsioned the resistance to the law, and bootlegging was not yet even a word, while racketeers might be a foursome walking onto the tennis courts. The thought of their favorite gathering place losing its character caused heads to hang and mourning to be sported. So my lads suggested a debate: "Shall Garavelli's when prohibition closes in become a drugstore or a museum?"

The debate was, naturally enough, spirited. The decision went to the museum, and the winning argument was this: Could we bear to think of our beloved tavern becoming a spot where women took over? Could we tolerate the thought of our beloved male "joint" profaned by women buying cosmetics and ice-cream sodas? Let the tavern remain exactly as it is, but let it take on the character of an historic museum; then we can walk slowly through, sorrowfully shed a tear at the beer-stained tables, and know that the flavor and atmosphere will be preserved forever, unsullied by the perfumed presence of the intruding sex.

How quaint and antiquated all that sounds!

In that period of transition, however, social life for students began to exercise a fascination. All our clubs had been organized for literary, athletic, or scientific groups. Social clubs flourished mildly in the professional schools. Not in arts and sciences, supposed home of the gay and the convivial. Parties under the auspices of the arts department were banned. There had never been a school dance. For that matter, during my years at St. Ignatius in Chicago we had one dance, a senior affair, which we managed for ourselves. It may interest this extravagant generation to know that each of us paid two dollars, which included the hall, the orchestra, a little mild punch (no alcoholic content), and one sandwich. Ah, we were roisterers!

So I used to regard my students speculatively. St. Louis was a town of much home entertainment in those days. But didn't the college need some social flavor?

Out in Webster Groves, a new and thriving suburb of the city, Loretto College had recently opened for the education of young women. Later it changed its name to Webster College and thrives today with a fine tradition. Then it had a minuscular student body, just about the size of our arts college. But it had a dean who was one of the finest and most farsighted women educators I have known, Sister Louise Wise. She was old enough to be my mother, yet she had come to some of our sisters' classes and we had struck up a great friendship. She had the wonderful gift of talking to anyone as if he or she stood on the same level. I watched the trick in her, trying to imitate it. Together we discussed the problem of Catholic marriages, then a much-debated subject. Why not more of them? We lamented that her girls and my boys did not meet and did not share a social life. So we did a little plotting.

First, she sent down two large automobiles filled with young ladies, pennant-waving and megaphone-wielding, to take part in our football parade through the city. The university students goggled. It was the first time a woman had taken part in any of our hitherto male demonstrations. Then Sister Louise invited out to her college my entire student body. Most of the lads went, and it was a joyous occasion.

Some of my young men, with a sense of the fitness of things, felt they must return this kindness with a party for their hostesses. I recall discussing this with my tireless Heithaus and Ryan. Yet the ban on social life remained. Authority had in some ancient day decreed that Girls were Girls and Boys were Boys and Never the Twain Should Meet. I talked the situation over with some of my student-minded priest friends on the faculty, notably the understanding Father Otto Kuhnmuench and the popular Father Theodore Schulte, whose love of laughter made him a great favorite. They listened to my plan, agreed it came within the law, and I plunged. In an informal meeting I suggested that the arts students form a club, call themselves the Bachelors, and run their own social affairs. Then I called on the Knights of Columbus of the Missouri Council, pointed out that they had a pleasant clubhouse and a very good dance floor, that they with their wives would make ideal chaperons, and that it was little less than their apostolic duty to see that our Catholic young people had an opportunity to meet and know one another.

The first dance under the new arrangements was an unqualified success, and, importantly, a financially inexpensive and yet successful one. It's a poor college dance in any era that doesn't leave behind a little rattling change in the till. Sister Louise and I congratulated ourselves. But we had forgotten one factor. Boys and girls do not like their social arrangements supervised by their elders. Actually I was not much older than most of my seniors. Still, the boys wanted to pick their own partners, and the girls insisted on being picked and not assigned by two stodgy faculty members. The Bachelors continued an anemic life. But the social relationships we had visualized for the two schools withered on the whine of protest. A good many young ladies from the college in the course of time were wooed and won by a good many young men from the university. But it was not done on any faculty-designed schedule. We were well-intentioned, Sister Louise and I, but we had forgotten that young people grow resentful when they think their social life is being managed.

My dealings with the other departments, notably the professional schools of the university, had taught me the strange isolation of each of them. St. Louis University, then as now, tended to sprawl. The arts-and-sciences building was in one location. Though the law school was not too far away, the two student bodies simply never met, nor did the students of commerce and finance. Far to the south, or so it seemed, stretched a great viaduct over the railroad tracks, and beyond it, as far away as if it lay on the Tropic of Cancer, were the medical and the dental schools. Because medical education was frightfully expensive and dental education not nearly so costly, the dents resented the medics. "Our tuition supports them," they used to growl.

So when I tried to sell them subscriptions to their university publications, tickets for the varsity shows, an interest in anything outside their own department, I was met with a chilly stare.

About this time the universities of the country were developing their student councils. I felt that this was precisely what the university needed. Could I sell the idea to the faculty? I had little doubt about the enthusiasm of the student body. At that time there had been a change in administration. Father William Robison, a very great philosopher, one of the most wonderful orators that ever charmed and compelled an audience, and a thoroughly attractive person, took over as president. Suddenly the normal reply "No" changed to a ringing answer of "Yes"! It was a startling experience for us who were trying to move a little scholastic world. So when I told him of the student-council idea, he took it to his board, and brought back clearance. I had nothing to do but sell the idea to the student body—a simple job.

Simple, indeed!

Little did I suspect the resistance that lies in the utterly conservative, rutted habits of a college student body. No one can dig deeper grooves than a collegian. No one is more reluctant to be jarred out of routine than a varsity man. My arts students were sure, should there be a university student council, they would be overwhelmed by the maturity, prestige, and numbers in the professional schools. The medics were totally uninterested in anything taking place north of their viaduct. The dents thought the idea was high-school stuff; in those days they prided themselves (there is always one such school in every university) on being the campus "toughies," slightly unkempt and with the hairy ears usually attributed to engineers. The law students had a schedule that brought them to class in the early morning and back again at night. Many of them worked through the day. And commerce and finance was still a stripling school.

So I tramped from department to department.

I took it on myself to interest the apathetic faculty of each school. I begged for assemblies, reluctantly granted me, where I poured forth young and enthusiastic oratory on what the council could do for the individual colleges and the whole university. Because I wanted to offer them something that sounded new and did not have that objectionable high-school flavor, I started calling it, not the student council, but the student conclave. And in the end I got a reluctant consent. The professional schools were convinced that the faculty would never give them any real power. Many of the faculty were persuaded that this would be just setting up an organization for student rebellion. Old King Selfishness and Queen Apathy clung to their ancient reign. And had it not been for Father Kuhnmuench and Father Schulte and a half dozen of my arts students, I might have quit. In the end, just as my term of teaching was over, the departments all voted to give the scheme a trial. They expressed scant hope. But they'd give it a whirl.

Then we held a first organization meeting. It was the only one I ever attended. But at that one meeting I put through, for the ease and convenience and comfort of my faculty successor and the students who were interested in university activity, one important measure only. Remembering the way I had constantly struggled without funds of any sort, and realizing that the conclave, if it were to function, must have some operating budget, I got the representatives of all the colleges to vote in a voluntary ten-dollar student tax. This would be put directly on their bill and collected by the university treasurer. But it would then be put into a fund for the conclave. Three dollars would buy the yearbook, the *Archive,* and make certain its continuance. A dollar would give every student a subscription to the *Billiken.* One dollar would be given to the university sodality. And the conclave would have five dollars for its operational expenses.

With a sigh I laid down my professorial status—though in truth I had never been more than an instructor. I walked away from the conclave and the Bachelors. The Bachelors promptly folded. Other spontaneous social clubs took its place, and the coming of the university woman to the campus made all the difference. But after struggles and sags and brief collapses the conclave took a firm grip on the university life and, when I pick up a current issue of the *University News,* I find it still operating successfully. The period of transition was, you see, rapidly melting into the period of the much more modern university. I was a weak link between the old and the new.

The fact that we had put on two musical shows was enough to create a tradition for the university. *Full Steam Ahead* and

Rouge and Rapid Fire had set a precedent. My second year teaching, I discovered that Frank Quinn was much too busy with his own students at St. Ignatius. Indeed, we had written a new version of *Full Steam Ahead* which he put on with a vigorous and talented Chicago cast. He had no time for the writing of a new musical score. So I did as many a producer has done before: I built up a new story and book, took the best of the songs out of our two preceding productions, added, with music by Frank Quinn, "Tiger Rose" and "Land of a Thousand Smiles," and presented *Over and Back*. It was a story based on the ending of the war and the collegians who went to Europe from class and came back wiser and slightly older men. Incidentally, we later sold "Land of a Thousand Smiles" to a musical publishing company which in the somnambulent fashion of all music publishers buried it in its files.

What a cast that student body handed me in those days!

There was Alphonse McMahon with his lovely baritone voice and his beautiful stage presence, who went on to become Admiral McMahon, medical aid to President Truman at the Potsdam Conference and then chief of staff at St. John's Hospital; and Lester O'Keefe, who turned professional and became one of the directors of NBC's better shows; and Lester O'Halloran, who died much too early as a great physician in Chicago; and Larry Clark, who is now a top pediatrician in Toledo; and Joe Hardy, now head of the obstetrical department of St. Louis University Medical School; and Hamilton Thornton, a leading St. Louis newspaperman.

Into our show walked the redoubtable Jimmie Conzelman, who did one of the trickiest dances I've ever seen, anticipating the way he would, on the Great Lakes teams and then in professional football, dance to touchdowns along the gridiron. Today he is one of the country's outstanding sports commentators, and a very popular after-dinner speaker. And Elmer Freimuth, now a nose-and-throat specialist in St. Louis, who stopped the show with his golden violin. And Ed Butler, who for years was my stage manager for our amateur shows and for himself manager of a dozen different professional shows and theaters.

But the year 1920, my final year as a formal teacher, offered me one of those rare opportunities which must be seized swiftly or lost forever. The university was celebrating its centenary. To celebrate the event, a campaign was planned to gather the then-enormous sum of two million dollars. I could see that the campaign needed the kind of show I felt we could do. But would the university agree?

In 1914 St. Louis, the city, had set a new pattern in civic entertainment and celebration by producing on Forest Park's Art Hill the first great pageant and masque. Percy Mackaye and Thomas Wood Stevens collaborated with the best of St. Louis talent to produce a show which set the standard for other cities and has been indefinitely copied since then. I had seen it with a thrill of approval; and now I dared dream that on a smaller scale we might produce a spectacle which would tell the story of the university and its beautiful history and bright promise for the city and the community. Without too much hope, I drew my plans. But Father Robison, whose lips were still shaped to say yes to any reasonable project, decided this was reasonable. I could do the show, provided I did not lose money or become delinquent in any of my normal duties to the students and the school. It took the courage and energy of youth to accept the conditions. The show was just something added to the rest of my normal assignments. But Jesuit scholastics are supposed to be built for heavy duty. When my father once in a jocose mood suggested to Father John Furay, president of Loyola University in Chicago, that the Jesuit course be speeded up, the Jesuit shook his head and with a twinkle in his usually austere eye said, "No indeed, Mr. Lord. We have a lot of work to get out of those young scholastics before we ordain them." They both laughed; I knew they were close to truth.

So we plunged into preparations for *Alma Mater,* the St. Louis University centennial pageant. It was my first experience in gathering a large cast and all the technical units necessary for a major production, writing the text, assembling the music, supervising the dances, and watching the show through to presentation.

My chief piece of providential good luck was finding precisely the actress who could be the very spirit and reincarnation of the university. She had come for two or three of my classes for nuns held at Maryville's parochial school; and when I began the casting, I knew that I would never be satisfied with anyone for the role of Alma Mater except Miriam Benoist. She had exactly what would represent the spirit of a university—beauty, dignity, a gracious manner, a deeply tender voice, and great acting ability. So through my very good friend, Mrs. William K. Morrison, who was helping me assemble the cast, I approached her. Would she please play the dramatic role of the university? She hesitated. Her plans called for a return to her farm in Virginia where "an onion patch is waiting for me and I have horses to be exercised." But the university needed her to represent it before the public on the occasion of its birthday; and in the end she stayed, and when in the finale the lights came up upon her, in a gown of the university colors, blue and white, her golden hair crowned with a diadem, and a faint smile on her face, the audience reacted with applause which was part tribute to the university and part to the girl who had represented it in vivid and memorable fashion.

The presentation of the birthday show at the Odeon for a series of nights combined with the establishment of the conclave to round off my days as a teaching scholastic. Ahead of me was a holiday, the first part of which I spent in fairly exhausted sleep. And then loomed the quiet and mental activity of theology. It had been three busy years; three wonderful years; three years when I had learned in the ruthless but invigorating school of experience; three years when I had served a great university gladly in the vigor of my willing youth; three years that I could never possibly forget, and for which I can never be sufficiently grateful.

Often I have heard people protest that the training of the Society of Jesus might well be cut. "Why not drop out the days when the young man is halted on his way to the priesthood to work as a teacher in your schools?" Please heaven, that will never happen. When for any reason one of the Jesuit scholastics must pass up that period of teaching, I feel a pity for him. Indeed, in talking to our diocesan priests I beg them to spend some time teaching. They are lucky if they are assigned to a high school or even can deal with youngsters in small catechism classes. There is no way to learn that compares with traveling the path of an interested teacher. And I am convinced that my years as a young teaching scholastic were years of intense personal growth, of learning the trick of dealing with people, of expanding my own knowledge of my fellows, of seeing the relationship between the theories of education and the very different job which is making people want to learn. I gathered unforgettable friends. I worked better and more closely with my fellow Jesuits than perhaps ever again. I knew what it meant to experience community of interest as with my fellow scholastics we devoted ourselves in genuine generosity to our school. My love of books became a new motive for sharing that love. And I was perforce obliged to learn how to handle money, to woo men into organizational operations, to make students work without resenting the work, and to turn wholeheartedly whatever slight talents God had given me into the service of others.

I envy young scholastics who begin their years of teaching.

I hope and pray that they may know the happiness which was mine far up on the fourth floor of the faculty building of St. Louis University. I used to climb those long flights a dozen times a day and always hurry back with eagerness and alacrity. For the work was wonderful and people were delightful and the service of God was full of joy.

TO SOME PLEASANT TEACHING SISTERS

Dear Sisters:

That was a sudden and convenient thunderstorm which opened our students' convention the other day, wasn't it? It forced our Jesuit superiors to lift cloister briefly, so that I had the pleasure of leading you through the living quarters of the Jesuits of St. Louis University. Of course, in proper nun fashion, you most carefully kept custody of the eyes. But you were not completely fooling the Jesuits who regarded you in surprise and amusement as you passed. I think your guardian angels smiled a bit when you could not help that quick glance into the Jesuit recreation room with its book-lined walls and its atmosphere of stale tobacco smoke. You could not fail to notice that some of the doors of the living rooms were slightly ajar; back of them, no doubt, mysterious Jesuits were living what there is of their private lives.

Once we had you safely out of the cloudburst and into the College Church, the rain with a sense of humor stopped. I think that providence intended you to have that detour through precincts normally reserved for Jesuits, very male and very traditional in their customs and association. Much before the public, the Jesuits relish the quiet of their slight time in cloister.

I imagine you were the only ladies who have ever walked down those corridors. But we just had to get you undrenched into the opening Mass of the convention, so superiors made their swift decision, suspended cloister, and gave you the unusual opportunity of going backstage.

Hollywood some time ago did a picture version of Emmet Lavery's Jesuit drama, *The First Legion*. The producers wanted to know exactly what a Jesuit house would look like. So they sent their scene supervisors on a tour of important Jesuit houses. They searched for a typical Jesuit recreation room, library, chapel, and private room. After much rubbing of chins and flashing of bulbs and comparing of notes, the scouts reported that none of the Jesuit houses were sufficiently Jesuitical. None of them looked the way a Jesuit house ought to look. They did not live up to their images in the popular imagination.

So Hollywood tore up the snaps that had been made and drew up designs for their own sets. These turned out to be a cross between Grand Central Station, a Benedictine chapter room, the main room of the First National Bank, tessellated overtones of Metro-Gothic-Mayer. When we Jesuits saw how we were supposed to live, we breathed wistful sighs and wondered what had happened to Jesuit architecture somewhere in the dim days of forgotten history.

Some years earlier still, René Fulop-Miller, a non-Catholic, wrote a book called *The Power and Secret of the Jesuits*. It made us out to be very powerful and very secret indeed. Most of us had to admit that we didn't find ourselves that way at all. It was rather a rehash of the traditions which puzzle us Jesuits, largely because they never seem to flow into our communities.

Since recently I wrote to a young priest-educator about the early days of my education, and since I feel you must have some curiosity about the Jesuits who set themselves to teach so many of you teaching nuns, I am taking this letter to talk, not about Jesuit educational training in general, but about what I found for my own mind when I had left brash, hustling Chicago for the studious calm and cloistered elms of St. Stanislaus Seminary in the lush Florissant Valley.

To religious like yourselves much of it will be old hat. After all, much of our training is exactly what any young religious, male or female, goes through.

The casual reader might do well to skip this chapter. For to my regret the Jesuits have no secrets imparted to them in darkened chapels while the candles flicker in the damp breeze blowing up from subterranean dungeons. The *arcana* of the Jesuits is—or are—pure invention of the predecessors of those imaginative creators of Superman, Tarzan, and Mandrake the Magician. At no place along the line does the superior summon you to a secret study back of the heavier books, which swing outward at the touch of a hidden button, to put you on your knees, bid you swear never to mention the events about to follow, and then, in hushed tone and with bated breath, let you in on what's really going to be your life. I doubt if any of them would even know how to bate breath.

Anyhow, it is not too easy to make exciting to the reader the record of long years of intellectual training. Einstein is a pretty exciting person, and with his hair standing electrically on end a fairly exciting-looking man. Who could make dramatic the story of how he got his mastery of mathematics, and how he could make relativity go into its dance? The career of a great physician is colorful; his years of study make dull enough reading.

The seminary training which makes up much of Jesuit studies is like that required for all future priests. Indeed, the laws of the Church leave little of this training to chance. The seminarians of every land and every race for a good many generations have been trained and will be trained with the same studies, with much the same type of texts, and for the same professional pursuits and a certain uniformity of priestly personality and character. Jesuits are religious with the novitiate training required of future religious; they are in the main to be priests who go through the studies of future priests.

Father John Talbot Smith half a century ago wrote a series of papers on what he thought the seminary of the future would be like. Evidently he was five centuries ahead of his day. Seminary training steadily advances and the training of priests constantly improves; but seminaries are still a long way from the idyllic blend of spirituality, apostolic zeal, social awareness, and fluent eloquence that he envisioned. But then, who has ever put into effect Newman's idea of a university?

The reaction of each young Jesuit to his training is completely distinctive. He remains highly individualized despite the easy conviction that all Jesuits bear a common stamp. Nothing has ever amused me more than the glib historic cliché, "All Jesuits are alike. They are all cast in the same mold." I've heard it said parrotlike in roomfuls of Jesuits so individualistic that you'd think the most surface observer would be puzzled to find what single factor binds them together. Ten years ago, in my own small organization, my fellow Jesuits made up a staff of the most completely specialized interests, the widest differences of disposition, temperaments that were hard to blend into a harmonious chord, and methods and manners that never had lost the flavor of the family backgrounds from which they came.

Actually, the long years of training give us common ideals and a loyalty to historic methods. But they seem also to accentuate the things which make us unlike.

So if you care to follow me in this swift journey through what were almost frighteningly swift years, please tag along. I shall lead you as I did through the cloistered corridors briefly uncloistered to save you from the thundershower outside.

At twenty-one I entered the Society of Jesus with highly cloudy ideas about the life I was accepting. But I was familiar with the popular legends of Jesuit intellectual attainment, though I certainly had not found it always justified by the teachers who taught me. Sister Mary Blanche and I once discussed the long period of Jesuit training. "Imagine," I said in youthful admiration, "the string of degrees that might follow their names if they took degrees." "After their names," she said primly and in the blind loyalty of some kindly nuns, "they write the most wonderful degree, S.J. So they need no other." That left me without comeback, even had I not been silently agreeing.

The result of too much praise from their friends and too much blame from their foes has been to create an almost fictional Jesuit. We are praised too much and damned too much. Some place in between lie the Jesuits whom I came to know as I reached the novitiate and became that very first day one of them.

The tradition of our very great learning rose out of a number of factors, I have decided for myself with the years. First there was the devotion of Jesuits to the classic ideals. Ignatius founded his order at a time when the Renaissance had created the dream of the universal man, the man whose mind was in the present but whose heart was in the classic past, who knew the great writings of the great cultural nations and was creating a new literature for the lands around him. Ignatius, himself no scholar, had the admiration which many a man without deep education has for men of real scholarship. He attracted learned men as only practical men can do. They trusted themselves, in their impractical devotion to learning, to his organizational skill. And he put them out for the world to see and admire. They spoke brilliantly before the courts and argued eloquently with believer and new heretic. They opened classrooms that soon were jammed with thousands. Where other men concerned themselves with practical affairs, they lived in the more rarefied atmosphere of ancient wisdom and its modern manifestations.

Ignatius knew, too, that the keen pseudotheologians of the Reformation and the reformers who made great protestation of high morality must be met with the double counterattack of saints and scholars. He aimed at high sanctity among his men. But as high sanctity is harder to attain than high scholarship, he demanded of those early Jesuits a profound learning, great knowledge of the Scriptures, and a zest for theology which the Church had not known since the days of the writers of *summas*.

To the classicists and the theologians were swiftly added the new scientists. This was largely the result of the missionary spirit of the Society of Jesus. The mere journeying to foreign lands gave the missionaries an enlargement of mind, a perception of lands and people with their laws and governments and customs of which western civilization had only vague notions. The Chinese and the Japanese, caring little for the classics, wanted instead mathematicians, watchmakers, men who could make a lens and explain the world about them, guides to the stars above and cataloguers of the plants and animals. So Jesuits were by turn missionaries and mathematicians to the Chinese emperor and to the mikado. They became astronomers-in-ordinary to pagan lords. For the delight of frivolous European monarchs and the spellbinding of the childlike pagans Athanasius Kircher invented the magic lantern. And the Jesuit reputation for science grew.

Later I shall take time to write a bit of my spiritual Odyssey. Now I am playing pedagogue as I lead you into the intellectual training that was mine as a Jesuit. But let me confess my surprise when in my novitiate I heard with amazement of the dumb oxen among famous Jesuits. Not merely the Dominicans could brag that their Aquinas had once been a dullard. The Society took satisfaction in deflating in its new members any haughty arrogance they might feel about a reputation for scholarship. My novice master told us how dull a student Pierre Jean de Smet had been, or the great Arnold Damen. We were taught to admire St. Alphonsus Rodriguez, the porter at the door whose concentration on God was so intense that he often seemed to play the simpleton. A favorite story concerned the ill-mated missionary couple, the brilliant preacher whose eloquence charmed a city and the lay brother companion who sat unnoticed on the pulpit steps, until the trumpet blast of an angel hailed the unseen brother as the source of the multiplied conversions.

Two years were meant for things of the spirit rather than things of the mind. One of my fellow novices, deeply in love with English style, did not surprise us too much when he protested to the novice master that he could not possibly spend forty-five minutes a day in spiritual reading. "That dreadful translation of the Spanish ascetic, Rodriguez! Two years of that and I shall have destroyed my English style." Yet, lest a concentration on the rules of holiness and the lives of the saints deflect future teachers and classicists from the love of words, an hour a day was promptly assigned to a refurbishing of our Latin and our Greek. We began at the very start, as if we were boys from the first year of high school. But we were challenged to move as rapidly as possible, to cover ground with ever-accelerating strides. And a sort of silent competition in racing through the fundamentals created among us an unacknowledged but very real sporting spirit, with the dead languages for our race course and no one but ourselves to pass down the decisions on who won.

On my very brief visit to Oxford University I learned that we had long practiced what was a great scholarly tradition. To obtain a degree in some of the great Oxford colleges a student need only take up residence at the college, pass final examinations, and eat a required and stipulated number of dinners in the great common dining halls. Some venerable tradition had linked food and examinations as the essentials of scholarship.

Only in the retrospect of years could a person measure the education which comes simply by being tossed into the ranks of fifty-seven dissimilar young fellows, studying with them in a common room, eating and praying side by side, elbows touching, sharing the order of a day, moving to the command of jangling bells, and ending the day in a dormitory where the beds formed long, cold, formal ranks as in some spiritual barracks.

The fifty-seven novices around me, of whom thirty-eight were of my year, had come mostly from the cities of the Middle West. A few of us brought our bachelor degrees along. All must have finished four years of Latin and two of Greek. Some had been teachers who had done a period or two of instructing in Jesuit schools. And when you said this and added that they all came under the impulse of the Holy Spirit and in an amazing spirit of self-devotion, you had touched on the only points of similarity among them. The rule and custom of the novitiate made it impossible to select the companions who were similar in background, disposition, or tastes. Each noon and each evening I found myself walking with what were called "assigned companions," two of them. We strolled in threes; it was not permitted to wander off with a single companion. And for two years one got the amazing education which consisted in being obliged to talk with men entirely different in almost everything, except a common dream of becoming good Jesuits. On a campus students clot together in an instinct which leads them to seek out those who reflect their own views of life, their own social conditions or ambitions, but here we walked with those whom chance and obedience assigned us. It was an amazing education all in itself. When one had learned to talk to fifty-six other young men and listen sympathetically to what concerned them, one had gained a great deal of sheer insight into human character and had circled a small but fairly complete universe.

And three times a day we followed the Oxford custom of eating together. Education progressed apace.

With the taking of our first vows, we were precipitated into the atmosphere of the juniorate: an intense calm, yet an excited leisure with time to study and much too much to be studied, a sense that the past was more vital and current than any newspaper headline, a coming to life of dead languages, an intimate companionship with authors dead for milleniums, a feeling that only the classic is contemporaneous, a resurrection of dead heroes and beauties, a summoning up of Troy and Athens and Rome till the sky line of nearby St. Louis lost its interest and we walked peacefully around the walls of civilizations and cities long since dust.

The juniorate was two years of intense study of what Ignatius and the modern pedagogue call the humanities, the study of man as recorded by men. Much was repetition to a young Jesuit who already had his arts degree; but there was a vital difference—a strange quality called zest, a sudden appetite for learning, a determination not to slip through culture, shaking off any stray drops that fell upon the shoulders, but to soak it up, to make it part of the blood stream. The class moved at a reasonable pace. The better-prepared and the more ambitious were dared to read fast and furiously. The hotly contested interclass games on the fields and the courts were far less exciting than the news that Mark Gross, former all-Kansas halfback, had just completed the entire works of Shakespeare, and that a minor genius named Leo Keeler had read Homer through for the second time, this trip without the need for referring more than three times to the unabridged Greek dictionary.

The faculty was small but devoted. Father Matthew Germing was a scholar who, stepping out of the normal course of Jesuit training, had been sent to Johns Hopkins University to take his doctorate in Latin. He loved the language and touched it with an affection that made the ancients seem the dear friends of his personal boyhood. Father Gilbert Garraghan was to become the outstanding historian of life in the Mississippi Valley; at that time he was leading us through the English classics, less as a teacher than as a guide who pointed out the books to be read and let the books speak for themselves.

Some strange fate had tripped me up again in my effort to master Greek. My hard luck started when a stretch of sickness kept me out of class at the very time when the others were getting the foundations of the language in St. Ignatius High School. After my return I had tried to follow along with the speeding class; but I was flying without wings and walking without feet, and translating without the necessary nouns and verbs. All through my college course I had passed the examinations by the complicated process of memorizing a pony. When I had a little time in the novitiate I settled down and memorized long Greek vocabularies, hoping through the accumulation of hundreds of Greek words to learn to read the Greek classics.

Then as I came to the juniorate, keen to relish the wonderful language that had given us the first great drama, the world's most completely unforgettable poets, and oratory at its most resounding, I ran into an educational experimentalist. He loved Greek, or so he said. But he had his own system for teaching it. Sitting at his desk, he read beautiful English translations while we sat with the Greek texts before us. It was altogether delightful. He read exquisitely. And as the rhythm of the excellent English fell upon our ears, we forgot to follow the Greek. In a semester I had lost all the Greek words I had so painfully memorized. I had listened to the English version of some Greek words. But of Greek each day I was learning less and less. Though today I am very fond of authentic Greek food and patronize Greek restaurants in strange cities, I order my meals from the English side of the menu, and listen wistfully while the waiter sings out my order in the lovely language of Homer, Plato, Pindar, and Aristophanes.

Well, the royal road of learning is not particularly exciting to tour in someone else's travelogue. It is hard to explain the thrill of finally catching the point and value of the three dramatic unities. It is difficult to show how a young fellow who had delighted in the theater of Shaw and Cohan and Pinero and Ibsen and Victor Herbert now sat enthralled with the slow unfolding of Victorian novels and the measured beat of classic verse. I used to stand in the midst of the riches which are contained in those generous purses known as books and sway under the pull of a dizzying series of attractions. Great thoughts of the great minds of the ages of history were mine for the taking, and I took in eager gulps, with much consequent indigestion, and not nearly the assimilation which I should have liked. My mental basal metabolism was not up to the vigor of my intake. I was not as yet aware that culture cannot be forced and the mastery of the masters cannot be crammed into a matter of months.

With the coming of Father Edward Bergin we were introduced to the university lecture method, and I learned one of life's important lessons. He was a real bookman. If he mentioned poetry, he followed the noun with every definition that had ever been given by any author worth noticing. He divided and subdivided the kinds of poetry and rattled off the names of poems which exemplified each. He talked in a droning but uninterrupted tone hour on end, and I sat, listening delightedly, feeling that I savored scholarship, and convinced that listening was the same thing as learning. When the course was over and examinations impended, I suddenly discovered that out of the course I had retained precisely nothing. My mind was a twelfth or thirteenth carbon copy, blurred, indistinct, with the words all running together and no clue to their meaning.

In an agony of apprehension I dashed to the library and boned up on books which gave me in synoptic form enough to pass an examination on poetry. But his classes were almost a total loss. I had forgotten the lesson faintly glimpsed in college days, that a good class has three elements: a satisfactory teacher, an attentive student, and *reaction.* I had had the first two; the third was entirely missing. From that hour on, I never attended any class without a notebook and a poised pencil. I became the delight and the despair of a lecturer. For my teachers soon came to know that one student in front of them was taking down everything they said. If the teacher was good, he was overjoyed at the compliment of my attention. If he was not good, he knew very well that I was making a record of his messy order, his muddy statements, and the fact that he had not mastered his material or organized it in convincing style. The lecturers knew too that I would bolt from their classrooms to make a fresh copy of the notes, and that, if there were a repetition asked on the next day, I was ready to give them back almost everything that they had given us on the preceding day.

I have often passed along this simple approach to reaction, and begged students to follow the lead. In my own classes I as a teacher demanded no less. To the classes of others I could only suggest the essential third element of good teaching—that the pupil be himself alive when the lecturer talks.

As always, I was rushing off into the fields of the cocurricular. The classes of the juniorate were encouraged to form themselves into informal and collateral groups. I shall talk later of the Five W's, the We Will Write Won't We? club out of which came a number of Jesuit writers. For a series of Sunday afternoons we produced scenes from Shakespeare. Sir Henry Irving, Richard Mansfield, Otis Skinner, and the other dramatic stalwarts of that day did not need to tremble for their spot in the center of the limelight; but we thought we were good and our audiences were kind—and it was great practice.

We matched the oratory of the great with debates among ourselves. We studied the classic essays and ourselves produced essays in the characteristic styles of the great. And, in the logrolling fashion later popularized at the Algonquin Hotel, we paid our friends to listen to what we had written with the guarantee that we would listen appreciatively to what they had produced. Walks were interrupted on holidays while we sat under trees, not unlike those of the Forest of Arden, to read poetry to one another. We paired off of a Sunday afternoon to preach to each other. We took turns being preacher and congregation, and a more persuasive preacher and a more critical and hardhearted congregation never faced up to each other. Twice in the year we juniors wrote and produced a full-length play for the community's entertainment; sometimes it was entertaining, sometimes it made a brave effort at entertaining. During the Christmas holidays we had a week of festivities in which we parodied the classics in absurd dramatic burlesques, did topical sketches that laughed at the mishaps and small misadventures of the community, and carried on the classic tradition of satire for the easiest audience that ever assembled to be amused and remained to roar with laughter.

I feel a little frustrated as I try to put into sentences the delight I had found in this new revelation of great literature. The minds and hearts of the most wonderful dreamers and thinkers all seemed to be opened for my personal revelation. I had always liked books; now I loved them. Learning to squeeze the juice from the fruits of Parnassus was fun and adventuring. The world that surrounded me was as if it did not exist. The dream world, the ivory tower, the cloistered garden for which scholars sigh, was mine. I did not become even a passable scholar. But I knew a little of the delights of scholarship; and from that hour great books were to be well-remembered friends and dear comrades of the road.

For a time I thought that the typhoid which we picked up during a summer picnic had ended my forward press toward education. I did not realize that my year on *The Queen's Work,* of which more later, was a time when I was learning the art of making books. I was printer's devil and copy boy and manuscript editor and on occasion author and sub-sub-editor. All to my own delight and further growth.

I warned you, my dear sisters, that this chapter—this letter—might make dull reading. The warmup before a race is not the race. The long hours of rehearsal before the play are not the drama. The grilling scrimmage is no equivalent for the thrill of matched play. And the years that go into the making of a Jesuit are not the Jesuit in action. Forgive me if my retelling of the days of preparation lacks color and drama. Perhaps they may seem the gray dreams of an old-timer. Perhaps they may seem exaggerations, badly remembered in tranquillity. Skip if you wish. For me, this chapter is important. I write it largely in tribute to the Society of Jesus, which does not believe its men should be sent out to do the work of the Lord ill trained and badly equipped. It is a task of personal gratitude.

My very good friend, inexorable critic, and model in the pursuit of philosophy, Father Robert Bakewell Morrison, seems to feel that I praise philosophy too much. I am sure he is convinced that I have the Socratic error: that truth is goodness and that the man who knows is therefore the man of virtue.

Perhaps in self-defense I may merely plead that the three years of philosophy and science were for me a high plateau, a series of mountain peaks, along the road of learning. I was blessed with excellent teachers. The full year of philosophy under Father Gleeson had prepared me to appreciate what was offered me. I seemed to have more time, more leisure, more calm of mind, than I ever was to know again. And somehow the bright clear light of philosophy shone for me with a warmth and a beckoning friendliness that has never quite faded.

Perhaps incorrectly I have thought the years during which I studied philosophy the best intellectual years of my life. Again and again, talking to young religious, I have begged them to get their philosophy thoroughly. You may not be able to talk religion to the pagan; you can go far along the road of truth in company with philosophy. He may resist the revelation of Christ; he finds the light of reason illuminating. He may object to religious truth; he finds it harder to struggle against the truth that comes from reason and the human intellect.

The thing that struck me when once more I plowed the fields of philosophy was the amazing unity and consistency of what I was learning. Philosophy, for which I had been prepared by the cold, logical approach of "Paw" Gleeson, seemed more and more the structural steel of life's edifice. It was the blueprint of human existence. It laid out a clear road map for man's progress. I liked the fact that what religion had taught, philosophy strongly affirmed. It was good to find the Supreme Being and the soul and immortality and free will searched out by Plato and Aristotle and Socrates as they were taken for granted by the clear-minded Christ.

I do not pretend to have become in any sense a profound philosopher. Indeed, I was often shamed by the depths my classmates reached; young Steve Rueve used to startle me by seeing difficulties which I had completely missed, and finding significant nuances of truth that I had not even glimpsed. I can only claim that philosophy became part of my normal way of thinking. To me it explained the world and life and myself and the complex relationships in which I constantly have found myself. It was the answer to fundamental morals, though certainly not the strength necessary for living as a moral man. It vaulted to the heavens and went into the atom before scientists began to break up the atom to the peril of civilization and the strange, wistful hope for a new and splendid future. It made truth and error luminously clear. It set the mind in a gymnasium and playing field of thought, where it could exercise muscles it had not suspected it possessed, and grow supple and accurate and sure-footed and skillful of hand. (My figures of speech are piling a little too high and looking a little too rickety. If you have shared the enlightenment of training in scholastic philosophy, you are following me even as I mix and muddle my figures of speech.)

At any rate, I had three wonderful years. Logic appealed to me, for I already had my dreams of some day writing. Ontology, which went right to the root of everything, was a new revelation in analysis. It was a deeply spiritual experience to lay God and man in the same theses, and grow to wonder at God and to marvel at His condescension to man.

The start of my second year threw me into the orbit of Father Hubert Gruender, who opened for me the world of the soul. He was an excellent rational psychologist, but he had done considerable work in experimental psychology, about which there was nothing like the common talk with which the modern has grown familiar. I found his rapid-fire blend of German, English, and Latin fascinating. He had a weird sense of humor which resulted often from his honest but completely wrong use of American slang. After a few days he commissioned me to sit in the front seat directly under his nose and note every mistake he made in the use of the American language. Wisely, he aimed at speaking American rather than English; and though I set myself faithfully to the task of spotting and reporting his slaughter of the idiom, he so fascinated me with the way in which he discussed mind and soul and spirit and will (I speak vaguely as if all these were completely distinct) that I forgot I was supposed to be sleuthing his grammatical errors.

His approach to psychology is one that I have often used since with young people. For almost two solid weeks he set himself to lay before us all the wild, wrong, misleading, half-correct arguments against the spirituality of a man's soul. He went after free will and human responsibility. He built up a terrific case against the soul, leaving us at the end of every class feeling pretty limp and helpless. I had many a questioning of myself during those days. Here I had come to the Jesuits in the hope of saving my soul and working for the souls of others; and it looked dangerously as if souls were a figment of the poet's fancy, wiped out by the science and philosophy of the modern age.

At the end of this period of blasting, he sat back in his chair to grin at us with mischief in his eyes.

"There!" he cried triumphantly. "I have destroyed your souls. You are mere animals, slaves to the laws of chemistry and biology, the end resultant of chance, without dignity or destiny. How do you like yourselves?" His grin grew into a sort of parody of the diabolic. "If," he continued, leaning forward closer to us and speaking out of his own personal experience in European universities, "if you were in many a modern university, you would be left right at that point, soulless automata, spiritless links in a brute evolution. Now, if you will sit back and relax, we shall begin something quite different. We shall prove to you that you have a spiritual soul, analyze and discuss its qualities, and put you back on your feet headed for a glorious immortality."

And that was the rest of the year.

Perhaps nothing surprised me more than the way in which my philosophy course took time out to present the philosophy of those who opposed scholasticism and the bases on which Christian thinking rested. In cosmology we spent weeks in analysis of evolution, studying the various systems (most of us had come to class thinking that Darwin had fathered the system and given it its only popularity), sifting out what might well be so and drawing a line where fact ended and theory began. Cosmology bothered me. I realized that I did not know enough chemistry and physics to be able intelligently to follow a discussion of how matter is put together and what makes the world tick. But I found the old Greek theory of matter and form fascinating, and it has been one of the great basic concepts which have influenced my far from deep but always interested approach to most of life.

Years later, as a train whirled me across mid-America, I talked with the president of a Methodist theological seminary. To my complete amazement what he wanted from me was an explanation of the scholastic theory of matter and form. I scraped the bottom of my shallow barrel to give him all that I could recall of the theory and what I had learned of the application of that theory to everything from painting to the sacraments, from government to human marriage. At the end he invited me to come and lecture to his Methodist seminarians, an invitation I regret I never got the chance to accept.

The final year brought me theodicy, and I found it a glorious subject—the struggle of the thinkers to penetrate the gates of heaven and come into the dim presence of God who shines in theology; the effort of man to make God his proper subject for study and research. Simultaneously we faced the problems of right and wrong, of human conduct in its great basic aspects, and the relationships of a man to his fellow man.

While the year I had spent at St. Ignatius with Father Gleeson had prepared me for all that these three years were to give, many of my fellow Jesuit students found the beginnings of philosophy a terrifying journey through dense thickets and against rushing streams of thought. One, who later became a brilliant professor along other lines and a charming public speaker to popular audiences, was so baffled by it all that he wandered the corridors of our house of philosophy as if one of the roof timbers had dropped on his head. That was my personal good luck. I offered early in our first year to study with him and coach him. He accepted gratefully, though the favor was from him to me. For I had hit upon the best possible way to study, to learn, and to retain forever. Following my recently discovered system, I paid the strictest possible attention in class. I took down faithfully the lectures of the professors, and rushing to my room after class, immediately copied them into permanent form. To these I added a careful synopsis of the texts and required reading of auxiliary books. And I made a carbon for my fellow student.

Indeed, in a short time a number of my friends had taken up the slogan invented by a very brilliant young philosopher, Remi Belleperche, "Carbon me, kid!" So my typewriter took a bulk of carbons and thin paper, and I was distributing them among the friends who found them helpful. The more profound scholars regarded them with a bit of rightful disdain. Those who knew something of struggle found them some slight aid.

Then, with special permission, each morning and late each afternoon I went to the private room of my associate and carefully went through the preceding day's lectures and the textbook assignment. He was quick, and my simpler presentation reached him. Once he said, in what was a quotation from a well-remembered German student, "I find philosophy hard because I haven't an abstract mind. You see, I have a concrete head." But selfishly, this was all the best possible opportunity for me. I was not merely a student seated in the benches; for two half hours a day, morning and afternoon, I was an instructor with an alert and interested class of one. And the double approach to philosophy meant that I got it with a thoroughness possible in very few other ways.

Because this was so good for me and not, I regret to admit, in any spirit of fraternal charity, I had begun a system which I continued until the end of my Jesuit training. In theology I teamed up with a young man to whom the doctors had calmly announced that he was losing his eyesight. He must not read or use his eyes beyond a minimum. So I did his reading and his writing, and each day put in an hour coaching him in all that he might have had to dig out for himself. It was wonderful for me, and it took him successfully through the difficult course. Incidentally, to the surprise and scientific bafflement of the doctors, his eyesight steadily improved, he went on to be a highly successful college dean and finally the president of a Jesuit college. The privilege of coaching him had given me a first-rate grip on my own theology.

During that final year of philosophy I tried something else. Would it be possible, I mused, to turn this abstract but fascinating subject matter into a form understandable by the man in the street? I had come remotely into the orbit of the famous Father Joseph Conroy, later one of the great deans of men at Loyola in Chicago. He taught the other half of poetry and rhetoric class, and I missed his magnificent training by an accident of fate. (Most unphilosophical expression, that, but I use it just for convenience.) He loved the concrete, the picture word. And he despised foggy thinking. Once when he asked a student to prove the existence of God to a motorman on a Chicago streetcar, the student used a form of argument for which Father Conroy evinced the greatest contempt. "That argument is useless, futile, false. What's wrong with it?" The young man thought that he saw his error. "I think it is a vicious circle," said he, proudly mentioning a famous form of bad argument. Father Conroy clasped his forehead in both hands. "So you'd tell that motorman that you were wrong; that you found you had been using a vicious circle! Don't you know that the only vicious circle with which he is acquainted is a prize-fight ring?"

Under the remote influence of this man and spurred on by my memory of Claude Pernin's "Make it picturesque; make your readers see it," I decided to enter on an experiment. Would it be possible for me to translate the terms and explanations and proofs of philosophy into simple and vivid words? Could I make a rushing reader understand the big high lights of scholastic philosophy? Patiently I tried. At the end of the year I had finished a series of short chapters that covered most of the big factors of a three-year course. These I mailed to Father Richard Tierney of *America,* and to my delight he published them and later issued them in a small book which he allowed me to call *Armchair Philosophy.* I still hear from people who have read it. I still am sure that because I forced myself to write it, philosophy for me became not a thing of cloister, library, and study, but of the streets, the countryside, and the town.

Since I have already inflicted upon you some record of my happy days as a teaching scholastic, you will skip along with me, my dear sisters, not losing your dignity, of course, but gathering a bit of speed, until after three delightful years on the staff of St. Louis University, I find myself in the halls of theology.

The Society of Jesus gave its priests from the earliest days a thorough and exacting course in theology. It believed that a priest must be a master of the sacred sciences. He must know the Scriptures well. He must be the repository of the great tradition of the Catholic Church. He must have walked in the company of the doctors of the Church and listened to the debates of the councils. He must be alert to new developments in faith and practice, of which there are a surprising number, but he must be in touch with the historic past that is rooted in Christ, and through Him in the long and unbroken history of God's revelation to His earth-journeying sons and daughters. A priest without theology would be like a doctor without medicine or a lawyer without law or an engineer without mathematics and physics.

In recent years, thank heaven, theology has ventured out of the seminaries and found its way into Catholic colleges, into Catholic study clubs, and, thanks to the reborn popularity of the *Summa* of St. Thomas, into the lecture halls of universities long alien to Catholic tradition and thinking. Dr. Robert Maynard Hutchins and Dr. Mortimer Adler have done a surprising job for Catholic theology without, to the regret of many, ever getting to know the joy of the full Catholic faith.

I found the first year of theology highly stimulating: apologetics, it was called; the preambles to revelation, a study of the Scriptures as history, of revelation not as a body of truth but an amazing fact in history itself, God's constant dealings with mankind. I had two excellent teachers, both of whom spoke Latin with a fluency that continuously amazed me. We came to see the Church as a great historic fact. We searched it for any possible mistakes it may have made and found no essential teaching and no fundamental practice that it had ever taken up and been obliged in embarrassment to drop. I recall that, at the end of the course, Father Robert Johnston turned to the class and said: "Do you see how anyone, facing this dovetailing of Catholic truth to human instincts, common sense, and the longings of the heart, could doubt it?" I am sure that mine was only one of the heads that nodded in complete agreement.

"I love religion," said a charming actress once; "but I cannot tell you how I hate dogma."

That was as silly as if she had said, "I am fascinated by the beauty of the human body, but I wish it didn't have a skeleton." The human body without that strong structural factor which is the skeleton would be a horrible suet pudding, an unjellied jelly, a building that crashed because it had no steel supports. Dogma in theology is as essential as the great natural laws that underlie science, the powerful codes that make law a unified and protective armor for human living, the findings of the great physicians and surgeons which give medicine its power for our good.

Simultaneously we took two years of dogmatic theology, the teaching of Christ, the revelations of God throughout the course of human history, and the decisions of the Church, speaking with the voice of God; and moral theology, the law of Christ applied to human conduct. I had great teachers and they made theology live. Here was not something that had been thought out in the solitude of the desert or the echoing libraries of the monastery, but something that God's prophets had called out in the cities of the old world, Christ had taught with compelling force from the mountaintop, and men had tried for centuries and found surprisingly common-sense and practical. The question was not what the human mind would be without God's revelation, but how long western civilization could exist if God's teachings and the law of Christ were abandoned and forgotten.

I lived to see two terrible experiments in precisely that—the Nazi paganism of Hitler and the awful movement of that human glacier which is soulless communism. We theorized about it then. I was to see it put into horrible practice within my generation. The theory of Catholic theology was amazingly beautiful. A world that lived without it was terrifyingly horrible.

The last semester of our four years was given over to direct preparation for our final examination.

At the end of each year of philosophy and theology we sat for one hour before a board of four professors who questioned us in an oral examination. At the end of our course in moral theology we were examined minutely on the law of God, and a series of sample confessions were made to us to test our ability as future confessors. The third year of theology terminated in a full hour of difficult quiz. Then the course rounded off in the fourth year when for two solid hours we were expected to be able to explain, present, defend, and know the chief objections against our Catholic theology and the great scholastic philosophy. For this final examination we were allowed four months of preparation. The four months were a time to revel in. No class. Plenty of time. Books at our disposal. Professors whom we could consult. And for me the companionship of my alert-minded if impaired-visioned fellow theologian with whom I rehearsed the entire course of seven years' continuous work. They were delightful days. Never again was I to know that expansive leisure, that immediate incentive to prepare my mind and muster my knowledge for so definite a use.

The third year of novitiate has always interested those who know anything of Jesuits—the return to the simple living of novices, the reburnishing of the soul's inner brightness. I skip that now, for just a final obvious remark. And all my life I have stressed the obvious on the principle that it is the thing most often missed.

When I had finished off the assigned course of Jesuit training, I said to myself, "Well, that's that! I am now what the Jesuit regards as a finished educational product. Education is over."

That is, of course, the most obviously stupid comment a man could make, the most foolishly complacent. I have lived well over a quarter century since I walked from the room of my final examination, pleased that it was ended and glad that the active life of a Jesuit was about to begin. And I doubt if there is a day since that I have not learned. What the Society had given me was not a rounded and complete education, but what it regarded as a sort of minimum. These were the essentials. In my mind the professors and studies had laid a foundation. Life and experience and the constant contact with people would build the structure—provided I cooperated.

So I have felt that everyone I have met and known has been an informal teacher. How can I estimate what I have learned from those thousands of young people for whom I have worked? How can I measure the value to myself of the constant preparation I have made for courses and lectures and sermons and retreats? The need of being keen and alert, to know today's problems as well as yesterday's history, to match the ancient truths to the morning's needs, to say to the young people and the older ones great fundamental facts in such a fashion that, though the truth was eternal, the language and illustrations and comparisons were not older than the last issue of *Time*—that has all been part of the continued education.

To meet and associate with and try to reach the wide gamut of Americans who flow through the life of a priest, that is training of a high order. To travel, to see new people and new cities, to keep scrap paper in one's pocket on which to jot down the interesting and unusual, to move with open eyes and senses alert . . . that is a struggle, and a most rewarding one. The flow of new books never dries up, and a Jesuit has the responsibility for at least noting titles, watching for new authors worth attention, and sensing the currents of what men think worth writing about.

I have lived through the most exciting and parlous times history has ever known. To keep watch on them, to note their almost electrical changes, to measure and evaluate the leaders and the misleaders, to recognize things that seem to be new truths but turn out to be old errors, to be in the currents that sweep along without being swept away by them, to see the shifts of customs and the rise of enthusiasms, the birth of new fears and the dawn of bright hopes—all that is education without pause or possibility of limitation. I cannot but feel that a person who has not been grounded on the rock of truth which Christ established may often be swept off his feet, tossed in a blanket, dropped from the clouds, exploded in the bomb of the moment, or tripped down dark wells. Without conceit and with much deep gratitude I have always felt that during these ages of shift and change, of fashions in thinking and fads in thought, my greatest natural good luck has been the Jesuit training. It has grounded me, given me fixed principles and polar stars. I have not navigated life's currents without a compass. I have not had to guess when Christ meant me to know. Because my thinking followed fixed certainties, I have not merely speculated when speculation became exciting.

God has been good. The Jesuit training has been wonderful. That I have not been far, far better, far more sure for myself and more confident as a guide for others has been, once more, my own fault and my own confessed failure.

TO A YOUNG JESUIT ABOUT TO BE ORDAINED

Dear Vince:

Legend has it that no priest, however skillful with the pen, has written well of his own ordination.

Apparently that is one of the things which God has meant to be kept secret. It is a joy He gives to the individual; He pours out an incredible sense of happiness and power and accomplishment upon the young man, and then makes it impossible for him ever to share it with anyone else. Men have written beautifully of their marriage on the poetic principle of emotion remembered in calm. Women have described the moment when the man of their heart asked them to wed. There have been attempts even to tell the emotions that filled the heart of a nun at the blessed time of her vows. But priests are inarticulate about their ordination.

It is too big. It is too significant. It has such intangible powers which nonetheless turn out to be the most real of all the possible things in life. It is a time when life reaches a climax; it is a kind of vital crossroads, toward which the whole of a preparatory life has been leading and from which the course of an entire career moves rapidly outward. Too much crowds into too little time. The intensity of realization is bigger than the emotions which should accompany it. All sacraments are outward signs of such tremendous inward reactions that they slip away from the pen that tries to capture them. But this is the sacrament which transforms a whole lifetime, which turns a layman into a priest and anoints hands with oil that they may smoothly pour forth blessings.

I do not expect to be able to do what no other priest has done. My approach to the happy hour of ordination is matter-of-fact. But since you are moving toward it yourself, you must read what I write and listen while I talk.

Must listen?

My apologies. You will be generous if you listen to an ancient who looks back wistfully over the years to a great day and the happy times that instantly followed the laying on of the bishop's hands.

After the intense activities of the life lived by a teaching scholastic, theology might be wearisome indeed. The sudden switch from the teacher's rostrum to the scholar's desk, from the professorial power to the student's subjection, is a trial. The longest possible walk is the one I made from the arts college of St. Louis University to the department of theology. In actual measurable feet it was about half a city block. In distance from all I had loved and lived with such intensity for three years, it was the crossing of a chasm of time and space. Once the final year of teaching was ended in June of 1920, I hurried away to the villa for a summer of leisure not altogether unwelcome after the delightfully exhausting labors of my scholastic teaching days. I came back to the university to find myself parked in a small room over West Pine Boulevard. Actually, I should have been relegated to the fourth floor; but one of the older men asked me to trade with him. He had fallen in love with a small under-the-eaves room, and when assigned to the noisy second-floor room he offered an exchange. For the next four years I lived there, with the rush of traffic pouring beneath me, with the tires whining and the brakes grinding and the gears creating strange, reassuring noises, and the children from the parochial school passing at noon to call to me and wave to me and keep me from submerging in the tomes that piled like building blocks on my desk. (Oh, how mixed I can get my figures of speech! Now I'm submerging in building material, a rough form of swimming!)

The spot in which I spent my years of theology was a little typical of the whole of my life. My room opened on the peace and silence of a Jesuit house of study. The windows opened on the fast currents of West Pine Boulevard, the Moose Club which staged parties lasting far into the night, two down-at-the-heel but enormous boarding houses in front of which parked jittery jalopies and through which raced tribes of transients. As so often in life, I was caught between the charm of cloistered studiousness and the rush and tumble of life.

But my separation from the arts college was as complete as if I had been moved to Bogotá in the Republic of Colombia. (That had been one of the theologates that had impended over my head. I never knew just why that threat was not fulfilled.) As a theologian I saw none of the boys whom I had taught or with whom I had worked. All my former associations were cut with one swift stroke of the knife of obedience. No more lectures. No more printers. No more organizations. Instead, a grinding routine of lectures, study periods, with an hour off in the afternoon for outdoor exercise, delightful recreations spent in the companionship of the hundred men who shared my studies, and books, books, and more books.

Theology itself was engrossing. But chiefly it seemed to me the guarantee of priesthood just ahead. One studied philosophy to understand human life. One studied theology to grip the fullness of the priestly life. Philosophy was walking with the God of nature, the God of reasonable truth, in the cool, almost abstract light of the human mind. Theology was walking with the God of revelation, the God who spoke through prophets and lawgivers and the world's most beautiful book and the fascinating lips of Christ Jesus the Lord. The light was the light of His face. It was warm and glowing, less the thoughts of the human mind than the imparted thoughts of the God of wisdom and infinite knowledge. Philosophy promised complete solutions. Theology would lift me to the Christlike powers and dignities of the priesthood.

Yet though all this was true, theology could be pretty dull and the classes would be conducted under the patronage of St. Anesthesia. I had long before learned to use a lecture class. Indeed, I had learned to use it so well that I bothered many of my professors. They were not too accustomed to seeing a theologian write steadily as they talked, and they suspected the worst. Was I writing poetry? Heaven forbid, I replied! Then I was writing for some publication? Indeed not! Correspondence? Of course not. What then? They found it, some of them, hard to believe, that as they lectured I was taking down their lectures as fast as I could. It seemed to me highly economical of my time if I caught on paper the well-prepared explanations which they were giving us. I saw no point in digging out of ponderous volumes what they had distilled for me in their lectures. So few young Jesuits ever worked harder in class than I did; and few of them were ever more suspected by their professors.

Indeed, I was so suspected that in my second year Father Bernard J. Otten, a very great teacher who rumbled along in magnificent Latin but in a monotone that was sleep-inducing, decided I was using his class to pursue some tangential literary interest. He called me to his private room and demanded to know what I was writing. "Your lectures," I replied. He shook a doubtful head. One week later he broke from all the theologate traditions. Repetitions and quizzes were conducted in strict order of seniority, and Father Otten was at the very top of his list. But when he sat himself heavily into his professorial chair, he surveyed the class with an ironical eye and then threw a complete surprise into us with this amazing departure from all precedent: "Audiamus hodie Fratrem Lord," he said, not disguising the conspiracy and purpose in his voice. "Today, let's hear what Brother Lord may have to tell us."

And to the amazement of the class he pitched into me, demanding a complete, detailed repetition of his lectures of the preceding week. He was not content with surface recollection. He pushed me, tried to corner me, asked trick questions, cross-examined me on all he had poured out for the past days.

Never did a student more completely relish his petty triumph. I had taken down all his lectures exactly. The moment I could return to my room, I had typed the lectures out with five carbons. The top copy went into my own personal notebook. The last four carbons I distributed to good friends among the theologians. The first carbon went to my friend Bill Manion, whose passing affliction was my great opportunity. He had, as I have mentioned, returned from a most successful teaching career under sentence of blindness. He would not see long enough to be ordained. But he prayed. The doctor's advice never to read a book for the succeeding years seemed to make theology impossible. But he had an astonishing memory; paid careful attention in class, and then with me as his coach listened while I reviewed with him, half an hour in the morning and half an hour in the evening, the notes I had carefully taken down and typed.

So Father Otten found me more than just fairly prepared. After half an hour of tough quizzing, he sat back, with a muttered "Bene!" That meant his begrudged "Good!" The moment class was over I went up to his desk. "You didn't believe I worked in your class and took down your lectures, did you? Well, I consider you a good teacher. I think it is my good luck to be able to take down the digest of your extensive studies. I hope you won't mind if I continue to follow your lectures pencil in hand. It is my way of complimenting you and saving myself vast stretches of time. But you may be sure I write what you say, only what you say, and gratefully what you say."

He smiled his slow, slightly ursine smile. We were good friends from that hour.

For all the enormous amount of theology and church history and Scripture and ancient language that was poured upon us by a succession of excellent teachers, I found I had still time on my hands. Hebrew baffled me. I never made head or tail of it. Moral theology under the charming and brilliant Father Francis O'Boyle had the instant value of preparation for the confessional. The basic truths of Christianity, the validity of the Bible, and the treatise on Christ and on His Church, all seemed to me to clamor for translation into the idiom of the people. I could feel that I was storing up endless material for sermons—I played with the idea of *Armchair Theology* to parallel my little *Armchair Philosophy,* but never, to my lifelong regret, settled myself to do it.

Everything I touched mentally seemed to have some bearing on the priesthood ahead. Yet there was time for so much else. I had discovered and been discovered by Father Louis B. Egan. First he introduced me to the apostolate of the deaf-mutes. Their language I never learned and their alphabet I fingered with slow and clumsy lack of skill. Yet I went down with him to work out deaf-mute dramas and to entertain the youngsters by thumping the piano while he alternated between catechism and a skillful handling of the drums. Together we rebuilt the stage of the university auditorium, preferring this type of manual and artistic work to the games in the theologians' playing field. Feeling that I might never again live in that leisurely atmosphere, I got leave to read "forbidden books," the famous classics which for one reason or another had been placed on the Index. It seemed to me that I could never be quite on the level of those who knew these books if I talked without personal contact with them; I wanted to be able to discuss them intelligently and to know precisely why they were condemned. It was a sort of return to the days of Dr. Bailey and his library filled with books on the Index; only now I was reading as a theologian and with a perceptive and assaying eye.

Father O'Boyle was deeply interested in the work of the Good Shepherd nuns. On Sunday afternoons he took me down with him, and we occasionally brought with us parish dramatic societies, films and slides, and my fumbling abilities at the piano.

I delivered my required sermon in the refectory, winning a reluctant permission to write a complete sermon and deliver it from a synopsis of my notes. Then, as later, I believed that sermons should be most carefully prepared. Then, as always, I felt that the sermon outline should contain almost twice as much material as one would have time to use. But then, as throughout my priestly life, I disliked memorized sermons, feeling that they lacked the spontaneity and contact with the people which a good sermon should show. I would guess it was the first unmemorized sermon ever given in our university dining hall. No one thought it worth his while to imitate my approach.

All the while, the bright lamp of the sanctuary grew closer and closer.

I learned to say Mass in a rather unusual fashion.

Father O'Boyle and I were driven back one Sunday afternoon from the Good Shepherd Convent. The car of some friends stalled on a busy uptown corner. I knew nothing of motors but plenty about what penalties followed the late return of young Jesuits who missed dinner and spiritual exercises. So, after a bit of restless waiting, I hurried away, caught a streetcar, and entered the theologate as the bells were ringing. Back on the corner, Father O'Boyle, a lighted cigar in his mouth, opened the hood of the auto. The fumes leaped up, ignited at the glowing end of his cigar, exploded to throw him back against a sharp curb and split his hipbone. We all deeply regretted this disabling accident. We missed him frightfully as a friend and a teacher. But once he returned from the hospital, he sent for me. He would be permitted to say Mass, but he would have to say it sitting down on a high bench. Would I like to serve his Mass in a small private chapel?

It was a most extraordinary opportunity and I seized it avidly. So each morning at six I knocked at his door, guided his wheel chair over to the tiny private chapel, helped him vest, placed him carefully at his bench, and then acted partly as acolyte and almost as assistant priest while he beautifully said Mass. For one solid year I watched a man say Mass with great devotion and precise liturgical care. Because of his lameness I had to be much closer to him than acolytes usually are; I had to assist him in his movements, and do the journeying to and fro that he would have done had he been able to walk. And little by little I discovered that I was almost saying the Mass with him. I did not need books on liturgy; I had the living example of a great scholar. I never read a line on how to say Mass; I watched a holy man saying Mass and imitated what I saw.

My direct preparation for hearing confessions was made with a holy young theologian, Father Louis Wheeler, whose eagerness for the priesthood expressed itself in frank wistfulness and open longing. He had counted the days to ordination as a child might count the days to Christmas. When we settled down for a session of "cases," those wonderful hypothetical instances that test the future priest's ability to handle moral problems, he would sigh and prelude our work with, "Just think! In two hundred and fifty-four days we shall be priests of God!" He said it with such emotion, such depths of sincerity, such a starry-eyed wonder, that nobody laughed. Instead, we found ourselves counting days right along with him. And in the corridors one of our year was likely to stop with, "How many more days, Lou?" to which he would answer by giving without hesitation the correct number.

The ordination of the men of the year ahead of my own seemed almost as much a thrill to me as the ordination of my own class. Bill Manion, whom I had been coaching through his theology, by special permission was ordained after his second year of studies. His eyes were the reason for that—those slowly closing eyes which would have sent him into his theological studies much sooner had it not been for the need of teachers during the days of World War I. I was present to watch him ordained. I had a kind of personal feeling of achievement in his priesthood. Little did I know that he would never go blind but would, instead, advance to be dean of Rockhurst College in Kansas City and then its very successful president. Instead, I knelt for his blessing, smiled up at him happily, and thought to myself, "This time next year, please God, I shall be where you now are and with the powers that are yours." We had suddenly become the "ordination class," we were those lucky people called "ordinandi"—"those who are about to be made priests."

That setback of my attack of tuberculosis, of which more later, bothered me very little. I wondered if it might hold me from the altar, and in the same thought was absolutely sure it would not.

With Father Gerald Fitzgibbons I had come to theology with an intense interest in the missions and a hearty desire to cooperate with the Catholic Students' Mission Crusade. Together, we had worked with the future Bishop Frank A. Thill on their educational program. We had built up for them their publicity, written pageants for them, and developed their ritual. Our enthusiasm for that fine program of mission training helped sharpen our interest in the priesthood and make what we would do as priests assume a pointed apostolic character.

Ordination! The ancient, wonderful rite of the laying on of hands! The transmission in unbroken succession of that Christ-given power of the priesthood from the Last Supper and the days following the Ascension to the latest young man to kneel before the outstretched hands of the bishop! The conferring of those Christ-ordained gifts which mean so much to the human race!

"Go, therefore, and teach the good news to every creature!" "Whose sins you shall forgive they are forgiven." "This is my body and this my blood; keep doing this in commemoration of me." "If there be sick among you, call in the priests and anoint with oil." "I shall be with you all days to the very ending of the world."

Ordination! Almost without knowing it, from the moment I had left mother and father and home and friends and headed off for Florissant, I had been moving steadily toward the altar. And now it was almost within reach of my outstretched fingers.

Neither my father nor my mother was well. Mother had gone through a period of inexplicable weeping and melancholia. The slow disintegration of my father's atrophy had begun. They both vetoed any thought of a celebration for my ordination. It would be enough if they came with my invalid brother for the ceremony and if the first solemn high Mass was sung with as little pomp and ceremony as possible. So I issued no invitations. Instead, from Loyola University Press I secured copies of the ordination ceremonial in a small booklet; wrote on the flyleaf my name, the date of my ordination, and the date of my first Mass. About a hundred copies of this booklet went out to my very few relatives, my small circle of friends, and a few of those with whom I had worked.

The great Father Joseph Spaeth preached our ordination retreat. I recall that it was characterized by deep simplicity, the baring of his own beautiful soul to us, and his magnificent love of the priesthood. We assembled for the subdiaconate in our lovely College Church, the first of the three successive days on which Jesuits by privilege receive all the major orders. And we waited. In panic, Father Alphonse Schwitalla, our master of ceremonies, reached the archbishop's residence. Archbishop Glennon had forgotten all about us. He was past the Offertory of his Mass. A messenger brought him to a halt; he rushed out in a car, and with his usual imperturbable calm went ahead to make us subdeacons. There was an element of the comic about this near slip, and those who were not sharing the feeling of panic were near to laughter. I have always been glad that my ordination was not delayed by a full day.

It is a solemn moment when the name of the young man is read out and he steps from the semicircle of his fellows and walks toward the bishop with a freely spoken, "Adsum!" That simple Latin word, "Here I am," has long been considered as the external expression of the clerical vow of chastity. It ends the young man's career in one state of life and precipitates him into the new career, so utterly different in all its aspects. He has joined the consecrated ranks of those men whose total life is dedicated to God and to the service of human souls. He has become by unretractable purpose God's man.

Fearing a return of the prevow scruples, I had determined that once I moved toward ordination, I would put all thought and all thinking out of my head. I'd done plenty of that in advance. Like any other man taking upon himself the responsibilities and duties of the priesthood, I had thought out in my own soul all the difficulties, my own personal unworthiness, the duties I assumed, the whole question of whether I was up to the standard of what I embraced. Knowing very well that I wasn't, knowing too that God asked willingness and not complete worthiness, I had determined to go ahead. Now I saw no point in letting the once-settled problems thrash around to make me miserable. Better to advance automatically. Better to put a pair of brackets around all thinking and feeling. Better to let God and the archbishop take over. Better to move with my fellow Jesuits toward the great moment. The priesthood had been wonderful in anticipation; it would be more wonderful still once the reality was achieved. In the interval I'd trust God and let long-established resolve carry me through.

Just as we came out for ordination to the priesthood, the heavens broke in one of Missouri's celebrated lightning storms. The flashes were fierce and blinding. The thunder roared around in incessant cannonading. Suddenly all the lights in the lovely College Church blew out. The building was plunged into gloom. Banks of candles were lighted, less for reasons of liturgy than for the need of illumination; and we walked into the sanctuary, feeling for all the world like the young men who centuries before had been made priests in the Roman catacombs. My mind remained a blank. I did not think. I did not pray. I did not worry. I was without concern to do exactly what I knew was being watched by a hundred careful, priestly eyes, the eyes of my fellow Jesuits. We moved together, we young priests-to-be. We knelt individually before the archbishop, who laid his hands heavily and convincingly upon our heads. We felt the hands of all the Jesuit priests of the St. Louis University community resting there with authority. I looked up to smile into the face of Father Pernin, who had come for my big day. I felt the slightly increased pressure as some dear friend laid his hands upon my head. And the men who touched me seemed vividly to represent and symbolize all that glorious Catholic priesthood from Peter to the young man ordained just before me.

Around my anointed hands were wrapped two beautifully painted ribbons, gifts of dear nuns who wanted to share my ordination. Later I cut those up into bookmarks and sent them or gave them to be placed in the prayer books and Missals of dear friends.

Then, in our wide half-moon, we knelt and with the archbishop said our first Mass. The Mass seemed to be his, but we knew that, as we said the words under the careful guidance of his cheerful and melodious brogue, we too were offering and we too were consecrating, and that the host we received at the archbishop's hands was the host transubstantiated by our words into the body of the Lord.

The first full sense of priesthood, however, rushed in upon me as I stood above my mother and father and blessed them with my newly priested hands. I bent to kiss them each, and we were crying together. Never should I have reached that altar without them. Never would I be able to repay them for their generosity and sacrifice except by what they most wanted of me, the life of a devoted priest.

My own first Mass was a solemn high Mass. To save Mother and Father the pressure of any celebration, I had arranged to say my solemn high Mass on a weekday, June 28, 1923, and to skip completely reception or celebration. The kind pastor of Resurrection Parish in Oak Park had begged for my first Mass there. As a youngster I had gone out with our St. Catherine's choir and dramatic society to put on the very first entertainment that brought in the very first money which he used to start the parish. He remembered and offered me the Mass, a breakfast for all I cared to invite, and a reception in the parish hall. Generous though this was, my mother had said no, and I had declined.

So, with perhaps a hundred people in the church, I sang my first solemn high Mass. I stress the "first" without too much reason. For I have often enjoyed surprising diocesan clergy with the facts about my celebration of Mass and my administration of the sacraments. I have in my whole life as a priest sung perhaps ten solemn high Masses. I have been deacon at the solemn high Mass less than five times and subdeacon perhaps twice. I have given the sacrament of baptism about five times, twice conditionally, and the last sacraments not more than ten times. But then I suggest that they ask me how many times I've preached, which is a quite different set of statistics.

At my own first solemn high Mass I sang wretchedly. This amused my associates. During my theology I had helped a great many tone-deaf Jesuits to master the music of the high Mass. When the time came for my own singing, for some absurd reason, I decided to sing low and soft. The palest whisper came forth. My singing voice, good for an occasional comic song, was not pitched for ecclesiastical functions. Said one of the young priests whom I had lifted from tone deafness to a reasonably satisfactory singing of the Mass, "Virtue must have gone forth from you; you gave us so much that you left nothing for yourself."

Father Pernin preached beautifully. And following the Mass we had a quiet family breakfast, with Father Pernin, the officers of the Mass, Mother, Father, and James.

A little incident made that first Mass memorable, however.

My immediate superior was the well-remembered Father Bernard J. Otting, fellow professor of theology with the constantly confused-with-him Father Bernard J. Otten. Coincidence was stretched too far when two men with names so closely alike were established in the same location. He had been my president when I taught at St. Louis University, then the dean of the theologate. Though later he became the most mellow and kindly of men, he lived under a sense of rigorous order that winced at any departure from the routine. As I came back from my first Mass,

I stopped by to thank him for his kindnesses and to ask his blessing on my new priesthood. Hardly had I got the words out of my mouth, "Father Otting, I stopped by after my first solemn high Mass to tell you I appreciate your many kindnesses to me . . ." when his famous jaw clamped and he glared at me.

"Your first solemn high Mass, indeed!" he said. "Do you mean to tell me that your first Mass was a solemn high Mass?"

I was rocked back on my heels. "Why, yes, Father."

"Who gave you permission to sing as your first Mass a solemn high Mass?"

He had me there. I had never thought a permission necessary.

"Why," I began, "I made the arrangements with the pastor of our church, but I never thought about the need for obtaining a permission . . ."

"In all my life," he fulminated, "I never heard of a man singing a solemn high Mass before he had first said a low Mass. This is unprecedented. I certainly would never have given you permission. I doubt if any superior would have . . ."

"But," I protested, stunned, "because of my parents . . ."

"Parents are no excuse for the violation of all established customs. First a Jesuit is ordained, then he says a low Mass, and then he sings a solemn high. Well, you've wrenched it all out of order now, so there is nothing further we can say or do." I waited for him to say, "Don't do it again," his usual formula for offenders. When he didn't suggest I never again make my first Mass a solemn high, I wanted to say, "I promise you that this will be the last time," but lost my nerve. One didn't crack jokes with Father Otting.

Off for Chicago I went. Sunday I said a parish low Mass in our little Oak Park church and suddenly found myself facing the people with the urge to preach. I did. It pleases me still that my first sermon was on the divinity of Christ and the wonder of possessing as our leader the God made man. The following Saturday I was permitted to hear for the first time confessions in a parish church. The day was hot. The penitents were few. But as for the first time I lifted my hand in absolution over an unseen, bowed head, I had the glorious sense of power. "Ego te absolvo," I whispered, repeating the formula I had used so often in practice confessions that prepared me for this moment. And as the unknown penitent left the dim box, I thanked God for the power over sin, one of the greatest powers God has ever granted for the happiness of mankind.

Jesuits are fortunate in the special permission which permits ordination after their third year of theology. For that quiet fourth year I lived the priestly life, knew the calm of scholarly days, began each day with the quiet glory of the Mass, and on occasion was sent out to act as an assistant priest in some parish church. Christmas brought me for my three Masses to old St. Malachy's, a run-down parish shortly to be transferred to the Negroes who had come in around it. It was one of the memorable Christmas days of my life . . . with confessions far into the evening, my own three Masses, a sermon at each of them, and a sense of the wonder that makes Christ's Mass the reality of Christmas Day relived, and brings all the loveliness of the manger under one's eyes as he stands at the altar.

Another masterly element in Jesuit training sends the young priest back to the tertianship for his third year of novitiate. St. Ignatius was a master psychologist. He restrained the unruly and slightly unkempt zeal of his young priests. He held them for a final year of theology and then for another year during which they would have leisure and quiet to relish their priesthood, and with the graces of the Mass and the obligation of the Office, they could prepare themselves directly for the difficult work ahead. Off I went with twenty more of our young priests to St. Stanislaus Seminary on the outskirts of Cleveland.

Jesuits sometimes forget that Ignatius saw an importance in his novitiate not always felt by the older orders. The Benedictines and those who follow their rule lived most of their lives in cloister. The Franciscans and Dominicans each day gathered for the discipline of the Office recited in common. But Jesuits were to be world travelers, men who returned to the cloister after harsh contact with the world, and who, in order to facilitate ease of movement and a wider range of immediate activities, said their Office privately and never in choir. So the older orders were content to give their men a full year of novitiate and trust to the constant graces of cloister and Office to keep high their religious ideals. Ignatius felt that his men had to be given two years to prepare them for far-flung missions and a life that would often enough be dangerously "on their own." And once they had been ordained, instead of releasing them for the excitements, distractions, and possible dangers of the apostolic life, he returned them for a third year of novitiate, a retempering of their spiritual steel, a reburnishing of their own characters.

I have felt that God was good to me. I really loved Florissant and the novitiate years. Some Jesuits find them hard almost to the point of being impossible. Some find them long and wearisome. I found them easy and pleasant. In the same way some Jesuits find the third year, the tertianship, a very great trial. To me it was one of the happiest and pleasantest years of my life.

The twenty-one of us arrived as August of 1924 drew to a close. The brick and frame buildings which made up the ugly little architectural unit of St. Stanislaus sat far back from State Road in a shadowy cluster of trees. It was an excellent spot for a hermitage or the scene of a murder. Each had his separate room. But once more we returned to group living. The buildings had once been the novitiate of the old German Province mission in the United States. When the mission was divided between the Missouri and New York provinces, the establishment became the tertianship of the Missouri Province.

Cleveland almost overlapped into our front yard. The strangely polyglot population that had assembled round Cleveland's steel mills, harbors, and burgeoning industries had gradually moved to little Parma, where the tertianship was located. But when the streetcar bumped to the end of the line, suddenly one found untouched woodland, deep, untrodden ravines, and country as primitive as if the nearest large town were a hundred miles away. We could in our rooms hear the swish of tires on the main highway. That was the only sound of modern civilization that reached us. A few steps took us back along forest paths, deep down into the heart of a wood through which burbled a brook fed by a luxuriant spring, and gave us a privacy and seclusion unguessed by those who motored past us with hardly a glimpse at the gaunt red houses set back in thickets of trees.

Father John J. Brown was our rector. Once on a time he had been appointed bishop of El Paso and had begged off the honor in abject fright. He had been superior most of his life and lived in the constant horror of making decisions. Few men have I liked more and found more amazing. For God had given him the cross of melancholia and he seemed to love it. He welcomed us with a face long as a cello. He told us the worst about St. Stanislaus, that its climate was enough to drive the rest of us into doldrums like his own. "It rains almost every day. And when it doesn't, the sun refuses to come out. Yet you'll have horribly hot weather just about the time you start your long retreat. Then the winter sets in, and you never see a bright day. It's one long, sunless season of snow and slush and overcast. With the spring you get more rain, more clouds, even less sunshine. I hope you don't mind bad weather too much. But I'm afraid it will create a depressing atmosphere you'll find hard to resist."

That made us look forward with real relish to the months ahead. Then one of the brighter among us remembered that Father Brown came from Colorado. People from Colorado, like people from California, are weather-conscious. Living in a land of sunshine and bright days, they grow totally dependent upon them. They dread the rain. They hate the overcast. Most of us tertians came from sections of the country where bad weather was no novelty and where we had learned to live equably under any type of skies. We had our share of bad weather, but not for a moment did it reduce us to the atmospheric hypochondria of Father Brown.

To our great good luck our novice master—that very important tertian master of our year—was the really great Alexander J. Burrowes. How we loved that man! Young Burrowes had come to the Society of Jesus without ever having seen a Jesuit. He had read about them, decided to join them, and came to the novitiate with no firsthand knowledge of either the life or the type of men he was joining. That was the Jesuits' good luck. When I was a lad at St. Ignatius in Chicago, he had arrived as our college president. He was utterly simple; I have seldom known a man more innocent and with less guile. He was not a great orator. He would have been a poor teacher. But he was a heaven-sent administrator. Every one of his faculty felt he had in the rector a father and a friend. He wandered casually among the boys and called them by name. He loved music, and wrote for the college two of the world's worst college songs. We sang them with gusto, even when an absurd lyric exhorted the student body to "cheer the ball nine crossing the goal line." That mixing of baseball and football into one charming incongruity never bothered the priestly author, though it tricked us into singing out the words with tremendous roars of ironic appreciation.

He had a great dean, Father Cassilly, and he let him run the school. He patted his teachers on the head and gave the boys holidays on almost any excuse. He was an ideal administrator, no doubt of that!

When I entered the Society the Missouri Province was ruled by a man who believed that authority should be ironclad and rigid as the laws of the Medes and Persians. I have always understood what was meant by "Prussian" when I thought of the famous Father Rudolph Meyer. He was himself a saint; but he felt it was his business to make every Jesuit a saint, and a saint according to the book. His sudden death brought to the seat of authority a man strangely unlike him but worshipful of his traditions and determined that the cast-iron character of his regime should continue to bear down upon the province. I have heard distinguished men of that era say they hesitated to send a young fellow to the novitiate, fearing he could not stand the rigors of this regime. I lived for several years under it, and in the resilience of youth never so much as suspected the iron hands in control.

But the Jesuit general in Rome knew conditions. So into office was shot Father Burrowes to bring calm and peace back to the Missouri Province. He was not as great as his predecessors in ability or perhaps in abstract character. But what a gentleman—and what a gentle man!

The typical story of his calm of mind became traditional. While he was in office and responsible for the welfare of the province, a frightened brother beat upon his door. "The philosophy building is on fire!" he cried. The St. Louis Fire Department regarded the entire university plant as a five-alarm fire. It was notorious for underground passages, for firetrap stairs, for corridors that were built with draughts in mind. So the news was alarming.

But Father Burrowes lifted his vast height to his feet, ambled down the corridor, arrived at the panicky philosophy department, and was surrounded by smoke and the frightened brethren. He regarded the scene with undisturbed eyes. "Oh," he said, gently, "a fire." Then, casually, "Have you sent for the fire department?" "Yes, yes!" the voices shrilled. He turned calmly on his heel. "Well," he said, "let me know when they come. I'll be back in my office."

The fire department came; no damage was done, but the utter and unshakable calm of the provincial permeated the community and brought back the province to peace and tranquillity.

We had two weeks to explore the novitiate and to get to know one another in our new surroundings. Father Burrowes brought out his famous, ancient, and battered gramophone. He delighted in Stephen Foster and a comic monologue called "Cohen on the Telephone." He sat and chuckled through the fiftieth repetition of this with more joy than he laughed at the first. He explained to us the meaning of the tertianship and the importance of our taking this last step in the training of a Jesuit. He was totally without eloquence or rhetoric or artifice. He spoke in such simplicity that it was the speech of a father talking to his beloved sons. Yet his eloquence consisted in a lack of eloquence, and his sincerity was transparent and convincing.

The Society of Jesus selects for its tertian masters men who, by prestige of former office, command the respect of the tertians. We knew this man had been a college and university president as well as our provincial. Rather vaguely we realized that here was one of those really great men who have a Lincolnesque character about them. With about three other equally great men Father Burrowes had transformed the Jesuit educational system of the United States from a series of small colleges and high schools into the university system that would eventually extend from Fordham to Santa Clara, from the University of Detroit to Loyola of the South. Treating us like the men we were, he began to talk about his own adventures with men and administration.

"We realized," he told us one day, "that this was a period when we could start universities on a nationwide scale, but it was a moment that might pass and never come again. So, though we had neither money nor resources, though we were inexperienced in the university forms, we built and annexed and ventured into new fields. We have a long way to go, and you young priests will have to push forward our work. But we had to act fast, courageously, and sometimes apparently against sound judgment and prudence. Now you have the Jesuit universities; what will happen to them is yours to decide."

He was paying us high compliment, we felt; and it woke us to appreciation and response.

After two weeks we plunged again into our long retreat. It was the second of our Jesuit training, the second time when for thirty full days we would make the complete Spiritual Exercises of St. Ignatius and see them in their logical context and carefully in each of their significant details. Again, Father Burrowes was perfect for the work. He gave us the Exercises as Ignatius had written them. His explanations were often stark and never imaginative. He did not try to spellbind us or charm us with flow of words. Here was the Foundation, God's plan for the universe; here was the effect of sin as mature men must see it and understand it; here was the glorious leader who spoke best when He was allowed to speak for Himself; there lay the challenging cause which must occupy our priestly lives. Now, as priests who each day said Mass, we must follow the suffering Christ into His Passion and offer to share with Him His cross. And now, as the ministers of His love and His grace, we must walk with the risen Christ, and feel with the apostles the certainty of ultimate victory.

The retreat had a new element of excitement for each of us; for out of the material we were getting we would during the course of the year fashion our own retreats which later on we would give as Jesuit retreat masters. We had been making retreats ourselves for fifteen and more years. Now we must so master the Exercises that they become our own personal property, things we understand thoroughly and could share with others. Though the Exercises were simple and basic, their treatment must be readjusted and redesigned for almost every type of retreatant. And we had some months in which we could think this through and plan the retreats we would give during a priestly lifetime.

The end of the retreat released us in a great burst of animal spirits. Our pent-up energies burst forth in an orgy of tree cutting and trimming, of manual work around the place, of long hikes over the primitive reaches back of the novitiate. Then we settled down for months of intensive training. The tertian master, Father Burrowes, brought in the complete Institute of the Society of Jesus and we read and studied comprehensively what we had thus far studied only in synopsis. There were no *arcana,* no secrets to impart. An enemy of the Jesuit and a hater of the Catholic Church would find the Institute dull and unexciting reading, with no undertone of plotting and mischief, and no single paragraph that taught the young Jesuit how to poison a monarch or hornswoggle a rich widow out of her money. There were no rules for betraying Protestants to the *auto de fe,* and no master plan for world treason and world domination.

Here were the common-sense regulations by which men had tried to adapt the poverty and obedience and purity of Christ to men living a very active life. Here were the ways in which some of life's greatest complications could be unraveled and the paradoxes of Christianity resolved into terms of routine living.

We studied how a man might give all he had to the poor and follow Christ and yet not starve or become a burden on society. We learned how the Christlike rule, to love one's neighbor as oneself, could be reconciled to a Christlike purity. We found that men had worked out a system by which perfect obedience always remained a noble, honorable, and dignified thing, and never degenerated into slavery. We discovered that it was possible so to orientate a complete life and a complicated network of colleges and parishes and publications into the scheme and pattern of Christ's plan for world salvation. We saw with mature eyes our duty to God, the Society of Jesus, and our fellow men; yet we were shown the benefits that came to us personally from the honorable and laborious fulfillment of that duty.

Each day we read or reread the lives of the saints and tackled the more profound works on spirituality and the Christian ideals.

Our library was rich in the writings of the fathers of the Church, to which we were directed as to the men who had kept alive the historic connection between their own age and the age of Christ and His apostles.

Little by little we reaffirmed our loyalty to the military obedience of the Society of Jesus. We were to move where we were sent. We were to realize that in effective organizations orders must be given and orders must be obeyed. We learned from a great administrator the reluctance he had always felt in issuing commands and the delight he experienced when his suggestions or hints were accepted and turned into achievements. We held tight to the Institute, which had been written by wise men, tested in the long centuries of human experience, approved by the popes, and integrated into the individual character of Jesuits and the far-flung works of the entire Society. The world opened to us was not a new one; but we were seeing it in leisure, almost from an objective point of view, now matching our own experience of the life against the theory that dominated it, and making plans for the more complete carrying out of our vocational ideals.

But if we soared to lofty heights of spirit, we were simultaneously doing some unintended physical penance. We were suffering, the first and only time it happened in my experience as a Jesuit, from poor food and bad cooks.

An amusing tradition of the Church holds that St. Dominic prayed that God would send his order bad cooks; that St. Ignatius prayed that He would send the Jesuits bad procurators and treasurers; and that both prayers were answered.

The jest is amusing but inaccurate. At least, I have known some excellent, almost miraculous, Jesuit treasurers. And never have I lived in a Jesuit house without delighting in good cooks. Except that one year. Ignatius had believed that his men must be well fed and comfortably housed. He knew the connection between a sound body and a sound mind, and he felt that the soul served God most effectively when it was not harassed by bad health or a wretched cuisine. So, though Jesuit meals had never been luxurious, they had always been abundant, varied, and well flavored. We took for granted the excellent breakfasts, the substantial lunches, the well-planned dinners. And feast days came round to give us, as Carissime Sontag said, "a foretaste of heaven." Himself an abstemious ascetic, he left with me from novice days an immortal saying: "I love feasts," he said; "they are a guarantee of the delights of the eternal banquet."

Well, we did not banquet in the tertianship.

The quality of the food that arrived in our kitchen was excellent. But the assignment of the good and willing brother who was sent to prepare it was one of those strange slip-ups of authority. He had been an excellent mechanic. He knew all about carburetors and nothing about skillets. He would reluctantly go into the kitchen, leaving the battered Ford lying around the back yard, to puzzle over the menu for the next dinner. In fact, we had a rumor that he would put motor oil into the gravy and that he used beef suet for the finer parts of his gasoline water pump. He could make a tough hamburger and send beefsteak onto the table so dry that we didn't carve it—we whittled it.

Painfully we came to the realization that our superiors had no idea how bad the food was. Father Brown accepted bad food as he accepted bad weather, as part of the general plan to enshroud the tertianship in clouds of gloom. Father Burrowes was by way of being a food crank. He never touched raw fruit. He never ate soup for fear of grease on the top. (Our soups had a thick crust of grease that needed breaking with a large spoon.) He liked all the juice cooked out of his meat. And he preferred his vegetables watery. As for Father Beeler, our father minister, he was simply indifferent to food; all dishes were the same to him.

Ice cream was so rare that it was an event; and it was manufactured by one of the brothers who normally ran the furnaces. When the pure cream and other ingredients were stirred together, he added a flavor that was like something an Italian barber might put on your hair if you fell asleep in his chair. It was redolent, emphatic, and sweetly sickening.

Now, food doesn't seem an important item in the life of an intelligent man, preoccupied, to all intent and purposes, with the higher things of life. Yet nothing can more swiftly upset the mind than bad food or throw a crowd of men into angry mutterings against fate. Young Father Quinn stood guard over the ice-cream freezer, refusing to allow the brother to poison it with his Woolworth perfume. And Father Lou Egan, in his fabulous mastery of emergencies, saved us from starvation.

Thursdays and Sundays and major holidays gave us a free afternoon, the chance for a walk, and leave to carry along a light lunch. Father Egan wangled his way into the affection of good old Brother Michael Jungfleish, who ruled over the dining room and storehouse, but not the kitchen. "Brother," he would say, "we are going for a long walk, and we shall need food. Will you please unlock the cupboard?" Brother Jungfleish would regard him out of ancient, humorous eyes: "Who," he would demand in his heavy Teutonic accent, "who is the boss around here?" "You are, Brother," Father Egan replied in mock humility. "So, you understand!" the brother would say. "Priests come and go; but in the tertianship it is the brothers who are the bosses. Understand?" "Completely," Father Egan agreed. Brother Jungfleish produced the keys. "Then we will open the larder and you may select for yourself."

Off we went into the hills laden with food. It was the sort of meal that tramps might assemble in their hobo jungles. But with the eggs broken into a deep skillet, the meat chopped fine, a bottle of ketchup added, and onions boiled and stirred into the mess, Father Egan produced the most healthy, hearty, and sustaining dish imaginable. And we lucky companions sat and gorged ourselves, laying away enough to keep us alive for the days of starvation until the next holiday and another tolerated raid on Brother Jungfleish's larder.

It was my one experience in the Society of poor meals. When the father provincial arrived for his spring visitation, every man who called upon him complained of food. The good young brother was happily restored to his motors and served them well. And we got a new cook, good food, and more contentment of mind. At that, we missed Father Egan's mysterious concoctions back in the hills.

From his arrival in September every tertian looked forward to the coming of Lent. Then we officially sallied forth to our first consecutive work as young priests. Each man was assigned to one of the Jesuit parishes or schools, to a mission or a hospital. And for the weeks of Lent he put in laborious days testing his priestly skills in the practice of the ministry.

My happy assignment brought me to our Gesu Church, attached to Marquette University in Milwaukee. What happy weeks they were! For once in my life I counted the number of talks I gave, and they totaled seventy-two. I gave the lenten course in our parish and another in St. Patrick's, a secular parish across the city. For the first time I gave a retreat, the retreatants being the high-school students of Marquette High. Then I had the joy of giving a retreat to the boys and girls of our parish school. The Novena of Grace in honor of St. Francis Xavier was a challenge to my youthful oratory. I heard several hundred confessions and each morning sang a high Mass. For the first time I was consulted on problems of vocation and marriage, and spoke out of secure theory and a total lack of practical experience. But it was a glorious time; I had the thrill of mounting a pulpit and looking down into the body of a jam-packed church. I knew the joy of giving consolation, advice, and absolution to penitents in the confessional. At long last I was a fullfledged priest, not yet with my final vows, but released to do the work for which through long years I had been trained.

Our return to the tertianship found Father Brown waiting for us, happy in his melancholia.

"Welcome home," he sighed. "Well, the tertians don't mind the tertianship too much up to Lent. They've got that lenten experience to look forward to. But once they come back after Easter, it's a dull time, and tough on the nerves. The spring rains, the overcast skies, the fact that it's all old stuff to you, the tiresome routine and monotony . . . I'm sorry, fathers, but you're in for a couple of slow, dreary months, and I just hope you won't let it get on your nerves."

It didn't.

I had my retreats to whip into shape. Experience with live audiences had taught me the difference between a sermon plan and a sermon that touched their hearts and influenced their conduct. We saw spring come to the woods back of St. Stanislaus, and one warm, beautiful day we stood and watched the little creek break as the ice melted and the water came slipping down, coyly but resistlessly. I had notebooks to put into order for future use, though I did not suspect how quickly I'd scrap them in the light of practical experience. For the last time in my Jesuit life I knew relative leisure, time to think and time to pray and time to plan and time to look forward to life and its possibilities.

During those days I met once more Father Charles Moulinier, the magnificent founder of the Catholic Hospital Association. "Look," he said, "you've got a name that appeals to me. Lord . . . Lord. It's not Irish. It's not German. It's not notably Catholic. Well, I'm getting to be an old man and soon I shall have to lay down the direction of the Catholic Hospital Association, even if the work has just begun. How would you like me to ask the provincial to assign you to me? I'll prepare you to take over when I resign. And you can direct and manage the Catholic Hospital Association."

I have often wondered how different my life might have been had I not thanked him and told him I doubted my fitness for the work. I was not a scientist. I was not sure I could deal with the temperamental elements of the medical profession.

Father Garesché, with whom I had worked long years before, called on me with a similar suggestion: "How would you like me to ask for you to come and work with me on *The Queen's Work?"* I answered with an even more emphatic negative. Neither of us knew then that most of my life would be along those Marian lines.

Then it was over and I was a Jesuit, fullfledged except for my final vows. They would come one full year later. I took the train for Chicago and my first assignment, which proved to be abortive—the chance to do a great dramatic show for the Eucharistic Congress. The Society had given me its best. It was now up to me to prove that I was not a totally unworthy son.

God had been very good to me.

Would I be good to Him?

I am embarrassed at the obvious answer.

TO A PERFECT SECRETARY

Dear Marian:

Shortly after the events that I am recording in this letter you became a member of our staff. You know all that happened from the end of this letter on. But I had always meant to give you (beyond the constant nostalgic backward glances I have made when I talked with you) a sort of picture as "it was in the beginning."

You and I spent a lot of time and energy and love on the Sodality of Our Lady. It was the work of a lifetime, really; certainly the preoccupation of more than a generation—allowing, as the historians do, thirty years for a generation. But you came into the work in 1926 when I was vaguely aware of what lay ahead and dimly planning for the developments that took place. Incidentally, but with very deep feeling, my gratitude to you for the work you have done for the sodality! There was little that I did which we did not talk over in advance and plan together. Once the sodality "movement" started rolling, we watched and nurtured and furthered it together. It was a great experience, often most heartening; we met great friends and wonderfully kind people along the ways and through the days. And this is just a little twice-told tale of the events which led into our work for the sodality. Be patient with me if I repeat myself.

Somehow, it seems to me that I was always connected with the sodality. I can't recall the time when I was not a sodalist of our Lady. But to put the fact correctly, I must have been received in the informal fashion of that day as soon as I received my first Holy Communion. Of course, first Communion came late in those pre-Pius X days. I was eleven in April and must have received my first Communion in May or June of that same year, the youngest of the group which approached the altar rail in the beautiful Holy Angels Church. From that moment on, I was a sodalist.

Truth to tell, the Sodality of Our Lady in those days was an extremely important organization. It was used, at least in Chicago, and I believe throughout Catholic America, as the medium for keeping monthly Communion alive. The battle of the Jesuits with the Jansenists had a number of practical effects. The Jansenist Pascal, for instance, wrote his famous and highly literate attacks upon my spiritual forebears and is partly responsible for our bad reputation among our enemies. He did not like us much and he communicated his dislike to successive generations of people, many of them very good indeed, and many of them looking for an excuse to hate anything notably Catholic.

The Jesuits, not having a literary genius to match words with Pascal, turned to something practical. If the Jansenists attacked frequent Communion and kept the Catholic faithful from the altar rail, the Jesuits determined to use the Sodality of Our Lady as the instrument to bring Catholics to Holy Communion. They shared that sodality with the zealous priests throughout the world; and for a very long time indeed made the sodality work to keep its members in touch with the Eucharistic Christ.

So it was in my boyhood that throughout Chicago's great archdiocese, each Sunday's parish announcements contained this or a similar notice: "Next Sunday, the first Sunday of the month, is Communion day for the married men's sodality. All the married men of the parish are exhorted to receive Holy Communion in a body." Or it would be the second Sunday, and the married ladies' sodality, or the third and the young men's and young women's, or the fourth and the children's sodality.

The sodality and frequent Communion were beautifully linked. When, later on, other religious organizations for the laity took over the practice of monthly Communion, I was entitled, it seemed to me, to a slight smile. They were reverting to an old custom which the sodality had kept sacred. They were, however, actually reverting to pre-Pius X days, before the plea of the saintly pope for "frequent and even daily Communion" on the part of all the faithful had been heard by the sodality as it had been meant to be heard by the whole Church.

The sodality which I joined in Holy Angels' Academy (as our little parochial school was rather elegantly named) was an excellent one. Sister Mary Blanche ran it with a great love for the Blessed Mother and a great devotion to us young people. She had the boys' sodality, and we met of a Sunday afternoon. Even in those days without movies or autos, getting boys out at three o'clock on a Sunday afternoon was a blend of suasion, magic, and great faith and love. She did it. As we boys met with Sister Mary Blanche, the girls in their sodality met with another sister moderator. If in later years I was to stress what nuns could do and should do for the sodality it was because I remembered what this nun (heaven bless Sister Mary Blanche!) did for the sodality and for me, the sodalist.

Strangely, I cannot recall that we had a priest director. I know that Sister Mary Blanche tried very hard to interest some of the fine young assistants of our parish. One may even have been, in proper canonical fashion, appointed. I believe that once in a while one of the assistants came to our Sunday meetings for a short talk; I remember neither the talk nor the talker; and when I close my eyes and struggle to reconstruct the scene of our sodality meeting, Sister Mary Blanche alone looms dominantly in the front of our meeting room.

But the meetings were good. We said the Office with genuine affection and devotion. Sister Mary Blanche communicated to us without ostentation her own love for our Lady. We were in the days before there was any talk about the lay apostolate, yet out of the sodality rules she had wisely selected the references to literary and intellectual interests and had begun to build up for us and in us a great love of books. Though the sodality met but once a month—and once for our monthly Communion—the sodality library was open continuously. We competed for the record in the reading of books; and as Sister Mary Blanche's taste was excellent and our own response genuine, she had us reading at a great rate. What Catholic books there were she bought for us and introduced to us. And where the Catholic books ended, wholesome books and classics began.

To buy the books she resorted to various expedients. I recall tramping the parish to get ten-cent chances from all my mother's friends. We of the sodality raffled off a "beautiful gold watch," and were richer by more than a hundred dollars when the watch was duly awarded. Sister Mary Blanche, who bought books with the economical skill of a housewife buying groceries, got a lot of books for that hundred dollars.

We paid our dues regularly, ten cents a month. I have no idea what was done with the dues, though we had a regularly elected treasurer. Perhaps it helped to defray the inexpensive but very important social life that followed the meetings. That social life was unofficial. But I know that Sister Mary Blanche smiled upon it approvingly. So, I hope, did our Lady. The boys' and the girls' sodalities, by happy coincidence, ended their meetings at precisely the same moment. We met outside the school, and instead of pairing off, formed groups that strolled down the quiet Sunday streets of Chicago's South Side, invariably heading for one of our homes.

Homes were large in those ample days, or large enough to welcome a cluster of six to sixteen boys and girls who suddenly arrived. Maybe the homes were not much larger than the present ones; but parents had a keener sense of the importance of welcoming their children and friends, mechanical entertainment did not claim our interest, and we knew how to have fun together.

I have often prayerfully thanked the sodality for the wonderfully wholesome friendships of my early adolescence. Many of them remained my friends for the whole of life. We had happy Catholic marriages out of our association. A loud, strident, wildly clamorous, and absolutely brainless game called "Pit" had just been thrown on the market. It simulated the buying and selling of the Chicago grain market, and we found it great fun. Approximately sixteen of us, equally divided between boys and girls, formed after the sodality meeting the Pit Club, and continued our meetings for years.

Indeed, the great tribute I can pay to Sister Mary Blanche's sodality is the fact that, though I moved to a far part of the city and joined the sodality at St. Ignatius High School, I came back month after month to her meetings, used her library, and met there the friends who were one happy center of my social life.

The sodality at St. Ignatius was not good.

Yet it met once a week and I attended with unfailing regularity. We too said the Office of the Immaculate Conception, but in a translation quite different from the one to which I had grown accustomed. There was usually a talk, spiritless and without any reference to our life or problems, by the director—a saintly priest who loved our Lady but had small ability to pass his love along to us. We dashed into meetings, checked a roll call, paid our dues of ten cents, said the Office like an express train rattling over an uneven roadbed, listened apathetically to the director's sermonette, and then bolted to resume the interesting and exciting things of student life. I cannot relate the sodality to anything in the normal life I led; I cannot see that it influenced the school or me personally. It did make me think of the Blessed Virgin for the length of a swiftly chanted Office of Our Lady. And I took a certain perhaps egotistic pride in the fact that I was one of the small number of students who took time out to attend the sodality meeting. When I became responsible for the sodality in America, I remembered the excellent sodality moderated by a nun and the ineffective sodality directed by a priest and drew inevitable conclusions.

May I pause for a second to recall that during my college days your beloved Pius X gave back frequent Communion to all the world? The effect of this upon the sodality was not good. Many a director felt that the sodality's work was over. It had been the instrument for frequent Communion; now frequent Communion belonged to all Catholics. The sodality's Common Rules were not to appear until 1910. The parish sodalists lost their spiritual purposes. Other organizations stepped in to assume the task of stimulating monthly Communion which the sodality leaders had thought was already passé. And I would guess that the sodality must have dropped to its lowest level.

Certainly the sodality as an efficient medium for anything slipped completely out of my mind during my early years as a

Jesuit. No one of my associates referred to it. No literature on it seemed to exist. I never bothered to think back to the two sodalities to which I had belonged. Never did I remotely foresee myself in any slightest sodality connection.

The end of my second-year juniorate at Florissant climaxed in a picnic with far-reaching results. Nineteen of us drank from a polluted spring, were laid low with typhoid, narrowly brushed the gates of death, and were late in appearing to start our philosophy course at St. Louis University. As one of the sickest, I lingered on at Florissant, waiting for the return of strength enough to tackle minor logic. Strength was slow returning.

At this time the Jesuit general had been laying new stress on the sodality. The coming of frequent Communion, he argued, did not mean the end of the sodality. There was a thing called the Catholic lay apostolate. He ordered every country in which Jesuits were established to start a central sodality office. Primarily this office was to edit a sodality magazine. Being a European, he had a great belief in the written word. If, he evidently felt, a good magazine would present the ideals and programs of the sodality, sodalists who read would accept and act on the suggestions. He was too, too trustful of the connection between print and practice.

Finishing his theology at the time in 1913 was a young Jesuit priest who had entered the Missouri Province with a law degree and some experience of practice. During his Jesuit studies he had written extensively for Jesuit publications and had just brought out his first book of poetry. He had real poetic gifts, and the superiors, on the principle that an acceptable author should be an adequate editor, gave him the assignment of starting a sodality magazine and opening the central office of the sodality for the United States. The assignments were in that order. Once more, a great faith in the written word made them feel that once a good magazine had been published the sodality would boom.

In the fashion to which religious become accustomed, Father Edward F. Garesché found himself with a new job, a nonexistent magazine, a room high over Grand Avenue on the third floor of the St. Louis University faculty building, a desk and typewriter, no assistants, and no money. Father Pernin suggested to him that out at Florissant was a young fellow who had some gifts for writing plus his personal training in handling a college magazine; since that young fellow was sick and not able to start his philosophy course, why didn't Father Garesché grab him for his secretary and assistant? So in the dark of a fall evening Father Garesché appeared, asked me how I'd like to work on a new sodality magazine, and left with my enthusiastic agreement.

It's odd looking back to see how small events shape the whole course of a life. If I had not gone on a picnic, if I had been one of the great majority who did not drink from the contaminated spring, if I had not been a little sicker than the others, I should have fallen into the routine of my Jesuit training. What would my life's work have been? Who can possibly know?

Now strength came pouring back. In two weeks I found myself occupying the room next to Father Garesché. We had one large, bare central room for an office; we each had a tiny bedroom. Mine overlooked the corner of St. Francis Xavier's Church. It was the College Church, and the parish church for our rapidly disintegrating neighborhood, but the piety of the people and the constant flow of the faithful gave a lovely background of Catholic loyalty for my whole year. I was given a typewriter, a desk, and a vague commission to help create a new magazine.

Father Garesché soon coined a phrase for his projected work: The Queen's Work, a Magazine and a Movement. I recall the afternoon when he selected the name. We had gone down to the public library to look through the magazines on the rack. He was caught by the title of *The World's Work,* an extremely popular magazine of international events. He said it over a number of times and then said: "Suppose we had a magazine that was not devoted to the work of the world but the work of the heavenly queen. Our Lady's Work . . . Mary's Work . . . The Queen of Heaven's Work . . . The Queen's Work . . . That's it. The Queen's Work." And The Queen's Work it became.

When, later on, I was put in charge, my good friend Wegman, musical critic and teacher, uninstructed Catholic and wit, remarked to one of his friends: "Father Lord has a new appointment. It's something to do with a magazine. I think it's called *'The Queen's Work.'* I believe it has something to do with bees."

While Father Garesché set the precedent of wide traveling, I remained at the desk working on correspondence, handling the trickle of manuscript which we wrote for and got, and practicing my hand at creating typical articles and stories for the future magazine. I handled all of Father Garesché's mail. Though unblessed with shorthand, I learned to type sufficiently fast to take down his letters directly on the machine. Then he tossed me a large number to answer in his name. I soon found myself private secretary, stenographer, copy boy, proofreader and copyreader, companion for occasional walks, altar boy for a late Mass when he returned from a trip, printer's devil, author and rewrite man, appraiser of manuscripts, Pooh-Bah to a lot of unaristocratic offices. It was a great experience. Father Garesché was away most of the time; and a young Jesuit was surprised to find himself with so many varied jobs dropping without anyone's intent or planning into his lap.

Father Garesché had discovered the revised edition of the Common Rules of the Sodality, published in 1910, and was building the policy of *The Queen's Work* about the first rule: Personal Holiness, Defense of the Church, Service of the Neighbor.

I had only to glimpse that first rule to see its enormous potential. What couldn't be done with a magazine that set itself to present holiness attractively, to defend and extend the Church of Christ, and to serve the neighbor without too much limitation or restriction? And if the sodality could formulate a program that would actuate that first rule, it would be really great.

Yet my job was merely the magazine. I found I had a great deal to learn. My knowledge of printing was sketchy. My dealings with the printers were those of a self-confessed amateur. I could not seem to find any sodality anywhere that lived up to a small part of that first rule. I got busier and busier with the mere routine of an office. I was handicapped by the fact that from the start of the year to its ending I never had a penny to spend. Indeed, I soon ran head-on into the province treasurer, out of whose hands nothing but a direct order of the provincial could pry a dollar bill.

Father Garesché left for one of his frequent trips and gave me orders to write one hundred letters to one hundred key pastors.

When the job was accomplished, I found myself without stamps. First-class mail was two cents in those days; and I went down to see the province treasurer and get one hundred two-cent stamps.

"What for?" he demanded.

I explained the hundred letters to pastors which waited to be mailed.

"Absurd!" he barked. "Are you writing to every priest in the United States? Indeed I'll give you no hundred stamps. No, and not ten either."

So, as I was very young and easily talked down, the letters remained unmailed until Father Garesché returned and got the stamps from a less reluctant source. After that he kept me supplied with essential stamps, though the generosity of my mother supplied me with the stamps which I needed for any mail of my own. For the rest, I lived a year and worked a year totally without money. When I went to the printers downtown, I walked. When I had an errand, I got concomitant exercise.

In early March we came out with the first issue of *The Queen's Work*. My name appeared on an article. My pen name appeared on a story. But I was not mentioned on the flag or the masthead. The issue was a May issue, the month selected to honor our Lady and properly initiate her magazine. We took plenty of time to bring out the June issue, and with that, I was through with my first connection with the sodality.

Quite honestly, I was not impressed. As far as I could make out—and I saw no reasons or explanations—the sodality was dead. Perhaps there was room for what *The Queen's Work* instantly became, a magazine of general Catholic interest. In those days there was not the forest of publications which now line the pathway of the faithful. *The Queen's Work* was one of the first; and when we set it to interest every possible Catholic along a wide variety of lines, we had plenty of waiting audience, little competition, and a fairly free field.

But the sodality did not impress me. Indeed, when during my tertianship I had occasion in retreat notes to list lay organizations to which I thought an energetic Catholic might well belong, I find I forgot to mention the sodality. In theory, the sodality looked good. In practice, I could find slight signs of its activity.

I had not as yet learned what it takes time to discover, that anyone can lay down a good theory, but that it requires tireless labor and ingenuity to put the theory into practice. Karl Marx could lay down the theory of communism in a vast volume; until Lenin and Trotsky and Stalin got to work putting it into the practice of the Soviets, it was a perfectly harmless spinning of cobwebs. Hitler was just a pointless lunatic when he wrote *Mein Kampf;* when he turned that prophecy into horrible reality, he was a peril to the world. The papal encyclicals on labor are beautiful documents; they begin to affect the condition of labor when someone has the courage to put their principles into economic practice.

I was convinced then, as I am convinced now, that the Sodality of Our Lady has a magnificent theory of effective Catholicity. I was not sure then that the theory would ever be so turned into effective action as to produce men and women with an inspiring love for Christ and Mary and a way of life that would make them real apostles. That would take terrific work, ingenuity, resourcefulness, and zeal.

In the busy years that followed, I doubt if I gave the sodality a thought. There must have been a sodality in the college of St. Louis University; I recall nothing about it or its impact on university life. I do remember that Father Kuhnmuench, for whom I had a great affection and respect, had developed a professional sodality for the professional schools that was doing great work among the medics, dents, and law students. I even managed to write him and his sodality into the student tax which the student council voted; getting him a dollar a year per student for his sodality activities. But it seemed to me that, with his zeal and affection for the students, he could have worked for them with any sort of organization. I grew convinced of something I later often stated: "A sodality will never rise above the level of its director. It may not reach the heights he sets for it; it will not exceed his ideals and his zeal."

During my tertianship in 1924-1925 I naturally wondered what lay ahead for me. Father Moulinier's offer of association with him in the Catholic Hospital Association made me flirt with the hope of working in a really live organization. Yet I declined. It seemed a little too much to hope that Father Louis Egan and I might be permitted to develop the great Catholic art movement of which we dreamed. I had enjoyed my teaching and would be glad once more to be assigned to the classroom.

Then Father Garesché came to see me. Would I like to return to *The Queen's Work?* I could manage the magazine for him while he worked on the sodality movement. I declined the offer with emphasis. I was not in the slightest degree interested. "Are you feeling that definite about it?" Father Garesché asked. "Perhaps I'm not stating it as emphatically as I feel," I answered. "Sorry; but it doesn't seem to me to have the possibilities that interest me."

Then came a letter from our father provincial, Father Francis X. McMenamy. It was a courteous and kindly letter, as he was a courteous and kindly man. Would I be interested in taking over the sodality's central office and editing *The Queen's Work?* I would be in charge.

Strange, isn't it, in view of the future that I wrote him an immediate refusal. Since he had not ordered me or even asked me to take the assignment, but had asked me what I would like, I was giving him an honest answer: I was not interested in the sodality or *The Queen's Work*. I would not like to be assigned to take charge of it. Sorry, but could I be excused?

Hardly was the letter in the mail when I got a second thought. It was not that I suddenly decided the sodality was attractive and *The Queen's Work* a possibility. It was just that I felt my letter an impertinence. He had been kind enough to ask me before he appointed me. He had been thoughtful enough to want my opinion. But evidently he had hoped I would accept. So I sat down and shot off a second letter: "Please pay no attention to my first letter. Though my feelings on the subject remain unchanged, I would prefer that the decision remained totally yours. Whatever you wish, I wish. If you appoint me, I will accept with the most sincere determination to do my best for the new job."

Neither letter was answered. But when the appointments for the year 1925-1926 came out, I was down to take over the sodality's central office and *The Queen's Work*.

The appointment was followed by a letter informing me that I could continue the summer's work of putting on for Cardinal Mundelein the eucharistic pageant. So up to Chicago I went to sit patiently and then impatiently waiting for instructions on the proposed show. Father Egan and I had prepared this gigantic show on the invitation of Monsignor Francis Clement Kelley. At the time he was expected to be executive secretary of the Eucharistic Congress and had commissioned us to do the biggest show possible. We had written the scenario, drawn up our stage plans, made our budget and had it approved, and during our year in the tertianship dreamed great dreams of the tremendous show we would do to honor the Eucharistic King. In the interval Monsignor Kelley had been appointed bishop of Oklahoma City, and Monsignor Quill, who succeeded him, had no slightest interest in the projected show. To take my mind off the matter while I was waiting for a decision, I taught a course in modern poetry for Loyola University's summer school. Then at long length we were dismissed by Monsignor Quill, Father Egan got orders to return to Loyola University of Los Angeles as its college dean, and I found myself at the doors of the sodality's central office and *The Queen's Work*.

What I walked into was a dying organization. Indeed, it was being gently smothered to death. Had I known conditions, I doubt if I should have written the second letter, for the situation was cheerfully moribund, happily on the verge of a pleasant funeral, with some flowers and no regrets.

All that came about rather simply. During the eleven years since my connection with the office, the heavy stress had been placed on the function of *The Queen's Work* as a magazine of general Catholic interest. The Catholic editors of the country had just discovered a weird institution known as the agency system, and the agents had covered the land like a plague of seventeen-year locusts.

I pause to pay my respect to honest agents, of whom there were and are many. I pause to recall that there were some honest businessmen who preferred to promote Catholic enterprises rather than to sell bobby pins and real estate and sausages and soft drinks. Some of them saw the possibilities of Catholic magazines and threw into their promotion fine abilities and a real zeal for Catholic truth.

But there were others, and they had written a story which had made the Catholic Press Association take a firm stand on the whole subject of how Catholic magazines could be advertised and sold. And the provincial and his consultors had decided that, for themselves, the whole matter of selling by agents must be dropped forever.

During the years of experiment while I was continuing my Jesuit training, Father Garesché and his associates had tried a variety of approaches to the difficult task of selling circulation for a Catholic magazine. Despite the relative lack of competition *The Queen's Work* knew the struggles that all religious publications must know. The sudden and highly approved rise of the "agency system" made Father Garesché attempt a modified version. I myself was far away, saw it only in remote operation, and can speak of it without authority. But apparently, as Father Aloysius Breen explained it to me when I took over, the central office hired its own agency manager, who in turn hired a small corps of house-to-house solicitors. The price of the magazine was raised from a dollar to three dollars a year. The agent who made the sale to the customer took the first dollar which was paid down. The manager and his office staff absorbed the second dollar. The third dollar went to *The Queen's Work*. For all that, the circulation zoomed to approximately 150,000, and the venture was financially profitable.

All this would, of course, be no concern of mine except for the fact that I had not been told I was to step into the office just after the agency system had been killed. Father Aloysius Breen remained on as business manager in charge of the funeral-director's assignment of burying the old magazine and its agency system. My arrival found the circulation already dropped from its peak to less than 50,000. The manager had gathered his tribe of agents, folded his tents, and silently slipped away. And all the profits made under the former system had been paid into the cause for which they had been made: the education of young Jesuits for the priesthood.

Father Breen used to love to tell stories of the amazing agency system. Apparently a distinctive breed of humans is developed by nature to sell magazines house to house. They do not need any particular magazine. Indeed, I saw letters in the files from agents to the manager reminding him that it made no difference whether the magazine was blank paper or something approaching *Harper's Bazaar*. "We need good premiums," he wrote. "We don't sell a magazine; we show the customer an attractive premium, and when he—or usually she—wants the premium, then we tell 'em they can have it if they also take the magazine." So the manager supplied the agents with rosaries, statues, pictures—any of the thousand premiums which would be bait for the magazine.

Naturally, that type of customer never bothered to renew his subscription for a magazine which he probably never took from the wrapper. Naturally, the falling off of circulation was prodigious. Each year the agents had to resell the magazine, and since each year they got the same commission of one third of the subscription price, that is what they aimed to do.

Along with the majority of honest agents there were some fantastic characters who served to give the system its bad name, no matter which magazine they sold. Father Breen described his rapid dash to Detroit on receiving from a Jewish merchant this inquiry: "When should I pay the second installment on the lot I bought in the Jesuit cemetery?" He found that the highly imaginative agent was selling lots in a nonexistent cemetery as premiums on the magazine. A similar character was offering those who bought a subscription the right to be buried in this cemetery clad in a Jesuit "habit."

One "fainter" sold by the simple expedient of collapsing on the doorstep when the lady of the house opened the door. When the charitable housewife had revived him, he was inside, able to appeal to her charity, and sold her his magazine.

Another left any neighborhood he visited in a turmoil. He would ring a doorbell; and when he had given his sales talk and been refused, he shrugged his shoulders and said, "That's what the lady next door led me to expect from you." The housewife demanded to know what he meant. "Well, your neighbor on the left, when she took a subscription, told me I would waste my time talking to you. She said you were too stingy to buy anything from anybody." The woman promptly bought to prove she wasn't stingy, and he tried the same story on the woman next door and so on down the block, leaving with an order book full of subscriptions, and a neighborhood on the verge of civil war.

For a good many years we Jesuits said Masses which had been promised as premiums to anybody buying a year's subscription to *The Queen's Work*. The offer of the Masses was just a bright idea thought up by the salesmen. When the central office discovered the promises, we Jesuits had to make good.

At any rate, the Jesuit managers were totally innocent of the various crooked rackets evolved. The lay manager was himself an honest and honorable gentleman. Most of the agents were honest men and women. But the whole system, regardless of what magazine used it, got a bad name, the provincials ordered its abandonment, and I stepped in shortly after the system had been closed out and the magazine's circulation was tobogganing downhill at lightning speed.

Around me as I came to take charge, in all innocence and unawareness, was a corporal's guard left out of the swarming office force that had been necessary under the old system. You must remember that we occupied a small section of the second floor of a wide sweep once filled by the bustling home office. It was in the Italian Fraternal Building, and our little remaining space was sandwiched in between stores on the ground level and clubrooms and dance halls on the third floor. The Italians, as a convivial and social-minded people, gave grand parties above us. There they put on gigantic receptions following their weddings and christenings. Every Sunday afternoon and evening the dance hall was packed. We mounted the stairs every Monday morning, and on many another weekday morning too, through the debris of revelers—hats and horns and confetti, bottles and boxes, the stale, chill, and greasy broken meats of the banquets and parties.

Across the street from us a flourishing blind pig or speak-easy operated, and from the window one warm autumn afternoon I watched while a car raked with machine-gun fire the tavern and its operator standing peacefully taking the sun.

The dirt and noise of Delmar and Vandeventer avenues floated up to our windows; and even before I had hung up my hat, I know I was fully determined as a first act to get our staff and our files out of those quarters and into something that did not reek of an abandoned ship and a neighborhood that was not merely down at the heels but running holes in its uppers. It took a bit of time to accomplish that; but we achieved it before too long.

Father Breen lingered on, conducting the obsequies. I liked him enormously. The eldest of three Jesuit brothers, he was calm, amused, never ruffled by anything that happened, destined to continue as superior in several Jesuit houses and enterprises, sincerely determined to clean up after the dishonest agents, kind to me, and convinced that there wasn't a hope for the future.

"If there were anything that could be done to save the sodality's central office and *The Queen's Work,* I'd do it. But the fact is, we've tried everything. The agency system worked well. We had a lot of subscribers" (he did not in all honesty say readers) "and we were financially solvent. Perhaps some genius can discover a way of keeping the place afloat" (he looked at me with his humorous smile, clearly convinced that in me they had not found the genius who would plug up the sinking ship and make for some safe and profitable port), "but I doubt that too. So I'm glad to listen if you've got any ideas; but remember I know too much about the business to have much faith in any new schemes or old." And he metaphorically patted me on the head and went off to put more red ink into his ledgers.

Father Garesché had moved on to head the already flourishing Catholic Medical Mission Board. This, with the foundation of an order of nursing nuns, has been his most successful lifework.

In the office I found a good and old-established friend, Father Isaac Bosset. Never was there a more delightful and baffling genius. I have already paid him tribute for what he did as editor of my manuscripts and copy for the following years. I should pause to pay him tribute as a sort of Admirable Crichton, a wonderful friend, and a rock of strength during the troubled times.

But before all else, I cannot forget that in this monument of good sense, this man of perfect judgment on matters of taste or conduct, I was to discover the most harrowing case of scruples I have ever known. Eventually they would kill him, though he seemed to die of Parkinson's disease. It was the constant scruples which from childhood had simply shaken his soul and his powerful body to pieces. On any question that involved others, his decisions were almost infallible. On any that concerned himself, they were fantastically wrong. He was a great theologian who never could see that the mercy of God and the truth of His revelation in the slightest way bore in upon himself.

Yet he was a genius in a dozen ways. In his youth he had led his classes at the University of Detroit with no effort. He was a champion intercollegiate wrestler, developing a beautiful physique. He played the clarinet like a symphony musician. He made exquisite photographs and painted a little. He had read everything worth reading and remembered it all. He came from a well-to-do Detroit family of old French Catholic tradition, and never lost the beautiful manners and perfectly modulated voice he had been given at home. His taste in what was correct along almost any line never missed. He could read a page of type while another man was reading the opening sentence, and then give it back to you almost word for word.

He had the kindest heart and the clearest head and the strongest hands . . . and the most harrowing, racking scruples that simply put the brakes on his whole personal conduct. He never wrote. He had been eloquent, but never spoke in public. He never missed when you asked for a fact or a decision unless these regarded himself, and then he was never right. I loved him and he was fond of me; and he did everything for me that he could do; and I never felt there was anything I could do for him. For to the day he died, his scruples were so bad that he could not convince himself he was properly a Jesuit under vows or even a priest with the powers given by an ordination he doubted he had ever received.

Along with me that first year came my very good and close friend, Father Leo Mullany. He kept us alive that first doleful year of collapsing circulation, pessimism around us, and vague doubts about our future. He laughed when things were worst. He wrote nonsense that delighted us even if we couldn't always find a place for it in the magazine. I turned over to him the last issues of the dying publication, and he sent the old format of *The Queen's Work* to its grave with a gay flourish to the music of pipes and tabors. He found the somewhat disorganized life of editor of a dying sheet and associate organizer of a nebulous organization, the sodality, amusing, lots of fun, but no job for him. He could have been the country's greatest humorist. He had a natural wit and sparkle that was a blend of Will Rogers and the later Bob Hope. Instead of settling down, he felt he should go elsewhere, and went on to take his Ph.D. at Fordham and to head the English Department of Creighton University at Omaha. What luck for the students he taught!

Of the once-flourishing lay staff only a handful remained. Again I pause to smile gratefully at Miss Clementine Stahlsmith who, even as I write, continues her unselfish service of the present staff of the sodality office. Clem was and is one of our most precious heritages from the former regime, a dear personal friend, and one of the unsung heroines of the Catholic lay apostolate. She was young in those days, but already a mistress of finances, with a degree from St. Louis University School of Commerce and Finance added to her natural gift for handling money. You know what she did for us during the years; how, often almost alone, she managed the hardest element in finance—a constant deficit. How she met payrolls when the treasury seemed empty. How she smiled with confidence when the financial horizon was black. How she handled our money with absolute honesty, complete disinterestedness, magic and mystery, and came through to our days of calm and growth and security.

Actually, I wonder if we would have had the courage in those days to face what lay ahead if we had guessed. We were entering into our new work when the country was lush with war profits and confident of its ability to put three or four cars in every garage and a couple of chickens plus a turkey or two into every Sunday stewpot. But just ahead of us lay the world's worst depression. We would have to ride it. Then, when we were beginning to feel confidence, we would go through the second World War. That we came through depressions and war and the revolutions which all unnoticed have taken place about us was due to

God's good gift, a lot of hard work, an almost blank innocence about the financial facts of life, a determination to work on the principle that, if we cared for the kingdom of God and His justice all else would be added, and the cooperation of people like Clem Stahlsmith. If I had not said "we" throughout, I should have added gratefully, "and the cooperation of people like Clem . . . and you."

Louise Boente I inherited from Father Garesché, whose secretary she was, unselfish, saintly, leading a life of heroic devotion to her motherless nieces and nephews, and destined to become Sister Mary Carmela of the Sisters of St. Joseph, efficient and kind. Mary O'Mara, now Mary Meyer, was hardly more than a child in those days and handled our mailing department. She left to get married, mothered two lovely daughters, and returned years later on a temporary basis—just to help out during the difficult days of World War II when efficient workers were flocking to war plants. The care of an invalid husband made it necessary for her to stay on, as you know, to become head of the present-day shipping department, which she runs in her calm, efficient, and helpful fashion. Helen Stokes, conscientious and meticulous in her care of circulation lists, was the only one of a large subscription department who remained. As I recall, she did the entire work of the department until her death several years later.

Well, we did not precisely sit down idly for those first months. I had everything to learn. My first questionnaire sent out hopefully to the sodalities on our list brought back nothing but the most frightening discouragement. Almost none bothered to answer. The few that did reported vagueness and doubts. I had asked for pictures. I recall that one school sodality sent us pictures of a play they had done some twenty-five years before. It seemed close to their most recent activity. The circulation of the magazine, apparently totally unrelated to sodality membership, fell off at the rate of six thousand to ten thousand a month. Each month our deficit mounted. When I talked money with Father Breen he was vague. Apparently it was my job to run the magazine and movement without giving thought to finances. Then I discovered that he had still about $20,000 retained from the profits of the "agency system" and that he was paying our monthly deficit out of that. The $20,000 shrank to $15,000 before I was able to stop the leak in the dike. Leak seems a simple word for the way in which everything was slipping away from us.

I only know that I knew time was of the essence. I had been handed a terrific job. I had not too much faith in the sodality itself. I knew that we could no longer get out a magazine of general interest. There had to be some formula found that would tie together those nebulous sodalists all over the land and keep them in contact with our office, our services (as yet nonexistent), and a magazine that would be theirs, meeting their needs and interests.

Then Father Breen shook hands and moved along to his series of rectorships; your very good friend and mine, Father Gerald Fitzgibbons, joined us as business manager; you came in February of 1926, and we were ready to begin. The days ahead beckoned promisingly. God would be generous and our Lady kind.

TO A MEMBER OF THE IFCA BOARD OF REVIEW

Dear Gertrude:

You were kind to ask about the origins of the motion-picture code. And you were even kinder to ask about my lifelong interest in motion pictures themselves. So here is the story, and I know that much of it has never been told before.

Let's, in an egocentric fashion, first go back to me myself.

Anyone who is interested in the theater is bound to be interested in the motion pictures. He may share the fierce resentment with which the legitimate stage first regarded the films. When Cecil B. de Mille, as he told me, first forsook Broadway for a barn on Vine Street in Hollywood, his family held a solemn conclave to determine whether they would hang crepe on the door and pronounce him dead. *Variety* (always subtitled "The Bible of the Entertainment World") reluctantly gave space in its pages to the upstart of the century's first decade, and watched with amazement while it reduced the "legitimate" to a place in the chimney corner. I recall how about 1907, John Pierre Roche, my theater-minded friend, and I talked of the future of the theater, and he predicted that in time the movies would be at least equal competitors with melodrama, musical comedy, and vaudeville. I laughed. I've swallowed that laughter many times since, as the movies took over the whole theatrical world outside New York except for a little gasping relict here and there.

Whether one thought the motion picture ruined the theater or made it accessible to more people than ever had the opportunity to see plays, it was impossible to be indifferent to the form of entertainment. The first films showed little promise of making Belasco or Klaw and Erlanger or the Shuberts worry. Who could guess that soon what remained of the theater would be subsidized and kept in business by the largess of the film magnates?

The first decade of the twentieth century, that era of incredible change and wonder, saw the real birth of the motion pictures. And I was standing on the side lines goggle-eyed.

My first motion picture was seen in a peep show. On State Street some pioneer in the entertainment world had opened what later became a penny arcade. By standing on a footstool I could crane into the eyepiece of a jumpy, staccato, badly lighted machine, the picture in which was propelled by the turning of a handle. Never shall I forget the wonder of it. It was the execution of Mary Queen of Scots, lasting, I'm sure, all of sixty seconds, but complete with the gruesome severance of her fair head, which dropped to the earth amid the tears of her friends and the cheers of her triumphant enemies.

Shortly after that the penny arcades prepared the way for the motion-picture theaters and for the coming of the code. They ran to prize fights, to crime pictures, and to naughty ladies misbehaving in yards and yards of petticoats and the stout stockade of corsets and the bold suggestion of brightly figured stockings. It was no entertainment for small boys, but small boys flocked to the penny arcades, the type of picture that they were seeing never being suspected by their trustful parents.

It would be my guess that most of these films came from France. Pathé Frères is a name contemporaneous in my mind with the very first films. The peep show was being paralleled by the screen (hardly more than a light-absorbent bed sheet) which was dropped down at the end of the vaudeville program or when the hero had slain the villain and clasped the heroine for the final curtain of the melodrama. Movies were popularly known in the theater trade as chasers. Vaudeville patrons had a way of coming early and staying late. Indeed, they brought their newspapers and their lunch; read the newspapers when they were bored by an act, and ate their lunch when hunger seized them. They would sit through the entire performance two, three, or even four times in the course of a single day. As this cost the management heavily, the shrewd theater operator picked on the motion picture to clear out an audience reluctant to leave.

So, when the headliner had finished to applause in his next-to-closing spot, and the acrobats who closed the bill failed to drive the audience out of the theater, the stagehands slowly dropped down the white screen, the audience groaned, the house went dark so that newspapers could no longer be read, and the motion pictures began. They were wordless, soundless, colorless, and chiefly chases. A boy would turn over the applecart of a gesticulating Italian; the Italian would pursue the lad, would be joined by all the dwellers in the block, and would end by falling into the river to the rhythm of great splashes and dismal silence from the audience. Or the plot was based on trick photography. A customer would enter the barbershop; with a great flourish the barber would use his razor to remove the customer's head. This head, still moving its lips and its eyes, would be placed upon a stand where it could in comfort be shaved by the barber. It would then be replaced on the customer's head, the customer would rise, pay his fee, and leave to the bows and smirks of the barber.

Yes, it was high-class entertainment.

But I can recall vividly when I sat through the wonder of *The Great Train Robbery*. As later critics were to discover, that brief film had everything: heartthrob, child pathos, danger, the rushing train, Wild West, masked men, horses (the real heroes of the movies), the chase, the final fight, victory! Along the streets the nickelodeons had started, impromptu little theaters that, as the wisecrack of the period went, were begun by renting a grocery store, pushing in the front of the building, and starting a gramophone. I sat in one of the most imaginative, built to resemble a day coach, while the film taken from the front of a locomotive gave the inexperienced audience all the sensation of a train ride. When Cinerama gave us a ride on a roller coaster and then in a plane across America, I had high hopes for its future development; the first American movies were shot off the cowcatcher of a locomotive.

In one of these primitive theaters I saw a strangely fascinating story, filmed into perhaps twenty minutes of drama, cast unnamed, author uncredited. Not for another five years did I learn that the fascinating story was Maupassant's *The Necklace,* good even when shot in a vacant lot against painted flats, with ball gowns flapping in the winds. The streets of Chicago in the middle of the first decade were the movie lots of a number of motion-picture companies. Chicago threatened to become the movie capital of the world; and we children watched for small companies of actors who suddenly appeared, used the front of a synagogue for a bank, shot a robbery, an escape, and the pursuit by police all at one's doorstep, and then folded their equipment and silently stole away.

The year 1909, which saw me on my way to Florissant, saw also the motion pictures still fumbling between hope and an unsavory past. When I returned to pass through Chicago some six years later, the dawn had broken. My mother told me of the wonder being shown at a downtown theater, a "regular theater at theater prices." Italy's genius Gabriele D'Annunzio had foreseen what American producers had not guessed, the sweep and scope of pictures that moved and a story that could be told on land, sea, and air. Enthralled I sat with my mother, I the young Jesuit in transit from studies to the summer villa, and saw *Cabiria.* All the history of Rome and Carthage, which had slumbered through the pages of my textbooks, suddenly came to life. The battles were not dusty wrestling matches between men in tin armor, but violent conflicts to settle the future of civilization and the world. I marched with Hannibal and his elephants. I watched Fabius as he fought his magnificent delays. And out of the film emerged a great comedian, a vast giant of a man, Maciste, whose contribution to the story of the motion pictures is now only too vaguely recalled.

Almost on the heels of Italy's triumph came the picture that sent the motion-picture industry leaping along its way. Once more, en route from studies to a holiday in Wisconsin, I sat with my mother and watched the wonders that would emerge from a can of celluloid. D. W. Griffith had produced the miracle which was *The Birth of a Nation.* One of my former college friends had purchased the "state rights" to the film and was making himself rich. Griffith, a great artist and a poor businessman, was selling his incredible picture state by state, making some money for himself but making others fabulously wealthy. I sat and sensed the beginning of a new era. Here was melodrama that made my beloved "Drury Lane" melodramas at McVicker's Theater seem static and without thrill. I watched and fell in love with the new race of actors and actresses who were to become the stars.

But deep down inside, I recall being troubled. Up to that moment I had not been even aware of a Negro problem. Now I walked from the theater wondering why the audience did not in a mob surge to the Negro district of Chicago's growing Bronzeville and burn the Negro dwellings about the inhabitants' ears. The deep hatred that Dixon had written into *The Clansman* had been blown high and hot in the film. Griffith, whether he meant to or not, made many persons hate Negroes and dread any emancipation given them. And I knew that I was in the presence of a medium so powerful that it well might change our whole attitude toward life, civilization, and established customs.

I had become acquainted with the Ku Klux Klan through Sherlock Holmes and his adventure of the orange pips. Now I thought of them as the Marines riding to the rescue of poor, oppressed, besieged, endangered whites. No doubt about it, the horrible bigotry of the KKK which sprang at the throat of the Catholic Church and American liberties not a decade later rode to its brief and ugly triumphs largely on a road down which had dashed Griffith's clansmen.

Years later, on a transcontinental train, I noticed that the drawing room was occupied by a strangely familiar figure. As he walked through the Pullman I realized that it was the great Griffith himself. But his fame was now historic and no motion-picture studio wanted him. He had not done a screen picture for years. He was a memory, and hardly that, to the average moviegoer. When he returned I stood up and said, "Mr. Griffith, do you mind if, without introduction, I speak to you?" He turned in complete surprise and delight. "Mind? I am delighted and amazed that anyone remembers me." I assured him that I for one certainly did, and that his title of "the old master" was well deserved. He told me that he was heading west. "Not a picture, though. But imagine this! Someone has located thirty thousand dollars of mine that I do not remember and had no idea I possessed." This man who had spent the first vast sums making a picture grinned wryly. "And I have reached a point in my career where thirty thousand dollars looks big as all the world."

He was just one of the many whom that relentless giant of the film industry has tossed up to greatness and then, callously and without a sigh, dropped into the largest scrap heap in the world.

Summer after summer I returned to find my mother and father more and more addicted to the movies. Two places claimed their pilgrimage: the parish church of a morning, the neighborhood theater of an evening. Many a fellow parishioner was inclined to genuflect on entering the local movie house and noticing my parents ahead of him. They were because of aging eyes keenly sensitive to the improvements in photography and projection. "You'd hardly know the movies," I recall my mother's saying; "all the shake and jump and wane of light is gone." They knew fresh delight when Chicago pioneered in the air-conditioned theaters. They had a great fondness for the current stars and an almost childlike knowledge of their better parts and current vehicles. But my mother, deep down a Puritan and always a loyal Catholic, began to express occasional doubts about the character of the plots and the lack of costumes and the general loosening of the moral tone. She had been brought up in an age of the theater that was rigorously decent. No comedian ever said damn or hell. Any improper suggestion was totally taboo. Virtue was virtue and vice was vice, and nobody in the audience had the slightest doubt when to applaud and when to hiss. The vicious attack of the immoralists which began when science decided that men and women were merely animals from whom only animal morals could be expected had not yet strayed over into the entertainment world. Sex was a gender and not a form of entertainment. Men and women were taught that they had self-control and that they became more human the more they developed it. Marriage was a sacred institution rather than a football and material for the Sunday-supplement writers. People went to the theater to laugh and not to snicker, to be amused and not bemused, to see young love fulfilled and not dying love go on its last ghostly and ghastly prowl, and the bedroom was a sacred spot and not the scene of slapstick and blue comedy.

A pleasant set of circumstances kept me constantly in touch with the motion-picture developments. Normally, during my long days as a Jesuit student and teacher, movies for me would have been rare enough. Usually I went once with my mother during the brief visits home to Chicago. About three times a year an exceptional treat meant that highly expurgated motion pictures were presented for the entertainment of the entire Jesuit community. Now, in those silent days a piano inevitably tinkled while the film unrolled. It became my pleasant assignment all through my three years of philosophy and four years of theology to be accompanist for the pictures. Naturally, I had to see in advance the picture I would back with musical effects. And naturally I wangled the invitation to be present when the films were shown to a small group of the faculty fathers who decided whether or not they were proper entertainment for the community.

Actually, few films were. It was a time when the films were running wild. Few films of adventure even in the windswept West failed to show a heroine cornered by a villain whose intent of rape was only too vividly displayed. The commonest thing in the films was for the innocent heroine, thinking herself totally alone (except for the director, cameraman, stage crew, other actors standing by, and a potential audience of several million), to pause at the brink of the sylvan lake, drop off all her clothes, and dive naked into the water. As Jack Warner said to me much later and in a surprising burst of confidence: "Whenever my directors are stuck for something to do, they make the heroine take off her clothes."

Triangle Pictures took its name from D. W. Griffith, Mack Sennett, and Thomas Ince. The Triangle plots were the constantly recurring theme of the newly popular problem pictures. Infidelity gave the heroines a fling at the gay life followed by a chance to emote their insincere repentance. The gay blade swished among his conquests. The comedians, when not verging on the obscene, were constantly playing around with the bodily functions.

So, to get a picture fit for a community of religious, the censors of the community would often shoot through twenty or thirty films and reject them all. They shot them fast, but not so fast that I, the accompanist, didn't get a chance to keep up on techniques, the current stars, and the fashion in plots. The fashions showed every sign of becoming cut to a standard pattern and of centering around sin and crime. Sometimes I have laughed as I recall how, about 1908, a critic writing in the *Chicago Daily News* solemnly declared that the motion pictures were practically through. "They have run out of plots," he explained, "and without plots how can they continue?" Little did he know that Minnie and Jake liked their dear familiar plots, and that the studios would continue to turn out exposed film as long as boy could meet, lose, and regain girl, and the West remained cinematographically unwon. A lack of plots would never even bring the film industry to a dogtrot. As the film joke put it: "That is a sheer inspiration. I'm so glad you thought it up. We've made a barrel with it every time we've used it."

By ordination time I found myself with a speciality unexpected and unusual. My youth in the theater audiences, my adolescence at the time when I could see the movies a-borning, my good luck in catching the first great pictures, the interest of my mother in the films, my years of watching films as I prepared to play the piano to accompany them, meant I was by way of being a minor authority on the subject. And in addition I had kept abreast of the theater, had read almost all the good plays that appeared on Broadway, and had contributed some articles on the theater to the *Catholic World*.

I was a very young Jesuit when I sent my first theater article to the great Paulist, Father John J. Burke, then editing the *Catholic World*. It was an unfavorable criticism of George Bernard Shaw's *Androcles and the Lion*. His answering letter was kind and encouraging, and he asked for more. He got what he had dared me to provide him. We struck up a friendship by correspondence, and I wrote to congratulate him when he advanced to become executive secretary of the National Catholic Welfare Conference. It was his presence in that post which occasioned my first official connection with the motion pictures.

A sudden volcanic interest in the Savior had resulted in several most successful books. Papini had given the world his internationally best-selling *Life of Christ*. Bruce Barton had written *The Man Nobody Knows*. Hollywood made one of its great discoveries, that biblical pictures simply never fail at the box office, and that the Scriptures are the richest of story material on earth. Cecil B. de Mille had produced the extravagantly expensive picture *The Ten Commandments* and proved that it could be the most generous money-maker up to that time. And the threat of disapproval from the Protestant churches as well as the danger of impending censorship turned the minds of Hollywood toward religious subjects.

So word went out that De Mille would do a story of Christ called *The King of Kings*. Wisely he determined to bring to his newly acquired studio a Protestant, a Jew, and a Catholic to guide him against the more obvious and dangerous blunders that might wreck his picture at the box office. Father Burke of the N.C.W.C. was asked to send a priest. He remembered the young Jesuit who loved the theater and had contributed articles on drama to the *Catholic World,* my provincial was asked to lend me for the advisory job, and I found myself heading for fabulous Hollywood.

Like every other mildly literate person in the United States, I was familiar with the name of De Mille. He had dramatized the bathtub. He had given me vast annoyance by filming the delightful little satire of J. M. Barrie, *The Admirable Crichton,* changing the name to *Male and Female*. He was supposed to "create" stars out of unknown actors and actresses of mediocre ability and then to cluster uncounted galaxies of them together into enormous spectacles and small plots that cost war debts and made motion-picture corporations richer than banks or life-insurance companies. *Vanity Fair,* Condé Nast's clever and sneerful publication, had sent its best cartoonist to the set of *The King of Kings* and ran a blend of Ziegfeld at his most sumptuous, Frank Buck at his most ferocious, Rome at its most luxurious, and a faint trickle of Scriptures struggling through a jungle of scenery and costume.

The company by the time I arrived was on location on Catalina Island, filming the carpenter shop of Nazareth and the highways of Galilee. H. B. Warner, playing the part of the Lord, was kept in a sort of tented cloister, addressed not at all until he was out of costume. An unfortunate lady, cast for Mary, was under a morals contract that she violated by divorcing and marrying again before the picture was well released; she slid into a blacklisting and disappeared from the world of the screen. All the orderly disorder, the batteries of cameras, the waving of armies of extras past thousands of feet of celluloid, the systematic confusion of the old silent pictures, burst upon my head. And De Mille welcomed me, like the emperor he is, to the fabulous empire which demands and receives more voluntary taxation than most of the great empires of history.

The Protestant minister had come and gone, and would return. The rabbi seemed to have disappeared once the Old Testament had dissolved into the New. And I settled down with the vast combination of tropic expedition, safari, transplanted Broadway, congress of the nations, great international dramatic stars and recent winners of beauty contests which was the company on location at the end of the lush period of American spending, soaring stocks, and 250-per-cent profit on any well-advertised motion picture. The company was a fabulous all-star assembly of all the great names De Mille had gathered around him when he departed from Paramount to start his own independent company. Never again was such a company to be gathered. Indeed, the part of Simon of Cyrene was played by William Boyd, a young star who a full generation later would become more celebrated still as Hopalong Cassidy.

I became aware of the slavery that attached to the office of an author in Hollywood. Jeanie Macpherson was the scenarist, swiftly killing herself with an intensity of work and a passion for precise detail that kept her on a sixteen-hour-a-day schedule during the long months of production. In a welded devotion to her work she had no time for anything—friendship, correspondence, hobbies, or care of her health. She died much too soon.

De Mille and I sat down to discuss his film story. He was a strange and fascinating blend of absolute monarch and charming gentleman, of excellent host and exacting taskmaster, of ruthless drive on the set and a complete letdown the moment that the day's shooting had come to an end; a Renaissance prince who had the instincts of a Barnum and a magnified Belasco; frankly in love with hokum (which he liked to discuss and reduce to terms of understandable basic emotion); a showman who in all his years has had only one failure at the box office; an excellent listener and a voice that spoke with the most compelling possible command; an Episcopalian whose mother (deeply beloved) was, I think, a Jewish convert to Christianity; a man with the Midas touch who couldn't in those days buy a stock without causing a boom in the market; a motion-picture director who made even more money in the banking business; extravagant and yet careful to invest money which he borrowed to put on his pictures. He loved to know that that borrowed money ran into the millions and that his backers were worried at his extravagance, while all the time he never lost sight of a penny or really wasted a single foot of film.

Because Mr. De Mille was basking in the box-office triumph of *The Ten Commandments* he was still deeply impressed with the two-part film. I talked with him about *The Ten Commandments,* the first half of which was the story of Moses and the giving of the Ten Commandments; the second, the story of their multiplied fracture by a group of very rebellious characters. It was my conviction that Moses and the commandments were the only interesting part of the film, needing no bolstering from the wholesale fracture of the laws. De Mille was convinced that the Moses story without the modern story of the commandments in collapse would not possibly have been a success. As I write, he is redoing *The Ten Commandments,* and of his own he has scrapped the modern half and kept to the fascinating story of Moses and the giving of the law through the Jews to the world.

Incidentally, he told me at the time how he and Jeanie Macpherson had gone to the most celebrated Jewish seminary in the country to consult the most learned modern rabbi on the commandments and Moses' connection with them. When the rabbi had finished, there was nothing left of the commandments and little of Moses. He was a modernist of modernists and he had little faith left for Moses and regarded the story of the giving of the Ten Commandments as myth and folklore. Said Mr. De Mille, "So when Jeanie and I got out into the open air, we paused on the seminary steps, looked at each other, realized that the rabbi had shot our story to pieces, and that there remained nothing to film. Said Jeanie, 'Let's stick to the Bible; it's a much better story.' I nodded and we did."

The two-part story of this film success led Mr. De Mille to plot a similar two-part story for *The King of Kings*. The first part would be the story of Christ; the second, the story of a modern man trying to live like Christ. But they had already discovered by the time I arrived that Matthew, Mark, Luke, and John were deceptively slim volumes. Even by the most careful picking and choosing of incidents they could never conceivably complete the story of Christ in less than a hundred thousand feet of film. Indeed, to this day some storehouse of forgotten film must hold five to ten times as much exposed film on the Savior than ever was shown in the complete full-length version of *The King of Kings*. I have often wondered when it would be rediscovered and released. Most of it was shot in technicolor as well as black and white, a pioneering enterprise in those days.

A careful scrutiny of the Gospels had failed to uncover any love story that Minnie and Jake (those mythical and all-powerful gods of the box office) would recognize. So to my horror I soon discovered that into the scenario had been written a love story that would satisfy the morons' desire for red meat. Out of some ancient and little-known German legend of the Middle Ages had been resurrected the love story of Mary Magdalene and Judas. Judas, a handsome young fellow with ambitions that the Gospels hint at, had fallen in love with Mary Magdalene, a courtesan in the very best Broadway, penthouse, or villa-on-the-Riviera style. He saw in Christ a chance to advance his own interests; but when Mary's acceptance of the Savior results in a complete change of her character, he resents the intrusion of Jesus into his plans and heart interest, grows to hate the man who took his mistress from him, and eventually betrays Him. There was even an indicated desert scene with Mary at the door of the tent of Christ and Judas raging in jealousy. I confess that my heart sank at the possibilities of this plot.

Late in the night or early in the morning Mr. De Mille and I sat and discussed his film. I began with a gentle suggestion. The first section ended with the recitation of the Our Father, which concluded with "For Thine is the kingdom and the power and the glory forever. Amen." Since the country is predominantly Protestant, I confessed that he was reasonable enough in using the Protestant conclusion for the Lord's Prayer. "But you have a vast foreign release. When you use that ending in France, Spain, Latin America, they won't recognize it; they will be totally unfamiliar with it, and you will give them a finale that none of them finds familiar or emotionally exciting." He thought it over for several days and came back to report they had rewritten the finale of the first section.

We sat together looking at the twenty-five hundred feet of the Judas-Magdalene sequence already shot. It was De Mille at his most De Mille-ish. A Roman banquet with roistering drinkers, dancing girls, ballets, animals on the prowl, zebras harnessed to a chariot, and a Mary Magdalene, played by the beautiful but soon-to-disappear Jacqueline Logan, who combined the charms of generations of females of the fatal stripe. I winced. Mr. De Mille patiently explained how essential it was that the Broadway audiences of the world be won over; how they could not be introduced to burlap and desert sands, but must have a sense of luxury and beauty, the kind of life they would themselves like to lead. "If they fall in love with Magdalene, then when she leaps into her chariot and says, 'I go to find a Carpenter,' they will go along."

Yet a strange thing had begun to happen, something which I have told and retold a hundred times since. Christ began to take over. It was a motion-picture Christ. It was a Christ of synthetic whiskers and grease paint. H. B. Warner was a good actor but by no means a great one. The figure of the Savior first appeared through the eyes of a blind girl to whom He restored sight. He moved about in His public life, quietly, effectively, miraculously, without too much emphasis on the divine nature (this was not eliminated but never underlined), and yet compellingly. Christ was doing to the film what Christ does to all life, once He has been given a chance. He was so dominating it that no one else mattered. His figure was becoming so overwhelming that the other characters faded into secondary positions. He was the Great Man, the compelling personality, the one in whom all the love and hatred centered.

We were sitting watching rushes one evening, when Mr. De Mille leaned over and touched my hand.

"He is great, isn't He?" he said.

"Warner?" I asked, pretending not to understand that he had capitalized the pronoun.

"Jesus," he replied. "He is great." There was a long pause, and then he spoke very quietly. "I doubt if we shall need the story of Mary Magdalene and Judas."

I grinned at him through the dim light of the projector.

"That is the wisest decision you have made," I answered, and we turned to watch Jesus Christ, played by an actor straight from Alias-Jimmy-Valentine roles, walk through make-believe scenery and yet dominate the hushed audience of actors, technicians, and make-up people, who watched Him and hardly breathed.

The Judas-Mary Magdalene story was trimmed down to a scant two hundred and fifty feet, and Christ was the hero who needed no fiction, no love story beyond His own historic love for mankind, no support by secondary personalities who, in His presence, faded to unimpressive or acted-upon shadows.

I have always been glad that this attempt to bring Christ to the screen resulted in a film that never has known a day since 1927 when it was not shown in some corner of the earth. I am glad that the critics praised and the audiences flocked to see it. We spent long days working out the subtitles, which were soon rendered almost useless by the introduction of the newly discovered sound-on-film. Eventually a sound version was produced to take the place of the silent film. The Resurrection was left in its startling technicolor. The rest of the film, except the introduction of Magdalene and her court, was in black and white.

The Protestant minister and I watched some retakes of the Resurrection. As we walked from the set, blinded by the fierce lights that flooded the figure of Christ as the stone rolled away from the tomb, the minister said to me, "How consoling that must be to those who accept the Resurrection literally." I think I blinked, but not with the strain of the lights. "I take it literally," I answered with as little emphasis as possible. "You do?" he said very much surprised. "Indeed I do," I replied, and he changed the subject.

My contribution to *The King of Kings* was singularly slight. At best, I was there on the set for brief days, as a protection against mistakes. So I had a great deal of time to watch the technical side of picturemaking, to get to know, less the actors and actresses, who are sometimes dull and preoccupied with their brief burst of fame, than the technicians and the cameramen, the musicians and the artists. It was wonderful to get to know the congress of nations which at that time assembled around the silent cameras: great character actors and actresses from Vienna and Prague and Budapest; artists from Paris and Berlin; musicians trained to interpret the masterpieces of the greatest composers. I said Mass regularly on the set while we were in Catalina. I heard confessions sitting on piles of lumber. Once I preached, using the carpenter bench of the Lord as my pulpit. I ventured onto other sets and watched some of the great directors at work, realizing how completely they dominate the actors, and why it is that the producers and directors come to feel that they can create stars out of stableboys and glamor girls out of waitresses. They exaggerate their own power; but there is reason enough for their feeling something like contempt for the majority of the big-name stars before whom the public burns its incense.

As Elizabeth of England said to her bishops, "I made you and, by God, I can unmake you!" The public never pays much attention to the names of the men who make and unmake the idols of the hour. I saw them made and saw them scrapped even in my short contact with Hollywood.

As in tragedy, I saw the stars of last year and a few years before haunting the casting offices begging for bit parts to pay overdue rent in cheap boardinghouses. The caprice of the public, the black-listing of the studios, a change in popular tastes, a disagreement with a powerful producer—and the lights of yesteryear burn out to greasy extinction. I came to Hollywood with great curiosity and zest. I left it with infinite relief. It burned up human life too fast. It was too much the Moloch for beauty and brains. And underneath the intense and fantastic operations of the studios ran an undercurrent of living as false as the façades of many a Hollywood stucco house. I made many friends and kept some of them; but I wanted no permanent part in what seemed to me the Waiting Room of Genius, the Distillery of Beauty and Ability, the Cuckoo Colony.

My brief connection with Mr. De Mille cast about me an unexpected glamor. I recall with amusement meeting for the first time since student days a good friend, who brought along his daughter. She regarded me with open, admiring eyes. Ah, thought I to myself, Harry has told her about his school-days' chum, retailed some of our pranks, and built me up in her imagination. Then she spoke, and there was a thrill in her voice; "Is it true that you know Cecil de Mille?" she asked.

Newspaper items about me continued for long years to mention the fact that I had been adviser to De Mille on *The King of Kings.* My small role as Catholic guide seemed to me blown up out of all proportion. At intervals my friendship for Mr. De Mille was renewed. I came to know the charming lady to whom he has been married for over fifty years; to write on occasion to his children; to know the hospitality of his beautiful establishment on De Mille Drive. In the end, I had to be the one to contradict him flatly.

He had been for a long time planning *The Queen of Queens* to complement or sequel *The King of Kings.* We had discussed this often, and I had taken the stand that he ventured on very dangerous ground. "If you do a film on Mary," I said, "you run the risk of offending both the Protestants and the Catholics. Protestants will think you pro-Catholic if you praise Mary and present her beautifully. But if you put into the film the slightest element that Catholics think unfitting to associate with Mary, you will hear such an outcry that you'll be forced to run for shelter. You see, we Catholics feel we own the Blessed Mother. And we'll permit nothing that lacks dignity and beauty and truth to be associated with her."

Some years later Mr. De Mille sent on his brother, William, to go over with me a scenario for *The Queen of Queens.* William de Mille is a sensitive and delicate artist who did some truly great films. He came from Broadway, where he had done beautiful work for the theater, was long associated with the silent pictures as one of the most esteemed directors, and then retired to the scholarly seclusion of the drama department of the University of Southern California.

Together William and I spent two days on the scenario for the Blessed Virgin film. It was completely dreadful. The story focused around the love affair of Judas, this time with Salome, the daughter of Herodias. The climactic scene occurred during the dance of the seven veils, with Mary in the garden outside the house of Herod, and the camera swinging back from the dancing Salome to the suffering Mother in the shadows as she tries to save John the Baptist.

"Frankly," said I, "the Catholic public will raise the roof!"

William had come to St. Louis chilly to the whole idea of the film. He knew that the scenario was a hash and a hazard, and though he presented it to me with objective justice and some show of enthusiasm, the moment I began to take it apart, he was entirely in agreement. After two days I sent to Cecil and William each a seven-page criticism of the scenario, with a statement of all the reasons why it must not and could not be done and a prediction as to what would happen in the Catholic world if that script ever became a screen reality.

When we had been working on *The King of Kings,* with considerable amusement Cecil showed me a cartoon of himself, labeled "The Man that Nobody No's." Indeed, I had been warned by many that to him you said yes. The one who corrected that was Jeanie Macpherson, who told me that I was to say no whenever the situation called for no. If I made any contribution to his great film, it was my constant use of the word no when I thought the scene simply would not do for the story of Christ. Now I was saying no to an entire subject. In the future when we met, Mr. De Mille regarded me a little sorrowfully and reminded me that I had blocked the production of *The Queen of Queens.* Personally, I think that was Mr. De Mille's good luck.

It seems to have been somewhat my fate to keep films about the Blessed Virgin off the screen. A good many years later Warner Brothers invited me out to work on the script for *The Miracle.* In the twenties Max Reinhardt and Morris Gest had imported the great German production to the United States and in vast auditoriums transformed into pseudocathedrals had staged the legend of the nun who elopes with the knight, to return years later and discover to her wonder that our Lady had taken her place in the convent and covered the shame of her defection. The story was bought by Hollywood, which found it too hot to handle. Eloping nuns are not box-office material, and the story, done other than on the most elaborate scale, would fall flat.

Stephen Vincent Benét and Samson Raphaelson (author of *The Jazz Singer*) were among the writers who had done treatments of the story. My advice at the beginning and in the final analysis was, "Don't! Protestants will call it Catholic propaganda; Catholics will think it anti-Catholic; and nobody will be happy." Rumor has it that a new treatment will bring it to the screen. When I had finished my work some ten years ago, the Benét, Raphaelson, and my own treatment were filed away without requiem or obituary. But it was a pleasure to work with Henry Blanke, a very great producer and a charming gentleman.

My plunge into work with sodalists took me completely out of the atmosphere of Hollywood. Because the heroes and heroines offered for their admiration had too often been tailored to admiration by the men who made the movies, I kept my eye on developments, saw all the pictures that seemed important, and watched the deterioration of the films. But my work was directly with the young people and only indirectly with the films, which were exercising a powerful influence upon the customs, manners, and morals of American life.

Up in Chicago, however, one of my really close friends, the great and generous Father FitzGeorge Dinneen, S.J., was up to his ears in the rapidly swelling threat of censorship. He was pastor of the great St. Ignatius Parish on the new North Side, and to protect his people against what he rightly judged the morally destructive influence of the pictures of that day, he had not hesitated to run a boycott against the vast Granada Theater only two blocks from his church. When he asked the management not to show an objectionable film, he was invited to mind his own business. Considering the rotten film paraded in his parish very much his business, he denounced it from the pulpit, initiated a boycott of the theater, and soon brought the managers to their knees with the film chucked into the garbage can where it belonged.

His militant attitude brought him to the attention of Cardinal Mundelein, worried, as most decent people and reputable leaders of the twenties were, at the rapid downsliding of the films. Chicago had an official board of censors connected with the Police Department. Like all boards of the sort, it admitted to frequent flounderings but sincerely expressed a desire to receive guidance. The police recognized the effect of bad movies on the adolescent and the potential criminal. They could see no difference between sex crimes and motion pictures that excited to sex crimes or actually glorified them. They felt it was a police duty to protect citizenry from men making money out of sex and crime in the films as it was to protect them against the sale of dope or the peddling of intoxicating drink to children. A lot of people disagreed with them then, as they disagree with them now. It is permitted to examine food to be sure that poisoned food is not sold in the groceries; it is not permitted to censor films to head off the corrupt who sell vicious sex on the screen. We are careful to safeguard the water supply; we think it an intrusion of freedom to stop the flow of rotten entertainment.

At any rate, the police in sincere if often-mistaken fashion were trying to plug off the obscene and crime-laden films of the era. They asked for guidance. Cardinal Mundelein asked Father Dinneen to sit in with them as, simultaneously, as many as four pictures (still silent) were rolled over the screens. Obviously it was a tiresome assignment. There was no entertainment value in watching simultaneously four films being screened. The object was not to enjoy a pleasant morning at a private theater but to prevent the showing of the scenes of passion and lust and brutality and precise crime methods which were so common in those pre-code days. If anyone, by the way, thinks that the code stopped artistry and sophisticated entertainment and adult films, he doesn't realize that the plots were puerile, that the thought content was less than zero, and that the scenes of violence had all the sophistication of an axe murder or a seduction in an alley.

Father Dinneen spent many a tiresome and disgusted morning sitting with the police censors. The more he saw, the more furious he grew and the more he feared for the youngsters of his parish, for whose entertainment and wholesome fun he had just built a beautiful gymnasium, remodeled a lovely auditorium, and started the Loyola Community Theatre. Father Dinneen was no long-faced Puritan objecting to fun. He made delightful recreation accessible to his parishioners. He constructively provided for their recreation on almost a seven-day-a-week program at the very time he was trying to staunch the flow of filth through the lens of the movie projector.

I had done considerable work with and for Father Dinneen. He had called Father Egan and me to Chicago to discuss with him the reconstruction of his recreational center. We had helped with the new stage, the new gym, the new clubrooms. I had written some of his first plays for him, and became a very close friend of Charles Costello, his dramatic director. Often we groaned together over the horrible stuff that came pouring out of Hollywood—always along with some excellent films and some high-type entertainment. I felt that Father Dinneen had the wise double approach: constructively he gave his people fine entertainment in the Loyola Community Theatre and backed with his approval the good films; furiously he attacked the evil films and worked with the police to keep them (along with dope, poisonous food, and spoiled canned goods) away from the public markets.

It was about this time that I was in New York and that I got word that the Will Hays office (established in an effort to fend off censorship and weld the wildcat motion-picture industry into a reputable business enterprise) was playing host to a large number of representatives of clubs and organizations. I dropped into the hotel where the meetings were taking place and sat far back in the auditorium. Around me were gathered the delegates, brought on at Mr. Hays' invitation, from societies and organizations which professed to represent some forty million well-intentioned men and women. They were lunched and dined and shown pictures and talked to by men from the Hays office. They were assured of the high purposes of the motion-picture industry and invited to let the industry know their likes and dislikes, their approval and their disapproval.

The meeting had far progressed when I dropped by. In the chair at the time was a man who became a good friend of mine, Mr. Charles C. Pettijohn, a very smart lawyer whom Mr. Hays had introduced into the Hays office. He was rounding off an eloquent report in which he professed the industry's acceptance of responsibility for clean entertainment, the desire of Mr. Hays to feel that he had the cooperation of the millions represented by these distinguished ladies and gentlemen, and an open ear that would be lent to their suggestions and complaints. He called for questions.

There were a few innocuous questions from timid clubwomen, and then one lady asked an important one.

"So often," she said, "the advertisement for the picture seems to me quite dreadful. Isn't something possible to stop that salacious advertising, the kind of theater poster and newspaper advertising that is evil and suggestive and vile?"

Mr. Pettijohn regarded her with surprise and gratitude.

"My dear lady," he replied, "you will do the industry a great favor if you will watch for that type of advertising. Let us know when you see it, and send us the clipping. We will bear down upon the theater showing our pictures and using that type of copy. We'll soon bring the exhibitor to time."

That was too much for me. I rose from my spot far back in the hall and said: "Mr. Pettijohn, how can you mislead the lady so completely? Why don't you tell her that all that advertising, with the rarest of rare exceptions, originates in the industry itself? The advertising is part of the product; it is got out by the company that produces the film. It is sent to the theater manager and the exhibitor. It comes from one central source on a national and a local-release basis. Why do you suggest that evil advertising is a surprise to you and that the rotten ads are originated by the local exhibitor when all the time you know the lady ought to be informed that they come right out of the same company that produced the picture?"

There was a moment of awful silence.

Mr. Pettijohn craned through the crowded hall to locate the tosser of the bomb. Then he saw my Roman collar, talked fast and ambiguously, and used words to cover up the unpleasant fact I was exposing. The moment the meeting recessed, he ran through the crowd like a broken-field runner, heading for me. We introduced ourselves and he assured me that I was right and that Mr. Hays would like to meet me, and could I call at their office. I liked him. He was a gruff, outspoken man, married to a Catholic wife, and willing to admit that he had been pulling herrings across an uncomfortably telltale trail.

All over the country in those early thirties—and earlier still—a wide variety of forces were bearing in on the motion pictures. The industry is prone to forget what an expensive process it was for them to struggle with the local censorship boards. Pennsylvania and New York and Ohio and Illinois were particularly tough. A film might have a thousand feet cut out of it in Pennsylvania, and another five hundred in New York. The Ohio censors, notoriously exacting, would throw out whole scenes for their state, and Illinois police censors would bear down on still more footage. The film got to look like ribbon that had been hacked by a child's shears. It cost the companies small fortunes to cut, to resplice, to take out, to put back, to satisfy digressing tastes, to see their positives hacked to pieces. Sometimes a single set of cuts in a single state might cost the company many thousands of dollars. And they knew little in advance about what the censors would order removed and what would happen to their precious positives. It was an expensive business, and the companies were not happy about it.

The rising tide of protest swelled and swelled. I have sometimes come across pictures of the period and looked at them with growing incredulity. It is hard to recall how rotten some of them were, how suggestive was the comedy, how frequent with nudity, how the plots had narrowed down to seduction and murder and rape and illegitimate children and immoral women and rapacious men. I have often felt it would do those demanding a repeal of the code a lot of good if they were obliged to sit through the uncut films released to women, children, the morons of the world, and the general public during those final days of Lust and Crime Let Loose. They are frankly incredible.

One man in the United States was doing his full share of worrying about the constantly worsening situation. Martin J. Quigley was a graduate of Georgetown University. He had become a member of the lay board of Loyola University in Chicago, the school which had blossomed forth from my small St. Ignatius College. He had a lovely Catholic wife and a growing family. And in the early days of the film boom he had wisely turned toward one branch of the industry hitherto neglected. He published *Motion Picture Herald* for the motion-picture theater owner and operator. He published similar trade journals to keep them informed of the product which would be offered to them. He had initiated and was bringing to high success an annual that was a kind of guidebook for the whole industry.

But in the pages of his publications he had to release the advertisements sent out from the Hollywood and New York production offices. And often enough they were starkly indecent. His reviewers in advance had to tell the theater managers and owners, in supposedly objective critiques, the quality and value of the pictures they would be asked to buy and exhibit. He had to run interviews with producers and magnates who were responsible for movie filth. He was the medium through which the tainted product reached the men who would retail it to the American and foreign trade.

It was a tough spot for an honorable and religious-minded man. I used to page through his publications and shudder. The ads were salacious in case after case. The mere outline of the plot as his reviewers presented it to the theater operators showed what kind of film they would be displaying. And I took it for granted that Mr. Quigley was not in a very happy situation.

Simultaneously, a surprising little man got out another journal for the trade called *Harrison's Reports*. He carried no advertising. He just reviewed the pictures for the exhibitors and told them exactly what they were getting. Often he described gutter events in the gutter language they rated. He called lust lust and not romance and rape rape and not gentle dalliance. He was not deeply loved by the industry, but a great many of the exhibitors felt he was their good friend.

Father Dinneen and I both subscribed for Mr. Quigley's weekly and for *Harrison's Reports,* and often in Father Dinneen's living room we read them together and shuddered.

Father Dinneen and I came to know Martin Quigley well. We liked him as a man and sympathized with the strange position that made him resent and be troubled by the very product his publications had to advertise. I believe Father Dinneen became acquainted with Harrison; I never personally met him. But in a short time Father Dinneen and Mr. Quigley were talking about what could be done, and the pressure of a great many events began to squeeze the situation into a manageable form. For a lot of things were happening.

Just for a convenient order, we might start with the coming of sound. When the Warner Brothers hit on Vitaphone, they were close to financial collapse. The pictures began first to squawk and then to talk and a new box-office audience rushed to hear the fantastic shadows blat and bleat.

But the sounds that now issued forth from the mouths of the cavorting shadows created a new situation. They had to speak some measure of sense. In the silent days nobody cared what any of the actors said. I have sat with my deaf-mute friends at the showing of a silent picture and seen them shake with unexplained laughter. What the lips of the actors were forming and what the sense of the scene demanded had no slightest connection. We who had ears missed the incongruity, but not the deaf-mutes, trained to read lips.

Amusing beyond words would be a scene in the silent pictures when men of different dialects talked together, their gestures and expressions caught by the camera, the words dying on empty air. In one scene in *The King of Kings* I recall Warner saying the word "fish" in an English accent; Torrence repeated the word as "fuuush," with a strong Scottish burr; and Schildkraut caught it up and in a Yiddish accent said, "Oi, feeeesh?"

Ray Graham of the Graham-Paige Motor Corporation asked me to go with him to the opening night of one of Vitaphone's first "part-talking" films shown on Broadway. Most of the film had been silent. Dolores Costello starred with Conrad Nagel in a stereotyped drama to which had been added a few scenes of dialogue. The audience sat pained through a quartet scene singing "Sweet Adeline." When the heroine spoke, the *s* sounds were prolonged hisses. Nobody had bothered to hire a dialogue writer, and the climax came when the villain broke into the heroine's room. He put his foot through the door and Vitaphone recorded the sound of a man shattering an empty orange crate. He tore a sheet of paper and the sound was the ripping of oilcloth. He moved toward the heroine, panic-stricken in the fashion of that day at impending rape, and then she opened her hissing lips and cried: "Don't look at me like that! Oh, don't look at me like that! You too may have a sister."

The Broadway audience howled. It was the old ten-twent'-thirt' melodrama at its worst. The word "sister" came out "shisther" . . . and the whole scene fell into the realms of low comedy.

So the transcontinental trains were packed with writers summoned to save the talking pictures with clever dialogue and brilliant conversation. But the men who came, along with the great dramatists and famous writers of good stories, were the very men whose smut drama, suggestive vaudeville skits, and blackouts for the musical shows had just slaughtered the legitimate drama of the United States. Outside New York the theater was totally dead. There had been a time when every small town had its opera house; now none remained.

New York with its large transient population of visitors could support questionable shows and obscene comedy. A man might leave his home town and "on the loose" take in that type of show. The same show would not be tolerated in the small American town. The reputable citizen would be embarrassed to be seen there. He would not permit his wife and children to attend. It would not be raw enough for the village scum, even if they had money to support it. The decent people stayed away. And the theater died.

I recall discussing this at great length with Pat Casey, for years the vice president and booking agent of the B. F. Keith Circuit. "The dogs! The dirty, filthy dogs!" he said, not sparing the profanity. "They've killed the theater. Every form of entertainment that goes bad goes out of business—the dime museum, the carnival, burlesque, the theater, vaudeville. There was a time when vaudeville was a gold mine. It was family entertainment. Every Monday afternoon one of our representatives sat in the stage box. If a comedian got off a shady joke, a damn or a hell, we slapped a ten-dollar fine on him. If he did it twice, his act was out and he was black-listed. Men came and brought their wives and children and Grandma and Aunt Suzie. If a dancer started pulling the rough stuff, she was warned, and then she was out. This was a decent place for decent people. But the dirty so-and-so's, they couldn't leave well enough alone. They had to spoil it and soil it and make it rotten with their smutty jokes and dirty sketches and nakedness and obscenity. And vaudeville is deader than a mule-drawn canalboat.

"And now those same dirty, filthy, stupid this-and-that's are ruining the motion pictures and nobody seems to care."

They piled out to Hollywood by the Chief-full. They brought along the blackouts and their risqué situations and their smutty dialogues. The movies had learned to talk and they would swiftly be taught to say mean, low, crude, and filthy things. Even Hollywood, clamoring for authors, grew alarmed over the authors who came and the material they began to inject into the films.

Silent smut had been bad. Vocal smut cried to the censors for vengeance.

Still another element was added to the complication, this time a fortunate one. The panic of 1929 and the early thirties hit nothing harder than it hit the expanding, slap-happy, prodigal motion-picture industry, which knew that it had found a bottomless mine of gold and that nothing could ever stop the cash from rolling into the box office. It's a fantastic story that only a financier could tell. But the motion-picture companies suddenly found themselves faced with bankruptcy, thrown into the hands of the banks, and suddenly handled by the bankers themselves.

The carefree days were over. Their booming stocks suddenly had the value of old Mack Sennett bathing suits. The bankers were not tossing them wads of money to put into pictures, name known, plot yet undecided. Indeed, the banks suddenly and exasperatingly found themselves in the motion-picture business. The stock was dumped back into their reluctant hands. The pants pressers and glove merchants turned financial geniuses were suddenly begging for lunch money. And the bankers had to take a first look at the stuff which they had been happily and heedlessly financing.

Now in a combination of circumstances that is a little too pat for easy credulity, a lot of things congealed.

Will Hays had got out a series of moral warnings called in the trade the "Do's and Don't's." These were things that must not be done, matters of good taste and common decency. They were isolated statements, unconnected, in no way complete or clear. But they were preliminary warning that the industry was aware it had better mend its ways and that the Hays office was prepared to help guide the companies to some degree of self-regulation.

Once a week Cardinal Mundelein of Chicago had lunch with the officials of Halsey Stuart and Company, one of the world's largest and most influential financial firms, bankers, handlers of stocks and bonds. Across the luncheon table the bankers told the cardinal how into their laps had been dumped the control of motion-picture companies. They were frankly shocked with what they now owned. They wanted no part of the crime and vice movies that were all too common from Hollywood.

The International Federation of Catholic Alumnae had long been issuing a list of approved pictures. They selected the good and praised these, though they pointedly ignored the bad. At least, someone was trying to sort out the good from the bad, and some sort of list was being drawn up.

Across the country federal censorship rose like a threatening storm cloud. States were tightening their censorship with constantly mounting expense for the producing companies. Censorship was a very real fact and no Supreme Court of those days dreamed of suggesting that a city or a state had no right to protect its citizens against moral filth and education to crime. The pure-food law had outlawed the making and marketing of rotten tomatoes and embalmed beef and arsenic in the beans and peas; and no one saw any reason why similar laws might not protect innocent children and decent family people from corrupt and rotten entertainment.

Meanwhile Father Dinneen and Martin Quigley held their meetings and dreamed their dreams. All the censorship in the world would not be the equivalent of cleaning up the films at their source. If the motion-picture industry, which had already adopted a series of business codes, could be persuaded to adopt a morals code, the reformation might be official, almost easy. It was a day when the cutthroat competition of American business was disappearing. Oil companies agreed to live in peace. Leather and cement companies signed pacts outlawing unfair business practices. And the motion-picture industry had followed these eminently sane procedures.

They had signed agreements forbidding the pirating of one another's stars, a practice of long standing. There had long been a practice, regarded as smart business, to watch for a big picture, and just before its issuance, slip out a similar picture with a like title and a similar plot to take the edge off the big one, and steal some of its audience. This was agreed upon as bad business. They began to copyright titles and plots and respected one another's properties. They started to liberalize their policy of working with labor. All this fell under the dominion of the Hays office and was paying off in better feeling, more reputable business dealings, and general improvement of conditions.

Martin Quigley was convinced that the time had now come for the presentation to the industry by the Hays office of a morals code, a code of responsibility for their relationship to the audience. The "Do's and Don't's" had been a beginning. He knew that a number of people had drawn up amplifications of these, among them the boy wonder of Metro-Goldwyn-Mayer, Irving Thalberg, and several men in the Hays office. None of them was complete, comprehensive, simple, and in a way foolproof.

If the cardinal of Chicago could become interested in more than just police censorship, if he could be sold on the value of the industry's assuming its own censorship, if he could bring this to the attention of the bankers who now controlled much of the industry, if he were ready with a morals code, not Catholic but basically decent, moral, and acceptable to all right-minded people, this might be the precise moment to present it to the industry itself.

Martin Quigley's belief convinced Father Dinneen. On his next meeting with Cardinal Mundelein about the rising tide of evil films, Father Dinneen suggested to his eminence that the time might be ripe for the industry to do its own censoring. Would his eminence propose this to Halsey Stuart and Company? He promptly did, and the bankers, relieved at the possibility of cleaning up the dirtiest and most annoying of their financial babies, agreed to pressure the companies. But who would give them a code that would cover the case and be acceptable to all?

Father Dinneen then sent for me. Far into the night Martin Quigley and Father Dinneen and I sat in Father Dinneen's rectory discussing what had to be done. The code must be so written that the follower of any religion, or any man of decent feeling and conviction, would read it and instantly agree. It must make morality attractive, and the sense of responsibility of the movies to its public clear and unmistakable. It must be a matter of general principles and their immediate relationship to the practical plots and situations of a film. It must cover all the essentials and go far enough into particulars as to be an easy guide for men who wanted to know precisely what was expected of them, how far they might be allowed to go, and how tightly they would be bound.

Father Dinneen turned to me. Would I be willing to attempt to write such a code? It was a challenge. Here was a chance to tie the Ten Commandments in with the newest and most widespread form of entertainment. Here was an opportunity to read morality and decency into mass recreation. Here was an industry that might be persuaded to avoid the police by a sane and honorable policy. Could the code be written that would stand up before the immoralist, the amoralist, the skilled dramatist, the producer who had risen from the slums, the auditor, the audience, the films of the day and of fifty years from now? I agreed most willingly to try. Then things moved swiftly.

Father Dinneen and the cardinal worked together and the bankers told their companies that they would be expected to act like moral men and reputable executives and not like dirty-minded small boys with chunks of chalk and a broad expanse of back fence.

Martin Quigley, who was very close to Will Hays, approached him with a most attractive proposition. The cardinal of Chicago would be willing to send his personal representative, on invitation from the Hays office, to offer them a morals code which, once accepted, would solve Mr. Hays' biggest problem and give the industry a guide which would make possible decent and at the same time entertaining films.

Mr. Hays and Martin Quigley carried the idea to the member companies of the Motion Picture Association, of which Hays was the head. The top men were impressed with the idea. The business and fair-practice agreements they had signed had been all to the good. A morals agreement might be equally profitable. They had been already warned by the threat of censorship. They knew that they were in a bad financial way. The bankers had begun to pressure them to clean up or close up. Indeed, the financial pressure was for the moment the big one, and they were listening.

Martin Quigley and Father Dinneen had one radical difference of opinion. Quigley believed that the companies would sign such a code and that, once signed, Will Hays would be strong enough to see that the code was enforced. Father Dinneen, out of his grim experiences with the films that flowed through the police-board censorship room, doubted that they would so willingly turn from easy filth to more difficult artistic enterprise. He thought they would sign. He doubted that they would keep their word.

In the interval, I had worked on the code.

The first draft of that code is still in my files with the A.M.D.G., B.V.M.H. at the top of the paper and my penciled notations on the margins. I set myself to write a code that beyond all else would be short and simple. Few people have ever bothered to read the complete code. Fewer still ever knew that it was divided into several sections.

The first section laid down the moral responsibility of the motion-picture industry as a "public service organization." We then considered the difference between the wide sweep of the films and the limited appeal of the other arts. General principles of morality followed in their bearing on entertainment. The code properly so called, the principles that would make good or bad pictures, were considered. A final section took up suggestions on the future approach to pictures and their making. I brought the code to Father Dinneen and Martin Quigley; Father Dinneen carried it to the cardinal of Chicago; and Martin Quigley relayed it to Will Hays.

Apparently Mr. Hays was delighted. With Mr. Quigley he set up a meeting of all the heads of the motion-picture industry. They were given advance copies of the code, and word flashed back to Chicago that I was to come out, present the code to the leaders, spend time explaining it in detail to the men in Will Hays' office who would put it into execution, and stand back while the signatures were affixed. So out I went with Father Dinneen's blessing, with the official backing of Cardinal Mundelein, to arrangements made by Martin Quigley, and on the expressed invitation of Will Hays.

Always it must be remembered that every step of actual initiative was taken by the industry. The code was forced upon them by no moral agency or religious group. The bankers were disgusted with the product which the financial collapse of the early thirties had given to them over their protest. The industry knew that censorship had been frightfully expensive, that the women's organizations of the country were rising in just wrath, that federal censorship might well be a possibility, and that growing state censorship was a fact they could not shrug off. Many of the decent men inside the industry were sick and tired of competing with the elements among them who fed the audiences red meat and then wondered that the pleasantly good pictures lost appeal.

It would be totally unfair to the good and honorable men in the production of motion pictures to suggest that they had not been disgusted with the tidal wave of filth and crime. But they were forced to compete with the ruthless and the unscrupulous.

Smut requires no brains and dirt comes out of the minds and hearts of the dullest and most illiterate. There is a sort of crude and compelling humor in the dirty joke which, tiresome and repetitious as it is, never loses its quick appeal. A beautiful woman willing to expose herself needs no talent or ability. Feed the audience blood and sex for a time, and they have known so highly seasoned a diet that a good story has almost no appeal for them. The child glutted with a diet of comic books and sensational TV finds the classics a great bore and poor entertainment.

Martin Quigley with Mr. Hays had gone far toward persuading the top men in the industry that the code would be good business. The decent among them were tired of constantly having to shape their product to match the films of the moral anarchists. They needed, however, precise and exact guidance. They confessed often enough that for all possible good will they got confused at the plots and situations offered to them by their authors, producers, and directors. Once the questionable scene was shot, it was expensive business to scrap it on moral grounds and do it all over again. With a code they would rid themselves of the confusion and fog and doubt in which they worked. They would have standards, their own personally accepted standards. They would not be groping and going down dark alleys and finding themselves in endless trouble.

The code looked like good business and certainly was magnificent public relations. They could calmly assert to the world that the motion-picture industry knew its moral obligations, accepted them, and would keep them with a solemnly pledged word.

It was an impressive group of leaders who gathered round the luncheon table for my presentation of the code. Mr. Hays himself presided. Mr. Martin Quigley could feel that the moment was largely of his management. I came with the code in my hand, and instructions to take half an hour to present it as only the actual author of the written document could do. For half an hour of the most rapid possible talking, I laid the code before them, explained what seemed to need explanation, and stressed less the actual "law" of the code than the reasons for its existence and what I thought could grow out of the acceptance of the code. To me it seemed to open possibilities for simply magnificent pictures that never would be done as long as the industry floundered and lazed about in gutters and dirt and crime.

At the end Mr. Cecil B. de Mille made a brief speech of thanks, stressing the fact that my work had been done through interest in the motion-picture industry, and with no financial consideration. Mr. Hays adjourned the meeting for whatever time and place would be agreeable for signing the code. The leaders of the industry left in agreement that they would sign and that the code would be effective almost immediately.

My work was then transferred to the Hays office, where I sat down at a series of meetings to explain to the men responsible for enforcing the code and explaining it to the individual companies exactly what each section of the code was intended to mean. I found this a charming group of honorable and well-intentioned men. They had been selected for personal honor and their ability to stand before the public and represent the companies of the industry in all matters of policy.

Carl Milliken, formerly governor of Maine, stands out in my memory. But I turn back with affection and high esteem to Colonel Jason S. Joy, with whom I was to do considerable work. More than any other one individual the work of explaining the code would fall upon him. He was a fine gentleman, a family man, enlisted into the Hays office because of his experience in dealing with social problems and public relations in their better sense. Even when, not too long afterwards, he became personal assistant to Darryl Zanuck, head of Twentieth-Century-Fox, our friendship continued. I never doubted his sincere desire to see the code effective. Even in the very dark days that followed the signing, when our hopes collapsed and the pictures worsened, I was convinced that Jason Joy was on the side of the angels, and but for one fact, not his responsibility, he would have put the code into operation. That "one fact" comes up shortly.

From the beginning of my connection with the code, I was surrounded with something which always bores me, a sort of "hush-hush" attitude, a "let's-not-talk-about-this"; an air of secrecy that was often annoying. Quite naturally, the industry did not wish the connection of the cardinal of Chicago with the code to be known. Mr. Hays rightly felt that it was most effective if the spontaneous nature of the code was stressed, the fact that it grew out of the good will of the industry. He was later willing to let the code be called the Hays code. And the industry never felt that the code would be stronger than when presented as their own expression of responsibility to the community.

As a consequence my connection with the code was very much played down. My name did not appear. The meetings of the leaders of the industry, my long sessions with the men in the Hays office, had no publicity whatsoever. I heartily agreed that it would be the greatest possible mistake to announce that the actual authorship of the code, the words in which it was expressed, could be laid at the feet of a Catholic priest, and a Jesuit at that. Authorship was not important. Acceptance by the industry, the public presentation of the document as their compact and professed agreement, was what mattered.

Much time and thought was given to the question of how and under what circumstances the code would be given to the public. I was back in St. Louis when the news broke, and not as the industry had meant it to. *Variety,* "The Bible of the Entertainment World," spread the whole code out over its front page and carried it into the mid-section. Who slipped the code to the editors of *Variety* I never learned. But the gallant presentation planned for a release to the whole country was spoiled. Martin Quigley was in an understandable rage. Somebody had blabbed. The industry was tricked of its chance to make a formal first presentation to the country. And Quigley's own *Motion Picture Herald* had been scooped by a rival entertainment journal.

My own connection with the code was kept almost unexplainably secret. It surprised me a little that none of the gossip columnists of the day made it a point. I was much relieved that bigotry got no chance to scorn the code because it was the product of a Jesuit. I agreed completely with the policy of silence, and for years never mentioned my authorship except in Hollywood, the Hays office in New York, or among close friends. The code seemed to me no occasion for personal claims. I had done it because the cardinal of Chicago had appointed me, because Mr.

Will Hays had invited me, because Mr. Martin Quigley had seen the attempted codes which had been written prior to this and found them wanting, and because it was a wonderful opportunity to do what seemed to me a worth-while job. Years later my name began to appear in connection with accounts of the code. The Luce publications referred to it, as did some of the Hollywood columnists. I continued to make no mention of it as mine. It belonged to the industry and it was much better that it be that way. At long length my name came into the context with growing frequence.

And then, as often happens, a sort of blur began to overcast the authorship. The idea of a code was not new. Dozens of industries had accepted responsibility in various ways by signed documents. The "Do's and Don't's" had carved a sort of precedent for the movie industry. The Will Hays office had made other agreements which turned out to be valuable and profitable to the industry. Mr. Martin Quigley felt sure that an adequate code would be welcomed by the motion-picture producers. My own continued interest in the theater and the films and my close connection with the very zealous Father Dinneen made me a "natural" to give the code its form and wording.

But "authorship" in Hollywood is a slightly disdained word. When there is question of a film, anywhere from three to ten men may be called upon to write the script. Usually the last man employed, or perhaps the last three, get the full credit for the completed job. I was always amused at the lowly position of the writer in the films. The author of the original book or play was not often encouraged to come to the studio and watch the metamorphosis of his work. His cries of pain were likely to interfere with the film's progress. Anyhow, it was taken for granted that he was the last person in the world who knew how to turn his written achievement into a moving film. The scenarists were well paid. But they were in general in the lower social caste. Rarely did one of them rise to the exalted level of producer or even director. So an "author" in the studios is seen but not heard; and the screen credits brush his name lightly.

Silence about my authorship of the code I took for granted. In fact, I agreed to the policy. It surprised me, however, when of a sudden I began to notice that others were credited with the authorship. Some of the claimants should, it seemed to me, know better. I even wrote to one claimant and told him that if it gave him any satisfaction to claim to have written the code, I would certainly not contradict him.

The final release of the code to the country met, as far as I can recall, real approval and enthusiasm. Almost a sigh of relief rose from countless men and women who loved the films and yet hated to see what had come over them by way of poisonous blight in the course of years. We all sat back with a feeling of "Now we have hope for decent pictures, lots of them, and a disappearance of the pictures that have done so much harm."

Among the things which I had done during my work with the Hays office was to outline whole categories of film subjects which it seemed to me had hardly been touched. I recall recommending such things as stories of business, great biographies, sports stories, skating pictures, stories of small towns rather than big cities or frontiers, stories directed toward women's interests. The list was long, and few of the fields had ever been touched. Because it seemed to me that there is an audience for problem stories, I urged that the motion-picture theater operators, besides their vast theaters and their neighborhood theaters reaching out to men, women, children, the young, the old, the educated and the illiterate, should think in terms of small theaters. I suggested they build or rent theaters to seat perhaps five hundred to a thousand, and for these theaters produce an inexpensive but well-acted story that would face problems, bring into discussion subjects that for vast, uncontrolled audiences would be taboo, charge almost theater prices instead of the mass-box-office rates, and cater to that "sophisticated audience" about which we hear so much.

It gave me some pleasure when the neglected categories I had listed, once the code became effective, began to be explored. I am sorry that the small theaters which since developed to a very limited degree are called by the unfortunate name of "art theaters." Art has a way of scaring off the average American. Yet I was glad when the small theater began to have a slight but recognized place in the motion-picture scene. Hardly a beginning has been made on this, however. And the vast audience of the churches and the schools is almost totally ignored.

The weeks rolled into months, and the months snowballed into years, and seemingly little or nothing was done to make the code effective. Crime, lust, the triangle situation, seductions, remained the normal plot of the films. I could see no slightest improvement. The signatures solemnly affixed by the heads of the companies to the code seemed to bind no one.

It did not take long to find the reason for this. The code had no agency for enforcement. The Hays office could advise; it could not oblige any company to follow its suggestions. Instead the industry had set up a form of enforcement which was the essence of ineffectiveness. Scenarios were to be submitted by the company to the Hays office, which, if it had any question about the conformity to the code, would submit the possibly offensive script to a committee made up of representatives from rival companies. Naturally, no company wanted to condemn the picture of any other company, since it in turn might find its questionable script submitted to the company whose picture it had condemned. So if Company A's film was submitted to Company B, C, and D, the three judges gave it a clean bill, winking an eye that said, "We've got a picture coming up that may be submitted to you, and when it does, remember we were gentle with your picture."

Actually there was not a sign of improvement. The cardinal of Chicago washed his hands briefly of the whole business. He felt he had been tricked. Father Dinneen went into one of his very rare but very just angers. Sitting on the police censorship board, he found the pictures if anything worse. I wrote a letter or two to Mr. Hays just asking if I could hear what was going on and when his office would begin to bear down.

Then one Sunday afternoon a neighborhood theater showed a picture about which I had been having a lot of doubts. It was first announced in a splash advertisement which I had noticed in *Motion Picture Herald*. *No Bed of Her Own* was the highly suggestive title. This was modified to *No Man of Her Own;* the improvement was not notable. I recall that Clark Gable, who in those days had a famous leer and a suave manner of seduction, played opposite the late Carole Lombard, a very great comedian, as they discovered later when code enforcement gave clean comedy a chance. I sat through the film and writhed. It was tough to take. The whole plot was a series of attempts at seduction. And "suggestive" was too mild a name for the dialogue and the situations.

Back I stormed to my office, and late that Sunday afternoon I sat down and burned up the typewriter. I wrote Will Hays a letter in which I let loose with what artillery I possessed. I told him that I had just seen a film that violated just about everything they promised by the code to observe. Then under the headings of 1, 2, 3 and subheadings of a, b, c, I listed exactly what I had seen and what had been seen by that Sunday-afternoon audience of teen-agers and younger. I called sins by their proper names, and used the bald, ugly words that properly expressed the bald, ugly things I had seen.

As a sort of background for mounting indignation there rose on the horizon of the land a sinister figure by the name of Howard Hughes. I knew nothing of his private life, but I had been invited by Mr. Quigley to see with him an early presentation of *Hell's Angels.* To counteract the simply magnificent scenes in the air, Hughes had introduced on earth about the most suggestive lines and situations that he could produce. Jean Harlow starred. Even the tough Broadway audiences winced when she appeared in costumes that were not only immodest but deliberately obscene, and when she set herself to seduce one of the aviators in the most candid and detailed fashion.

I'm sure I was only one of the many who had had hopes for the code and who was mad through and through.

I began to make an analysis of the films produced in the months since the code, and the results of the survey were terrifying. Into a small booklet called *The Motion Pictures Betray America* I put the cold statistics on the rapes, the seductions, the illicit loves, the illegitimate children, the murders, the brutality. I named names and mentioned in detail what I thought of important producers (named) who used their wives (named) to star in a series of pictures that presented them as filthy, immoral women. I accused the industry of faking observance of the code. I said that they were, these companies, a menace to the decencies, with no slightest regard for the future of America, ambassadors of bad will and national slander to the European nations, and an irresponsible lot of money-loving scamps who would sell their sisters to make a fast buck.

Mr. Quigley wrote that the booklet contained some mistakes. He listed two slight mistakes in company organization that I had made. He then told me that Will Hays and the industry were thinking of bringing me into court to sue me for this booklet. Nothing ever pleased me more. I answered that I would be delighted to appear in court. I had been saving up a lot of things that I would be happy to spill out for the general public to hear. And any time the Hays office wanted to sue me, let them sue.

All the time Father Dinneen and I kept feeling that our approach to the industry had been wrong. Like the International Federation of Catholic Alumnae, we had tried to work along, to cooperate, to praise their occasional magnificent pictures, and to pat on the head any company which produced a small, innocent film. These men did not seem to understand cooperation. It was about time that somebody got up and told them off and put in a demand for that very dangerous thing which is a boycott.

I had been invited to talk to five thousand young people in Buffalo. My assigned subject was the motion pictures. But when I walked out on the stage of that vast auditorium and looked at the thousands of boys and girls before whom the motion pictures were parading their lustful scenes and undressed women and crime and vice and seduction and rape, I threw the outline for my speech away. Instead I talked quietly to that five thousand about the code, about what Hollywood motion-picture companies had promised, about what they had failed to do, about their betrayed signatures. Then, without being specific, I reminded them what they were seeing when they went to the theater, and what effect it was bound to have upon adolescents like themselves.

Then I think my tone rose slightly for I was, without preparation, on the verge of a challenge:

"Nobody else seems to be willing to tackle the job," I said. "How would you like to clean up the movies?"

There was a moment of surprised silence, then somebody cried out, "Yes!" then the place thundered with applause, and then we worked out our plan.

At the time I was editor of *The Queen's Work,* and I knew that it reached practically every Catholic high school and college in the country and several thousand parish sodalities for young people. So I promised them that, beginning with the next issue, we would start to black-list. By name we would mention the producing company, the stars, and the picture, listing two of the worst from each company.

"Stay away from the ones we list. Write indignant letters of protest to the companies responsible. Get your parents to stay away from them. Make it so hot for the offenders that they'll stop in sheer self-defense. Will you?"

They roared their agreement.

The next day I made a similar appeal to Jesuit high-school boys of Toledo with the same response. Back I went to the St. Louis office, and we began our black-listing. Each month we selected two or three of the most obnoxious pictures, listed them on the front page of our magazine, demanded protests, and begged the boys and girls to stay away. Perhaps to the amazement of some, they did just that.

I got some indignant letters, some threats of more lawsuits, and some hurt protests. A good many of my former associates took the attitude that black-listing bad pictures was simply a means of publicizing them. I retorted that, if mentioning bad pictures was wrong, then the Index of Forbidden Books ought to go out of business. And if our people were just looking for the names of bad pictures in order to patronize them, religion might as well close up shop. Martin Quigley and I flatly disagreed on the subject. He wanted a continuance of the IFCA policy of praising the good. I maintained that years of praising the good had left the bad worse than ever.

A letter from Mr. De Mille followed the appearance of his film *The Sign of the Cross*. I had loved that old melodrama when it appeared in my boyhood in Chicago. When Mr. De Mille decided to film it I congratulated him. The film version, with its sadistic cruelty, its playing up of Roman lust and debauchery and crime, seemed to me intolerable. An executive of the company told me that the picture was taking a beating, and mentioned a large financial loss over a brief period. Could I do anything to get the young people to change their attitude? I answered that I was largely responsible for their attitude and hoped it would continue.

Mr. Quigley showed me a batch of letters that had been sent to him by one of the producing companies. A sister in one of the lower grades had sent on in protest about thirty juvenile letters. They were almost identical. Said Mr. Quigley, "What possible effect can this have on the companies but to make us seem ridiculous? Obviously the sister wrote the master letter, and obviously all the children slavishly copied it." I answered in what I believe was the simple truth: "Believe me, if I were in business, and if I discovered that a sister in fourth grade had her class copy out and send to me a letter telling me that my business was rotten and that my product ought to be banned, I'd be scared stiff. If my business was so bad that it was a horrible example held up to the scorn of little children, I'd start examining my conscience and my product."

Meanwhile, however, the influence of Cardinal Mundelein, now aroused, was beginning to reach out to the bishops. In young Bishop Bernard J. Sheil, auxiliary bishop of Chicago, he had a firebrand waiting to explode in holy indignation. The gathering indignation only needed to take focus. I recall that Father Dinneen and I talked over a nationwide boycott that would really make the industry pay attention. If our small black-listing, effective principally among the adolescents, had accomplished so much, how about a national protest and cutting off of patronage? Chicago's cardinal and the already champing-at-the-bit Bishop Sheil would throw the power of Chicago's Catholicity back of a movement. "The Legion of Decency" had been thought of (I honestly do not know by whom) as a title. The Legion of Decency was launched with Archbishop McNicholas of Cincinnati in charge. Bishop Sheil of Chicago put on his vast young people's march of protest, which I watched from the side lines.

The story of the Legion is not mine. I often got credit for what was the work of others. But our sodalists had proved the value of the boycott. The pressure of the Legion on the box office was so instant and so effective, the moral temper of the country was so ready for this movement, that non-Catholics joined it with enthusiasm, and in a matter of days Hollywood knew it was licked . . . to its own salvation.

For the code became effective. The companies gave the Hays office the power to pronounce on scenarios, to say that this script conformed and this did not conform to the code, to order specified changes, and to give or refuse its seal of approval as it saw fit. Largely at the suggestion of Martin Quigley, Mr. Joseph I. Breen was put in charge of this new and powerful department of the Hays office. He brought to it high integrity, fine personal courage, a great belief in the value of the code for the industry itself and for the audience, and a technique that made the recalcitrant among the producers come to time.

The films now had a chance to do decent stories without having to compete with the salacious and the evil. *San Francisco* was filmed and proved so successful that the producers grasped the fact that films which conformed in every detail to the code were probable box-office smashes. The audiences notably increased. The good directors got a chance to do stories that had long been held in abeyance. The whole industry learned that good morals are good business.

I returned to Hollywood at times to work with Joe Breen and his associates. We had some modifications, very few, to make. We had to write in a section on suicide when sloppy and lazy directors started to solve their plots with the suicide of some uncomfortable character. As late as 1953 I sat in with the board of the Breen office to listen to scripts and to watch the formulae that grew out of the code applied to questionable situations. Joe Breen has told me that a situation seldom arises which the code does not cover.

I still believe in the small theater and the film for the limited audience. The fault of the motion picture is not mentioned in the code; it is in the desire of the producers to have enormous audiences, to get out films that will please everybody, to aim at the universal man who simply does not exist. When the day comes that films are produced for various levels of intelligence and culture, as books are or music or paintings, or magazines or food or clothing, the films will grow up.

It is my conviction that, were the companies themselves to work on a revision of the code, they would turn up with a stricter one than they now work by. Notably they would exclude the horrible cruelty which has become too much a part of modern films. And I fancy that in the excitement over communism and subversive activities they would write a highly restrictive and perhaps a not-too-wise section on patriotism and the way in which motion pictures should lash out at our country's enemies.

Once I was called to Hollywood on what seemed a wonderful opportunity. John Adams and John Healy, under Colonel Joy of Twentieth-Century-Fox, were assigned to the task of measuring the religious educational field. J. Arthur Rank in England had discovered and was doing films for the churches and schools with real effectiveness. Spyros Skouras thought his company could do the same thing for the United States. The Twentieth-Century-Fox Company bought three of my stories and I spent two weeks in their studio working on potential scripts for twenty-minute pictures to be shown to the new audiences in churches and schools. But the fear of TV, the sudden preoccupation with three-dimensional films, and the coming of cinemascope knocked this new project into a discard. Someone will again pick up the idea and do extremely well with it. Now it lies dormant.

In my long and pleasant life the films and Hollywood have been just an incident. Characteristically, the fascination of the films has made me blow up the story to proportions not justified by what little I did. But you asked about it, and here is the record. Some time you may want to check it all in my very complete files. The files are exact and comprehensive; even in this long account I have done considerable synopsizing.

TO A YOUNG CATHOLIC WRITER

Dear Ginny:

Many young people in the course of my life have written to ask me questions about my writing. I am always flattered, just as I am flattered now that you should have asked me. I always answer as promptly as possible. I tell them what they seem to want to know. But when they begin as you do with a request for statistics, I am stuck.

You see, I never count. I have always had the weird superstition that, the day I begin to count what I have done, I shall have finished doing anything. I shall stop being a writer and become a bookkeeper. And I don't want that to happen. So I don't know how many pamphlets I have written. And I don't know how many of them have been distributed. I have no idea how many books I have published. As for the plays and dramatic sketches of varied types, some time back, at the request of Mary Kay Barmann, doing a graduate thesis on my dramatic writings, I tried to recall all I had written. Maybe the catalogue was complete. When I finished it I did not go back to count what I had written.

Once I made a sort of estimate of how much I write each year. Overwhelmingly the vast mass of my writings turns out to be letters—all kinds of letters. Of these, more later. I have long written a syndicated column a week, and usually a second column. For years I did about eight pamphlets a year, and at least one book. I've no record of the number of articles I do, for most of them are request articles, written because some editor is kind enough to want them. When you ask me, however, how I write and why I write and what value I place on my own writing, you've got me started. Prepare for another cataract of words. And blame yourself if you are swept off in the flood.

I am beyond all else an occasional writer. Most of my writing grew out of a need. Because I was working with young people, I wrote for young people. Because I felt and to some extent understood their needs, I found myself with plenty of subjects to write about. Indeed, my writings long supported the sodality movement, at least in its main developments. I had a sort of double purpose in writing: I wanted to write the answers to questions that seemed to trouble those with whom I worked; and by selling the articles, booklets, and books, I hoped to earn enough money to be able to do something practical about those problems. The writings grew out of my work; my work was supported by the writing. A sort of circle, isn't it? Let's hope it is not what is called a vicious circle.

As a youth I wrote for the joy of writing and for the love of literature. I cultivated the "forms." Before I had finished college I had tried most of them. I spent a lot of time writing light and nonsense verse; and I often encourage young people to follow that lead. You really learn a lot about writing if you can cram your thoughts into the tight container which is smart, concise, carefully rhymed verse. I tried my hand at short stories and sold one of my first to the *Black Cat,* a fiction magazine of my youth. The *Woman's Home Companion,* by the way, bought one of my light verses when I was a sophomore in college. It was called "Excelsior," was a parody on Longfellow's old favorite, but concerned a man who gets lost unpacking china from a package stuffed with excelsior.

Mr. Pernin egged me on to do criticism, which meant that I had to read carefully some very excellent authors before I dared to write about them. I did short dramatic sketches for our parish, and tried my hand at a full-length drama, which was frankly terrible. I wrote debates and speeches, editorials for the school paper, some drama and music criticism, and a bit of serious poetry —which turned out to be verse or worse.

The whole fact of the matter is that a reader is almost bound to try his hand at writing. And when I became a Jesuit, I knew that writing could well be one of the most effective apostolates.

I had dreamed, as all young writers do, of creating literature. I soon found my right level in turning out reams of words, always with some purpose in mind, always with an audience before my eyes, always in the hope of advancing some work that seemed important, always for what I hoped would be the slight improvement of my readers. I have never written, for long, long years, just to please myself. Perhaps that is why I am not an artist.

For years I have gone about with my eyes open and my senses alert. It seemed to me rather dreadful that people should confess that "they would like to write but they can't really think of anything to write about." I guessed early that the world is full of the most fascinating subjects. Early, too, I read how Charles Dickens traveled London taking down the fantastic proper names he saw over the shops of the city. They became the fascinating names of the characters in his books. So, still early, I began to carry small blocks of cheap paper. On these I endlessly jot down things that happen around me, stories I hear that are true, little incidents that amuse or impress me, and questions I'm asked by friends or chance acquaintances.

I return from a trip with sheaves of these notes. Some of them have been jotted so rapidly that they make no sense to me. Others are just a single word that, nonetheless, suggests a whole line of events. Some I use immediately in a form that I can publish. Some no longer seem interesting. Some turn out to be problems that are pretty general at the time and will become the basis of further study and finally a sizable treatment. Many I use at once. Others I toss into the top drawer of a table that stands beside my typewriter.

For years it was my custom, come spring, to houseclean that top drawer. Strangely the notes had grown into a large accumulation. But I did not throw away the notes and scraps of paper—parts torn from letters, questions I had had sent up to me when I was lecturing, little notes from boys and girls on the corner of an envelope, questions, objections, suggestions, "Why don't you write about . . . ?" or "We need somebody to tell us about . . ."

These I sorted of a springtime day, and when I had finished, I jotted them down, just subject headings and topics, and there before me was enough matter to keep me going for years. I could tell, for instance, from the number of times any topic appeared whether or not it was "hot." It recurred often? Ah, a lot of people were interested in that subject. It occurred only once, but the writer evidently was highly intelligent. It rated attention.

I am one of those lucky authors to whom his readers write. This means that a surprisingly large number of people send me suggestions. The pamphlets grew out of such suggestions. Almost never did I write about something that merely interested me; I wanted first to be sure that it also interested a good number of other people. Once sure of that, I knew I had a real topic.

Yes, in my youth I dreamed of writing literature, perhaps good literature. I am not such a fool as to feel that a failure to write literature is a sign of virtue or a self-renunciation. Newman's essays will be read centuries after my for-today's-purpose writings are not even wrapping paper. "The Hound of Heaven" probably did far more good than my hundreds of thousands of words. I should love to be able to write as Evelyn Waugh writes, or to create a novel like Bruce Marshall's *Father Malachy's Miracle*. Was it ever possible that I might have? I doubt it. I don't feel that I have that inner fire, that flair for the precise word, that tireless willingness to polish and repolish, to write and rewrite, which makes a literary artist. I was always more interested in what I was going to write next than in what I had just written.

It is a simple fact that once anything I have written is in print, I cannot bring myself to read it again. I imagine that first-rank literary artists, like Oscar Wilde, reread their stuff and instinctively cry out, "What genius then!" Genius is a thing of which I find no signs in my manuscripts; I dare not expect to find the least glimmer of it in my printed work. I have few illusions about my writings.

Once I had set my sights and determined to write for definite people on a definite subject in the hope that it would do them a definite good, I adopted as my style the letter and good conversation. I mentioned that the overwhelming mass of my writing is letters. That letter style is bound to dominate my more formal writing. But often to me the task of writing is really the pleasure of one-sided conversation. I fancy that across the table from me sits someone in whom I am interested, and to that person I pour out the ideas that seem important.

In writing, I have tried hard to keep to one subject at a time. I like to get a single subject and give it as full a treatment as possible. To me a man who can write a great short story or a gripping play is a fine writer. He has one thing he wants to put across, one plot that is all tightly knit together. When the reader finishes he has been given one impression. He leaves the book or theater with one emotional experience, but a deep and lasting one. That is what I'd like my writing to do—give the reader one new idea, emotion, experience, fact . . . and then send him away holding tight to that.

To me a subject is interesting when it is "of today." I am strictly a topical writer. Today has always been to me the really wonderful day. I am of course interested in that potential today which is still tomorrow. Yesterday? Well, if yesterday helps me understand today, I like it. Yesterday just for the sake of memory leaves me chilled. I have read history only insofar as it makes me understand the world around me, and, because history repeats itself, gives me a clue to what is likely to be taking place soon. I find historic figures worth my attention when I can stand them beside the great of today and make comparisons. All the past to me is just a preparation for my precious today. So it is that I tend to write in such a fashion that almost in a matter of months what I write is likely to seem dated. The figures of speech are stale, though at the time I used them they might have been right on the nose. I never have written anything with my eye on posterity. Like the famous cynic, I feel that posterity has done little for me; the reader who will read me while the ink is still smudgeable is the reader who claims and gets my hardest work.

It's fun to luxuriate now in a sort of retrospect over what might, in a careless use of words, be called a writing career. Vividly do I recall my first experience trying to write a short story. I must have been in my preteens, but saturated to the ears with stories of adventure. So for my subject I took nothing less than the adventures of a boy my own age lost in an avalanche in the Alps. I need not tell you that the story was never written. I had never seen an Alp; I had only the most third-hand knowledge of how an avalanche operated; I had no racial sympathy or connection with a Swiss lad; and though I did some intensive reading in the encyclopedia which I borrowed from Dr. Bailey's library, I got nowhere.

Later I settled down to write some fairy stories. I created for myself a little girl to whom the stories were to be told. But she never even heard her first. I had nothing to tell and did not know how to tell it.

Elsewhere I have paid tribute to Sister Mary Blanche, who gently urged on my pen, and Brother Baldwin, the Christian Brother, whose criticisms of my work in first-year-high were precious. It was Mr. Pernin, however, who really sent me madly in pursuit of the fugitive noun, the often static verb, and the illusory and usually unnecessary adjective. Prior to his arrival at St. Ignatius High School I had written faithfully. I tried out all the story and essay contests and won none of them. I offered the moderator of *The Collegian* bales of my manuscripts, and out of them all he finally selected one.

Ah, the thrill at seeing one's name in print! The joy in reading the opening lines that miraculously have passed from one's brain to a sheet of paper and through the medium of type to the glorious printed page! Some little germ must rise up out of the printer's ink and bite the victim right on the back of the wrist. He may well be lost for life, a writer, or someone who knows that he could write if "he had a mind to do it." In the words of the immortal Charles Lamb, "Ah, yes, only the mind is lacking."

With the coming of Father Pernin, then Mr. Pernin, a young and highly volatile scholastic, a small cluster of us were caught and held and chained and changed by his love of letters and his patience with us semi-illiterates.

He was made moderator of *The Collegian,* which promptly became my great extracurricular enthusiasm. I began that writing for publication which seems to me one of the finest possible trainings. Years later I wrote an article for an English journal suggesting that the best place to learn to write was a newspaper office, with a definite deadline that had to be met, a certain amount of space into which one had to tailor his material, and a subject that was concrete, definite, and capable of clear reporting. An eminent professor of English hit out at me with sentences that stung and scorpioned. He didn't offer a substitute, but to him newspaper writing was the bane of all literature, and any man who was subjected to its discipline was doomed to eternal mediocrity. Maybe he was right for geniuses. I know that every time I have had to meet a deadline, the discipline has been good for me; every time I had to cram what I wanted to say into a limited number of words instead of into all outdoors, every time I dealt with something I could touch and feel and appraise with my own experiences, I improved my writing just a little.

So writing for *The Collegian* was great practice and a wonderful training. And writing under Mr. Pernin's careful, kindly, and yet ruthless eye helped beyond all the classes I ever attended.

Never for a moment did I suspect I might have great poetic gifts. Just the same, Mr. Pernin subjected me to the exacting training of writing verse. He introduced me to *The Bab Ballads,* and I grew to love them. He pushed me back a bit to bring me to *The Ingoldsby Legends,* wonderful minor masterpieces of nonsense verse. He made me for a time write limericks, and then the French verse forms.

Time and again I have advised young writers to write verse. They did not have to be poets. They did not need to be discouraged by the obvious fact that in them the poetic spark never flares. I have never, I'm afraid, written any verse that moved over the line into poetry. The bright light of genius never burned. Yet writing verse was a great experience and a wonderful training. As writing for a newspaper or a magazine forces a person to meet a deadline and to cram all he has to say into a limited number of words, so writing verse forces a person to cut out the extra words and to finish the thought on the fourteenth line of the sonnet. The trickier the verse form, the more a writer is obliged to juggle words, to cut out what is not absolutely essential, and to jam his thought into a limited number of syllables. My thanks to Mr. Pernin for that too.

Under his stern eye and kindly hand I began to think a little about style. He scorned affectation. He shouted at me on all occasions the famous aphorism (of the French Comte de Buffon, wasn't it?), "Style is the man himself." That wasn't too flattering for me; for he insisted that I write short sentences; think first of the thought and then of the style—"Be sure you've got something to say and say it as rapidly and as succinctly as possible. A good sentence is like a good whip. It has a real crack in it. Make it snap." He loved picturesque speech and doted on O. Henry, who was writing his one-a-week short stories in those days. "Find the unusual comparison, the fresh figure of speech, the historic or fictional character who hasn't been run to death, and put them into your writing."

He was a tough, tough critic, the sort that a writer ought to have as long as he lives. Once I submitted to him the sort of story he detested. It revolved around an outlaw of the West who, on Christmas Eve, finding himself without money to buy presents for his children and his wife, gave himself up, claimed the reward, gave his family one delightful Christmas, and then went off to jail. Mr. Pernin read it and tossed it to me with disgust.

"Bathos!" he said, scathingly. "Cheap bathos!"

I winced.

"What do you know about outlaws? What do you know about how a man feels on Christmas Day when it has lost all that makes it wonderful? Never mind the Wild West. Stick to the campus here and the suburb in which you live. Don't hand in junk like that again."

On the other hand, when I submitted "Wanted: A Homely Girl!" for his publication, he called me back. "This is too good for the college paper. Send it to the *Black Cat;* I hear they pay attention to young authors." I did; they promptly bought it, and I was absolutely sure that I was launched on a writer's career. The editors just as promptly rejected the next three I submitted. Mr. Pernin had not advised my sending these in. In fact, he shook his head doubtfully when he read them in the manuscript form they never left.

My junior year saw me editor of *The Collegian,* one of the moments of glory. A senior by rights should have been editor, but by one of those strange circumstances the senior class had no one interested in writing or publishing. So I got the job . . . and did it badly. In juvenile enthusiasm and lack of judgment I thought that an editor was the man who wrote the magazine. The first issue appeared with a literary criticism, a short story, two light verses, and a department all signed with my name. One of the exchange editors of another college publication in his criticism of our journal suggested that it should be called "The Daniel A. Lord Edition." I took advantage of my position as editor to get my own stuff published. I did not scrape the campus for potential authors. Very bad, indeed.

For a time, because of Mr. Pernin's enthusiasm for the current authors, I was by turns each and all of them. Bert Leston Taylor, in the *Chicago Tribune's* "Line o' Type or Two," had invented the column. He had the wit and the knack of gossip which the later columnists never knew. I tried hard for his smart style, his epigrams, his wit, his topical comment. One of his contributors was the later famous Franklin P. Adams, who was bringing back into fashion light verse and the classic poets in his brilliant translations. That too I imitated. In my heavy-handed fashion I was O. Henry and W. W. Jacobs of the breezy English sea yarns, and James Barrie and Henry Harland and even Oscar Wilde of the lovely fairy tales. Mr. Pernin and I both knew we were a million miles from any of these stalwarts of contemporary literature, but it was fun running even a thousand yards behind them.

When I headed for Florissant I carried along my love for the writer's career. It seemed to me that the apostolate of the pen was just about the most fascinating possible. But in the novitiate there was little time for writing. If I got half an hour a week, I was lucky. At that, in the half hour I wrote self-consciously and stiffly a full notebook of odds and ends. Along with this stilted "practice writing" I was also doing an enormous amount of writing that was an invaluable experience. I had transcribed from memory each meditation of the long retreat, storing up the richest possible material for later writing. I often swiftly jotted down the talks given by Father Finn, always pointed, always exquisitely worded, always a fine wedding of sound to sense.

My arrival at the juniorate brought me into happy companionship with the world's greatest writers. But it also threw me under the influence of a teacher who came close to wrecking whatever chance I had of writing. Let him be nameless. Let his advice be a horrible warning to all young writers.

He called me to his room one day and in his nervous, staccato fashion said: "Now, I notice that you are interested in writing. You have something to say. Sometimes you say it well. But usually you run to short sentences. You are—well, too athletic in your writing. You should try for style. Write long sentences. Learn how to form a periodic sentence. You must cultivate a grand manner, elegance, the classic approach."

I went off bewildered. His advice contradicted apparently all that Mr. Pernin had insisted on. I thought of an experience which Mr. Pernin loved to tell with biting irony. "So this fellow," he said, "who wanted to write a book on psychology, called me in and handed me a manuscript. 'Take this,' he said; 'it's my new book. See if you can put some style into it.' The idiot! As if you could add style to content! Style flows out of a blend of content and the man himself."

The library was full of classics. I found Washington Irving and his periodic style too simple to copy. Soon I was writing, "Perched high on the side of the lofty cliff, fanned by the wings of eagles and looking down disdainfully on the little village nestling beneath, was the great castle of the Prince of Noodlepate and his princess, the lovely Gretchen Poddadumplings." It was too, too easy. The deuce with the thought! Down with short sentences and up with long, crawling paragraphs, that twisted their winding phrases through hurdles of commas and semicolons! Down with the Anglo-Saxon words and up with the lush Latin polysyllables! I had dedicated myself to St. Sesquipedalia. And the "compositions" I handed in were ten, twenty pages of closely written script. Not a thought to a ream of paper! Not a memorable idea in the padding of literary sawdust!

Fortunately for me, the fell (but oh, so well-intentioned) professor was moved in the middle of second semester. His successor had a trick of reading aloud selected effusions from us young Jesuits. One day in class he read one of mine. He read it well—

that is, exactly as it deserved to be read—rapidly, without any sign of expression, with no glimmer of interest, and at the end, no comment. He didn't need to make any. The paper had all the nutritious content of so much cotton candy. It was words, words, and no Hamlet to speak them or comment on them. I blushed throughout. At the end I heard my name read as the author and wanted to die. My shame was burning and I wondered that the flames didn't come pouring from my ears. But it was the beginning of a swift return to Mr. Pernin and the authors he had loved. I might never be a stylist. No book of "famous selections" would list one of mine. But from that moment on, I would write only when I had something to write about; I would say it as simply and directly as I could.

Throughout my life I have written much and apparently rapidly. "Oh, Father Lord just dashes stuff off," I've been told a dozen times a year. I wish I could take young writers back to those holiday afternoons when twice a week I stole two hours to write painfully and consistently. If at the end of two hours I had completed one paragraph that seemed acceptable, I was content. I wrote and rewrote, and crossed out and substituted. I tried saying it this way and that. I whipped up my enthusiasm for the subject before I tackled it; but when I had become emotional, I subjected that emotion to the exact words and the sentence that put it as clearly and simply as possible.

I recall growing deeply interested in Shakespeare's Jaques of *As You Like It,* and doing a psychological study of him. The puns on my name had finally irritated me to a point where I worked hard on a semicomic essay on "The Man Who Puns on Names." I did a few stories which were terrible and a few pieces of literary criticism which were fair, and some verse that forced me once more into the tight structure of the well-chiseled stanza. Nothing I wrote was worth publication and none of it was printed. It was the last time I ever wrote just for practice. And I doubt much that practice for practice's sake ever makes perfect.

In another chapter I have told how the typhoid that hit almost a score of us at the end of my juniorate threw me out of course. Mr. Pernin, in St. Louis, heard that young Father Garesché had been appointed to start a sodality magazine which he had christened *The Queen's Work*. He suggested to Father Garesché that the young scholastic and semi-invalid might make him a hard-working and not incompetent assistant. So instead of going on to my philosophy, I was deflected to a room in St. Louis University high over rushing, noisy, grimy Grand Avenue, where I had ten months of service to the new editor and a chance to pound the typewriter.

For the consolation of young writers let me say that I worked like a galley slave to turn out acceptable copy for the new magazine. And let me whisper that, of the first nine manuscripts which I turned out, eight were ignominiously rejected by the Jesuit censors. Father Garesché, himself a poet, laughed a little at the verse I submitted. The ninth was accepted, a simple account of an outing home for children from the slums conducted by a sodality in St. Louis. It was factual; it was from my heart, and it was a beginning of writing from what I knew, saw, felt, and had experienced. The tenth was a story which concerned one of the "lightning artists" who in my youth sat in the windows of picture stores and turned out "masterpieces in oils" in a half hour. On the factual account I put my real name; to the story I affixed one of my many pen names. So the first issue of *The Queen's Work* found me twice in its pages.

When Father Garesché was away on his promotional trips I was left with the typewriter, a slight trickle of business mail, and time to write. So I wrote avidly. Most of it never reached the censors. Most of it I destroyed myself. But it was once more great practice and painful moving toward fluency and some moderate craftsmanship.

A young Jesuit writer soon learns that there are a good many hurdles to leap on his way to the publisher. Fortunately, Jesuit publications are eager for contributors, and the editors are their own censors. So a manuscript sent to them gets a quick response and, if passable, an eager welcome. Manuscripts sent to any but a Jesuit publication must first go to the appointed Jesuit censors. For manuscripts that are designed for magazines or newspapers these censors will be designated men in one's own house. For books they will be men appointed by the provincial, often from among the professors of philosophy and theology, or the specialists on that particular subject.

For the guidance of Jesuit censors an admirable and objective set of standards had been designed. The manuscript must be judged objectively. Did it contain anything that was against Catholic truth or would even slightly vitiate morals? If so, it was marked with its offense and returned, either for a rewrite of the offending section or to be dispatched to a wastepaper basket. Was it, in the censor's opinion, up to a reasonable standard and quality? Would publishers be interested in accepting it?

Jesuit censors are not supposed to know the name of the author they censor; nor is the author supposed to know the names of the censors who criticize his writing. But once my style of writing became fairly well known, the Missouri Province was good enough to assign to my work Father Robert Bakewell Morrison. In his censorship I have been extremely fortunate. He is a brilliant scholar and a sound theologian. He is tough with me and I like that. Every manuscript that goes through his hands is given no cursory glance but a thorough study. It comes back to me sometimes with pages of comments. If I have a shade of meaning that seems doubtful, he points it out. If my sentence is slightly ambiguous, he objects. He calls my attention to new statements from Rome or new scientific facts that I may have missed. We do not always see eye to eye, but his eye seems to me remarkably clear and honest; and I prefer it to my own in any matter that is doubtful.

Censoring my writing must have been for him a hard chore. It has meant that I have sent out my manuscripts with a calm assurance. He would not let me wander even slightly from the truth. He would not let me write in any fashion that was careless or inaccurate.

During that year on *The Queen's Work* I wrote my first novel. Like all firsts, it was autobiographical; but unlike all firsts, it was very bad. I laid it at Mr. Pernin's door in the theologate and waited for his criticism. It did not come. I waited and waited, puzzled, since I knew what a fast reader he was. Here was what I thought was the charming story of the dramatic club to which I had belonged back in that delightful suburb of Chicago. Here was the beginning of what I hoped would be a career as a Catholic novelist. And the answer was silence.

At long last, unable to stand the suspense, I went to see him, and the truth was out. He spared me none of it. The characters were lifeless, the men impossible, the women incredible. The action was slow and listless. The story never moved, and would never move anyone who read it. "You seem to be able to report well," he said; "I like your exposition and your discussion and your criticism. But your narrative has the one unforgivable fault. It is dull."

I staggered back to my room under the burden of my leaden manuscript. The saddest part was that I knew he was right. The book was deadly tiresome. Down into my trunk it went and there it still slumbers—or so I think. I was to try fiction over and over again. But as a novelist I knew he had pronounced sentence.

Even as I rocked under this blow, a letter came from New York. Mr. Pernin's close friend, Father Paul L. Blakely, had been recently added to the staff of *America,* the Jesuit weekly review. Mr. Pernin had suggested me as a possible contributor, and Father Blakely wrote me an invitation to send on a manuscript. Would I care to write? Would I?

In no sense am I complaining; yet as a young writer I used to wonder if my Jesuit superiors ever noticed that I wrote. No provincial ever referred to the fact that I was publishing. Indeed, the only times I was called about my writing was when I was stopped. Because of the fear that my writing would interfere with my studies (instead of, as was the case, helping to spur me on to study harder) I was brought to an abrupt pause both in my philosophy course and my theological studies.

The invitation of Father Blakely had opened to me the pages of *America.* I was soon a regular contributor. No greater inspiration could possibly be given to a young writer. Writing only on holidays and never for a moment neglecting my studies, I was contributing to *The Queen's Work;* I had done an acceptable article for the *Catholic World,* and Simon Baldus of *Extension* had bought a Christmas story of my making. Father Francis J. Finn, heaven bless him, noticed my writing and wrote me a little congratulatory note which was dropped right from the pearly gates. He was like that, always watching for young fellows who dared to write; remembering the chill that surrounded the publication of his own *Tom Playfair,* and the superior who had advised him never to write again. How close we came to missing those classics of our youth!

Well, in the middle of my second year of philosophy I was called by my superior.

"When do you do all this writing?"

"On my holidays only."

"It will interfere with your studies."

"If I may disagree, I think it helps me study."

"Whether it does or not, you must discontinue publication while you are a young philosopher."

"Did you say I must discontinue publishing or writing?"

"Publishing."

That was the clear order. So I turned myself to the task of writing a series of articles on my philosophical studies. The day I completed my course, I was ready to mail them to Father Richard H. Tierney of *America,* who had by that time taken me under his wing. Off they went; he ran them in series in *America,* and later published them as my first book. Ah, how can one forget so great a kindness!

The same thing happened during my theology. On the supposition that writing would turn me from my studies, I was ordered not to publish—during the school year. So during the summer vacation I wrote like mad. The articles were published by Father Tierney and the other editors when they got around to them. But if no *Armchair Theology* appeared to parallel *Armchair Philosophy,* I think it can be attributed to a brief discouragement. The order was not to publish. I think now, as I thought then, that the order was shortsighted. But it was obeyed. It could easily have been obeyed so well that there would have been an end to the habit of writing.

For writing is almost more than anything I can think of a habit. A writer never finds writing easy. It is simple nonsense to pretend that even the most deft and fluent writer doesn't find his work a chore. Each time a man sits down to write, he groans.

Almost anything can turn him aside. Almost any distraction is welcome and welcomed. To put one's mind on precisely the right subject, to visualize the audience for whom that subject should be treated, to block out the treatment that seems called for, to break through the sound barrier that blocks off his first written words, to pick the introduction that has an instant grip, and then to continue the laborious work of finding the precise words for the precise thoughts—it's a job, and nobody with sense pretends it isn't.

But some people force themselves to develop the habit of writing. They stick to it because they feel it is their job. They want to reach out to the thousands they cannot personally meet. Limited in their ability personally to see and talk with people, they try to reach them through the clack of their typewriter. They have truths they feel worth sharing. They know that the revelation of Christ and the glory that is Catholic doctrine must be given to mankind. They are a bit ashamed that the men with nothing to write write it beautifully; and that lies and filth are so often exquisitely presented. They wonder if they can possibly sit back, hoarding their truth and beauty, God-given, Christ-taught, while the multitudes are hungry and often deceived.

The habit of writing takes a long time to settle itself deep in human character. It never means that writing is an easy task. Ask any editor how the greatest and most successful writers are about the book that must be finished to meet a deadline. I remember years ago discussing this phase of authorship with Mary King, who at that time was buying all the fiction and the cartoon strips for the *New York Daily News* and the *Chicago Tribune*. She laughed as she told me of the way authors groaned as she demanded their first chapter. They would think up a hundred excuses to postpone the start of that promised book. Finally she would almost have to back them into an office, shackle them to a typewriter, and lock the door before they would, with loud groanings and protesting sobs, start to work.

We must remember that the greatest poems of Francis Thompson were written after the Meynells had locked him in his room and refused to feed him until a poem was slipped out under the door. O. Henry, his money exhausted, showed up at his editor's early in the week, wrote the introduction to a short story, took away half the fee, and turned up again at the end of the week to claim the second half and write the other section of the story. If the O. Henry stories sometimes have slight connection between introduction and conclusion, blame this fact.

Many an author, just as soon as he has made enough money, simply quits the slavery of writing. And if an author can find some excuse for discontinuing—such as a posh job in Hollywood or a break in the advertising world—he quickly slips away from the typewriter and his treadmill to forget he ever had the habit of writing.

I say all this simply because not one tenth of the men and women who could write ever do write. They never get the habit. Or, with the habit beginning, they are frozen by some unjust criticism, or by the neglect of those who should have given them a small pat on the back. I had determined to write, not because I thought I would ever be a great writer, but because I felt that Catholic truth and the decencies of life needed even the writing of the mediocre. Yet the silence of superiors often made me wonder. The fact that most of my Jesuit confreres quite obviously never even looked at what had been written was a form of deep freeze. And when direct orders came forbidding publication, one had to examine on his knees whether or not it was worth while to go on cultivating a habit that was not always pleasant, that meant hard work, and that in the end reaped largely the reward of silence. I write this merely in the hope of smoothing the path for young Jesuits and young clerics and religious who may come my way. I got my chance and used it all too badly. Others must get the same chance, or a better one.

During this period of my early struggles with the typewriter I ran across the trail of George Bernard Shaw. He had just written *Androcles and the Lion*. To me it seemed a bitter attack on the Christian martyrs whom I loved. For me it was a new incentive to write. In giving advice to young people I have often told them that as a stimulus to writing a real sense of indignation is sometimes better than a warm enthusiasm or a love. Enthusiasm or love may make a young person turn maudlin. The desire to hit somebody over the head with the club of a manuscript may inspire him to write well, sharply, and out of his heart.

I bow respectfully and gratefully to the late G.B. My dislike for him, my anger at his sneers and sophistries, my fury at his smearing of martyrs and the Christian virtues, made me write many a hot, indignant page of script. It left Shaw unharmed. Only time has thawed him down to the pale image of his greatness. He gave me a subject and motive for indignation. And that's a great help to writing.

While I seem to be dishing out advice to young writers, let me add something that I find vital. Always write for publication. Never write just to practice or for self-indulgence. If you are a genius, you do not need my advice. Write as the spirit moves you. But the rest of you ordinary, intelligent, and aspiring authors should write everything you write with publication in mind. You'll write for an audience, then. You'll know from the reaction of the editor whether you are good or bad. You'll write the word limit that the magazine or periodical wants.

Next-best to that is to join with a small group of ambitious young writers and write for them to criticize you. During my second-year juniorate a small group of us young Jesuits formed the Five W's (We Will Write Won't We?) Club. We read our writings to each other; we pulled them to pieces; we were alternately author and critic. Yet even there, my own writing notably improved when I persuaded the authorities to let us edit a typewritten biweekly. Even that very amateur periodical sharpened the point and purpose, the style and content, of the writing.

It's strange how the saints enter into our lives. And it's surprising, as one looks back, how a small event, totally unpremeditated or unforeseen, will affect life's full progress.

We were in our third-year novitiate, young priests in the tertianship, and formal writing for us was taboo. The mere fact that I was carefully preparing the talks for my future retreats and working out sermon outlines was preparation for writing. But publication was not encouraged. And our day was too full for practice writing.

Then through the mail came an unexpected letter. Benziger Brothers, the famous Catholic publishers of Father Finn's books, wondered if I could undertake an assignment. The Little Flower was undoubtedly going to be canonized. Their firm would like to be ready with a pamphlet life of the wonderful young saint. Would I undertake to write such a life for them, and had I any idea where they could get an illustrator who would match my style?

My enthusiasm for the Little Flower was precisely nil. They had read her life in our St. Louis University dining room, and she had seemed to me juvenile, a bit spoiled by the favors of God, sentimental, and in general of slight concern to me. But the publishers needed the manuscript badly. Besides, this might be a chance to cement a combination which had been long a-building. Father Egan and I had been doing theater together. Could he turn his clever pencil and brush to the making of books?

We talked it over and he was intrigued. I suggested that, instead of realistic illustrations, we work out a series of symbolic drawings, black and white, with perhaps a suggestion of William Blake or Dürer. The acceptance depended upon the decision of Father Burrowes, and he, to my surprise, gave it without hesitation. Yes, I might write the book, and yes, Father Egan might illustrate it. I shot the answer back to Benziger, got the Little Flower's autobiography from the library, closeted myself for three days with the life story of this holy youngster, and came out a raving maniac. This is exaggeration for a complete enthusiasm, a realization that here was sanctity at its most attractive, great suffering leading to great sacrifice, a modern saint who would fascinate any modern man or woman of good will.

Under the heat of this emotional enthusiasm I wrote like mad. Father Egan and I blocked out his illustrations and he did a set that were symbolism and suggestion fitted to the highly imaginative and slightly poetic prose I was writing. We hurried our results on to Benziger, who accepted them without hesitation. As usual, the author got the second-best financial reward. My check was for the stipulated $300; Father Egan for his drawings was paid $450. I took considerable ribbing for that.

The little booklet came out in plenty of time for the canonization. It was tiny vest-pocket size, with a slightly embossed cover, a frontispiece, and then alternation of my text and Father Egan's drawings. I must confess that I liked it a lot. During the course of the succeeding summer I dropped into Benziger's Chicago store to be greeted with open arms by the manager. "Aren't you Father Lord? Well, I'm certainly glad to meet you. Your book on the Little Flower is the biggest seller we've ever had. We sold as many as twenty thousand copies of it in a single day."

Of course I was honest enough to attribute the sale to the prairie-fire popularity of the Little Flower. Yet at that, I measured the intake of the publishers against the fee they had paid me and decided I should have done much better on a royalty gamble.

I did not know it, but the pamphlet bug had bitten me. That booklet on the Little Flower taught me what pamphlets could do on the market with a popular subject and a popular format. A brace of years later, when I had determined to publish pamphlets through *The Queen's Work* and for the sodality, I thought of Benziger and their success with that booklet. I wrote to them and asked them if they were interested in publishing for us. They answered that they were. As that booklet had been fifteen cents, I wrote back that I'd be delighted to make them our official publishers if they would give me a ten-per-cent royalty. They replied that they would give me five per cent. I had not expected ten per cent, and I felt we could compromise on seven and a half per cent. I so suggested. They stuck to their five per cent. So I let it go at that, decided to do our own publishing, and found myself in the business, not merely of writing, but of publishing, pamphlets.

We should have got them all out under the patronage of the Little Flower. I could not but feel that she had put me in business and given me the means for years of supporting the sodality movement. That was one of her sweetly gracious, if lesser, miracles.

I cannot drop the subject of that important-to-me pamphlet without recalling that it was the reason for the most devastating criticism ever passed upon me. The pamphlet fell into the hands of the very erudite and unemotional English Benedictines. They liked nothing about it, neither the high emotion under which I was writing about the Little Flower nor the symbolic illustrations of Father Egan. In their review they tore me limb from limb. I recall that they said I had committed the intolerable crime of mixing talcum powder with good wheat.

It recalled the famous story which O. Henry wrote about authorship. The young author fails to write a good love story because he has never been in love; he falls in love and the story he produces is the depths of mawkish bathos. Then a girl falls in love with him; he watches her objectively, sees her suffer, and writes a magnificent love story. But he decides it's not worth while to learn about emotions at the expense of others, and he gives up the dishonest craft of authorship. I had written about the Little Flower under the impulse of a simply tempestuous enthusiasm. I had expressed my emotion with fury and unrestraint. Apparently the public liked the result. The Benedictine critics were probably more correct. Some day I hope I can ask the Little Flower what she thought of our product.

Once I was assigned to the central office of the sodality and *The Queen's Work,* I found myself in a magazine-publishing house. Like many another author, I found myself under the sharp compulsion of the bread-and-butter urge. The sodality was supposed to be a national movement giving service on a wide scale to anyone who asked it and with no charge to him. The sodality had no dues or membership fees to its central office. Yet it was expected to pay its own way and handle all the expenses of the Jesuits assigned to it, as well as the salaries of the lay staff. Again this is a subject that recurs later; just now it is interesting only because it drove me into the pamphlet business.

I wanted to get out booklets that would have a varied purpose. First they must be on subjects of interest and value to sodalists, notably young sodalists. Then each pamphlet must cover one subject in such a fashion that it could be read as the reader ran, and would leave at the end that unified impression which was with me a preoccupation. The subjects should supplement our sodality ideals and programs. Yet they should be broad enough to interest the educated Catholics who now were pouring forth from our great Catholic school system.

The format of these pamphlets was a subject to which I gave a lot of thinking. The Paulists for years had got out a most successful pamphlet, usually with the convert in mind. But their pamphlets seemed large to me, as did the few published by America Press.

Our pamphlet should be small enough to fit into the inside pocket of a man's coat, into a woman's purse or handbag, or into an ordinary correspondence envelope. It should be something that could be read through in an hour by a reader of normal speed. It must be inconspicuous enough to be read without self-consciousness on a streetcar or bus, in a railroad station or on a train; and yet the cover must have appeal sufficient to make a casual passer-by stop and reach out to investigate it further. The title must tell the story of the content in a few stimulating words. The buyer must know exactly what he is getting. Hence tricky titles, ambiguous titles, to me were bad. The style should be such as would be clear to a mildly intelligent teen-ager and yet no insult to the intelligence of an adult.

We did a bit of working on that design. Father Gerald Fitzgibbons was our business manager, and he got into contact with a clever young printing salesman named Clyde Hilton. Father Fitzgibbons went on to authority in the Society of Jesus. Clyde Hilton remained my close associate in the publishing business for long, happy, and successful years. He designed the first format of our pamphlets. He managed to get the first photographic cover, and then shifted to the conventionalized designs in color that became our basic pattern. Eventually our style of pamphlet was the form adopted by almost all the successful pamphlet-producing companies. The Paulists and America Press retained their old formats. All the others adopted our form.

When I was in my Jesuit training, I had lunch one noon with the editor and biographer of Joyce Kilmer, the very clever Robert Cortes Holliday. A lady at the luncheon table asked him one of those eternally stupid questions: "Mr. Holliday, how does one become a success as an author?" At the time I laughed at his reply: "I should advise any young author to become a reader for a publishing house, to submit his manuscripts to himself, carefully to read them, and with alacrity to accept them!" That turned out to be in measure my own formula.

I was in the publishing business. I was an author. I would submit my manuscripts to myself, design the format in which they would appear, accept the works of my favorite author, and publish them. The only point at which the formula did not work was the royalties. I did not pay myself royalties. Instead, we adopted a policy and formulated a statement of policy from which we never departed: "Any financial profit made by the Central Office of the Sodality will be used for the advancement of the Sodality Movement and the cause of Catholic Action."

The first pamphlet was written, as almost all the pamphlets would be, on request. I wrote it on the train bound for California, and mailed it when I reached Los Angeles. It was *Shall I Be a Nun?* On the cover was to be a photograph of the leading lady in a play presented by Sister Mary Louis at Ursuline College, Louisville. Clyde Hilton turned the manuscript into our first booklet and we were in the pamphlet business.

Time and again I have been asked to tell about our pamphlets. They are the result of a good many ingredients.

First, I was convinced that the modern just does not read long books. He may buy them; often he does not remove the dust jackets; seldom does he read them through. So we designed the brief compass of a booklet, something that could be read on the bus as one traveled to work; something to read in bed before turning out the light. Father Edward Dowling is convinced that modern reading habits have so changed in the past few years that our little pamphlets seem as formidable to a present-day reader as a three-volume novel did to Victorians.

Usually the subject was chosen as the result of a suggestion. Letters asked questions. Friends were perplexed by some problem. Some sudden rise of interest in a popular topic would bring a sheaf of queries to my desk. When at the end of the year I sorted out the papers I had tossed into it, a topic or two was bound to recur several times, the index of current interest.

Almost invariably, before I came to write one of the pamphlets, I tried it out as a talk. In fact, I would often try it out several times, reshaping the development of the subject in response to the interest or lack of interest which I observed in my audience. It has happened that some of the pamphlets were written only after they had been given twenty to fifty times as a talk. However, once I had given the talk permanent form in a pamphlet, I never used it as a talk again.

If I wrote the first booklet on a California-bound train, I was setting a precedent for future work. Many another would be written on trains, or ships, or in railroad stations as I waited for a change of cars—started perhaps in Chicago, continued on the train for New York, and ended as I went on to the South. In the depression days the almost-empty Pullmans meant I could write without interrupting the quiet of fellow passengers; there were almost no fellow passengers. I have carried a portable typewriter for over a quarter of a century, and longed for the time when portables would also become silent. The portable silent was never a particularly good typewriter; I could type much faster than it could record on the paper. So for my own comfort and the peace of my fellow passengers I rejoice in the invention of the roomette, my typewriter on my knees and hours of complete absence of interruption making possible great spurts of labor.

Incidentally, I have often wondered what difference it would have made had I not given that time during my summer vacations to learn to type. I am, as I have often stated, the world's most inaccurate typist. But having mastered the touch system (great writers, I was to discover, invariably write hunt-and-peck) I could really grind out copy when I set myself to it. As my handwriting is completely illegible, as no editor on earth could have possibly read a handwritten manuscript, as I could copy my own scrawled notes and rough-hewn manuscripts at a swift pace, and as my thought processes could continue without the slightest energy expended on the problem of typing, the blessed fact that I constantly am accompanied by a typewriter and that I am its master has made just all the difference to the quantity if not the quality of my writing.

Because of my work I had to write much, and so I got the reputation of writing very fast. A lot of snap judgments were made on the basis of that supposed fact. "He writes too fast. He writes too much. He couldn't possibly give thought to what he writes and turn it out that way."

First, because it seemed to me that the work I was doing demanded the backing of a literature, I considered creating that literature part of my normal day's work. It was a very unusual day when I did not put in two hours writing. Often I would put in as much as five. Anyone who has done any writing is aware of the vast quantity of material that can be turned out by a person writing two hours a day. I recall that Thomas Mann in an interview on writing said that he wrote mornings, for perhaps three hours. Despite the fact that he wrote and rewrote in the expectation of writing an average of five hundred words a day, he still turned out his vast, voluminous, tomelike novels. Somerset Maugham wrote throughout most of his productive life just mornings, about three to four hours. We know the volumes he produced. Dickens had time for lecturing, traveling, and a series of rather fervid romantic adventures; he still in systematic husbanding of time turned out (I keep using the words "turned out") his enormous library. Most writers who are responsible for slim volumes, and few of them, stop writing. Or they write when the mood is on them, and the mood is seldom on a writer. Inspiration is a rare event in the life of the greatest. I forget which writer said that the art of writing consisted in the ability to apply the seat of the pants to the seat of a chair. Father James J. Daly, who was an instance of great genius which produced the thinnest of thin volumes, in a life that reached into the eighties, early in my Jesuit life said to me in effect: "If you wait for inspiration, you will seldom if ever write. Writing is a craft. Learn your craft and exercise it as any other craftsman does. When you have something to say, settle down to your tablet and write it. Rarely in life does the genius produce the work of genius. Generally he is content with good craftsmanship."

It seemed to me from the beginning that, after the happy life which had been mine and the years of Jesuit training, the reading, the travel, the experience, the amazing content of the Catholic faith and practice, I, like any of my fellow Jesuits, had a great deal to tell to anyone willing to read.

I am not one who believes that what is written must never have been written before. My professor of psychology, Father Hubert Gruender, used to say that, if once in a lifetime a man hit upon an absolutely new and different, fresh and original, idea, he was a genius. It seemed to me that the philosophy and history and theology of the Christian religion was a simply inexhaustible mine. It had been written magnificently by Augustine and

Thomas and Suárez and Bonaventure, but largely in a language and usually in a style that made it almost inaccessible to the average reader. The modern man, even the college graduate, does not know Latin well enough to read it comfortably. The style was not intended to entertain and to ingratiate the saintly authors with their readers. To me this was a source of "raw material" that had never even been scraped. I did not feel it necessary to make some new discovery in truth. Too many people were unfamiliar with the things which lay in the great books of the Catholic tradition.

I felt that the eternal truths constantly needed a new statement that tied them in with the current year. I believe it is Ben Ames Williams who claimed that, as long as he could take his plots from the Bible and dress the ancient characters in the fashions of the day, he would never run out of plots. The application of God's great law to the situations of the present year of grace makes an author rich beyond any possibility of exhausting his store of material.

Without shame I have confessed myself the master of the obvious. And without condescension I claim that the obvious is what most of us badly need and constantly miss. All my life I have been astonished that so much of what people "learn" in school they later have completely forgotten. That is as true of the secular subjects as it is of religious education. We lose what we have learned at a down-the-iced-slide speed. I felt it was my job less to lay before my readers brilliant new truths than to keep reminding them in the language of today of truths which they knew, had forgotten or half-forgotten, and could remeet with a sense of renewed friendship.

So it was, when the doctrine of the mystical body was regiven to the Church, I did not for a moment place myself in the rare ranks of the Belgian curé who restated it for mankind. It was a joy to be allowed to take that truth, old as the parable of vine and branches, older than St. Paul's conversion, and state it for the modern reader to grasp and make part of his mental equipment and workaday life.

I do not think I have discovered any dogmatic truth that was not old as the Sermon on the Mount or any moral principle that was not included in Moses, the statements of the Savior, and the experience of Christian civilization. Instead, I set myself to present them as they were meant to be presented (or so I believe), as the foundations of current civilization, the bases of today's right living and happy conduct. I make no pretense to being a profound philosopher; I should rather be a man who writes philosophy in such a way that the reader does not suspect he is reading philosophy but feels he is recognizing what he has always suspected was good common sense. I am certainly no erudite theologian; but to me theology has always been an exciting and contemporaneous subject, and I have wanted to share with my readers the truth of God and the simple, beautiful structure of the Christian faith.

So, no matter what I have written, I have tried to make sure that it somehow contained the light of philosophy and the divine teachings of theology. I have seldom quoted Scripture directly. Instead, I have tried to put into modern words and phrases the tremendous truths that God gave to all. I do not think for a moment that Charles and Mary Lamb, when they wrote *Tales from Shakespeare,* even slightly rivaled the greatest of the dramatists. Gratefully I recall that they introduced me to the wonders which later I was to read in the original. My mother wisely read me in rapid sequence Lamb's tales and then the plays as Shakespeare wrote them. If I could be a Charles Lamb for the greatness of revealed truth, if I opened paths and touched vestibule doors, if the reader went on from me to the great authors, the doctors and the saints, Christ Himself, and the very words which God had used, the progress could not be sufficiently fast and complete to please me.

It has always seemed to me that the great authors have a way of laying down the syllogism's major. They give the reader the tremendous truth, the basic fact, the fundamental principle. In the vast, comprehensive minds which are theirs, they see the minors; they do not bother to present them. They serenely remain convinced that all see as clearly as they do, and can write their own correct minors and draw their own conclusions.

That was as true of the Ten Commandments as it was of the papal encyclicals on labor. The command "Thou shalt not kill"—which I believe would have been more correctly translated "Thou shalt not murder"—was very clear to Moses. It has taken a lot of thinking to add such phrases, such minors as "But just wars are not necessarily murder" or "But killing in self-defense is not murder."

I doubt if I am even a writer of good minors. I have tried only to draw the conclusions that the modern man and woman would understand. "Therefore this and this and this are wrong for me," "Therefore this and this and that are right and I must do them."

A man who has had the education which provident parents and the Society of Jesus have given me is supposed to have vast mines of material at his disposal. I must be forgiven if I have been a little impatient with fellow Jesuits who confess they have not too much to write or talk about. We incline to groove. We incline endlessly to ring the changes on the same subjects. We tend to write what others have written and to say what others have said or to choose for our subject matter topics already threadbare. The vastness of Catholic truth can be an endless challenge. One does not need to pioneer far or dangerously to discover the most fascinating subjects, both from the viewpoint of the writer and from that of the reader. And after all, when I sat down to write, I had been for years preparing myself with subject matter of endless possibility and provocativeness.

For years I wrote slowly and painfully. But, as I insist, writing is a habit, and the muscles of the brain used in writing can become as pliable and trained as any other muscles used by their owners. I had early adopted the habit of having my tablet and pencils ready, a typewriter open and within reach, paper, carbons, clips, all the paraphernalia of the craft at my quick disposal. A great deal more time than one imagines is spent in the mere physical chore of assembling the tools. My tools were always ready and waiting.

The subject on which I launched was something in which I had a personal interest, the combination of former studies and the fact that others had asked me about it. Often I had given the subject a fairly comprehensive treatment in a talk. If I found the talk worth repeating, it might be given anywhere from ten to a half-hundred times.

For years I wrote my first copy out painfully by hand. I forced myself to this because when I typed that first copy I found that I hated to spoil the clean typed page with corrections and changes. The scribbled first draft in pencil seemed to demand changes, lines through whole sections, and the angry jabs of a correcting pencil. Now I usually write on a typewriter even the first draft, for it is physically less tiring and easier and faster than my painful pushing of the illegible pencil. Before a typewriter I find my mind released for the concentrated work of "composition." Typing comes easily; the text stands out before my eyes clearly; I no longer hesitate to make corrections and changes; and I have in emergencies been able to grind out, on some very familiar subject, as much as fifteen thousand words in a day.

All my writing of more than a page length is written from a careful outline. The outline in turn is drawn up after I have jotted down all that I find I know or need to look up on the subject from the particular aspect I intend to treat. As I write this, my eyes are on the rough, full outline beside me, my fingers are on the keys, and my mind is surprisingly free to concentrate on the thought I try to express.

All my writing, even of the slightest and most negligible character, was for years rewritten with every needed alteration, correction, and change. Today all writing of more than the most transient value is thus rewritten. Most frequently, I carefully went over the second draft and rewrote it into its third and final form.

Until very recent years all that I wrote was then fine-combed for errors, bad constructions, and better arrangements, first by Father Isaac Bosset and then by Frances Bittner, whom Father Bosset had trained. Never did a writer have a more exacting and relentless critic than Father Bosset. Himself a man who had written beautifully in his youth, a wide and catholic reader, with exquisite taste and the finest possible knowledge of correct form, he was for years a slave to my manuscripts. I say it with gratitude. When I had finished my corrected draft, I laid it with all docility on his desk. I stepped aside while he picked it up, poised his blue pencil (a large and literal one), and went to work.

Deep down, we were very different in our approach to writing. He knew exactly what the rules required and he demanded obedience to the laws. I felt that language was a medium to be used as one wanted to use it. He had a great respect for language. I felt that language was meant to be our slave. The laws of syntax to him were sacred; fortunately, I had been given an excellent training in syntax and continued to think that, when the laws cramped the thought, they were meant to be broken open to let the thought come through. If there was no word to express something I wanted to say, I never hesitated to invent one. It seemed to me perfectly clear in context, nothing that would cause the reader even an instant's pause. Father Bosset never let the word appear. We would wrangle for hours, pleasantly but furiously, over my deliberate use of words not in the dictionary, of sentence structure that seemed to me stronger than the laws permitted in a violation of syntax which to me served to underline the thought. Out they all went. And in his presence I was honestly humble. He invariably prevailed.

We fought, too, about what was sentiment and what was sentimental. He thought me egregiously the sentimentalist; and he drove his pencil through anything that seemed to him mawkish and hyperemotional. I recall days on end when we battled over a little booklet called *When Mary Walked the Earth.* He would not allow Mary what he thought was the sloppy emotionalism of ordinary human mothers. He did not think she would be visibly moved by the departure of her Son to His public life. He insisted that she would not have cherished His baby clothes or His carpenter's tools, but would have quickly disposed of what ordinary mothers might regard as mementos.

In the end he always won. Out of my manuscripts went the unusual word, the sentence construction that was not strictly orthodox, the deliberate wrenching of syntax to draw a line under some meaning I wanted to stress. He regarded the thought with a cold, emotionless eye. And he wielded the scalpel of his blue pencil till my manuscripts were the patients of a difficult but successful operation.

I am endlessly grateful. Certainly he kept me from making gross mistakes. His taste was meticulous and precise. When he had finished with a manuscript, his slashings and cuttings, his substitution of the correct word for the picturesque one, the exact syntax for my free-swinging sentence, the grammarians would be pleased, the purist would nod an approving head, and it would be hard to pick out mistakes in the manuscript.

But I have often wondered if, in the long run, my freer approach to writing may not have had something in its favor. By the time he had drilled me for years, his taste prevailed. The law had triumphed and the dictionary was honored with no breaches. I still wonder . . . I still would like to go back sometimes and compare my original manuscript with the precisely correct manuscript which he finally developed. Of course, I never shall. It's more fun just speculating and speculating.

Father Bosset trained as his assistant for my manuscripts Frances Bittner. She was a brilliant young college graduate, a Jewish convert, with a rapier mind, a vacuum-cleaner memory, and an enormous respect for the positive genius of Father Bosset. From him she learned his approach to my writing. She too followed the book, the dictionary, the rules, and the laws. So when his hand, stricken with Parkinson's disease, could no longer hold a blue pencil, she sat beside him, took his orders, was his eyes and his hands but not his brain, and continued the incisions and deletions and substitutions. When he died she took over and continued to handle my manuscripts precisely as he had done.

Occasionally we had a few of the hot battles that I had once vainly fought with Father Bosset. In every case I retired from the field. I lacked sufficient confidence in my writing to hold out for the unusual against anyone who could quote the correct grammatical or syntactical law. I had yielded too long to Father Bosset to rebel against the logical successor to his law and dominion.

It gave me a great deal of confidence to recall that hardly ever in anything I wrote and published was there the suggestion of heresy, theological, philosophical, syntactical, or grammatical. I was sure that whatever I had written and rewritten would be subjected to the most objective and relentless scrutiny. I was permitted to get away with nothing. The truth must be stated. It must be presented in exact word and precise sentence form and with due regard for the book. How different would my writing have been had I not written under these salutary but restraining wraps? I don't know.

With gratitude and affection I pay tribute to Father Bosset and Frances Bittner. They knew their craft; they were the world's best copyreaders and revisers, the best possible proofreaders, completely sure of (or willing to look up) the facts involved; completely convinced that accuracy was better than freshness and the correct word and sentence more valuable than the sparkling and unusual one.

When Frances Bittner moved on to become proofreader for one of St. Louis' greatest printing and publishing houses, I had so fallen into agreement with her policy and Father Bosset's that change would have been difficult and probably impossible. I can only speculate in some amusement on the effect of exactitude on a somewhat gay and too daring mentality.

It is not easy to take seriously a pamphlet writer, and this I became in the eyes of those who paid any attention whatsoever to my writing. The circulation of the pamphlets boomed. We were pleased when they reached a million a year. They were to go far beyond that. When the USO came across the booklet that we had developed for the young draftees of World War II, they circulated around four million copies of that one khaki-covered booklet. That they ever saw it was largely due to Clyde Hilton, still my faithful printer and close friend.

From the beginning I took the policy that the pamphlets were our missionary and apostolic approach to the wider audience than the sodalists. For that reason we gave freely to all who asked for them. Foreign nations asked for translation rights; and unless the country and the publishers seemed to be financially well off, we gave the permission with little enough thought to royalties. Missionary countries always got the right to reprint without any financial consideration.

I have not bothered to look up the records of translations, but I know the pamphlets have been turned into French, Spanish, German, Portuguese, Italian, and many of the unusual dialects of mission lands. It is something of a joy that some of the pamphlets which I wrote twenty years ago have almost as wide a circulation today as they had the year of publication. Evidently the subjects suggested by letters and friends were basic and remain fundamental. Many of the booklets are long since out of print. It had been my idea to build up a library of pamphlets covering all the popular subjects, those of wide interest and those of more limited appeal. I knew what a simplification of my own correspondence it was to be able to answer a letter of inquiry with a brief note and a fairly comprehensive pamphlet.

Time and again I have been asked if Dick and Sue, the Bradley twins who figure in many of the "conversational" pamphlets, are real. In a sense they are. I wrote *The Pure in Heart* because parents of whom I was very fond wrote me about the problem of explaining sex to their growing children. Visualizing the boy and girl whom I knew and loved, I wrote the booklet. But from that time on, Dick and Sue were likely to be the last interested teenagers who asked me a vital question. Often I have replied to youthful questioners and reviewers: "Dick and Sue might turn out to be you, if you happen to ask me a particularly interesting and timely question." They in the concrete represented that character across the table for whom I was always writing. They were intelligent, alert, attractive (or so I hoped), of good middle-class environment, with the normal problems, the constant interferences and distractions of modern life; they probably paged through *Time* and *Life,* read an occasional story in *Collier's* or the *Saturday Evening Post,* hadn't much time to read a book, but might be coaxed into a rapid-fire pamphlet.

The books for which I have some responsibility were mostly occasional writing. *Armchair Philosophy,* my first, was of this nature. Then I had written, as a very young scholastic, a series of studies of Catholic nuns at work. For this I had visited the typical convents, schools, orphanages, hospitals, and institutions of St. Louis and Chicago. The articles appeared in *The Queen's Work.* The book christened *Our Nuns* was brought out by Benziger.

When my mother died I felt that I owed her a monument. As she had vetoed the possibility of a monument in stone to mark her grave, I gave her instead the literary monument of her life story. *My Mother* has been widely distributed and apparently read with relish by those who found in my mother many reminders of their own. When John Considine, one of Hollywood's most successful producers, stumbled across the biography, he got in touch with me and bought an option on it. Shake-ups in the company caused him to let the option drop.

Father Robert Bakewell Morrison, Father Gerald Ellard, and an occasional friendly associate spent a good many evenings discussing a modernized series of religious textbooks for colleges. I brought out the first of the series through Bruce of Milwaukee, *Religion and Leadership*. Father Morrison and Father Ellard followed with texts still widely used. My book, meant for freshmen, was in synoptical form, demanded work on the part of the teacher and the student, and aimed at teaching first-year college religion as a sort of orientation course. I experimented with a special kind of book that would present philosophy in outline form. *The Brief Case for the Existence of God,* still published and used, was an experiment, meant to be the first of many. The "many" never materialized.

The other books came out of a very happy trip to Europe, interest in young people and their guardians, courses I had myself given to thousands of auditors, sudden spurts of interest in subjects which seemed to be perplexing the current mind.

The book-publishing business is a complicated and specialized one. Bruce of Milwaukee did well by my books when they published them; one of them, *His Passion Forever,* was chosen by their Catholic book-of-the-month club. Benziger sold well the two books they brought out. Yet my peculiar financial position and the pressing demands for money for the sodality movement made me feel that we must sacrifice circulation for financial return and bring out our own books. We did this because we were in touch with the audience which we felt needed the particular books I wrote, and then because we needed the financial return that came from a publication house and not just through the often slight royalties.

So, producing our own books, we lacked the know-how and persistence, that preoccupation with circulation and that access to the markets which the professional publisher has. We were strictly a mail-order publication house. We had no salesmen on the road. We found that by mail the Catholic bookseller probably would consider three to five books a large order. Most booksellers used their book department as a mere service connected with the real business of profitable church goods. Some of the slightly high-brow sellers cared for nothing but foreign translations. Some felt that booklets and pamphlets just cluttered up their store.

As I have never reread anything I ever wrote, my opinion of my own books would be untrustworthy. I usually wrote them out of a deep interest, partly in the subject and partly in the audience to whom I felt that subject might be important. Some, like *Some Notes on the Guidance of Youth* and *Some Notes on Guidance for Parents,* have been textbooks rather than books merely to be read. Every book was written after a great deal of planning, and usually rewritten two to four times.

I never read criticism or comment on what I write. My incomparable secretary, Marian Prendergast, keeps a record. Perhaps it would pay me to go back and see what the kinder critics have written, as perhaps they have. My criticisms have come to me in letters from readers, in questions inspired by what I wrote, or, nicer still, in letters that have this tone: "I have read a book (or booklet) you wrote, and you seemed a little kind. Would you mind answering this personal question for me?" If my writing made people think I was kind, I was grateful and content. Indeed, the hundreds of letters which come to me every year from readers, invariably asking for further help, have been the form of criticism that has been most heart-warming. I like it when one of my readers writes and asks for help or guidance or some explanation of the problems we all face.

Into my writing experience came some fifteen years ago a delightful novelty. I, who had published as my first book a small volume on philosophy, was invited to write books for preschool children. The blessed opportunity came about through the farsightedness of a Jewish gentleman with whom I struck up a lasting friendship. Mr. Samuel Lowe, hardly more than five feet high, short of breath and long on ideas, was top production man with the Whitman Publishing Company, makers of children's books. As he surveyed the field, he noticed that there was a great dearth of inexpensive books for Catholic children. Sending out on the road a research expert, he discovered that the Catholics of the United States are the top book buyers, and that the books published for them tend to be adult, somewhat profound, and decidedly expensive.

He sent his representative to see me. Would I be interested in helping him produce books for Catholic children? We held a preliminary meeting, and he laid down his ideas, which I found fascinating. He wanted to produce a Catholic book that would be able to compete with the comics. It would not, however, be a comic. It would sell for ten cents, be equal parts of pictures and texts, illustrated throughout in color, and reach not merely the boys and girls in the parochial schools but Catholics who just dropped into the "five-and-ten" and non-Catholics who might want to give their youngsters fundamental religion.

Sam Lowe had arranged to strike out for himself. He would operate his own company, which would give him elbowroom for ideas he felt would be of service as well as of profit. He had begun life as a Jewish social worker in New York. An opportunity to work in his chosen profession took him to Racine, Wisconsin. There he came to know the need of youngsters for good literature. An invitation to join the Whitman Publishing Company put him into a field in which he was an unquestioned master. He started to produce children's books for the country's largest company. Almost his last act before leaving this firm was to tie up Walt Disney with a contract which still must be enormously profitable both for Whitman and for Disney.

We decided to test the market for books written for Catholic children. Sam Lowe contacted Mr. Vincent J. Hirten of Barclay Street, who happened to own a number of color plates that were lying under layers of dust in his storeroom. We blew off the dust, looked at the plates, and found we had a large assortment of saints and angels, with a few of the Savior and our Lady. We could not possibly afford the cost of new color plates for our first venture, so we decided to write a text around these uncorrelated pictures. I suggested a family picture album under the title of *Meet My Family,* produced the texts to face each picture, and sat back while Lowe got out his first Catholic book, and with the aid of Vince Hirten marketed it.

It skyrocketed. The first edition of 250,000 sold at once. A French Canadian edition of 150,000 met the same heartening reception. When the Woolworth store in downtown Chicago was high-pressured to put the book on their counter, they sold several thousand in a matter of days. Evidently the Catholic public was ready for booklets printed with colored pictures and selling for ten cents.

In collaboration with Mr. Hirten and then the Seffert Company of New York, these books continued to appear. It was a joy to write the texts with children in mind. Often it was my additional job to design the illustrations. Though I have no slightest ability to draw, I found it easy to imagine what would please children and to write the texts and to suggest the picture ideas for books on the sacraments, the Church, God and His saints, the life of our Lady, the Bible, and correct conduct for children. A fairly sizable library developed which soon ran into a circulation of a million or more copies a year. I always felt it was a pleasant sort of climax—to begin writing philosophy and to end with my eyes on the eager young faces of preschool children.

For more than twenty years I have been writing a weekly column called "Along the Way." I began it to force myself to keep alive, to watch the world around me, to take notes on the pleasant events that came within my range, and to present a somewhat happy view of life in short comments and stories, with an emphasis on the smile and an occasional glisten of a tear. The diocesan newspapers which have used this column have won my real gratitude. I have made many happy friends through this deliberately simple and almost "homey" column. And it has served to keep me looking for the bright and cheerful, the gay and happy things in the world around me.

As a writer I have never for a moment been other than Catholic. As a Catholic I have tried to be consistently optimistic. I find myself completely out of sympathy with the school of Catholics who like their Catholicity subtle and concealed; or the other Catholics who seem to think that the faith is almost fatal, that the constant atmosphere of Catholicity is midnoon on Good Friday, that St. Paul's injunction to play the fool for Christ consists in acting just a little queer, being profoundly melancholy, dragging through life without a smile or a jest. Perhaps being a fool for

Christ was meant to consist in playing the jester, singing like the troubadour, following the footsteps of the minister of God, who loved the hard things of the Gospel and yet was the center and source of much of the beauty and gaiety of the Renaissance. Francis of Assisi has always seemed to me much more the saint than Savonarola.

I have read and failed to like much of the modern French Catholic literature. It seems to me much more like Jeremias than like John the Divine. I do not find Christ repellent or gloomy or the center of constant storm clouds. The daily carrying of the cross is a personal assignment, not the commission to insist that all others be aware of its shadow and weight.

I have said that the facts about God are to me always simple, though the explanations of these facts may be beyond the most profound intelligences. These facts seem to me joyous enough to make a writer want to sing of the glory of the love of God and the beauty of Mary and the wonder of grace and the charm of the person of Christ. I have not found the shadowy pattern of human sin an absorbing subject. Nor have I felt the urge to write of gloom and doom and the appalling consequences of evil. The pagan authors seem to me often more competent to handle the shadows of the human scene than the Catholic authors. The best pictures of sin have been painted by notable sinners; maybe it was meant for the Catholic writers to write eloquently of grace and virtue and the beauty of God's world and the wonders that have been promised to those who love Him.

I have never written with any hope that my writings would live. On the contrary, I am content that they die with the vast body of topical writings which profoundly affect the moment and the hour. I do not expect to be rediscovered in a hundred years by commentators who will discuss me learnedly and embalm me in footnotes. Who cares? I wrote for the Dicks and Sues I knew and loved. I wrote in the hope that someone who ran as he read might, because of my writing, run with a little more security and read with a sense that I had confirmed what he had hoped for and known without quite being able to put it into words.

I have yet to write without putting at the top of my paper the Jesuit A.M.D.G. To that, I like to add B.V.M.H. What I write would not be likely to contribute much to the glory, much less the greater glory, of God; and our Lady has had such wonderful troubadours that what I wrote would add but little to her honor. Yet since I felt that writing was an apostolate and my trust from God, I keep on writing. The author who called his books little ships was wise. Mine have been little ships with cargoes of the commonplace. Most of their names have been lost in the registry office. Many have slipped quietly under the waves. Again, so what?

I could wish that I had written beautifully and brilliantly. I am content to have had the friendship of generous readers and the letters from people who from my writings judged that I was interested in them and would be willing to add in the form of a letter to what I had already written. I expect my writings to be forgotten completely. Not, I hope, entirely by the Author of the universe.

TO A YOUNG HOSPITAL NUN

Dear Sister:

Ahead of you there is, I hope, a long life, a life very important to a lot of people who are sick, will be sick, or think they are sick. You'll meet many a discouraged soul in a weakened body. You'll try to say the proper word to the person for whom a serious illness seems the end of the line. You will watch the light pulled by the patient to whom the doctor has just brought the definite word of fatal illness. You'll be with the families of patients who hover between life and death.

So do you mind if I write to you about my own sicknesses and health? Both have been important to me. Both have always seemed clear gifts from God. The experience of one man sometimes helps others who suddenly look into the eyes of a major illness and find it hypnotic and frightening. You will know sickness professionally. I'd like to talk to you as one who has known it as an arrant amateur, found it sometimes a nuisance, always an apparent roadblock, usually more of a trial to others than it is to himself, but invariably, by the wonderful providence of God, a blessing.

Imagine the luxury of this letter! Imagine a man calmly sitting down and saying to himself, "For a bit of time, now, I shall talk about my operations." When in my early Jesuit days Irvin Cobb wrote his famous essay, "Speaking of Operations," the whole country rocked with laughter. How absurd! How ridiculous to imagine others would be interested in my hospital experiences!

A few of us made brave resolutions at the time: "I solemnly promise I shall never discuss any of my illnesses save with my doctor." I doubt if anyone kept the resolution. Like food, sickness is much too fascinating a subject to be forsworn. And I am indulging myself to the limit.

May I warn away those possible readers who want to talk about their own ailments? May I remind them that, if they hear me out, they will not have the compensatory satisfaction of saying, "I went through that and worse. Let me tell you!" The only fun in listening to the account of another person's sickness is to know that, when he pauses for breath, we can cap all that he has bragged about.

I have often in recent years marveled at the fascination people feel for sickness. Many a magazine adds another hundred thousand monthly circulation by the simple process of describing ailments and the miraculous cures discovered to end them. Universal good health, like universal good weather, would deprive us humans of one of our great universal subjects for conversation. What a thrill it is, when someone has presented the horrors of his late hospital experience, to say with a contented sigh: "I know exactly what you went through, for when I had my gall bladder out ten years ago . . ." And because you listened to him, he has to listen to you.

So if you insist on making my minor ills take their proper proportions by placing them alongside your major woes, please skip this chapter. I shall not be around to listen; and I don't want to cheat.

One thing I can say with emphasis: God in His goodness has just never let health or the lack of it seriously affect my life's work. I've had perhaps more than my share of illness, and yet, looking back, it seems to me that each sickness was a brief interlude, a breather, a pause on the way, no serious deflection, no reason for a wide detour, no closing of a chapter or ending of a work. In fact, I would guess that I had a reputation for abounding health.

A quarter of a century ago I came back from one of the work journeys which filled my year. I had done perhaps twenty towns in a month, talked at least five times a day, interviewed and been interviewed by more people than I could count, and continued from the road my normal routine of office work and writing. In the corridor of the Jesuit residence where I lived I met the great English stylist, Father James J. Daly. He was bundled, as he was bundled winter and summer, in a vast greatcoat; he moved along the hallway with ancient and unsteady steps; he had just been torn by a violent attack of coughing. He asked for and got a brief synopsis of the trip which had still left me tingling with excitement, and then, looking at me through watery eyes, he said in honest envy: "You must have a tremendous constitution. What health! What physical energy!"

Father Daly lived to be one of the oldest men in our province, dying at last in his advanced eighties. At sixty-six I have been told of my cancer, and doubt that any normal course of events will bring me to the pleasant port of my golden jubilee.

Yet he was right. I often felt that I had such an excellent constitution that I need not give health a second thought. Constantly traveling, I could eat anything at any hour of the day, regular meals or pickups or sandwiches caught before the midnight hour, and digest them like an anaconda. I might sleep in a different bed every night and miss not a wink of sleep. I could often talk seven times a day in vast gymnasiums heated by blowers, without the courtesy of public-address systems (something that developed with the advance of my work); at the end of the day I was not more than normally tired. I have on one trip been in twenty different cities in twenty-one days. On one tour of Canada with my good friend and lecture manager, Father Thomas J. Walsh, we did thirty cities in thirty-five days, ranging from Quebec to Victoria and Vancouver, talking at least four times each day; and I felt no notable strain and no real taxing of my strength.

That is one side of the story. I almost regret that I cannot join Ignatius Loyola in what Francis Thompson calls "the world's great dyspeptics." Yet under the developed calm which characterizes a practiced public speaker, I have known such attacks of nerves that following my lecture I have rushed to the nearest toilet to be violently sick at my stomach. I have so completely lost my voice that in the wings I could not speak above a whisper, gone out onto the platform, given a talk of an hour and a half in a perfectly normal tone, and returned to lapse back into paralyzed whispers. It's the triumph of mind over matter, I suppose—another instance of the thing called the psychosomatic. I have had my full share of illness and appreciated it all.

Never has a sickness really held me back from work that needed to be done. Sometimes it delayed the work a little, but in the end the work was finished, usually on schedule. Every major illness has been followed by a notable blessing. It was not just a case of "Post hoc, ergo propter hoc"; the blessing grew out of the sickness.

Sickness brings back again and again the unfailing kindness of friends. Sickness naturally excites friends to a spontaneous burst of goodness. You are a novelty to them and they greet you with the interest reserved for novelties. But when I returned to the hospital, usually four times a year as I have for the past near decade, kindness might grow tired and friends could become impatient with the chronic patient. Mine have never been that way. I marvel at the generous response of friends—and many generous strangers—to my illnesses.

Sickness has taught me to be deeply grateful for the magnificent science of the modern doctor and the vast advances which have been wrought in modern medicine. I have lived through the generations that regarded hospitals as slaughterhouses and doctors as quacks, when decent families thought it a shame to exile patients from comfortable homes to noxious infirmaries. I have seen with my own eyes the wonders of modern surgery, the power of the X ray, the development of the antibiotics and the miracle drugs, the elimination of diseases which once were as common as the common cold—scarlet fever, typhoid, mastoids, pneumonia. To me the modern physician and the modern surgeon are the great inventions of an age of great inventions. And no discoveries can match the discoveries of the medical laboratories.

Had I not been a priest, my youthful ambition to be a doctor seems a most sensible and advisable choice. I should be happy to carry with me into eternity the good which great physicians and skilled surgeons and the self-effacing general practitioner have done for the human race.

Through sickness I have come to regard hospitals as my normal second home. St. John's Hospital in St. Louis is a place to which I turn in constant need, and it has never failed me. And I know that it is a pattern of uncounted other hospitals which have graciously admitted me as patient, entertained me as visitor, let me say Mass in their devotional chapels, or permitted me the pleasure of talking with the nursing sisters and their student nurses.

Health, I suppose the medical texts must agree, starts with the right ancestors. I seem to have come from a healthy strain. In the main, my ancestors were the tough Irish who had the good sense to migrate to lands of wider opportunities, or the English who came to America long years ago to settle in the hard climates of northern New York and Pennsylvania.

My father always seemed to me a man of abounding physical strength. He bragged that he had been a tireless farm boy who would without weariness carry his invalid brother on his back across the Herkimer hills. Modesty personified, he never appeared without a shirt and vest. The nude-from-the-waist males of the present would strike him as the depth of bad taste. Yet when he fed coal into an overhead hopper in our basement, I could not fail to see the ripple of his muscles and the ease with which he swung aloft a cast-iron shovel heavy with hard coal. I cannot recall his ever missing work for a day because of illness.

He had almost a disdain toward illness. For years he had carried a growth on his neck that was the size of a half-egg. One afternoon he took time from work, visited a surgeon, ordered him to lance and drain the swelling without anesthetic (he had a fear of heart ailments and dreaded any form of ether), went through the operation, took the cable car home, and sat down to eat a normal dinner with the family. I shudder when I recall this, even though I admit to an honest admiration.

He died of retirement. Had he in the prime of his physical strength continued his work, as his father had done, like his father, he would have been hearty and alert at seventy-six. Instead he slipped into the featherbed of retirement, and knew precisely the reaction that comes to active men deprived of their activity:

he withered, body and mind, atrophied before our eyes, and died not of disease but of the sloughing off of his powers.

My mother matched his health day for day. I cannot recall her taking to her bed for even a day of sickness. She never had the migraine headaches notably popular among the women of her generation. She was up before any of us and to bed when the rest had all retired. She brought to her cooking and to the care of her home a sort of buoyant strength. She could nurse the rest of us without need for any care of herself. In the end I have always felt she died because she willed it. She had lost her zest for life. A broken limb handicapped her in movements and healed badly. She was tired of battling with the problems of existence and calmly willed to die. Evidently she willed effectively.

Both my mother and my father shared a fear of dentists. Somewhere along the line they had fallen into the hands of the stonecutters who often enough in those days hung out a dentist's shingle. As a consequence both of them had bad teeth. I stood beside my mother while she had all her teeth extracted and plates made for complete dentures. My father to the end of his days champed on stumps that were miraculously hidden behind his walrus mustache. They passed along their vain fears to me; and I was twenty-one and a young novice before I submitted myself to a dentist for the first time. I have paid for my neglect with the long hours in dental chairs while skillful oral surgeons battled to save my teeth. Fortunately I am literally one of those people who can sleep in a dental chair. And when, a very few years ago, I was invited by the Michigan Dental Association in Detroit to address their summer meeting, I was pleased to stand before the dentists, pay tribute to them for what they had done for me, and announce myself as a living monument to modern dental skill. Only recently has the seesaw game in my mouth gone in favor of the outs rather than the ins.

We ate extremely well in our family. Yet I never heard the word "diet," and I doubt if any of the current health-food fads ever penetrated to our household of good substantial courses and plenty of delicious desserts.

Breakfast was a sort of English institution among us. I do not recall any form of fruit juice or cooked or uncooked cereal. I do recall bowls of fruit, platters of chops and steaks and sausages and bacon, eggs in all their forms, a variety of breads (no toast), sweet rolls, and limitless preserves.

For the children meals occurred four times a day, for the substantial afternoon lunch following school made the fourth meal. My mother was an excellent cook who believed that all God's raw materials could be turned into attractive, palatable dishes and who demonstrated her belief in a wonderful ritual of changing meals. My father insisted that any food placed on our table was fit for all of us to eat; and we never were permitted to push a dish aside with "I don't like that." I ate it and liked it. As a consequence I have gone through life with a great relish for food, all kinds and varieties of food. From a menu in a restaurant I am most likely to select the dish which I never tried before. In foreign cafes I always eat the specialty of the house without bothering to ask what it is. I have enjoyed southern cooking and New England cooking; I grow enthusiastic about Chinese dishes and discovered with great relish authentic Greek food. My brief wanderings in Europe made me know the delights of French cuisine, and I reveled in the little Italian restaurants which everywhere and at any time offered fresh flavors and new combinations of meat and vegetables.

On the other hand, my own universal interest in food has made me pitying and contemptuous of those who like only a limited number of dishes and who flatly refuse to adventure in food. They seem to me like those illiterates who read only the books they read when they were children and who decline to leave their native village to see the rest of the world. God filled the world with flavors and the means of combining those flavors. Though I like some better than others, I am always discovering new tastes, new dishes, new menus, new ways of preparing foods, ancient national foods, and the latest developments of the modern kitchens.

We children got a minimum of eight hours sleep. We did not nap in the afternoon. But we were in bed by eight and asleep shortly afterwards. Even as an adolescent, that eight hours of sleep was mandatory. I've never recovered from my need of sleep; on the other hand, I can hit a strange pillow, do the reading I always do before sleeping, turn off the light, and fall into a deep sleep that lasts until the insistent alarm clock wakes me up.

From the aspect of mental health, my companionship was excellent. I was surrounded by youngsters my own age with whom I played and danced and progressed from the games of make-believe to amateur dramatics. From the viewpoint of physical health, I decidedly lacked sports. My father had no time for sports. He took his exercise shoveling snow, stoking the furnace, and running a balky lawn mower. Once, when he discovered a vacant lot next door, he brought home a baseball glove for each of us, a bat, and a ball. We went out and played exactly once.

My mother had been brought up in an age when women did not expose their precious skins to the rough fingers of the sun. I doubt if she ever played a game more strenuous than skipping rope or playing jacks. She saw no value in sports for me. Dancing was her equivalent. And when, later on, I could play tennis, she was all for it. But she had a real distrust for "gangs" and thought small boys a pretty dangerous lot. So I missed all the physical give-and-take, the hardening and development of baseball and football and shinny, and the rough-and-tumble on the city's vacant lots. At St. Ignatius I played on the subordinate class teams . . . badly and by courtesy of my generous classmates. But I played without zest and with little effect upon my physical development.

As a result I reached twenty-one weighing a scant 150 pounds scattered over my five-foot-eleven frame. I was embarrassed when the tailor measured my chest. I had learned to swim, breast stroke and laboriously; played a fair game of tennis; could dance endlessly; and could outrun and outwork most of my associates. But I had missed the development that comes with sports.

I am sure I looked delicate. And I recall that I had more than my share of illnesses. My clinical record at St. John's Hospital makes me a fairly complete textbook. I was never to be without some sort of illness, recent or impending; and illness was never to hold me back from anything I thought worth the doing.

The cold little cottage into which I had been born must have been a spot to test the survival of the fittest. After battling with frozen plumbing and rats from the neighboring freight yards, my parents decided to advance in the domestic world. My diphtheria at the age of two was the final deciding factor. I hovered on the brink of death, came out of it bravely, and we all moved to far better living quarters on the South Side.

Had I not run the peril of death by diphtheria, would my parents have dared what for them was a long financial stride?

Perhaps the icebound cottage, perhaps the diphtheria, perhaps some congenital weakness left me with chronic throat trouble. Every year from then until mid-college days I was laid low with some form of throat disease—tonsillitis, as it was called, or a racking croup, or whooping cough, or a steady siege of sore throat. Each winter I knew two to six weeks in bed, missing class, very sick and very miserable.

Yet my mother withstood any suggestion to have my tonsils out; I have them, healthy and useful, to this day. I learned to grow up with a physical weakness, to be patient with myself, and to make as few demands as possible upon others. When the time came for me to start my work that involved much public speaking, I found myself with what is called "a weak throat." After my first year of steady talking I had developed what is often called a speaker's chronic throat. It was sore most of the time. After a bout of talking, I was hoarse and reaching for the iodine.

I had already taught myself to be clearly articulate. I wondered if I could teach myself to talk without constantly racking my throat. I did. It took only a matter of weeks until I had discovered the secret of talking far up in my mouth, using my teeth to cut the sound clearly. I talked from my diaphragm and the roof of my mouth, with almost no strain on my throat.

As a result I have been able for all my active life to talk hour on end, day after day, under the most difficult circumstances, without a sign of throat weariness or soreness. If I had not had chronic throat trouble, I doubt if I should ever have bothered to learn how to talk without fatigue and exhaustion. Out of sickness came a new strength.

Thirteen and the summer following grammar-school graduation brought me my next major illness. I have written of this at length in the story of my mother, simply because it seemed to me an amazing instance of a mother's determination pulling a son back from the gates of death. The doctors never agreed what struck me down. The consultation around my bed decreed an operation. My mother, despite my fever of 104 and my complete coma, begged for one night to make her own last try. That try consisted in feeding me, during the course of ten hours, a quart bottle of olive oil. The results were startling and rather terrifying. For when the doctors arrived with the ambulance in the morning, they found me too weak to move; I should be dead before I reached the ambulance. So Dr. Bailey and my mother settled down to fan the faint flame—and did. Unlike the famous twin in Mark Twain's story, I was not the boy who died. But I was too weak to attempt school in the fall.

Once again, the fact that I stayed out of school that year meant the switch to a classical education, the Jesuits at St. Ignatius, and eventually my Jesuit vocation. It was a tough way to be turned toward a life's work; but that is the way it proved to be.

From thirteen to twenty-one I was a delicately healthy and a substantially frail youngster. I lost my two to six weeks each winter with throat troubles. But I can't recall missing an examination or a party or a play or a dance or a club meeting or an issue of the school paper or any of the things that were the consuming concerns of my life. The Jesuits when I applied for admittance never bothered to ask me about my health. They just took it for granted that I was sound of wind and limb and likely to give them a few years of service.

Florissant was a wonderful place into which to plunge a young fellow of my slight build and notable nervous energy. The life was rugged, which was very much to the good. Sleep on slats and a corn-shuck mattress is not too different from what doctors now prescribe for possible bone trouble and heart conditions. The food was excellent and abundant, and physical exercise plentiful enough to make me continuously hungry.

We went for those long walks, pulling our legs out of mud and muck. I played my first complete baseball game. My comrades in all charity promptly rated me in the minor, minor leagues, from which, despite considerable effort, I never emerged. Yet I found I could study as hard and harder, carry my burden of physical work, keep on my feet for a holiday's fun as successfully as they, and be no more weary than the most stalwart among my associates.

For the time of so-called "probation," which we spent doing the work of a novice brother, I had expected to be assigned to the garden. That usually happened to the slightly delicate. I was much flattered when I was sent to work in the kitchen and the dining room. Later my novice master sent me for six more weeks to work in the garden and chicken yard. That was to "build me up" for the years of study as a junior. To me it was a complete novelty and a six-weeks picnic.

Actually, I took my studies, as I was later to continue to take them, in easy stride. However much a mental strain, they were no physical burden. So the two years of juniorate were easy. I remained the same hundred and fifty pounds stretched over a long frame. I was pale and inclined to occasional rashes of pimples. But I missed nothing along the line. Then the now obsolete disease, typhoid fever, struck down nineteen of us.

The entire juniorate had gone for one of its annual picnics. Some days before a flood had sent the small river overflowing its banks; we did not realize that it had contaminated the spring from which we got our drinking water. Some drank. Some did not. Of those who drank, the victims started dropping over like plague victims. I was among the early ones to fall. I found myself in an infirmary room with young Mr. Francis Yealy, while every available bed was filled with fellow sufferers.

The great Brother Caspar Saeger was our infirmarian. What a man! Small, with a head of white hair, and a German accent that was soft and gutteral and played strange tricks with the English language, he had the heart of a mother, the hands of a great machinist, and the patience of a master of research. Into his spotless infirmary eighteen of us were dumped. One was caught in St. Louis and hospitalized there. For six weeks, with only the assistance of novices assigned to help him nurse his patients, Brother Saeger fought the typhoid.

I believe that a doctor came out occasionally from Florissant. Hazily, through fever, I seem to see him early in the siege. I never saw him later. Brother Saeger pulled us all through, but by the hair of our heads. Typhoid was cured in those rugged days by the simple regimen of starvation. So we were given each day castor oil topped with orange juice, the white of an egg, and plenty of cold water. After that stimulating diet I have always understood the feelings of the victims of the concentration camps! For within a matter of days food became an obsession. I lay in bed planning vast meals. I was Lucullus and Gargantua and the Cornish giants all rolled into one enormous, enveloping appetite.

But our diet did not change for almost a full month. I lay abed, planning the exquisite care with which I would eat the first soft-boiled egg that was to break the pattern of our starvation. I crunched imaginary toast and savored its delightful flavor. I got a craving for graham crackers and chocolate peppermints.

When the fever grew high, each of us in turn walked the long corridor from our beds to a cold bath, sat in it until the fever was reduced, and then, bouncing off the wall, made our shaky ways back to our pillows. But Brother Saeger pulled us through. I rose at last, weighing a hundred and ten pounds of skin and bone; and again I can look upon the victims of totalitarianism and understand how they feel.

With the closing of the six weeks of ordeal, we went back to food, slowly and then rapidly and ravenously. We had a special table for us victims and plowed our way through incredible meals of steaks and chops and eggs and great pitchers of whole milk and corn bread and biscuits and butter and roasts and vegetables. We were a miserable-looking football squad in training for a hard season. And we took on weight like balloons puffed up at the gas-station pump.

Once more out of the illness, a blessing: I was deflected from my regular course to the beginnings of *The Queen's Work*. For a year I had the chance to write, to read, to study things that interested me, to think through what might capture the fancy of young Catholic Americans, and to prepare, however remotely, for an unexpected life's work.

But the year was physically hard. Despite vast intake of food, I stopped gaining weight. I knew there was something wrong, something that failed to heal. So I was sent across the street to the office of young Dr. William Paul Glennon, recently from Ireland, youngest brother of the city's great archbishop, and since then a lifelong friend and benefactor. He was a stripling of a lad when he opened his own office door to admit me, the gangling, pale, sickly-looking young Jesuit. But his hands already had the skill that was to make them famous and oh, so beneficial. And his examination was gentle, thorough, and exact. I was to go to St. John's Hospital for the first of the many visits which would from that hour on punctuate my life.

Civilized America was at that period emerging from the dark ages of the hospital. My mother had communicated to me her fear and distaste for hospitals. I can recall stepping inside the lobby of one to hear her mention in disgust the proverbial hospital odor. She did not use the word stench; but her tone indicated that was the word she covered with a gentler synonym. Father Charles Moulinier was in the midst of his magnificent struggle, triumphant in the end, to standardize Catholic hospitals so that they could meet any tests imposed upon them in the near future by the state, the government, and the demands of the rapidly growing American Medical Association. St. John's itself had just moved from its venerable cluster of buildings on the edge of St. Louis' downtown into beautiful new quarters on the margins of Forest Park. Hospitalization was not as yet invented, so that the Sisters of Mercy at St. John's made continuous novenas, not that people would get sick, but that, in the event they did get sick, they would think of coming to the new hospital.

When a patient walked in over the red carpet always spread for his arrival, he was allowed to pick his own room, selecting from any of a half-dozen different styles, all newly finished and all beautifully empty. Some of the older sisters saw the long corridors and ample operating rooms and shook doleful heads; Sister Mary Theresa had brought them out to starve to death in the midst of a vast, empty hospital. There would never be patients enough in the whole state of Missouri to fill these hollow, echoing wards and private rooms! But with the distaste and distrust that still hung over hospitals, who would possibly foresee that golden age of American hospitals which was just opening in the land?

I arrived afraid of hospitals, convinced that operations were the end of all, without friends in the big city, sick and miserable and totally unhappy. I sat down in my beautifully homelike room waiting for a vague fate. It was Sister Mary John, the supervisor of my floor, who wandered in to smile her shy smile, reassure me with her quietly calm voice, take my fears into her womanly hands, and give me the feeling that all would be well with my world. For years Sister Mary John has been stationed elsewhere. I have never forgotten that saintly little nun who saw me through the preliminaries of my operation, and sent in a vast, great-hearted orderly, Joe with the unpronounceable Hungarian name, who made me think of a gentle trained bear and who assured me in gutturals and massacred English that all would be well.

It seems strange to think there was a time when the prospect of an operation could so unnerve me. It is part of the scientific revolution that all fear of hospitals has been banished from the contemporaneous mind, that we rush to the hospital for any ailment if they have a spare room for us, and that I go up to an anesthetic without a tremor or more than the most casual forward glance.

Yet the first journey down the corridor to the operating table probably remains for each of us an unforgettable experience. I do not recall that I was given the hypos which now float the patient off into a comfortable coma. I know that I was fully alert as the cart was wheeled down the empty corridors of St. John's Hospital, and I was affronted when the student nurse leaned over to ask me if I had any false teeth . . . movable dentures, I think she elegantly called them. The elevator that carried me toward the complete mystery of the operating room was a chill and fearsome thing, and the opening vista of the operating room as seen by the prostrate patient was . . .

The visual memory is keen to this day—the ghostlike figures of the nurses hurrying about, the banks of lights in the ceilings, the skylights through which one got a sort of wistful glimpse of the sky, the smell of ether, the strangely shrouded figures of the surgeons, and horrific instruments that seemed to be waiting for the closing of some awful nightmare.

I wanted to close it all out by shutting my eyes. I could not because of the mesmeric fascination all the strange objects had upon me. I wasn't afraid now; I was plain scared stiff.

Then over me loomed a vast, tall, white, laughing figure. "I'm Sister Mary Loyola," she said, and caught and pressed my hand. "You're perfectly safe up here with us and we'll send you back a well boy. I'm helping with the operation and the sisters are praying while Dr. Glennon works." I smiled back in a sudden burst of confidence. The face of Sister Mary Loyola, incredibly effective supervisor of the operating rooms, has remained one of the bright spots in a long life of happy memories.

Well, operations are operations, and successful operations are among man's great gifts to his fellow men. And mine was a success and the pain was slight and the aftermath softened by the gay nurses who cared for us, by the skill of Sister Mary John, by the nightly visits of Sister Mary Malachy, who patrolled the entire hospital as night supervisor, and the newborn friendship for Sister Mary Theresa.

I never can forget the student nurses who had willingness, skill, and apparently all the time in the world. My second morning was begun with the shy entrance of Miss McQueeney. She was fresh from Ireland, with a magnificent brogue that I can imitate in speech but not on a typewriter, and she came with the equipment for an early-morning bath.

"I've been sent in to wash you," she said in her delightful accent, "and I don't know which of us is more embarrassed."

That dissolved my embarrassment in a burst of laughter that irritated my fresh wound but relieved my soul.

"What do they call you young Jesuits?" she asked. I told her. "That's easy. I was taking care of a young Passionist lately. They call the poor young things confraters. 'Oh, glory,' I said to him; 'never in the world could I remember that. Confrater, indeed! I might call you Con, which sounds Irish but would be disrespectful. So I'd better be satisfied calling you brother.' "

She had washed away our embarrassment as she had washed away the accumulated sweat and lint of a day after the operation.

Almost thirty years later, now Mrs. Klocker and a widow, she came back to solve my week-old problem of hiccups following a double-hernia operation. She taught me what the medical world has long known, that half the cure rests in the hands of a good nurse.

In Sister Mary Theresa I found my second mother. "My St. Louis mother" I called her until death. She was one of the Highland McDonalds who, suffering for the faith, had carried the Catholic Church from Scotland to the New Scotland that we know as Canada's Nova Scotia. She came from the town of Antigonish, now famous as the home of St. Francis Xavier University, the school that economically through cooperatives and credit unions saved an entire Canadian province. She had reached a beautiful and dignified old age, passing quietly from the post of superior once she had moved her Sisters of Mercy from the old to the new St. John's. Now she was the sacristan, destined in years to come to build the present lovely chapel. But between visiting the Lord in her chapel and the patients in their rooms, she put in a busy day. She was almost my only visitor. She came bringing me the Antigonish *Casket,* the paper of her home town. She talked wistfully of Scotland and the Scots of Nova Scotia. Then she came with delicacies from the kitchen, tiny sandwiches that only a woman could confect, and candy and cold drinks and fancy ice creams, things which I had, or so I thought, years before put out of my life. She encouraged me to talk to her about myself, my youth in Chicago, and my dreams as a young Jesuit. Indeed, she was the first woman I talked to as a Jesuit, bringing me a woman's sympathetic listening ear and her firm love of religious life and her zeal for the souls of her patients.

During my convalescence my youthful curiosity made me ferret out all that I could about hospitals. Medical people respond to interest on the part of the laity, so I found myself the invited guest at a series of operations. I watched the great Dr. John Young Brown remove a fifth nerve, and almost fainted as through the hole in the temple for the first time I saw the pulsings of a human brain. I watched Dr. Glennon remove gallstones and an appendix. I gritted my teeth while a leg was amputated. It seemed to me that as a future priest I should have the edge taken off the possible horror of surgery and be ready to stand by if ever I were needed.

Two weeks in the hospital passed like a lovely dream. No doubt of it, I had caught a severe attack of hospitalitis. For the first time in five years people fussed over me. The night nurses came by with premidnight snacks that even, I recall, included lobster sandwiches. I had the exhilarating experience of seeing my wishes catered to and my wants anticipated. In two weeks I was completely spoiled.

So when, at the end of the two weeks, I mounted the three long flights of stairs to the little room over Grand Avenue from which I was slightly helping to develop *The Queen's Work,* I looked around my grimy little room, saw the stacks of work that had accumulated while I was in the hospital, and sat down on the edge of my bed to cry tears of loneliness and weakness and unexplained distress.

So, to cover the lapse, I plunged that evening into work. I worked long and hard for two weeks trying to make up for lost time, and then collapsed. Fortunately the vacation period was close at hand. So I dragged my way about my work. Dr. Glennon recalled me for regular shots of what I later learned was tuberculin. Once I arrived at our island in Lake Beulah, Wisconsin, health came flowing back in sunshine and fresh air and gentle exercise and good food. And I moved along to the three years of philosophy and the three strenuous years as a teaching scholastic on the crest of very considerable health and strength.

Oh, yes. Like the rest of the war-stricken world, I got the Spanish influenza which we contemptuously abbreviated into the "flu." I got it twice. The second time I learned the full power of mind over matter. For anything this side of an operative case or a fatal disease, we Jesuit teachers remained in our rooms. Brother Hoffmann was our infirmarian, another wonderful brother who brought us our meals and carried out the orders of the doctor, and brooded over us with affectionate care. But in the intervals between his visits the patient lay with his face to the wall, or, if he had any energy and love of books, read the day away, fever or no fever.

My second attack of flu laid me very low indeed. I was as sick as people got with that mysterious disease, sick at the stomach and too weak to totter to the window for air, aching and sore and not much caring to live or to die. I had been too sick to notice the false armistice. But the compelling blasts that welcomed the true armistice brought me abruptly upright. My fever was still high.

My pulse was wobbling. But when I staggered to the window the whole impact of that incredible burst of national frenzy that ended the First World War rushed up from Grand and Pine to make me forget everything but that the war was won.

Somehow I managed to get into my clothes. Somehow I got on my hat and topcoat. I had to get out and into the heart of the celebration that was rising in a phrenetic cyclone of sound all around me. So, sick as I was, I managed the stairs and got out into the street. I meant to take a streetcar down to the heart of the celebration in St. Louis' downtown section. But the car was jammed with howling, screaming passengers. I began to walk, slowly at first, and then swirled along by the clamoring crowds. With my fever still raging, I walked the thirty blocks to the downtown streets, milled around with the mad mobs who were making carnival everywhere, and as evening came on, fought my way back against the tides that in continuing flow poured downtown to celebrate. I reached the university more excited than I have often been before or since. And the "flu" was gone. The fever had broken. I could walk in to supper on my own firm legs.

I do not understand psychosomatic medicine, but it makes very good sense to me.

Out of these illnesses I had won a deep appreciation of the wonderful thing which is a modern hospital. I had developed a great faith in the medical profession. And I had given my friendship and gratitude and loyalty to the nursing sisters of whom the Sisters of Mercy were a gloriously unselfish pattern.

Ordination was drawing happily near. Actually, it was less than a year and a half away. I was a second-year theologian, interested in my studies, but moving along with the lights of the altar growing ever brighter. Yet in the winter of that year my old throat trouble seemed to return in concentrated form. I coughed continuously. I felt sick, and hot and cold by turns. I managed to get to class but without much zest for study.

St. Louis University remained still without an infirmary. And in a large community of busily occupied men, believe me, a cough or a cold or a slightly feverish forehead is a matter of slight interest to anyone but the victim. I had come to be very close in friendship and affection to Mr. and Mrs. Vol C. Turner, the parents of an almost-grown family, and they had been very kind to me during my teaching days. It was Mrs. Turner who discovered my condition, pounded the table in our little visitors' parlor with her small gloved hand, and demanded that I do something about it—*at once*. So I dragged my languid form to Brother Hoffmann, who used a thermometer, put me on the scales (I was down to a scant 145 pounds), and sent me down the street to Dr. Raemdonck, our house physician. He made a few tests, sent me out to St. John's for some more, and I returned to my classes and my regular life.

Three days later the provincial sent for me. I walked into his office without much idea what he might be wanting, but his grave face was telltale.

"Sit down, Mr. Lord," he began in his gentle, sympathetic voice. "I find this a little difficult to tell you, but . . ."

I recall that I interrupted him.

"Oh, I've got T.B.," I said. "Haven't I?" It had not dawned on me that all through my life I had been expecting and waiting for this minute. I was always sure I would some day be told I had tuberculosis of the lungs, and now the moment had arrived.

"Why, yes!" he said in surprise.

I laughed. "Well," I said, "with ordination less than eighteen months away, I haven't a lot of time to get it cured." I was not being smart aleck, but just completely confident and assured. "How long did the doctors say I'd be out of my studies?"

"Six months at least," he answered.

I laughed again. "I'll make you a bet I can get back into regular order, cured, in three."

With that he sent me off. He called for me again the next day.

"Where would you like to go for your period of cure? I was thinking of sending you to Creighton University in Omaha."

"Oh, please," I begged, "not Creighton. It would be terrible to sit taking care of my health in the midst of a hard-working community. I'm afraid I'd feel such a parasite that it would hold back my recuperation."

"Where would you like to go?" he asked in characteristic consideration.

I could think of a dozen wonderful places . . . any of the Jesuit houses in Florida or California or the lovely Northwest, for instance. Yet it seemed to me that I should place myself at his disposal rather than make a choice. So I put it negatively: "Any place you select, except the novitiate at Florissant. You see, it would be so hard to live among all those bells. You realize I shall have to be lazy and out of order, and I'd shock the young novices with my care for my health. Any place but Florissant will do."

He was a kind man, a great provincial, but one of those who hears nouns and never notices whether or not there is a negative before them. Two days later he recalled me. "I've been thinking it over, and I'd say that Florissant was the best place for you to go." My heart sank. I was baffled that he had completely forgotten or chosen to overlook our conversation. But I said in a low, back-in-the-throat voice, "Thank you, Father," and went to pack my bags.

Mr. and Mrs. Turner offered to drive me to the novitiate. They arrived in the early afternoon and deflected to the Odeon, where the St. Louis Symphony was playing a program which included Tchaikovsky's sixth symphony, the *Pathétique*. I sat with my good friends while for the first time I heard that magnificent work of hope and despair. When the glorious march which is the third movement was played, I knew that it would only be a matter of days before I had licked my illness.

And then Tchaikovsky plunged me down into the depths. For the first time I listened to that dreadful final movement which the composer must have written in clear anticipation of his own impending death. It is often played as the requiem for great musicians. All around me beat the dreadful death march, the awful chords that cried aloud in despair and hope forsworn, the slow diminuendo that seems to tell, as few pieces of music do, of the inexorable approach of death and the futility of striving against it. We went from the hopelessness of the music out into the bleak darkness of an overcast February night, and rode the muddy miles to Florissant in silence. I was as near to despair as I have ever been in my life.

Once more it was the incomparable Brother Saeger who greeted me. He installed me in a delightful room in his immaculate infirmary. With a hand which recently had been mending the plumbing and probing novice teeth he patted my head. "Don't worry, Carissime. We'll fatten you up . . . and heaven knows you can stand it, and have you back on the way to ordination in no time at all."

With that I began three wonderful months. I ate Gargantuan meals—five meals a day. I was back on the diet with which he had built us up after typhoid. I slept late and slept each afternoon. For the rest I was on my own. Three times a day I was checked for temperature. Around me was the mud and the melting snows of early Florissant spring. I was alone, since the novices and juniors were busy with their fixed routine, and the faculty of priests were a very small club of scholars into whose rarefied atmosphere I should have been slow to intrude.

So I discovered Charles Dickens, heaven bless him! Each day, except in downpours of rain, I sat on a bench under a cluster of evergreens, wrapped in a sweater and a greatcoat and wearing high boots, to read my way through those wonderful novels. In the company of his characters I completely forgot myself and my sickness. It was escapism at its best.

Then from one of the faculty I borrowed a .22 rifle for which my mother provided the ammunition. My best and closest friend, Lou Egan, came out and taught me the fundamentals of shooting. So with the gun under my arm I tramped back into the woods, prepared to shoot my way out of my ailment. The first purple grackle at which I aimed fell in a shower of feathers to the earth. On my return I found his dead carcass overrun with predatory ants. I never again could shoot any living thing. Instead, I found a dump in the woods, and shot bottles and tin cans, as later I sat on the banks of the Missouri and shot the floating logs and boxes that came slipping down the river.

I can't see that I did any of the things which modern medicine prescribes for the cure of T.B. But within three months I had kept my promise to myself and the provincial. I was back in St. Louis and able to make up all the work of the lost months, pass my examinations, and move on to the summer's vacation. The plates showed healed lungs. The sputum tests were negative. My temperature was normal. And I was a well young man. Incidentally,

I weighed 175 pounds, for I had gained thirty pounds in the three months.

It has been a wonderfully reassuring thing during the course of my priesthood to meet invalids close to despair.

"Do I look healthy?" I'd ask.

They would take a quick look at my healthy color, my chest that had fairly barreled with so much public speaking, and agreed that I did.

"A year and a half before my ordination," I would go on, "I had to stop everything and take care of a pronounced case of tuberculosis." Invariably they looked their incredulity. "Every test was positive and I have seen the plates since, as have my doctors. So, you see, sickness isn't necessarily fatal. It may have been the prayers of friends. It may have been God's good providence. I don't know. I just know that I was cured and am as you see me now." And they have walked away with new courage.

From that illness came the usual catalogue of blessings. I came to value health and to do a little to protect it. I think that ordination itself and the priesthood took on a new value when I came so close to missing the goal of a Jesuit's ambition. I developed a queer confidence that illness could be conquered and that no sickness need be final and fatal until God so planned it. And the sickness was actually a prelude to the wonderful years of health that followed. For I walked on to ordination. I finished my preparation as a Jesuit. I was assigned to my life's work and gave to it a good many years of continued and exhausting service. Once I paused while that double hernia was submitted to Dr. Glennon's infallible hands. But out of sickness came health. And I was grateful.

The forties laid a good many burdens on a good many backs. I was climaxing my years of service to the sodality. We had fought our way through the world's worst depression and an era of national despair. Now we were working under the difficulties of a second world war. To the responsibilities of the sodality had been added the financing and management of the Jesuit Institute of Social Order. My superiors had given me permission to buy a building to house our developing work; so Marian Prendergast, my infallible secretary, and I haunted the real-estate agents, and went prying into any building that seemed to promise a satisfactory shelter for our future developments.

The agent had sent us on a wild-goose chase. The building he suggested had been the garage of an automobile company. It had no windows above the first floor, no heating, no sanitary facilities, and was in a bad location. So we looked at it and turned away annoyed at the waste of time and effort. As we walked back to our offices on West Pine, suddenly the most mysterious thing happened to me. We were crossing the busy intersection of Olive Street when I knew I had gone totally blind. I laid my fingers on Marian's arm and, letting her guide me, I managed to get back, up the stairs, and into my office. There faint streaks of light came back. But I sat in my big chair, holding my head in my hands. She found me there in a half daze. I was rushed to the hospital, put to bed, and Dr. A. P. Munsch took over. Just everything was wrong. The pulse was down in the upper fifties. The blood pressure registered fitfully. The thyroid seemed more or less exhausted. I was in the depths of what was once called a breakdown. Even the temperature, normally low in my case, was in the mid 96's.

The way a skillful physician can build a man's resources back again may make interesting medical reading. The patient himself hardly pays attention to what goes on around him. I just know that for five months Dr. Munsch and St. John's Hospital worked on me, giving me back what I had lost. And at the end I left, feeling top of the world, able to take up the full work assigned me, and ready for strenuous years ahead. Even during the sickness we found and bought the building now occupied by the sodality and *The Queen's Work;* I managed to keep up the essential work of my office; and I knew that, thanks to my efficient staff and particularly to Marian Prendergast, the lapse had not meant the collapse of work.

TO A TYPICAL CHILD OF THIS AGE

Dear Young Friend:

Everyone seemed to enjoy your school dramatic production, which you so kindly invited me to attend as your guest. In our day we probably would have called that a vaudeville show. On television I think they are bringing back the old name, variety show. Yours was one of those recurrent shows of the Gay Nineties, and I laughed along with your cast and your audience at what I am sure you felt was a very, very funny period of history.

Happily, I confess that I was born in the year 1888. My parents selected as my birthday the Feast of St. George of England—a tribute, I'm sure, to my father, whose name was George, and who, despite two centuries and more of family background in America, had a great many English characteristics. April 23 is also the birthday of William Shakespeare, but the connection between myself and the bard is purely coincidental. Years later the movie magazines made much of the day because a moppet briefly blocked out the horizon and Shirley Temple became such a rage that thousands of girl children borrowed her name and hoped for her fame.

The years since 1888 have not been incredibly numerous. The events since 1888 have moved so fast that no shelf of histories could record them, and no period of man's memory could possibly match them in number, variety, or impact upon the earthly scene.

For a good many years now I have been saying in public something which I sincerely believe. This has been the most interesting period of human history. For good or evil it has moved faster and more excitingly than any former age. To you those years from the time of my birth to, let's say, the year of my entrance into the Society of Jesus in 1909 may seem a little funny. You may laugh at them condescendingly. You may think them a little absurd and sweetly ridiculous. You may, and I'm sure you do, feel closer to the age of George Washington than you do to the period of the high-wheel bicycle, the handle-bar mustache, the kerosene street light, and the Bowery at its peak of fame. You may think that our clothes and our customs, the multitude of petticoats that tented the very pretty girls of the period, the hansom cabs, the two-step, the chaperons, were a little pitiful.

Actually, it was a time when a full century of American freedom and experimentation, the daring of pioneers and the cleverness of inventors, the success of democratic ideals which few people ever thought would succeed, and the impact of raw, sprawling America upon the world were moving into a new and different age. There was nothing funny about all that, and a lot that was frighteningly rapid, excitingly adventuresome, and whirling with such speed that no one has been able to chronicle the revolutions or say with certainty who and what was responsible for which of the vast changes taking place.

I can look back to the days of my boyhood with nostalgic affection. I do not find them amusing. I can see the swift rush of invention and be amazed. I have had the good luck to be born into a simple age and to move along with the science which has resulted in this highly complicated age. Fireworks were enough to give me a thrill back then; you are a little blasé in the presence of the exploding atom.

As a matter of fact, you irritate me a little with your calm acceptance of the wonders that my age and the brief years before it have achieved with vast labor and infinite ingenuity. You are the children and the grandchildren of the ages which I saw. You possess the wonders that came into being in the fastest spurt of man's creative genius. You have yourselves done nothing yet to augment the world's greatness or to profit by our gadgets and the spread of simply wonderful ideas. So when you are amused and condescending toward the Gay Nineties, incredible years of achievement and glory, when you use the word Victorian as if it were the synonym for stuffy, stilted, reactionary, and dull, you will forgive me but, while I may smile a slightly wry and forced smile, I am, in the famous phrase of the great Victoria herself, "not amused."

The America into which I was born was an exciting and nicely isolated spot. We had not had a European war since 1812, and we had strangely managed to win that. We had grown from a little strip along the seacoast into a land so vast and inexhaustible that any man could become a millionaire (or set himself that goal); and Horatio Alger, Jr. was spinning for us the strange fairy tales of bootblacks who, by saving on the polish and going strong on the elbow grease, loving their mothers, and eventually, without the slightest glimmer of romance, marrying the daughter of the local banker, grew fabulously rich. At least, I never caught on, until half a century later when I lectured on that Chronicler of Rags to Riches, that his heroes ended the book fabulously rich to the sum of about fifteen thousand dollars. That was big, big money in those days.

The Civil War—renamed in recent years, in one of our efforts at widespread conciliation, the War between the States—was a very vivid thing to me. Not, please let me hasten to correct you, that I was a drummer boy in one of the battles. But my father had been a youngster growing up when it raged; New York was one of the fiercely loyal states; and in the twilight story hour that made memorable our Sunday evenings, he talked much of the backwash of war as he felt it with the intense sensitivity of a small boy. He used to love to tell how he would drive into town, or ride there astride a farm horse, to pick up the papers that brought first news of Bull Run and Gettysburg and Vicksburg. His voice dropped in the sincere sorrow he had felt then, and could easily recapture, as he talked of the horrible page after page, framed in black, that listed the deaths of northern boys on the battlefield. The farmers, he told me, would be waiting at their fences and he would ride fast, tossing them the paper and rushing on if the name of a son was among the missing or the dead.

We did not look back to the Revolution through the fierce barrages of two world wars. It was a living thing to us from our class texts, from the stories which made up much of our juvenile literature, and from the intense distaste with which my Irish maternal ancestors regarded the British. One of our most popular nickel weeklies, predecessors to your comics but with pages of action and dialogue and a minimum of pictures, ran on year after year under the general title of "The Boys of 1776." Washington and Howe and Arnold were our familiars. And England was our hereditary enemy and more than likely our next battle foe.

At the same time Russia was a land for which we had mixed feelings; we were taught that the Russians had been almost our sole friends during the Civil War and that a threat from the czar had kept some of the big nations which wanted southern cotton from throwing in with the Confederacy. Yet we were fascinated by those remote ancestors of the Bolsheviki and communists who were known mysteriously as nihilists. And we found ourselves sentimentally on the side of young smooth-faced conspirators who met in the cellars of Moscow and of a city then called St. Petersburg to plot the overthrow of bearded grand dukes and to free the serfs who were victims of a strange, remote tyrant ruling in the Kremlin. The terms were not too different in those days; the setting remained when the characters of the story changed.

Around me was a vital and fiercely alive America.

Chicago had miraculously sprung once more from the ashes of the Chicago fire, which, among other structures, had burned down the Presbyterian church on Prairie Avenue, served before the fire by my grandfather Lord. We loved to dine in a North Side restaurant built, by some host with a sense of the picturesque, from the fire-scarred bricks and rubble of the fire itself. We touched the walls tentatively and recalled the tales of flight in the night, and of stupefied displaced people carrying away their chief treasures, which, likely as not, turned out to be a parrot in a cage, a bed mattress, a lamp without oil, or one of the family portraits.

On the South Side, brick by brick and stone by stone, some impresario had rebuilt the Civil War Libby Prison; and we regarded it with something of the horror later transferred to German concentration camps. I even managed to squeeze my small frame, when the guards were not looking, into the hole through which a cluster of heroic Union prisoners had managed to burrow and tunnel their way to liberty.

Around me was a land without any doubts about itself.

The Civil War had ended in a burst of national vitality that flung the lines of railroads across the country. J. P. Morgan (or was it great James Hill?) had not as yet pronounced railroad bonds the Rembrandts of securities. But every lad was swiftly initiated into the Great American Secret: "Any boy can become president; but with real luck, any boy can earn his first million by thirty."

We were beginning to hear rumbles about terrible things called trusts; but as my father was a staunch Republican and as my mother, Democratic like ninety-nine per cent of the Irish, had no vote, I could hear a counter rumble from a father who thought that trusts might well be the kind of big business which our big country needed.

Trains had started to travel forty-five miles an hour. When the New York Central years later announced that it would put in a run which, en route to New York, topped a mile a minute, we all gasped, for the last stride in speed had been made.

If our land had a foreign policy, nobody in my status of society had ever heard of it. For that matter, thirty years later, Calvin Coolidge could confine his remarks on foreign affairs in his state-of-the-Union speech to one small paragraph hinting that all was very well indeed. The uncrossable moats of two gigantic oceans surrounded the castle of our land, and Mr. Geddes, who had escaped from Germany to avoid military service and become the martinet manager of the Grand Theater, could shake my small hand and congratulate me in a heavy accent on being a boy in a land which had no army and needed only the small fleet that made good-will visits round a peaceful globe.

On the other hand, while the handful of regulars marched in the Decoration Day parades and shot off salutes on the Glorious Fourth, I often persuaded my mother to take me down to the Labor Day parade and, hardly at the age of reason, came in contact with the growing ferment of organized labor. The floats impressed me, with their tableaux of the honest workingman standing at the door of his shop under a huge sign that read, "No scabs need apply." I found the marching men in overalls dull in contrast to the smartly stepping regulars in their blue military uniforms; but I sensed that here was something at once grim and hopeful, fraught with promise and maybe a little dark with threat. I was still very young indeed when, coming home from school, I saw the union strikers stone two "scabs" or strikebreakers, and watched from behind the shelter of a friendly tree when, bloody and terrified, the men ran madly down the street with the pack in full cry.

The Pullman strike laid down its picket lines across the railroad tracks I must pass on my way to third grade. Then, when the strike grew violent, the National Guard threw up an encampment in the center of Grand Boulevard, and we small youngsters came close to "real soldiers" (as we thought the clerks and carpenters, the druggists and salesmen, in uniform were) to our own thrilled delight. We were not so thrilled when in the early dawn a roar of explosion broke the silence of our peaceful South Side, and as we ran to school we saw death and destruction in the semblance of a miniature battlefield after the final charge. The ammunition caisson which had blown up during the night had wrecked the district and scattered the fragments of these volunteer soldiers in horror and death and agony over that peaceful boulevard. I have never heard of bombings since without feeling that too early I had come in personal contact with the dread thing which is high explosive.

I was a very small boy when the Spanish-American War worked its transformation upon the nation. A strange racking possessed me. At our Catholic school there was pity for Catholic Spain. My mother had learned that this was the personal war of Mr. William Randolph Hearst, then in the early stages of his journalistic jaundice. Somehow I heard how the queen regent of Spain had begged President McKinley not to go to war, and how the pope, a strangely muffled voice in world affairs of that day, had interceded in the interests of a peaceful compromise. Against this I had come into contact with the power and fury of propaganda. The *Maine* exploded in Havana's harbor. In no time at all we kids had bought small postal cards that presented a sinister Spaniard lurking in the cellars of Morro Castle, with a trail of powder running direct to the sea beneath the battleship. By touching a match to the Spaniard's hand, we could watch the powder spurt and fizz along the train until it reached the miniature torpedo, and the picture of the *Maine* burst into flame. Vividly do I recall newspaper pictures of Spaniards, dressed in what I later discovered was seventeenth-century attire, tearing to pieces between oxen one of their victims. "Cuba libre" was not yet a powerful drink, but a battle cry that we kids shouted as we played in the schoolyard. I discovered that a school on the West Side (my later beloved St. Ignatius) had for its colors maroon and gold; I was in an infantile fury that these so closely resembled the Spanish red and yellow. And with the coming of the Glorious Fourth, we turned our firecrackers from rockets hurled upon the advancing British to bombs placed under carefully located tin cans, now representing the fortifications of dastardly Spaniards.

With news of the battles we gathered a new race of heroes. Teddy Roosevelt charged San Juan Hill in a battle chiefly remembered by the participants for the plastered signs advertising the beer that made Milwaukee famous. Sampson and Schley, our admirals, were pictured on lapel buttons which we wore proudly; and once the Battle of Manila had been fought without loss of a man, we calmly decided that Admiral George Dewey was the greatest hero our world had ever known.

Little did we suspect that in the world of the pre-Spanish War days the "experts" bet two to one that the Spanish navy would wipe the American Navy off the seas, and that even the remnants of the once world-straddling Spanish empire would make mincemeat of a stripling called the United States. Foreigners didn't think much of our military might in those days.

Loudly and boisterously we bragged of our national might. Words like imperialism and anti-imperialism for the first time cropped up in the language. We sang the war songs of the period, sentimentals that ended, "One kissed a locket of thin gray hair, One kissed a lock of brown, Bidding farewell to the Stars and Stripes, Just as the sun went down"; songs of renunciation like "Good-by, Dolly, I must leave you for the front to fight the foe"; "You're only a volunteer; but Uncle Sam will take off his hat, to you, Mr. Volunteer." We had, like the rest of America, discovered that there was a Europe; opened our eyes to find that we had been whisked into the heart of the Orient; and suddenly got our first glimpse of the vast world outside our hitherto adequate and self-sufficient America.

While you find it easy to imagine yourself in a world of spinning wheels and tallyhos, of powdered wigs and sedan chairs, you find it incredible that the lifetime of a single man should extend from horsecars, their floors covered with straw, to jet planes. Central heating was much of a novelty; people could be a little vain about the fact that they had constant hot water flowing through their plumbing; newspapers were a penny, bargains at the price, and a city like Chicago would have eight or ten papers proclaiming the might of the press. Telephones were so rare that a hilarious story of the period told of the unlucky family which put in the first telephone in their district and became a sort of service station for the entire neighborhood, no rest by day and no peace by night. News reached you by "extra" papers shouted along the streets in the early hours of the evening. Hospitals were places to which the heartless sent their unwanted sick to die. Medicine was a struggle between allopaths and homeopaths, whose main point of difference, as far as we youngsters could tell, was that the homeopaths gave us sugar candy for medicine, and you had to clamp your nose and make a horrible face when you swallowed allopathic medicine. Of the boys who graduated with me from grammar school only two of us continued to high school; and we both went in for a business course. Vaccines were regarded with deep suspicion; and antibiotics were half a century away.

We were right in the middle of one of the world's great revolutions, and of course didn't know it. Communication and transportation were breaking out the accustomed grooves of some six thousand years to transform our sense of the size of the earth and the proximity of our neighbors. We talked in great mirth of the passing of the horse, and meant that he was constantly passing the stalled horseless carriages which lined the ditches of the few paved highways. In fact, "Get a horse!" was the ironic shout we hurled as a gasoline buggy snorted down the street. Even as late as 1910 a trip in an automobile meant changing tires as often as once every twenty miles. And five punctures in the course of a fifty-mile tour was by no means unusual. If you took a trip in a motorcar, you spent much of it seated on the greensward watching your host and car owner sweating as he forced the thin rubber off the tire and wrestled a new tire into place.

I have been accused indignantly of being a gadget lover, and I am inclined not to contest the accusation. You see, I lived from the period without gadgets like good plumbing and plenty of hot baths and easy transportation and a desk telephone and fountain pens and typewriters and Pullman roomettes and a plane to take you in a matter of hours to a spot you once reached in days and even weeks—and I like gadgets. I have never let myself become a slave to them. I frankly confess I should find it almost impossible to do my work without my portable typewriter, even though I know that Shakespeare wrote *Hamlet* with a quill pen. I prefer crossing the continent on the *Chief* to rolling along in a covered wagon. I am glad that women today can cook on electric ranges rather than chop wood for brick hearths. I think canned goods and frozen foods are great timesavers which, rightly used, might give our age much more time to do important and worthwhile things. Elevators that carry us upstairs should cut down the number of heart troubles, even if other events incident to our swifter civilization may keep the heart failures high on our mortality records.

I have never had the use of an automobile except occasionally when I could borrow one from a kind friend; yet I have known what it meant to be rushed to a hospital in a cab when minutes meant the difference between my life and my death. I like it that the art of the world can be so reproduced that, when I saw the Mona Lisa in the Louvre, I was a little disappointed it was not infinitely better than the color prints that had introduced me to that masterpiece. It seems to me an advantage that the great music of the world can be recorded and dropped under the magic of a sensitive needle.

Quite willingly I concede that a great book is still centuries ahead of a good radio or TV program; yet I can well believe that Bishop Fulton Sheen, addressing his fifteen million of an evening, would be the frank envy of St. Paul, reaching only those within the throwing power of his unaided voice. I myself have been constantly grateful for the loud speaker and the public-address system, for in my early days as a priest I knew what it meant to talk for five hours in a drafty gymnasium with fans blowing and five thousand young people daring me to control them by the articulation of my words and their interest in what I had to say to them.

It would be easily possible for a person who like myself has spanned the period of the great bulge in inventions to grow wordy on the subject. From charcoal to atomic energy, from the high-wheel bike to the sports-model car, from the first typewriters to the dictating machines and the mathematic devices of the modern scientific laboratory, from quick death by pneumonia to penicillin and later "miracle" drugs—the swift progression is fascinating. And it took place largely in the era at which you, my genial and not-too-well-informed young friend, are inclined to smile. You find a tintype funny; it took men millenniums to develop reproduction from the scratched figure on the wall of a cave to a daguerreotype. And it has taken us only half a century to progress from the tintype to the magnificent perfection of color photography. I peeped into the eyepiece of the early kinescopes to see Mary Queen of Scots lose her head. From that to Cinerama is a vast stride taken at a rate of speed that a thousand years from now will dumfound the historian. We had a wheezing gramophone, without tubes and with a minimum of bass reproduction; it seemed a vast forward stride from the wide steel disk of the music box and its tinkle. But what a primitive toy it was! And what an incredible scientific advance when compared to all that had gone before it in the centuries of relative soundlessness!

Economics? I think back to twenty-five-cent haircuts, children on weekdays fifteen cents. The best candy in the city twenty-five cents a pound, a beautiful five-pound box for a dollar. A Sunday chicken for a quarter. The best pair of boy's dancing pumps, two dollars and a half; a boy's good suit, five dollars. The top and absolutely best seats for an all-star play, two dollars. A dinner in the best hotels, which meant all you could eat of everything you wanted from the menu, one dollar. Rent for an eight-room apartment thirty-five dollars a month. An ice-cream soda five and ten cents—the latter if you wanted fresh crushed-fruit flavor.

But on the other hand, incomes about one fifth of what is the current average. Office boys at three dollars a week. A good male clerk for fifteen dollars. The home visit from your physician, a dollar. A half an hour's music lesson from a private teacher, who came to your house to give it, fifty cents.

Whether people are better off with larger incomes and larger living costs is not something to debate now. I feel they are, but there is another side. All I am indicating to you is the obvious spread of events in the lifetime I have known. The economic world into which my contemporaries were born is so different from your world that you might be more at home in medieval Paris. Can you imagine that in 1905 the debating teams of St. Ignatius College debated: "Have labor unions been a benefit or a detriment to the laboring man?" And the judges decided that they had done more harm than good. The shift of interest has been from money to power. There was no income tax then; indeed, it took a decision of the Supreme Court to decide that the government could tax an income. I can recall as late as the twenties hearing a Hollywood magnate protest violently that on an income of $450,000 a year the government had robbed him by charging a $15,000 income tax. The government has come to love the big-income people simply because they are such an aid and comfort to the treasury department.

The leveling off of Americans' income has been one of the revolutions through which I have lived. With no income myself, with a vow of poverty which means all I have "earned" goes into my work, I have been in the position of a calm observer. I have liked it immensely that poor people get so much more income and rich people get so much less. I like it that the whole national level of income rises and rises, and that more workers have more wages and more professional people have more income than ever before in the history of mankind.

Often I have been asked whether the world grows, to my observation, better or worse. To me it has seemed in so many ways better.

I have not failed to notice the Spectacular Sins. The newspapers have made us fiercely conscious of them. I have seen and hated the cruelty of tyrants and the awful oppressions of the dictators. I have watched with dread the advance of the totalitarian governments, their brain washes, their contempt for truth. I have shed my silent tears and done my best to train young people against broken homes and wrecked marriages. I have "tutted" over necking and the casual attitude of young folks toward modesty.

Yet deep down, I have a happy conviction that, under the providence of God and the wonderful work of the Church, the revolutions have been progressively upward. It is marvelous to realize that, in our country and lands like Canada and the countries "down under," more people have more part in the gracious goods with which God filled the world than ever before in history. It is good to know that humanity is at least aware that it cannot indulge in the luxury of wars without destroying the very things for which wars pretend to be fought. Once on a time men fought what they called wars of conquest; now they know that there are only wars too costly for anyone to afford them.

I like it that the workingman can raise his head to the dignity which must have characterized two carpenters of Nazareth. While I am aware of the evils to which labor racketeering has brought the unions, I have a somewhat contradictory pleasure that the evils are not all on the side of the employer. Two evils do not make a right; but once on a time the evils were all the evils of industrial capitalism and a mad desire to make as much money as possible by the exploitation of the laborer. I am glad that the laborer has been put in the position of fighting back. When the already successful development of labor-management is pushed slightly further, the war between the employed and the employer, the age of the sweatshops into which I was born, the ruthless and unchecked swelling of fortunes and the shrinking of subexistence wages, may largely end.

Social legislation is part of the revolution, and all to the good. Christ would smile His approval on old-age pensions and unemployment insurance, and laws that prevent the crushing out of small young lives in the interest of big hereditary fortunes. I am glad that laws on labor and wages guarantee decent conditions under which men and women can work and mean that their income is in some sense proportioned to the expenditure of their energies and the use of their hands and brains.

When I hear people moaning sorrowfully over the eagerness with which the "poor" long for TV sets and autos and good clothes and higher education for their children and more chance to play golf for themselves, I cannot add my crocodile tears to their wailings. To me that is a part of the revolutions I have seen that is very good. Too long was it accepted that the good things of earth were the hereditary right of a very few. The phrase "privileged class," like the other parasitical phrase "leisure class," can well be ended forever. I have never believed that the lovely and comforting things of earth were created by the good Father in heaven for some small clique of select society that just happened to be born that way. I have never liked inherited class. And when a taxi driver along the streets of New York can without boasting or ostentation tell me that of his children he has raised one to be a physician, one to be a lawyer, one to be a high-school teacher, and one to be a successful merchant, I thank God for the revolution which made it possible for a child to set his sights high and climb and climb and climb. Social climbers, as they were discussed in the early decades of my life, I dislike; men and women with the courage and opportunity to climb to better homes and richer education and more civilized and cultured living I admire. Thank heaven for an age and a land that has given them their chance!

It was with considerable complacency that I discovered for myself the pleasant fact that in the United States we have almost no such thing as a proletariat. The communist upset that threatened our land did not rise out of a vast, submerged, oppressed understratum of society but from men and women of the intellectual class whose consciences bothered them and who were trying to substitute the theoretic religion of "humanity" for the tough and taxing practice of loving God and sacrificing in personal service for their fellow men. The rise and advance of the Negro (who threatened to become our proletariat) has been one of the proudest revolutions I have seen. I have watched it as one of the great and hopeful signs of our upward climb.

The worldwide viewpoint of the Church and my deepest inner conviction that God meant humanity to be "one fold with one shepherd" has made me delight in the progress of mankind toward one world. I did not hesitate to throw in my slight efforts with the Americans interested in the League of Nations. Poor as that effort was and poor and full of holes as was the League itself, I find encouraging its effort to substitute arbitration for war, and the fact that nations could at least sit down side by side without planking sabers and muskets and grenades on the table before them. The struggle for the United Nations seems to me on a par with the struggle of our colonies for the United States; and no Catholic can be bitter against any honest attempt to make the nations lay aside their fierce and often senseless animosities, to substitute the council for the battlefield, discussion for bombings, and an ultimate union of interests for carefully cultivated and artfully whipped up hatreds.

To me it has seemed that the shrinking of the world, thanks to the marvels of transportation, our easy access to the ears of our fellows through modern communication, and the constant meetings of the representatives of divergent nations with contrasting civilizations (however ineffective their immediate consequences may seem) is a reason for hope. The Romans, we are reminded, had no thought in building their military roads that they were preparing for the apostolic journeys of the early Church and the conquest of the empire by Christendom. Along the lines laid down by modern transportation and communication the new apostles of the kingdom of God may well make their most effective advance. I never think of the meetings of the United Nations without dreaming that in God's plans and providence the representatives of His universal Church may one day meet to fulfill Christ's prayer that we may be one as He and His Father are one.

You, my dear young friend, taking for granted your Catholic education, hardly realize that it is one of the wonders of the age and the invention of very recent times. But then, the whole concept of universal education, which makes possible the wider sweep of our American democracy, is something very new in human experience. So are the modern hospitals which have been called, and rightly, the greatest invention of modern times. They grew out of the ideals and courage of the Gay Nineties. Laugh at those simpler ages, my dear young friend; but laugh only if you are willing to recognize how a somewhat silly age turned out to be a master of invention, a dreamer of dreams it had the courage to bring into reality, an incredible period of history that has changed the face of the earth.

I lived through exciting times, times that have seen a great upswing in Christianity. I was born into a period of science that had set itself coldly and recklessly to destroy religion. The men who set up the graven idol called evolution thought they had found a first-rate substitute for God. The word "soul" had largely disappeared from scientific literature. The heavens were emptied of God. Religion was the superstitious hangover from dark periods of history. Man would make for himself the only heaven to which he need aspire, a new heaven on an old earth.

I lived my youth in an age that was ruthless in its attack upon morality. Men were animals without free will or any moral obligation. The law of the jungle which had made the animals fight to see which one would survive was the law of human society too. World War I was a sort of gigantic laboratory experiment to see which culture deserved to survive and which nation would, in the struggle for survival, prove itself deserving of world domination.

God is strangely back in His world. His name has begun to appear in the speeches of public officials. Hitler and Stalin have driven us back to the need for morality and the sanctions of religion.

Fortunately, atheism linked itself with communism and, hating communism, we have come to dread atheism as its inevitable ally. The churches have never known such swelling memberships. Whereas in the days of the American Revolution hardly half a dozen students on the small campus of Princeton University professed any formal religion, even the most pagan of campuses today, at least in America, pays passing respect to God and makes church membership reason for commendation. Recently one of the scientists engaged in the atomic projects lectured on a midwest campus. He told the non-Catholic students how a very considerable majority of the physicists who entered the project had been at least skeptical about the existence of God. Contact with the miracle and wonder of the atom, a study of the exact planning and blueprinting that made its universe in miniature possible, contact with the power that had been thrust into the heart of the atom, had sent an overwhelming majority out with a deep certainty that God exists and that the best man can do is slightly to modify the amazing creation which is His.

I was a boy in high school when there took place what I sincerely believe to be the greatest single event of the twentieth century. A simple little man had gone to Rome to help elect a pope. His return-trip ticket was in his wallet. He would return to be the devoted bishop and priest who loved his parishioners in utter gentleness and unselfish service. Instead he remained in Rome to become Pope Pius X and then Pope St. Pius X. During his pontificate he gave back to the Christian world frequent Communion. Though he foretold the saints whom this reunion with the Christ of love would give to the world, he himself could not foresee the things which frequent Communion would mean to the immediate future.

I think I have made it abundantly clear that I came from a stalwart Catholic family and home. Before I had finished my college days my non-Catholic father had become a Catholic himself. Except for two years in Forestville Public School mine was from third grade through senior college a complete Catholic education. I was a faithful parishioner sharing the parish life in a measure unusual among young fellows. I was early initiated into Catholic reading, such as it was in those days. Yet I know that there were words common today and practices with which even casual Catholics are familiar which were as unknown as the new scientific terms of our current era.

Frequent Communion took the place of the once-a-month Communion practiced by the more devout Catholics. The liturgical movement with the return of the Missal to the laity blossomed. I had made retreats in college, but I can recall as a novice listening with astonishment to the fact that in Spain they had begun closed retreats for laymen. The lay-retreat movement so familiar to educated Catholics in our land is something that is of recent origin and development.

We had some Catholic books, juveniles and translations. Who could have foreseen the Catholic resurgence of literature of which a fine scholar (even if he was a former pupil of mine), Father Calvert Alexander, wrote eloquently? Who fifty years ago would have dreamed of Catholic books on the lists of popular best sellers? Who would have guessed that we would know writers like Chesterton and Belloc and Graham Greene and Evelyn Waugh presenting Catholic truth for a general audience?

My slight contact with the missions consisted in listening once to some of the famous White Fathers of Africa telling of their work. It was a generation later before the tremendous sweep of the propagation of the faith and the great growth of the Catholic missions became one of the standard elements of contemporary Catholicity.

We of the laity had heard no invitation to the Catholic lay apostolate. The phrase Catholic action had not yet been coined.

Catholic education was in its swaddling clothes of red brick and rough painted frame. Few in the year 1900 would have dared to suggest that the current year, hardly more than half a century later, would know Catholic educational triumphs like our universal grammar schools, our Catholic high schools that match the public tax-supported institutions in classroom, laboratory, gymnasium, and playing field, campuses such as Notre Dame and Fordham and Catholic University and Villanova; the lovely Catholic academies and colleges which welcome future Catholic womanhood; St. Louis University Medical School, Georgetown Law School, the teacher-training colleges of a hundred and more religious communities, the excellently equipped nursing schools of our Catholic hospital system, and glorious clerical seminaries like those of the archdioceses of New York, Chicago, St. Louis, and San Francisco.

Our struggling periodicals of the nineteenth century would not have guessed their expansion into such things as the *Register* chain of diocesan newspapers, *Our Sunday Visitor, Extension,* the *Catholic Digest, America,* and the *Commonweal.*

The National Council of Catholic Men and Women, as part of the National Catholic Welfare Conference, had not even been blueprinted. Nor had the Catholic Hospital Association, the Catholic Educational Association, and the flourishing and effective organizations devoted to Catholic social improvement, family life, art, literature, democratic action.

The seminaries bulge with clerical vocations. While we hear of the pressing need for priests, brothers, and nuns, actually our novitiates have increased fivefold and each contains far more than any one of them did in the year 1900.

The voice of the holy father, long silenced in world affairs, now speaks with compelling authority and the world listens when he speaks, even if it turns away from the common-sense and idealistic courses which he indicates.

I cannot be pessimistic about a world which during my single lifetime repudiated the idea of colonies and master races, of inferior people and the white-man's burden. No author ever grew obsolete more swiftly than that poet of imperialism, Rudyard Kipling. We accept our responsibility for world betterment, but not with the condescension of a master race bending to the needs of subjugated people. We accept the freedom of India just as an incident of history instead of the revolution that it was. The Dominion of Canada becomes the Canadian nation and the news hardly makes a headline. The United States gives independence to the Philippine Islands without expecting plaudits or the oh's and ah's of history.

I feel high hopes for a science that has increased the life expectancy of a baby born today by thirty years over the life expectancy of a child born in my 1888. I am happy that medicine has conquered malaria, typhoid, mastoids, scarlet fever, smallpox; and through the discovery of the wonder drugs has promised the elimination of pneumonia and diphtheria and the social diseases. I am a little humble in the presence of the geniuses who gave us the gasoline engine, and the spread of wings that lift the plane, and tractors, and streamlining. I am grateful to the men who make it possible for me at the table in my Jesuit community to eat delicacies which a hundred years ago scarcely found their way to the banquet boards of kings.

Chemistry astonished me. Physics served me as no spirit from a brass bottle served the sultan of *The Arabian Nights*.

I have had brought to me the world, so that in my armchair the printing press, the lithographer, color printing, the radio, the motion picture, TV, the incredible service of the international news companies, make all mankind my near neighbors and place me within earshot of all mankind.

Universal education, the training that fits mankind for decent living, could be realized tomorrow if the United Nations ever becomes what God's providence may intend it to be.

Dignity has clothed the workingman and the craftsman. The farmer walks his fields knowing that science is his slave and the nation his beneficiary. The artist is well paid after his long centuries of the garret and the cellar. Unions have banded the exploited into real power. Wealth has been taught its social obligations and tyranny finds itself destroyed by the might of the vote.

All this I have seen happen since the day of my birth.

And as a Catholic I am deeply proud and happy that my Church has advanced with the same giant strides.

I cannot agree with those who wag despondent heads over these evil times. Even in communism I have seen a foe which Providence has allowed to plague us for our sins and wake us from our apathy and challenge us to match our zeal for justice with its zeal for human slavery. And the horrors of totalitarian nazism and oppressive fascism have made us love democracy the more and cling with fiercer loyalty to our Christian truth and freedom.

The evils of the generations just gone I know. I admit that I too have been part of them. One could not have lived through two world wars and a depression, seen the onrush of communism, and known, however remotely, the ugliness that is nazism and fascism, and still question the terrors and ills of that span of years. Yet God has had a singularly miraculous way of wrenching from the evils created by mankind wonders and benefits beyond counting. It is something to know one has lived through a new age of martyrs; and though I have missed martyrdom by the widest possible margin, I have been proud of the willingness of thousands to die for their faith. It is a lovely thing to have been part of what history will know as the Age of Mary. It has been glorious to watch the Church at work, its emergence from the exile into which Protestantism had pushed it, into the great spiritual force even of large sections of mankind that do not admit its leadership or accept its truth. Mahatma Gandhi would never have done his work had he not learned of the poverty and purity and gentleness of Christ through the Catholic tradition. Mohammedanism in our century would not have repudiated such fundamental teachings of Mohammed as polygamy, slavery, and bloody slaughter of its enemies had it not tried to copy the Christian virtues without accepting Christian truths. And if, after the pounding and assault of paganism reborn, mankind still shrinks from the tyrant, hates the exploiter, is sneakingly ashamed of its sex sins, and practices a gentle charity and human qualities which are totally at variance with the materialistic theory of brute evolution, it is because the Church keeps stressing Christian virtue and demanding that men live like men no matter who tries to teach them that they are animals.

Over and over I have said, "To me this is the most exciting period of history. I am glad that I have known it. I would not willingly have missed it for anything." You may smile at the Gay Nineties if you wish. Human beings, even in their moments of heroism and greatest achievement, sometimes give reason for laughter and jeers. But if your age can produce as much, my dear young friend; if at the end of your life you can see the advances I have seen, yours will be a lucky age and a blessed one.